T0190458

IFIP Advances in Information and Communication Technology

660

Editor-in-Chief

Kai Rannenberg, Goethe University Frankfurt, Germany

IFIP – The International Federation for Information Processing

IFIP was founded in 1960 under the auspices of UNESCO, following the first World Computer Congress held in Paris the previous year. A federation for societies working in information processing, IFIP's aim is two-fold: to support information processing in the countries of its members and to encourage technology transfer to developing nations. As its mission statement clearly states:

> *IFIP is the global non-profit federation of societies of ICT professionals that aims at achieving a worldwide professional and socially responsible development and application of information and communication technologies.*

IFIP is a non-profit-making organization, run almost solely by 2500 volunteers. It operates through a number of technical committees and working groups, which organize events and publications. IFIP's events range from large international open conferences to working conferences and local seminars.

The flagship event is the IFIP World Computer Congress, at which both invited and contributed papers are presented. Contributed papers are rigorously refereed and the rejection rate is high.

As with the Congress, participation in the open conferences is open to all and papers may be invited or submitted. Again, submitted papers are stringently refereed.

The working conferences are structured differently. They are usually run by a working group and attendance is generally smaller and occasionally by invitation only. Their purpose is to create an atmosphere conducive to innovation and development. Refereeing is also rigorous and papers are subjected to extensive group discussion.

Publications arising from IFIP events vary. The papers presented at the IFIP World Computer Congress and at open conferences are published as conference proceedings, while the results of the working conferences are often published as collections of selected and edited papers.

IFIP distinguishes three types of institutional membership: Country Representative Members, Members at Large, and Associate Members. The type of organization that can apply for membership is a wide variety and includes national or international societies of individual computer scientists/ICT professionals, associations or federations of such societies, government institutions/government related organizations, national or international research institutes or consortia, universities, academies of sciences, companies, national or international associations or federations of companies.

More information about this series at https://link.springer.com/bookseries/6102

Amany Elbanna · Shane McLoughlin ·
Yogesh K. Dwivedi · Brian Donnellan ·
David Wastell (Eds.)

Co-creating for Context in the Transfer and Diffusion of IT

IFIP WG 8.6 International Working Conference
on Transfer and Diffusion of IT, TDIT 2022
Maynooth, Ireland, June 15–16, 2022
Proceedings

 Springer

Editors
Amany Elbanna (iD)
Royal Holloway University of London
London, UK

Yogesh K. Dwivedi (iD)
Swansea University
Swansea, UK

David Wastell
University of Nottingham
Nottingham, UK

Shane McLoughlin
University of Maynooth
Maynooth, Ireland

Brian Donnellan
University of Maynooth
Maynooth, Kildare, Ireland

ISSN 1868-4238   ISSN 1868-422X (electronic)
IFIP Advances in Information and Communication Technology
ISBN 978-3-031-17970-9   ISBN 978-3-031-17968-6 (eBook)
https://doi.org/10.1007/978-3-031-17968-6

This Springer imprint is published by the registered company Springer Nature Switzerland AG
The registered company address is: Gewerbestrasse 11, 6330 Cham, Switzerland

Preface

The adoption and diffusion of information technology has passed through decades of developments and major shifts. Recent world events have brought particular emphasis on the inherent and increasing diversity, complexity, and uncertainty of context(s) influencing the diffusion of emerging IT. This challenges our academic community to acknowledge and better address such context in our methods, theories, and practices of research. It further welcomes avenues of co-creation in research to better unpack and understand context, by bringing together a diversity of different expertise, stakeholders, and forms of data, information, and knowledge.

Not only are IT artefacts becoming more complex, so too are the environments which they inhabit (e.g. smart homes, smart cities, Industry 4.0, Agriculture 4.0, etc.) and the contexts influencing their use (e.g. sustainable development, global pandemics, disruption to supply chains, etc.). Key interrelated challenges requiring understanding and solutions include technological advances (e.g. IoT, AI, and blockchain) enabling increasing diversity, volume, and fluidity of data flowing amongst actors (technical and non-technical) to create value; public sentiment and political policies shifting priorities of research; IT enabled servitization delivering new value, markets, and market influences; deepening IT penetration into various life domains (from governing cities to transport, housing, and farming); and innovation ecosystems that enrich, enlarge, and intersect with each other (e.g. platform-based ecosystems, new transport modalities such as driverless cars, etc.).

This book presents the post-proceedings of this year's International Federation of Information Processing Working Group 8.6 (IFIP WG 8.6) Conference on Transfer and Diffusion of IT (TDIT 2022). IFIP WG 8.6 focuses on the diffusion, adoption, and implementation of information and communication technologies. The conference was held in Maynooth, Ireland, and was hosted by the Innovation Value Institute (IVI) at Maynooth University. We are grateful to IVI for their commitment and effort in producing such a well-organized and memorable conference.

The theme of the conference, "Co-creating for Context in Prospective Transfer and Diffusion of IT", acknowledged the importance, richness, diversity, uncertainty, and complexity of today's IT adoption and diffusion context. TDIT 2022 welcomed research specifically tackling the conference theme. For example, co-creating with practice in capturing what is happening on the ground and at the precipice of digital transformation, harnessing the collective intelligence of citizens in devising and/or offering solutions, or converging interdisciplinary expertise to gain new or greater insight. This is in addition to IFIP WG 8.6 longstanding themes on IT adoption, implementation, and use. In total, 60 submissions were received after a call for papers. After initial screening, all papers were subjected to a two-way anonymous reviewing process with at least two expert reviews per paper. We followed a constructive reviewing process to develop papers and direct authors to other types of submissions when the criteria of full papers were not sufficiently met. This resulted in the acceptance of 19 full-length papers and ten short papers to be included in the proceedings and other papers to be presented at the conference only to benefit from scholarly development. The acceptance rate, therefore, was 48%. Authors of selected papers are affiliated to institutions in five continents, which is a good reflection of IFIP WG 8.6 membership. To serve authors, in this conference and due to COVID-19 conditions and world contingencies, we developed a new model of open submission and agile reviewing of papers on a rolling basis so that authors could submit as travel opened up in their countries and as they saw possible within their existing challenges. We further developed a hybrid model for the conference itself, with approximately a third of registered authors attending, participating, and presenting their work remotely. We are indebted to the Program Committee members, for their hard work in reviewing and assessing submissions on a rolling basis and in a timely manner which made this event possible, and to the local organizers and presenting authors for harmonizing the online and in-person presentations.

This book is organized into five parts to reflect the themes of the conference and papers. Part I includes papers that examine different IS concepts and theories that could provide the basis for future research. Part II includes papers that address the theme of the conference on co-creation in design, implementation, and use. Part III presents papers that discuss IS use and impact in different contexts. Part IIII includes papers that examine the recent emergence and interest in blockchain and cryptocurrency technologies in different contexts. The final part includes papers that investigate the use and impact of social media in different domains.

Events like these cannot be staged without considerable help and advice from others. Our meeting would not have been possible without the hard work of Niall Connolly leading the local organizing team and Carol Connolly from IVI for her careful assistance and support. A special thanks must also be given to the IFIP WG 8.6 members and authors for their resilience and rising to the different challenges of making this conference a success despite the global circumstances. We hope that our meeting and the collection of papers included in these proceedings progress our understanding of the diverse, complex, and uncertain context of the adoption and diffusion of technology and inspire further research.

June 2022

Amany Elbanna
Shane Mcloughlin
Yogesh Dwivedi
Brian Donnellan
David Wastell

Organization

General Chairs

Brian Donnellan   University of Maynooth, Ireland
David Wastell   University of Nottingham, UK

Program Chairs

Amany Elbanna   Royal Holloway University of London, UK
Shane Mcloughlin   University of Maynooth, Ireland
Yogesh K. Dwivedi   Swansea University, UK

Organizing Chair

Niall Connolly   Maynooth University, Ireland

Program Committee

Richard Baskerville   Georgia State University, USA
Peter Bednar   University of Portsmouth, UK
Richard Boateng   University of Ghana, Ghana
Debra Bunker   University of Sydney, Australia
Kieran Conboy   University of Ireland, Galway, Ireland
Edward Curry   Maynooth University, Ireland
Brian Donnellan   National University of Ireland, Galway, Ireland
Yogesh Dwivedi   University of Swansea, UK
Amany Elbanna   Royal Holloway, University of London, UK
Guy Gable   Queensland University of Technology, Australia
Anna Sigriour Islind   Reykjavik University, Iceland
Karl Kautz   RMIT University, Australia
Satish Krishnan   IIM Kozhikode, India
Banita Lal   University of Bradford, UK
Henrik Linderoth   University of Jonkoping, Sweden
Giovanni Maccani   Ideas for Change, Spain
Lars Mathiassen   Georgia State University, USA
Lorraine Morgan   National University of Ireland, Galway, Ireland
Peter A. Nielsen   Aalborg University, Denmark
Jacob Norbjerg   Copenhagen Business School, Denmark
Markus Nuettgens   University of Hamburg, Germany

Adegboyega Ojo	Maynooth University, Ireland
Savvas Papagiannidis	Newcastle Business School, UK
Jan Pries-Heje	Roskilde University, Denmark
Abhinay Puvvala	National University of Ireland, Ireland
Nerpanda Rana	Qatar University, Qatar
M. N. Ravishankar	Loughborough University, UK
Sven Rehm	Université de Strasbourg, France
Ulrika Lundh Snis	University West, Sweden
Sujeet Kumar Sharma	IIM Trichy, India
P. K. Senyo	Southampton Business School, UK
Richard Vidgen	University of New South Wales, Australia
Grace Walsh	Maynooth University, Ireland
David Wastell	University of Nottingham, UK
Eleanor Wynn	Intel, USA

Contents

IS Use and Impact in Context

Metaverse and Social Media

Blockchain and Cryptocurrency

Concepts and Theories in Context

An Interdisciplinary Review of Ephemerality for Information Systems Research

Ronan Doyle[1,2(✉)], Kieran Conboy[1,2], and David Kreps[1,2]

[1] University of Galway, Galway, Ireland
r.doyle28@universityofgalway.ie
[2] Lero Science Foundation Ireland Research Centre for Software, Limerick, Ireland

Abstract. Ephemerality should be a significant concept for the information systems (IS) discipline but has not been developed as such. On the one hand, ephemerality is considered a characteristic of the IS "core" and focus, of data, information, and knowledge, and of digital material and the experience of digital technologies. On the other, IS reference to ephemerality is relatively scarce, and use of the term tends to implicitly rely upon the dictionary definition only. As a result, ephemerality is not well defined in the IS literature. Our aim in this study is to contribute to broader and deeper IS understanding of ephemerality. This is important because systems of people and technology are reformulating the meaning of ephemeral. Reformulating our understanding of ephemeral can improve our understanding of diverse, fast-paced, and quickly changing contexts for transfer and diffusion of digital technology. While our ultimate focus is ephemeral in digitalised contexts, our overarching focus is ephemerality as a standalone concept. We conduct an interdisciplinary review of the temporal and material qualities of the ephemeral in disciplines including sociology, philosophy, organisation studies, performance studies, new media studies, and IS. Out of this review, we propose a definition for ephemeral and develop a conceptual framework of ephemeral dimensions and characteristics, in which ephemerality is not only characterized by short-lived, unstable duration, but also by repetition, recombination, and durability. We conclude by briefly situating the framework in an IS context.

Keywords: Ephemeral · Information systems · Interdisciplinary · Review

1 Introduction

The Oxford English Dictionary (2004) defines 'ephemeral' as 'lasting or used for a very short time.' Ephemeral phenomena and materials shape human experience of the world (Döring et al. 2013). Indeed, it is routinely assumed (Conboy et al. 2020; Kavanagh 2007) and theorized that our increasingly digitized world is particularly ephemeral (e.g.: Urry 2000; Bauman 2000; Castells 1996). The lifespans of digital technologies, of digital information and its circulation, of work and news cycles, and of popular culture and market trends seem progressively evanescent. In the information systems (IS) context, ephemerality is considered characteristic of the IS "core" and focus (Lytinnen and King

© IFIP International Federation for Information Processing 2022
Published by Springer Nature Switzerland AG 2022
A. Elbanna et al. (Eds.): TDIT 2022, IFIP AICT 660, pp. 3–23, 2022.
https://doi.org/10.1007/978-3-031-17968-6_1

2004; Niederman et al. 1990), of digital material (Yoo 2010; Lytinnen 2021), and of the human experience of digital technologies (Yoo 2010). Ephemerality is now emerging in IS as an intentional design choice (Xu et al. 2018) in areas like the Internet of Things (IoT) (Huang et al. 2019), blockchain (Henry et al. 2018), and social media (Morlok et al. 2018), not least because the technical, regulatory, and social scenarios that require ephemerality are seemingly escalating (Giallorenzo et al. 2019).[1]

The problem is that the concept of ephemerality is not well defined in the literature. Ephemerality is most frequently applied in IS as an adjective but with little qualification (e.g.: ephemeral online communities (Quintarelli et al. 2019), ephemeral blockchain functions (Gisdakis et al. 2015), and ephemeral design knowledge (vom Brocke et al. 2020)). Yoo's (2010) impactful and insightful experiental computing paper notes ephemerality as one of three characteristics of digital but does not delineate what ephemeral means. In such cases, IS researchers are informed only by the dictionary definition and the context of the individual study. If digital is the future of IS (Burton-Jones et al. 2021) and ephemerality partially characterizes digital, we believe that a broader and deeper understanding of ephemerality will benefit IS stakeholders.

Bødker (2017), for example, suggests that IS must 'move towards a more general concern with how ubiquitous and pervasive computing is *entangled* with mundane "being".' Broader and deeper conceptualisation of the everyday ephemeral can augment theorization of digital. As Taylor (2007, p.4/5) puts it, 'digital technologies… further ask us to reformulate our understanding of… the ephemeral.' The challenge is to determine not only how digital is ephemeral, but also how digital is reformulating the meaning of ephemeral. IS researchers are well positioned to provide new theoretical perspectives on, for example, the ephemerality of digital transformation boundaries (Sandberg et al. 2020), of information and knowledge (Salovaara and Tuunainen 2015; Alavi and Leidner 2001), and of organizations (Prester et al. 2019), as well as the ephemeral nature of the sociomaterial and processual (Orlikowski and Scott 2008; Mousavi Baygi et al. 2021). Enhanced understanding can also contribute to disentangling the ephemeral from associated (and similarly elusive) digital-related concepts such as social acceleration (Fichman et al. 2014) and fluidity (Malhotra and Majchrzak 2021).

On the other hand, lack of conceptual depth stymies development of normative principles around ephemerality, raising potentiality for ephemerality-related risk (McPeak 2018; Shein 2013). The ephemeral highlights, for example, regulatory and corporate compliance concerns around the technical preservation of knowledge (Kelly and Baron 2019). Ephemerality-based social media[2] are implicated in US election interference (Mueller 2019) and Uber has directed employees to no longer use such platforms for Uber-related business. We will not adequately regulate for the consequences of digital

---

[1] Technical scenarios include storage constraints around IoT systems. Regulatory scenarios include concerns around persistence of data. Social scenarios include user desire for more authentic forms of digital communication. Mark Zuckerberg claims that ephemeral-type social media 'are by far the fastest growing areas of online communication' (Zuckerberg, 2019).

[2] Examples of 'ephemerality-based platforms' (Morlok et al., 2018) include Snapchat, Telegram, Wickr, Clubhouse, and Confide. Other apps are also adding ephemeral functionality to their platforms, such as Facebook and Instagram Vanish Mode, TikTok Stories, WhatsApp View Once, and Twitter Spaces. Web-tools like TweetDelete enable automatic deletion of tweets.

ephemerality without better understanding what the ephemeral implies. Enhanced understanding may also help disentangle the ephemeral from issues like privacy, anonymity, and trust (Welsh 2020; Schlesinger et al. 2017).

However, despite noteworthy IS reference to the ephemeral, to the best of our knowledge no IS study characterizes the concept in depth. Ephemerality *is* receiving attention in other fields. In the humanities and social sciences, the ephemeral informs interpretations of modernity and postmodernity (e.g.: Simmel 1900; Harvey 1989; Castells 1996; Bauman 2000; Rosa 2019). There is a rich lineage of ephemerality as a concept in the performance arts (Reason 2006) and in media studies (Grainge 2011). Philosophers (e.g.: Bergson 1911, 1946; Buci-Glucksmann 2003; Grosz 2013), artists (e.g.: Purpura 2009), and urban planners (e.g.: Lefebvre 1970; Crane 2015; Vera and Mehrotra 2015) have been motivated by ephemerality. Ephemerality is also a feature of studies in philosophy of science (Glennan 2009), organisation studies (e.g.: Bakker et al. 2016; Elkjaer 2017; Sydow 2017), computer science (e.g.: Schlesinger et al. 2017), consumer research (Bardhi and Eckhardt 2017), cyberpsychology (Utz et al. 2015), marketing (Belanche et al. 2019), and communication (Bayer et al. 2016; Kaun and Stiernstedt 2004). The contexts of digitalisation are common to most recent studies.

We suggest the IS perspective on ephemerality should be widely and uniquely informative, not least because ephemerality is seen to challenge both social and technical norms (Haber 2019; McRoberts et al. 2017). For example, with the rate of digital innovation, product introduction, and diffusion accelerating (e.g.: Gunther McGrath 2013), we might consider how ephemeral materials, spaces, timelines, and interactions challenge traditional theory around technology diffusion (e.g.: Rogers 1963). The objective of this research, therefore, is to contribute toward overcoming the issues and realizing the benefits outlined above by providing a rich definition and characterisation of the ephemeral based upon an interdisciplinary literature review of the term.

The remainder of this article is structured as follows: in Sect. 2, we discuss the theoretical background relevant to the review; in Sect. 3, we outline our methodological approach; in Sect. 4, we present our interdisciplinary review, develop a conceptual framework of ephemeral dimensions and characteristics, and propose a definition for ephemeral; Sect. 5 situates our conceptualisation of ephemeral in an IS context.

2 Theoretical Background

As per Merriam-Webster (2022), the etymological roots of 'ephemeral' are found in the Greek word *ephēmeros* from the stems *epi-* (meaning 'on' or 'in') and *hēmera* (meaning 'day'), which, in combination, yield the adjective *ephemeron* (meaning 'lasting (only) a day'). Young (2003) provides an excellent account of the historical development of the term and its derivatives, noting *ephemera* (plural of ephemeron) as the source of our contemporary 'short-lived' understanding. Today, *ephemera* is largely employed as a noun for things that exist or are used for a short time only. Early usage includes Aristotle applying *ephemera* to insects of very brief life span and the astronomical and astrological use of tabulated texts called *ephemerides* (plural noun derived from the adjective) to identify the regular placement of celestial bodies on specific days. It is not until the 1800s, however, that an increase is noted in the use of the adjectival form *ephemeral* through its 'application to transitory objects and abstract ideas' (*ibid.*).

'Ephemeral' thus emerges in the nineteenth century as a 'signifier' of modernity (Marcus and Saka 2006). Baudelaire (1863), characterizing modernity (in part) as 'the ephemeral, the fugitive, the contingent,' worries about 'a riot of [ephemeral] details'. As such, the task is to 'distill the eternal from the transitory' (*ibid.*), which sets an antagonistic and dualistic template of sorts, particularly in Western thinking, for the modernist relationship with the ephemeral. In modernity, the ephemeral is 'that which is resistant to meaning' (Doane 2002, p11). For Marx, Dostoevsky, and Goethe, the ephemeral must be 'confronted' and, as is possible, 'dealt with' (Harvey 1989). And even though, for Benjamin (1918, p.100) 'the integrity of an experience that is ephemeral' must be established on its own terms, for he too the perceived rise of the ephemeral in modernity is a form of 'hell' (Osborne and Charles 2020). This negative, acutely modernist sense of the ephemeral is borne not only of its problematic 'representability' (Doane 2002, p.11), of our inability to fix and quantify ephemeral value, but also of an emergent sense of the implications of ephemerality for stable societal structures, processes, and relations. In ephemeral digital contexts, for example, where the ephemeral is 'commonly seen more as a problem than as a solution' (Cotta et al. 2015), 'fixing' the ephemeral remains the predominant objective. The imposed aim for technologies, in the main, has long been to 'de-ephemeralise' the ephemeral (Evans 2011).

The ephemeral is perhaps most directly confronted in postmodern thinking. Given its basis in a 'weak' ontology of *becoming* (Chia 1995), postmodernism 'wallows' in 'total acceptance of... ephemerality' (Harvey 1989, p.27). In challenging the logic of language and organizing, the postmodernist aims to more adequately express 'the ephemeral aspects of process' (Chia 1995). It is not surprising then that the ephemeral receives particular attention in research traditions that, firstly, are significantly defined by their relation to the transitory and, secondly, wrestle with postmodern perspectives. For example, Artieri and colleagues (2020) note that ephemerality is a core focus in performance studies (e.g.: Phelan 1993) and in media studies (e.g.: Grainge 2011). On one level, the primary research challenge of the ephemeral is to 'write time' (Reason 2006), which, as we know, can be exceptionally difficult (e.g.: Dawson 2014). However, time is not the only concern when considering what counts as ephemeral.

Across the literature, two dimensions of the ephemeral reflect dictionary definitions: the temporal and the material. The temporal refers, as per standard definition (*ephemeral*), to experiences or perceptions of short duration: the perception of a rainbow, the experience of verbal interaction, the brief timeline of an ephemeral digital text. The material refers, as per standard definition (*ephemera*), to objects or things of time-limited and insubstantial value: train tickets, event programs, the content of an ephemeral digital text. In our view, it is essential to consider both the temporal and material aspects of the ephemeral for three reasons. Firstly, because digital is theorised to have material properties (Yoo 2010; Leonardi 2010). If digital is ephemeral, it is ephemeral in material and temporal ways. Secondly, because the qualities of material ephemera 'reflect the fact that they [are] only designed for short-term existence' (Crowther and Mac Cumhaill 2018). In other words, the material qualities of the ephemeral shape the temporal qualities of the ephemeral, and vice versa. And thirdly, because conceptualisation of the ephemeral as solely temporal (or material) will be complicated by several additional factors. As will be developed in Sect. 4, the ephemeral is not merely time-bound, singular, and insubstantial: the unstable ephemeral is also repetitive, recombinatory, and durable, with agency and meaning distributed in time.

3   Methodological Approach

Motivated by an interdisciplinary IS review (Smith et al. 2015) of another 'hard-to-fix' concept (privacy), the three-stage, concept-centric review approach proposed by Webster and Watson (2002) is followed. First, we performed a broad search spanning the information systems, social sciences, philosophy, humanities, marketing, management, and organisation theory literatures. We queried relevant library catalogues, journal databases, and conference proceedings. Search terms included 'ephemeral', 'ephemeral AND definition', 'ephemeral AND information systems', and 'ephemeral AND digital'. Secondly, working *backward* to broaden the scope further (*ibid.*), we reviewed the citations for the articles identified in step one, identifying literature of potential interest in other disciplines, including performance and media studies. Finally, we used Web of Science to work *forward* (*ibid.*), identifying further candidate articles citing the key articles previously identified. In total, 135 articles and 26 books were selected.

4   Interdisciplinary Review of the Ephemeral

Sub-Sects. 4.1 through 4.4 present our interdisciplinary review of the ephemeral. A tabulated conceptual framework of ephemeral dimensions and characteristics follows in sub-Sect. 4.5. A definition for the ephemeral is proposed in sub-Sect. 4.6.

4.1   Short-Lived: Speed, Compression, Limitation

Ephemeral timespans can range from split seconds, through minutes, weeks, and months, to years (Doring et al. 2013; Datry et al. 2017; Vidal-Abarca et al. 2020) and millions of years in, for example, geological contexts (Rohr and Furlong 1995). Nevertheless, in any specific context, the ephemeral always seems relatively short-lived (Schneider and Foot 2004), always conveys 'connotations of brevity and evanescence' (Grainge 2011, p.3). For example, ephemeral products (such as ephemeral hygiene products (López-Forniés and Sierra-Pérez 2021) or ephemeral digital products, like Snapchat (Villaespesa and Wowkowych 2020)) are 'short-term oriented' (Janssen et al. 2014). Approached as form, process, or perspective, the ephemeral always seems short-term (Bakker et al. 2016). Ephemeral 'briefness', however, is not only defined in terms of duration. The short-lived quality of the ephemeral is also shaped by interrelated forms of speed, compression, and limitation.

Firstly, social theorists have described the ephemeral in terms of an accelerated (and accelerating) pace of change and life (e.g.: Bauman 2000; Urry 2000; Rosa 2013). Ephemeral speed is evident in the turnover of technologies, fashions, products, labor processes, ideas, and images (Urry 1995, p.177); in the 'high-speed temporality' of social media practice (Arda 2021); in ephemeral organizations having to 'quickly convert decision into action' (Lanzara 1983), and in the speed of access to ephemeral forms of consumption (Bardhi and Eckhardt 2017). Ephemeral speed is further illustrated in relationships that are quickly formed and disbanded (Biraghi et al. 2018), in the speed of production and circulation for various types of new media (Grainge 2011, p.3), and in the acceleration of sociotechnical innovation (Heylighen 2007). However, Chun (2008) advises that we need to 'think beyond speed' because 'flow and segmentation do not quite encompass digital media's ephemerality.'

Secondly, the ephemeral compresses perceptual boundaries of value to timeframes localised to the present. As Young (2003) puts it, 'immediacy binds the ephemeral object more tightly to the occasion.' This compressed relationship of the ephemeral and the present time reinforces its short-lived nature. That the ephemeral 'inhabits the present' (Chun 2016, p.160) and is perceivable in the 'here and now' is not only 'essential for [its] effectiveness' (Grudin 2001, citing Toda 1991) but also intensifies the impact – both immediate *and* longer term – of the ephemeral. High-level social theory abstractions like 'time-space compression' (Harvey 1989), 'timeless time' (Castells 1996), 'liquid modernity' (Bauman 2000), and 'instantaneous time' (Urry 2000) theorise this quality of the ephemeral. Liquid modernity, for example, describes a rate of change so short-lived, quickly changing, and present-oriented that effective stabilisation of societal structures is no longer feasible. Eckhardt and Bardhi (2020), drawing from Bauman to develop a framework of 'liquid consumption' around three constructs (one being ephemerality (Bardhi and Eckhardt 2017)), note that the ephemeral refers to 'the expiration date of value increasingly shortening'. In characterising the ephemerality of 'instantaneous time', Urry also observes (2000, p.125) that time-horizons for decision-making are dramatically compressed.

Thirdly and consequently, the short-lived ephemeral is by nature limited. 'Anchored in the present' (He and Kivetz 2016), the nature of ephemeral time is 'fundamentally perishable' (Reason 2006) and the ephemeral moment seems materially 'constrained' (Bayer et al. 2015). The ephemerality of live performance is one clear example (Kirby 1974; Barba 1990; Schieffelin 1998). Dance, for instance, is said to exist at a 'perpetual vanishing point' (Siegel 1972) whereby, 'at the moment of its creation it is gone.' Phelan (1993) and Auslander (1999) note that ephemeral live performance is predicated upon disappearance; ephemeral organisations 'are there to disappear' (Lanzara 1983); for Grainge (2011), the ephemerality of web content means that 'digital materials are always under threat of disappearing'; ephemeral digital texts can be materially restricted to a specific number of views or a pre-determined span of viewing time (Chen and Cheung 2019; Vazquez-Herrero et al. 2019), and ephemeral edge computing proposes computation limited by 'stringent time constraints' (Lee et al. 2020).

In sum, the short-lived (durational) quality of the ephemeral is characterised by speed (of change), compression (of space, time, artifact, action, experience, value, and/or relevance to the present), and limitation (of space, time, artifact, action, experience, value, and/or relevance).

4.2 Repetitive: Anticipated, Varied

Ephemeral time is a time 'of repetitions and variations' (Buci-Glucksmann 2012). Performance scholars illuminate the repetitive quality of the ephemeral through the logic that 'ephemerality [is] 'repeated each night of a repeated live performance' (Reason 2006). For media scholars, television programs are 'ephemeral in the sense of being both fleeting and repeated', with the *most repeated* programs considered particularly ephemeral (Uricchio 2011, p.28–31). And Schneider and Foot (2004) write that digital content is 'ephemeral in its construction' because it must be reconstructed or reproduced to be experienced. The ephemeral is also cyclically repetitive. Brassley (1998) describes ephemeral cycles of change in the study of landscapes, ranging from twice-daily (i.e.: the movement of tides) to the progression of the seasons. Archaeological ephemeral art-works related to rites and performances are cyclical (López-Bertran 2019). And for Vera and Mehrotra (2015), the cyclically celebrated religious event in the ephemeral city of Kumbh Mela expresses 'a range of [material and temporal] ephemeral configurations.' In such places – and others, like humanitarian camps, natural disaster shelters, work settlements, and music festivals – the life cycle of the material ephemeral object (be it city, camp, shelter, settlement, or festival environment) – aligns with the duration of the activity so that objective start and end times are predictable. Applying the same logic to theatre spaces, we might say that ephemerality is repeated, Wednesday through Sunday, from 8pm to 11pm, for three months.[3]

Ephemeral repetition, therefore, not only infers orientation to the ephemeral 'past' but also anticipation of the ephemeral 'future'. Anticipation can range from the relative certainty of '*anticipated ephemera*' (Brassley 1998) (that is, ephemeral repetition we fully expect to occur) to the uncertainty of the ephemeral as 'a space of projective antic-ipation' (Crane 2015). For example, we may accurately anticipate the future repetition of tide movements, the upcoming run of a play, or the materialisation of a revisited webpage. Similarly, 'anticipation of the future embodied actions and activities', or *how* ephemerality *might* be repeated, is an important feature in ephemeral work settings (Hindmarsh and Pilnick 2007). The ephemeral is 'full of anticipation' (Purpura 2009). Drawing from Lefebvre (1970), Crane (2015) describes the ephemeral urban space as one of 'projective anticipation', where 'groups take control of spaces for expressive actions and constructions, which are soon destroyed' (Lefebvre 1970, p.130). Pop-up spaces, demonstration or celebration spaces, walls or hoardings displaying flyers and graffiti, and virus-testing or vaccination clinics are illustrative instantiations of ephemeral urban space. The ephemerality of these spaces is characterized not only by being short-lived but also by the anticipation that the ephemeral will be repeated *in* the space.

Finally, ephemeral repetition is further evident in the habituation of ephemeral actions. Consider, for example, the ephemerality of a mouse-click or the ease with which the ephemeral is enacted through taps, swipes, and scrolls on mobile digital platforms. 'Repetition breeds expertise,' writes Chun (2016). In this sense, following Bergson and Deleuze, repetition through the habitual enables forms of stability 'in a universe in which nothing truly repeats' (Grosz 2013). For Deleuze (1994), to repeat 'is to behave in a certain manner, but in relation to something unique or singular.' Using the example

---

[3] Opposing this perspective is the view that the ephemerality of performance is ontologically unrepeatable; the idea that 'a gesture, once made, can never be made the same way twice' (Artaud, 1938, p.75). Albeit an extreme example, the staging of the 20,000th performance of *The Mousetrap* in London on 16 December 2000 challenges the demonstrable practicality, if not the essence, of this perspective (Reason, 2006, p.16).

of festivals, Deleuze writes that repetitions 'do not add a second and a third time to the first, but carry the first time to the 'nth' power.' Hindmarsh and Pilnick (2007) reflect this understanding in their study of ephemeral workteams in surgical settings, where actors '(re)produce the routine or normative character of activities *for the first time again.*' We might say in summation that ephemeral repetition orients to the past to stabilise the present in a variation of that past, and, simultaneously, anticipates the future in repeated and varied forms of the ephemeral present.

Consequently, the short-lived limitation of disappearance does not negate the possibility of ephemeral repetition. For Phelan (1993), repetition marks the repeated as 'different'. In other words, the ephemeral repeats in ephemeral ways: there is always some variation, something unique, in repetitions of the ephemeral.

4.3   Recombinatory: Multiple Possibilities

The short-lived ephemeral is recombinatory. Ephemeral recombination repurposes the 'old' ephemeral artifact, action, space, or experience in a 'new' ephemeral present. The ephemeral city is dismantled and its material components 'recycled or repurposed' (Vera and Mehrotra 2015). Ephemeral architecture' is a 'system in which entire fragments of the building may be reclaimed and preserved' (Armada 2012). And 'old' ephemeral media texts are recombined again and again in 'new' ephemeral sequences and contexts (Urrichio 2011, p.28). Digital technology intensifies the ephemeral capacity for recombination. For example, the ephemeral recombination of prodigious volumes of diverse and ephemeral digital texts (Grainge 2011, p.3; Chun 2008) is endemic in copying, cutting, pasting, splicing, and circulation *of* ephemeral digital texts. Mashup applications similarly enable recombination of diverse functionalities from multiple web domains (Kreps and Kimppa 2015).

We distinguish the ephemerally repetitive from the ephemerally recombinatory in two interrelated ways. Firstly, where the meaning or knowledge gained from the ephemerally repetitive is sufficiently *similar* to the past or 'first' ephemeral, the meaning or knowledge gained from the ephemerally recombined is sufficiently *different*. For example, the roof of a food stall in the ephemeral city is recombined as one wall of a dwelling in a work settlement. Or the rerun of a television series recombines the ephemeral meaning of the artifact (the 'framework of coherence' (Urrichio 2011, p.28) for both old and first-time viewers. The ephemeral not only implies 'degradation or disappearance, but... is also productive, transformative' (Purpura 2009).

And secondly, where the ephemerally repetitive *anticipates* the future, the ephemerally recombinatory opens up the future in *multiple possibilities.* Lefebvre (1970) defines the urban ephemeral space as 'multifunctional, polyvalent, transfunctional' (Crane 2015). In the ephemeral city, there are 'infinite possibilities for recombination' (Vera and Mehrotra 2015). Guillaume and Huysmans (2018) suggest the ephemeral 'introduces a multiplicity of political temporalities.' In ephemeral organisations, the 'possibilities for action and response are multiplied' (Lanzara 1983). And in the context of consumer entrepreneurship, for Biraghi and colleagues (2018) it is the ephemerality of digital platforms that 'holds together the whole business model, throughout creating, de-configuring, and re-configuring.' In the examples cited, however, there remains a sense of linearity and succession, which the ephemeral is theorised to disrupt. Time is also recombined through the ephemeral.

In its future orientation, the ephemerally recombinatory is more fragmented and disjointed than the ephemerally repetitive. For Castells (1996), the temporality of 'timeless time' disorders succession and fosters simultaneity, creating what he terms 'structural ephemerality' (Castells 2004, p.57). For example, remote and non-linear work-day models (Gibbs et al. 2021; Dong et al. 2021) disorder the traditional segregation and linear flow of the working day, highlighting the overlap between 'ephemeral computing' and 'ubiquitous computing' (Cotta et al. 2015; Camacho et al. 2018). In a similar vein, media scholars note that as the digitized file can be recombined (that is, stopped, repeated, rearranged, edited, catalogued, and discarded (Kompare 2002, p.1)), it disorders the traditional, linear temporal logic of broadcast flow (Williams 1974). In cultures organized around systems of electronic media, the various forms of 'ephemeral symbolic communication' (Castells 2000) become a productive constituent of ephemeral 'timeless time' (i.e.: reality) (Castells 1996; Buci-Glucksman 2012). Fundamental to these systems, through digitalization and recurrent communication, is their recombinatory ability (Castells 2004, p.12). While the digitized media file should, in theory, resist ephemerality, online streaming of files is ultimately considered ephemeral because, in part, files are amenable to external recombination.

In sum, recombination of the 'past' ephemeral (space, time, artifact, action, or experience) enables repurposing *of* the ephemeral *from* the ephemeral in fragmented, disjointed ways that opens up the future in multiple possibilities.

4.4 Unstable, Durable

The short-lived ephemeral is unstable. Ephemerality is directly associated with organisational instability (Bechky 2006; van Marrewijk et al. 2016). Ephemeral art is 'inherently unstable' (Purpura 2009) and ephemeral digital art 'utterly unstable and prone to endless transformations' (Denoit 2014). Digital is ephemerally unstable because, for example, software and hardware 'constantly change, manically upgrade' (Chun 2016). Ephemeral computing environments are unstable and ever-changing (Cotta et al. 2016; Camacho et al. 2018). And ephemeral time is 'unstable time, made up of fragments' (Guillaume and Huysmans 2018). In processual terms, 'ephemeral emergence' (Sawyer 2005, p.210–214) cannot be known in advance because it occurs within 'episodic interactive encounters' (Tsoukas 2016). In postmodern terms, the ephemeral 'is interested in following traces, glimmers, residues, and specks of things' (Muñoz 1996, p.10).

The instability of the ephemeral underpins the modernist challenge of 'fixing' the ephemeral. Archivists have a difficult time categorising, storing, and defining ephemera (Young 2003). Political scientists suggest the ephemeral cannot be represented statically (Guillaume and Huysmans 2018).[4] The concept of 'stage detritus' highlights the 'unstable' state of live performance (Reason 2006, p.54). And in media research the ephemeral has been used to signify 'moving image detritus' (Grainge 2011, p.2), such as out-takes, outdated television sets, and the trash associated with movie theatres (Hastie 2007). Finally, the ephemeral as a concept is somewhat passed over in the processual literature

---

[4] Performance art scholars directly address this tension through, for example, critical review.

(Kreps et al. 2020), where reality is ephemerally unstable and stability, not change, must be accounted for (Chia and Nayak 2017). The Bergsonian, not 'short-lived', sense of duration applies in processual thinking, where 'temporariness' is 'centerstage' (Bakker et al. 2017) and 'the ephemeral and dynamic becomingness of human experience as a continuous flow of creative action' is the focus (Garud et al. 2015).

However, the short-lived, unstable ephemeral is also durable. For archaeologists, the ephemeral is 'embodied or materialized in durable objects' (López-Bertran 2019). Anthropologists note that ephemeral objects of value are also 'the durable material of cultural resilience and continuity' (Lepani 2012, p.75), with the short-lived limitation of such objects catalysing their durability (MacCarthy 2017). Ephemeral architecture sustains cultural meaning (Armada 2012) and legacy (Colfer 2019). 'Resilience' is a key property of any algorithm operating in ephemeral environments (Camacho et al. 2018). And the limitations of ephemeral social media content result in 'less loss (or forgetting)' of ephemeral content than of content perceived as more stable (van Nimwegen and Bergman 2019; Bayer et al. 2016). Digital technology intensifies ephemeral durability, complicating 'any clear division between technology as *either* permanent *or* ephemeral' (Evans 2011, p.157; *italics added*). Chun (2016) writes that digital information is 'curiously undead, constantly regenerating'. And media scholars note that although the 'configuration of space/time constructed through online media' is unstable and fragmented, the ephemeral fragments 'are so abundant as to be inexhaustible' and 'connect us into a network' (Grainge 2011, p.224). In the workings and experience of this network, the ephemeral is 'made to endure' (Chun 2008).

Ephemeral durability attunes us to the anticipation and possibility *in* the ephemeral and distributes the ephemeral in time. Repetition and recombination prolong the durability of the ephemeral by extending or repurposing the 'prior' ephemeral in the 'new' ephemeral present. The past of a primary ephemeral text (e.g.: a tweet) is 'reactivated' through 'knowledge that has since been acquired' (Uricchio 2011, p.29/30). Or the 'affective ephemera of likes and comments' (Haber 2019) stimulates what has objectively passed, regenerating new agency, meaning, and durability in the ephemeral.

Finally, the durability of the unstable ephemeral guides us toward the idea that the ephemeral is not only short-lived but 'eternal' (e.g.: Benjamin's 'eternal ephemerality' (1920/21, p.281); Castells' 'eternal ephemerality' (2010, p.497), and what Jameson (1991, p.64–68/71–2), after Lacan, calls the 'eternal present' (the unification of past and future with present)). In a landmark new media paper, Chun (2008) observes that digital technology originates non-linear temporalities that move 'simultaneously towards the future and the past', proliferating what she terms 'enduring ephemerals'. When digitalisation facilitates the ephemeral gathering of 'everything into the present' (Chun 2016), the modernist tension inherent to the unstable ephemeral is no longer a dualism but a duality, no longer 'either/or' but 'and': the ephemeral is fleeting *and* persistent (van Nimwegen and Bergman 2019), old *and* new (Chun 2008), 'open-ended *and* constrained' (Tsoukas 2016), short-lived *and* durable (Pimlott 2011; Gale 2009). We are given a sense of this perspective in Prado and Sapsed's (2016) study of ephemeral innovations in project-based organisations, where 'permanence is only realized through activation in the temporary.'

Husserl emphasizes that no experience is ephemeral merely in the sense of being short-lived or momentary (Moran 2011). The short-lived ephemeral 'is not fleeting' (Haber 2019). Rather, lived experience and 'the objective moment constituted in it, may become "forgotten"; but for all this, it in no way disappears without a trace... it has merely become latent' (Husserl 1948/1973, p.122). Husserlian traces are afforded material and temporal durability in the digital network. In the material documentation of ephemeral live performance, it is noted that representations of the ephemeral 'contain something of the thing itself... which are not the thing itself' (Reason 2006, P.232). The unstable ephemeral, in ephemeral ways, endures.

4.5   A Framework of Ephemeral Dimensions and Characteristics

The dialectical tension (Van de Ven and Poole 1995) between 'ephemeral' being short-lived *and* durable is not, in our view, a condition to be resolved but rather that condition which epitomises the ephemeral. This *logic of opposition* (Boudreau and Robey 1999) identifies the ephemeral as short-lived and durable by incorporating repetition and recombination. Below, we characterize the ephemeral through the four dimensions of Yoo's (2010) schematic for experiental computing: space, time, artifacts, and actors. We consider the schematic appropriate for three reasons. Firstly, experiental computing is concerned with 'computing in everyday life experiences' (*ibid.*). The ephemeral is that which is processed and encountered in the everyday (Guillaume and Huysmans 2018). Secondly, experiental computing describes a spatiotemporal context 'that is temporary and unfolds over time' (Yoo 2010). The material and temporal ephemeral is both short-lived and distributed in space and time. Thirdly, we consider the schematic an appropriately broad structure for conceptualizing the ephemeral in IS research (Table 1).

Table 1. Conceptual framework of ephemeral dimensions and characteristics

Ephemeral dimensions	Ephemeral characteristics			
	Short-lived	**Repetitive**	**Recombinatory**	**Unstable, Durable**
Time	*Speed:* of change *Compression:* of and to the present time *Limitation:* by transience, disappearance	*Repetitive:* recycling of past in repetition; ephemerality increased through repetition *Anticipated:* looks to future repetition *Varied:* present stabilized in variation of past	*Recombinatory:* repurposing of past in present; repurposed present sufficiently different to past; repurposed time disordered *Multiple possibilities:* future is open, uncertain	*Unstable:* emergent, volatile, non-linear, fragmented, fleeting temporal traces *Durable:* duality of ephemeral time as short-lived *and* durable/ 'eternal'
Space	*Speed:* of spatial transformation *Compression:* of space and the present time *Limitation:* of spatial value, use, and relevance	*Repetitive:* recycling of space; ephemerality increased through repetition *Anticipated:* ephemeral will be repeated in the space *Varied:* present space stabilized in similar variation of past	*Recombinatory:* repurposing of space that is sufficiently different to past use or form of the space *Multiple possibilities:* future ephemerality of the space is open, uncertain	*Unstable:* short-lived spatial limitations *Durable:* ephemeral materialized and extended in space through repetition and/or recombination; endurance catalyzed by being short-lived
Artifact	*Speed:* of material production, circulation, and consumption *Compression:* of material value, use, and relevance *Limitation:* of social and technical functions	*Repetitive:* recycling of artifact; ephemerality increased through repetition *Anticipated:* ephemeral will be repeated through the artifact *Varied:* present artifact stabilized in similar variation of past	*Recombinatory:* repurposing of artifact that is sufficiently different to past use or form of the artifact *Multiple possibilities:* future ephemerality of the artifact is open, uncertain	*Unstable:* short-lived material limitations *Durable:* ephemeral materialized and extended in artifacts through repetition and/or recombination; endurance catalyzed by being short-lived
Actor	*Speed:* of perception, experience, agency *Compression:* of perception, experience, agency to the present time *Limitation:* of perception, experience, agency to the present time	*Repetitive:* recycling of agency, experience; ephemerality increased through repetition *Anticipated:* looks to future repetition of agency, experience *Varied:* present agency, experience stabilized in variation of past	*Recombinatory:* repurposing of perception, experience, agency that is sufficiently different to past perception, experience, agency *Multiple possibilities:* future ephemerality of perception, experience, agency is open, uncertain	*Unstable:* short-lived limitations of perception, experience, and agency *Durable:* ephemeral embodied and extended in perception, experience, and agency through repetition and/or recombination; endurance catalyzed by being short-lived

4.6   A Definition for Ephemeral

Out of our review and framework, we propose the following definition for 'ephemeral': *the ephemeral refers to unstable times, spaces, artifacts, and actors that are both relatively short-lived and repetitive, recombinatory, and durable.*

5 Conclusion: Situating the Ephemeral in an IS Context

Ephemerality can help describe the diverse, fast-paced, and unstable contexts for transfer and diffusion of digital technology. For example, the periodicity between major innovations in traditional theories of diffusion (e.g.: Rogers 1963) is less plausible in ephemeral conditions where innovation, adoption, and diffusion can quickly be undone (e.g.: SEJ.com 2019). Even if delays remain determinable, they are compressing because of accelerating innovation (Heylighen 2007). As cited in Sect. 1, ephemerality is referenced in multiple IS contexts, including digital transformation (Mousavi Baygi et al. 2021) and social media (Urquhart and Vaast 2012). Dictionary definition of ephemeral, together with study context, implicitly informs most IS reference to the term.[5] This is problematic, as we outline below in the context of social media.

In IS social media research the ephemeral is routinely conceptualised as short-lived only (e.g.: Morlok et al. 2017, 2018; Browne et al. 2017; Xu et al. 2016). The degree of ephemerality is subsequently determined by the perceived duration of the singular ephemeral event, with shorter timespans denoting 'stronger' ephemerality and vice versa (Morlok et al. 2018; Xu et al. 2016). Through this lens, a three-second Snapchat 'snap' is more ephemeral than a ten-second 'snap' (Morlok et al. 2018). However, the ephemeral characteristics of repetition and recombination attune us to ephemeral durability, with practical implications for how ephemerality is described in research and design. That ephemeral social media content is, for example, subject to screenshotting, is characteristic of ephemerality, and not its conceptual 'other'.

However, the short-lived-only conceptualization sees the ephemeral set against, rather than containing, its perceived opposite: persistence or durability (Xu et al. 2016; Faik et al. 2020). Too rigid categorization accommodates excessively technical conceptual approaches to sociotechnical problems, whereby 'ephemerality is perceived as a technical remedy' *for* its perceived opposite (Morlok et al. 2018). Ephemerality is not merely 'an artificial technical restriction' (Morlok et al. 2017). Ephemerality-based IS research must necessarily address durability as constitutive of the ephemeral.

Unchallenged assumptions around the meaning of ephemeral result in a social media literature base that is user-centric, focusing on user characteristics, rationale, and experience in relation to ephemerality-based platforms at the expense of the ephemerality concept. Users, however, are very much 'cogs in a machine', and increasingly 'part of the applications that emerge and disappear' (Kreps and Kimppa 2015). The behaviours and experiences of people should not be offset against ephemeral technical affordances but factored into conceptualisation *of* the ephemeral.

In conclusion, systems of people and technologies are reformulating the nature of the ephemeral. We suggest that the unstable ephemeral is not only short-lived, but also repetitive, recombinatory, and durable. In their organizational study of subjective time, Shipp and Jansen (2021) note the importance of 'studying the past, present, and future simultaneously.' The ephemeral as characterised here offers such an opportunity.

---

[5] Notable exceptions include conceptual association of the ephemeral with malleability (Yoo, 2010; von Briel et al., 2018), editability (Kallinikos et al., 2010; 2013), fluidity (Lytinnen, 2021; Ahuja & Choudhury, 1999), and performance (Marabelli et al., 2016).

Acknowledgement. "This work was supported with the financial support of the Science Foundation Ireland grant 13/RC/2094 and co-funded under the European Regional Development Fund through the Southern & Eastern Regional Operational Programme to Lero - the Science Foundation Ireland Research Centre for Software (www.lero.ie)".

References

Ahuja, M., Choudhury, V.: Evolution of Virtual Organizations Over Time: An Empirical Examination. In: AMCIS Proceedings. 209 (1999)

Alavi, M., Leidner, D.E.: Review: knowledge management and knowledge management systems: conceptual foundations and research issues. MIS Q. **25**(1), 107–136 (2002)

Arda, B.: Ephemeral social media visuals and their picturesque design: interaction and user experience in instagram stories. Sapientiae, Film And Media Studies (19) 156–175 (2021). https://doi.org/10.2478/ausfm-2021-0010

Armada, J.: Sustainable Ephemeral: Temporary Spaces with Lasting Impact. Syracuse University Honors Program Capstone Projects (2012). https://surface.syr.edu/honors_capstone/111

Artaud, A.: Theatre and its Double. In: Richards, M.C. (ed.) Trans. Grove Press, New York (1958). (1938)

Artieri, G., Brilli, S., Zurovac, E.: Below the Radar: Private Groups, Locked Platforms, and Ephemeral Content—Introduction to the Special Issue. Social Media and Society, Sage (2021)

Auslander, P.: Liveness: Performance in a Mediatized Culture. Routledge, London (1999)

Bakker, R., DeFillippi, R., Schwab, A., Sydow, J.: Temporary Organizing: Promises, Processes, Problems. Organization Studies 1–17 (2016). https://doi.org/10.1177/0170840616655982

Bauman, Z.: Liquid Modernity. Polity Press, Cambridge (2000)

Barba, E.: Efermaele: "That Which Will Be Said Afterwards." Drama Rev. **36**(2), 77–80 (1992)

Bardhi, F., Eckhardt, G.: Liquid consumption. Journal of Consumer Research **44** (2017). https://doi.org/10.1093/jcr/ucx050

Baudelaire, C.: The Painter of Modern Life and Other Essays. In: Mayne, J. (ed.) Trans. Phaidon, London (1964)

Bayer, J.B., Ellison, N.B., Schoenebeck, S.Y., Falk, E.B.: Sharing the small moments: ephemeral social interaction on Snapchat. Inf. Commun. Soc. **19**(7), 956–977 (2015)

Bechky, B.: Gaffers, Gofers, and Grips: Role-Based Coordination in Temporary Organizations. Organ. Sci. **17**(1), 3–21 (2006)

Belanche, D., Cenjor, I., Pérez-Rueda, A.: Instagram stories versus facebook wall: an advertising effectiveness analysis. Spanish Journal of Marketing - ESIC. Emerald Pub. (2019)

Benjamin, W.: In: Bullock, M., Jennings, M. (eds.) Selected Writings, vol 1, pp. 1913–1926. Harvard University Press (1920/21) (1996)

Bergson, H.: Time and Free Will. George Allen and Unwin, New York (1911/2005)

Bergson, H.: Creative Evolution. Random House Modern Library, New York (1946/1992)

Berthon, P., Pitt, L., Parent, M., Berthon, J-P.: Aesthetics and Ephemerality: Observing and Preserving the Luxury Brand. California Management Review 52(1). University of California (2009)

Biraghi, S., Gambetti, R., Pace, S.: Between tribes and markets: the emergence of a liquid consumer-entrepreneurship. Journal of Business Research. Elsevier (2018)

Bødker, M.: "What else is there...?": reporting meditations in experiential computing. European Journal of Information Systems **26**(3), 274–286 (2017). https://doi.org/10.1057/s41303-017-0041-6

Brassley, P.: On the unrecognized significance of the ephemeral landscape. Landscape Research **23**(2), 119–132 (1998). https://doi.org/10.1080/01426399808706531

Browne, O., O'Reilly, P., Hutchinson, M.: Ephemeral returns: social network valuations and perceived privacy. In: ICIS Proceedings 10 (2017). http://aisel.aisnet.org/icis2017/Economics/Pre sentations/10

Buci-Glucksmann, C.: Esthétique de l'éphémère, Paris, Galilée, quoted in: Denoit, N. (2014) "Showing Time": the Ephemeral Made Sublime. Hybrid [Online], p. 13 (2003). https://doi.org/ 10.4000/hybrid.1153

Buci-Glucksmann, C.: Time spirals: from the immemorial to the ephemeral. Translator: Jonathan Pollock (2012). http://dombis.com/wp-content/uploads/2012/11/CBG_Time-spirals.pdf

Buci-Glucksmann, C., Quinz, E.: "Ephemeral Heritages", For an Aesthetics of the Ephemeral. Interview with Christine Buci-Glucksmann. Trans. Heft, S. Hybrid, n° 1 (2014)

Burton-Jones, A., Butler, B., Scott, S., Xu, S.: Next-generation information systems theorizing: a call to action. MIS Q. 45(1), 301–314 (2021)

Camacho, D., et al.: From ephemeral computing to deep bioinspired algorithms: new trends and applications. Future Generation Computer Systems (2018)

Cavalcanti, L.H.C., Pinto, A., Brubaker, J.R., Dombrowski, L.S.: Media, Meaning, and Context Loss in Ephemeral Communication Platforms: A Qualitative Investigation on Snapchat. In: CSCW, pp. 1934–1945 (2017). https://doi.org/10.1145/2998181.2998266

Castells, M.: The Information Age: Economy, Society and Culture, 2nd ed. Blackwell, Oxford UK (1996/2010)

Castells, M.: Materials for an exploratory theory of the network society. Br. J. Sociol. 51(1), 5–24 (2000)

Castells, M.: Informationalism, networks, and the network society: a theoretical blueprint. In: Castells, M. (ed.) The network society: a cross-cultural perspective. Edward Elgar, Northampton, MA (2004)

Chen, A., Karahanna, E.: Life interrupted: the effects of technology-mediated work interruptions on work and nonwork outcomes. MIS Quarterly 42(4), 1023–1042 (2018)

Chen, K.-J., Cheung, H.: Unlocking the power of ephemeral content: The roles of motivations, gratification, need for closure, and engagement. Computers in Human Behavior. Elsevier (2019)

Chia, R.: From modern to postmodern organizational analysis. Organization Studies 16, 579 (1995). https://doi.org/10.1177/017084069501600406

Chia, R., Nayak, A.: Circumventing the logic and limits of representation: otherness in east–west approaches to paradox. In: Smith, W., Lewis, M., Jarzabkowski, J., Langley, A. (eds.) The Oxford Handbook of Organizational Paradox. Oxford University Press (2017)

Chun, W.: The enduring ephemeral, or the future is a memory. Critical Inquiry 35(1), 148–171 (2008). The University of Chicago Press

Chun, W.: Updating to remain the same: habitual new media. MIT Press (2016)

Colfer, D.: The legacy of the ephemeral. Building Material, 22, Public, pp. 207–214. Architectural Association of Ireland (2019)

Conboy, K., Dennehy, D., O'Connor, M.: 'Big time': An examination of temporal complexity and business value in analytics. Information & Management (2018)

Cotta, C., et al.: Ephemeral computing and bioinspired optimization, challenges and opportunities. In: Proceedings of the 7th International Joint Conference on Computational Intelligence (IJCCI 2015), 1: ECTA, pp. 319–324 (2015)

Cotta, C., et al.: Application areas of ephemeral computing: a survey. In: LNCS 9770, pp. 153–167. Springer-Verlag, Berlin Heidelberg (2016). https://doi.org/10.1007/978-3-662-53525-79

Crane, S.: The Conundrum of Ephemerality: Time, Memory, and Museums. In: MacDonald, S. (ed.) A Companion to Museum Studies. Blackwell Publishing Ltd. (2006)

Crane, S.: Rewriting the battles of algiers: ephemeral tactics in the city at war. Space and Culture 18(4), pp. 387–410 (2015). Sage Journals

Crowther, T., Mac Cumhaill, C.: Perceptual ephemera. Oxford University Press (2018)

Datry, T., et al.: Flow intermittence and ecosystem services in rivers of the Anthropocene. Journal of Applied Ecology (2017). https://doi.org/10.1111/1365-2664.12941

Davies, R.: Digital intimacies: aesthetic and affective strategies in the production and use of online video. In: Ephemeral Media: Transitory Screen Culture from Television to YouTube. Palgrave Macmillan (2011)

Dawson, P.: Reflections: on time, temporality and change in organizations. J. Chang. Manag. **14**, 285–308 (2014)

Deleuze, G.: Difference and Repetition. Trans. Paul Patton. Athlone, London (1994)

Denoit, N.: "Showing Time": the Ephemeral Made Sublime. Hybrid [Online] (2014). https://doi.org/10.4000/hybrid.1153

Doane, M.A.: The Emergence of Cinematic Time. Harvard University Press (2002)

Dong, R., Wu, H., Ni, S., Lu, T.: The nonlinear consequences of working hours for job satisfaction: The moderating role of job autonomy. Current psychology (New Brunswick, N.J.), 1–22 (2021). Advance online publication. https://doi.org/10.1007/s12144-021-02463-3

Döring, T., Sylvester, A., Schmidt, A.: A design space for ephemeral user interfaces. In: Conference: TEI 2013 (2013). https://doi.org/10.1145/2460625.2460637

Doyle, R., Conboy, K.: The role of IS in the covid-19 pandemic: a liquid-modern perspective. Int. J. Info. Manage (2020). https://doi.org/10.1016/j.ijinfomgt.2020.102184

Eckhardt, G., Bardhi, F.: The value in de-emphasizing structure in liquidity. Marketing Theory **20**(4), 573–580. Sage (2020)

Elkjaer, B.: Organizations as real and ephemeral. Zeitschrift für Weiterbildungsforschung **40**(1), 53–68 (2017). https://doi.org/10.1007/s40955-017-0086-0

Evans, E.-J.: 'Carnaby Street, 10 a.m.': KateModern and the Ephemeral Dynamics of Online Drama. In: EPHEMERAL MEDIA: Transitory Screen Culture from Television to YouTube. Palgrave Macmillan (2011)

Fichman, R., Dos Santos, B., Zheng, Z.: Digital innovation as a fundamental and powerful concept in the information systems curriculum. MIS Q. **38**(2), 329–353 (2014)

Frisby, D.: Fragments of modernity. Cambridge (1985)

Fuller, R., Summers, J.: The impact of virtual team consistency on individual performance and perceptual outcomes over time. In: Proceedings of the 50th Hawaii International Conference on System Sciences (2017)

Gale, T.: Urban beaches, virtual worlds and 'The End of Tourism'. Mobilities **4**(1), 119–138 (2009). https://doi.org/10.1080/17450100802657996

Garud, R., Simpson, B., Langley, A., Tsoukas, H.: How does novelty emerge?. In: The Emergence of Novelty in Organizations. Perspectives on Process Organization Studies, 5, pp. 1–24. Oxford University Press, Oxford (2015)

Glennan, S.: Ephemeral mechanisms and historical explanation. Erkenn **72**, 251–266 (2010). https://doi.org/10.1007/s10670-009-9203-9

Giallorenzo, S., Montesi, F., Safina, L., Zingaro, S.P.: Ephemeral data handling in microservices. In: IEEE International Conference on Services Computing (SCC) (2019). https://doi.org/10.1109/SCC.2019.00048

Gibbs, M., Mengel, F., Siemroth, C.: Work from Home & Productivity: Evidence from Personnel & Analytics Data on IT Professionals. University of Chicago, Becker Friedman Institute (2021)

Gisdakis, S., Manolopoulos, V., Tao, S., Rusu, A., Papadimitratos, P.: Secure and privacy-preserving smartphone-based traffic information systems. IEEE Transactions on Intelligent Transportation Systems (2014)

Grainge, P.: Ephemeral Media: Transitory Screen Culture from Television to YouTube. Palgrave Macmillan (2011)

Grosz, E.: Architecture from the Outside: Essays on Virtual and Real Space. MIT Press (2001)

Grosz, E.: Habit today: ravaisson, Bergson. Deleuze and Us. Body and Society **19**(2–3), 219 (2013)

Grudin, J.: Group dynamics and ubiquitous computing. Commun. ACM **45**(12), 74–78 (2001)

Guillaume, X., Huysmans, J.: The concept of 'the everyday': ephemeral politics and the abundance of life. Cooperation and Conflict. Sage Journals (2018)

Gunther McGrath, R.: The pace of technology adoption is speeding up. Harvard Business Review (2013)

Haber, B.: The digital ephemeral turn: queer theory, privacy, and the temporality of risk. Media, Culture & Society. Sage (2019)

Harvey, D.: The Condition of Postmodernity: an Enquiry into the Origins of Cultural Change. Blackwell, Cambridge, Mass (1989)

Hastie, A.: Detritus and the Moving Image: Ephemera, Materiality, History. Journal of Visual Culture **6**(2), 171–174. Sage (2007). [1470–4129]

He, D., Kivetz, R.: Blink and you'll miss it: the consequences of ephemeral messaging. In: Moreau, P.M., Puntoni, S., Duluth, M.N. (eds.) NA - Advances in Consumer Research, pp. 470–471. Association for Consumer Research, USA (2016)

He, Y., Xu, X., Huang, N., Hong, Y., Liu, D.: Preserving user privacy through ephemeral sharing design: a large-scale randomized field experiment in online dating. In: ICIS 2021 Proceedings (2021)

Henry, R., Herzberg, A., Kate, A.: Blockchain access privacy: challenges and directions. In: Co-published by the IEEE Computer and Reliability Societies (2018)

Heyman, J., Campbell, H.: The anthropology of global flows. Anthropological Theory. Sage. **9**(2), 131–148 (2009)

Hindmarsh, J., Pilnick, A.: Knowing bodies at work: embodiment and ephemeral teamwork in anaesthesia. Organ. Stud. **28**(09), 1395–1416 (2007)

Huang, K., Zhang, X., Mu, Y., Rezaeibagha, F., Du, X., Guizani, N.: Achieving intelligent trust-layer for IoT via self-redactable blockchain. IEEE Transactions on Industrial Informatics (2018). https://doi.org/10.1109/TII.2019.2943331

Husserl, E.: Experience and Judgment, investigations in a genealogy of logic. Northwestern University Press (1948/1973)

Janssen, C., Vanhamme, J., Lindgreen, A., Lefebvre, C.: The Catch-22 of responsible luxury: effects of luxury product characteristics on consumers' perception of fit with corporate social responsibility. Journal of Business Ethics **119**(1), 45–57. Springer (2014)

Jameson, F.: Postmodernism, or The Cultural Logic of Late Capitalism. Duke University Press (1991)

Kallinikos, J.: The making of ephemeria: on the shortening life spans of information. The Int. J. Interdisciplinary Sci. **4**(3). Common Ground Publishing (2009)

Kallinikos, J., Aaltonen, A., Marton, A.: A Theory of Digital Objects. First Mondays (2010)

Kallinikos, J., Aaltonen, A., Marton, A.: The ambivalent ontology of digital artifacts. MIS Q. **37**(2), 357–370 (2013)

Karlsson, M., Sjøvaag, H.: Content analysis and online news. Digital Journalism (2015). https://doi.org/10.1080/21670811.2015.1096619

Kaun, A., Stiernstedt, F.: Facebook time: technological and institutional affordances for media memories. New Media & Society **16**(7), 1154–1168. Sage (2004)

Kavanagh, D., Lightfoot, G., Lilley, S.: Running to stand still: late modernity's acceleration fixation. Cult. Politics **3**(1), 95–122 (2007)

Kelly, J.T.: Beyond the broadcast text: new economies and temporalities of online TV. In: Grainge, P. (ed.) Ephemeral Media: Transitory Screen Culture from Television to YouTube. Palgrave Macmillan (2011)

Kelly, T., Baron, J.: The rise of ephemeral messaging apps in the business world. The National Law Review **XI**(249) (2021)

Kirby, M.: The New Theatre: Performance Documentation. New York University Press (1974)

Kirçova, İ., Pınarbaşı, F., Köse, Ş.G.: Understanding ephemeral social media through instagram stories: a marketing perspective. BMIJ **8**(2), 2173–2192 (2020)

Kompare, D.: 'Flow to Files: Conceiving 21st Century Media'. In: Conference Paper, Media in Transition 2. Cambridge, MA (2002)

Kotfila, C.: This message will self-destruct: the growing role of obscurity and self- destructing data in digital communication. Bull. Assoc. Inf. Sci. Technol. **40**(2), 12–16 (2014)

Kreps, D.G.P., Kimppa, K.: Theorising web 3.0: ICTs in a changing society. Information Technology & People **28**(4), pp. 726–741 (2015). https://doi.org/10.1108/ITP-09-2015-0223

Kreps, D.G.P., Rowe, F., Muirhead, J.: Understanding digital events: process philosophy and causal autonomy. In: Proceedings of the 53rd Hawaii International Conference on System Sciences (2020)

Lanzara, G.F.: Ephemeral organizations in extreme environments; Emergences, strategy, extinctions. J. Manage. Stud. **20**(1), 71–95 (1983)

Lee, G., Saad, W., Bennis, M.: An Online Framework for Ephemeral Edge Computing in the Internet of Things (2020). https://doi.org/10.48550/arXiv.2004.08640

Lefebvre, H.: The Urban Revolution. In: Bononno, R. (ed.) Trans. (2003). University of Minnesota Press (1970)

Lehmann, J., Recker, J.: Offerings that are "Ever-in-the-Making": post-launch continuous digital innovation in late-stage entrepreneurial ventures. In: ICIS 2019 Proceedings 11 (2019)

Leonardi, P.M.: Digital materiality? how artifacts without matter, matter. First Monday (2010)

Lepani, K.: Islands of Love, Islands of Risk: Culture and HIV in the Trobriands. Vanderbilt University Press, Nashville, TN (2012)

López-Bertran, M.: Ephemeral Art. Encyclopedia of Global Archaeology (2019). https://doi.org/10.1007/978-3-319-51726-1_2825-1

López-Forniés, I., Sierra-Pérez, J.: Ephemeral products: opportunities for circularity based on ideation for reuse. In: An Experience. International Conference on Design, Simulation, Manufacturing: The Innovation Exchange ADM: Design Tools and Methods in Industrial Engineering II, pp. 365–372 (2021)

Lorino, P., Tricard, B., Clot, Y.: Research methods for non-representational approaches to organizational complexity: the dialogical mediated inquiry. Organ. Stud. **32**(6), 769–801 (2011)

Lyytinen, K.: Innovation logics in the digital era: a systemic review of the emerging digital innovation regime. Innovation (2021). https://doi.org/10.1080/14479338.2021.1938579

Lyytinen, K., King, J.: Nothing At The Center?: Academic Legitimacy in the Information Systems Field. Journal of the Association for Information Systems 5(6) (2004). https://doi.org/10.17705/1jais.00051

MacCarthy, M.: Doing away with Doba? Women's Wealth and Shifting Values in Trobriand Mortuary Distributions. In: Hermkens, A-K., Lepani, K. (eds.) SINUOUS OBJECTS, Revaluing Women's Wealth in the Contemporary Pacific. Australian National University Press (2017)

Malhotra, A., Majchrzak, A.: Hidden patterns of knowledge evolution in fluid digital innovation. Innovation (2021). https://doi.org/10.1080/14479338.2021.1879653

Marabelli, M., Newell, S., Galliers, R.: The materiality of impression management in social media use: a focus on time, space and algorithms. In: Thirty Seventh International Conference on Information Systems (2016)

Marcus, G., Saka, E.: Assemblage. Culture & Society. Sage Publishing, Theory (2006)

McPeak, A.: Self-destruct apps: spoliation by design? Akron Law Review **51**(3) (2017)

McRoberts, S., Ma, H., Hall, A., Yarosh, S.: Share First, Save Later: Performance of Self through Snapchat Stories CHI 2017, May 06–11. Denver, CO, USA (2017)

Merleau-Ponty, M.: The Visible and the Invisible. Northwestern University Press (1968)

Merriam-Webster.com Dictionary: (2022). https://www.merriam-webster.com/dictionary/ephemeral

Moran, D.: Edmund Husserl's phenomenology of habituality and habitus. Journal of the British Society for Phenomenology **42** (2011)

Morlok, T., Schneider, K., Matt, C., Hess, T.: Snap. Share. (Don't) Care? Ephemerality, Privacy Concerns, and the Use of Ephemeral Social Network Sites. In: Proceedings of Twenty-third Americas Conference on Information Systems (2017)

Morlok, T., Constantiou, I., Hess, T.: Gone for better or for worse? exploring the dual nature of ephemerality on social media platforms. In: ECIS Completed Research Papers. Paper 15 (2018)

Mousavi Baygi, R., Introna, L.D., Hultin, L.: Everything flows: studying continuous socio-technological transformation in a fluid and dynamic digital world. MIS Quarterly **45**(1) (2021)

Mueller, R.: Report on the Investigation into Russian Interference in the 2016 Presidential Election (2019). Retrieved from https://www.justice.gov/storage/report.pdf

Muñoz, J.E.: Ephemera as evidence: introductory notes to queer acts. Women & Performance: a Journal of Feminist Theory **8**(2), 5–16 (1996). https://doi.org/10.1080/07407709608571228

Nayak, A.: On the way to theory: a processual approach. Organ. Stud. **29**(2), 173–190 (2008)

Niederman, F., Brancheau, J., Wetherbe, J.: Information Systems Management Issues for the 1990s. MIS Quarterly (1991)

Orlikowski, W.J., Scott, S.V.: Sociomateriality: challenging the separation of technology, work and organization. Acad. Manag. Ann. **2**(1), 433–474 (2008)

Osborne, P., Charles, M.: Walter Benjamin. Stanford Encyclopedia of Philosophy (2020). https://plato.stanford.edu/archives/fall2021/entries/benjamin/

Oxford English Dictionary (OED) Oxford: Clarendon Press; Oxford University Press (2004)

Phelan, P.: Unmarked: The Politics of Performance. Routledge, London (1993)

Pimlott, H.: 'Eternal ephemera' or the durability of 'disposable literature': the power and persistence of print in an electronic world. Media Cult. Soc. **33**(4), 515–530 (2011)

Prado, P., Sapsed. J.: The Anthropophagic organization: how innovations transcend the temporary in a project-based organization. Organization Studies **37**(12), 1793–1818 (2016). https://doi.org/10.1177/0170840616655491

Prester, J., Cecez-Kecmanovic, D., Schlagwein, D.: Becoming a digital nomad: decentered identity work along agentic lines. In: 11th International Process Symposium (2019)

Purpura, A.: Framing the ephemeral. African Arts. **42**(3), 11–15 (2009). https://doi.org/10.1162/afar.2009.42.3.11

Quintarelli, E., Rabosio, E., Tanca, L.: Efficiently using contextual influence to recommend new items to ephemeral groups. Inf. Syst. **84**, 197–213 (2019)

Reason, M.: Documentation, Disappearance, and the Representation of Live Performance. Palgrave Macmillan (2006)

Robey, D., Boudreau, M.: Accounting for the contradictory organizational consequences of information technology: Theoretical directions and methodological implications. Information Systems Research **10**, 167–185 (1999). https://doi.org/10.5539/mas.v6n4p49

Rogers, E.M.: Diffusion of Innovations. Free Press, New York (1995)

Rohr, K., Furlong, K.: Ephemeral plate tectonics at the Queen Charlotte triple junction. Geology **23**(11), 1035–1038 (1995)

Rosa, H.: Social acceleration : a new theory of modernity. Columbia University Press, New York (2013)

Rosa, H.: Resonance. A Sociology of Our Relationship to the World. Trans. J. Wagner, Cambridge: Polity (2019)

Salovaara, A., Tuunainen, V.: Mediated sharing as software developers' strategy to manage ephemeral knowledge. In: ECIS Completed Research Papers. Paper 158 (2015)

Sandberg, J., Holmström, J., Lyytinen, K.: Digitization and phase transitions in platform organizing logics: Evidence from the process automation industry. MIS Quarterly **44**(1), 129–153 (2020). https://doi.org/10.25300/MISQ/2020/14520

Sarker, S., Sahay, S.: Understanding virtual team development: an interpretive study. J. Assoc. Info. Sys. (4) (2003)

Sawyer, K.: Social Emergence. Cambridge University Press, Cambridge (2005)

Schieffelin, E.L.: 'Problematising performance'. In: Hughes Freeland, R. (ed.) Ritual, Performance, Media, London, pp. 194–207. Routledge (1998)

Schlesinger, A., Chandrasekharan, E., Masden, C.A., Bruckman, A.S., Edwards, W.K., Grinter. R.E.: Situated anonymity: impacts of anonymity, ephemerality, and hyper-locality on social media. In: Proceedings of the 2017 CHI Conference on Human Factors in Computing Systems. Denver, CO, USA (2017)

Schneider, S., Foot, K.: The web as an object of study. Sage. New media & society **6**(1), 114–122 (2004). https://doi.org/10.1177/1461444804039912

SEJ.com (www.searchenginejournal.com): R.I.P. to the Top 10 Failed Social Media Sites (2019). Accessed online 05 May 2022 at: https://www.searchenginejournal.com/failed-social-media-sites/303421/#close

Shein, E.: Ephemeral data. Communications of the ACM **56**(9), 20–22 (2013)

Shipp, A., Jansen, K.: The "other" time: a review of the subjective experience of time in organisations. Academy of Management Annals **15**(1), 299–334 (2021). https://doi.org/10.5465/annals.2018.0142

Siegel, M.: At the Vanishing Point: A Critic Looks at Dance. Saturday Review Press, New York (1972)

Simmel, G.: The philosophy of money. Routledge, London (1900/2004)

Smith, H.J., Dinev, T., Xu, H.: Information privacy research: an interdisciplinary review. MIS Q. **35**(4), 989–1016 (2011)

Sydow, J.: Temporary organizing – the end of organizations as we know them? Rutgers Business Review **2**(2) (2017)

Taylor, D.: The Archive and the Repertoire. Duke University Press (2007)

Toda, M.: The urge theory of emotion and social interaction. Unpublished manuscript. Chukyo University (1999)

Tropp, J., Baetzgen, A.: Users' definition of snapchat usage. Implications for marketing on snapchat. Int. J. Media Manage **21**(2), 130–156 (2019)

Tsoukas, H.: Don't Simplify, Complexify: From Disjunctive to Conjunctive Theorizing in Organization and Management Studies. Journal of Management Studies **54**(2) (2016)

Uricchio, W.: The Recurrent, the Recombinatory and the Ephemeral. In: Grainge, P. (ed.) Ephemeral Media: Transitory Screen Culture from Television to YouTube. Palgrave Macmillan. (2011). and: manuscript version at: https://web.mit.edu/uricchio/Public/pdfs/pdfs/The%20Recurrent.pdf

Urquhart, C., Vaast, E.: Building social media theory from case studies: a new frontier for is research. In: Thirty Third International Conference on Information Systems (2012)

Urry, J.: Consuming Places. Routledge (1995)

Urry, J.: Sociology beyond societies: mobilities for the twenty-first century. Routledge (2000/2012)

Utz, S., Muscanell, N., Khalid, C.: Snapchat elicits more jealousy than Facebook: a comparison of Snapchat and Facebook use. Cyberpsychol. Behav. Soc. Netw. **18**(3), 141–146 (2015)

Vaast, E., Boland, R., Davidson, E., Pawlowski, S., Schultze, U.: Investigating the "Knowledge" in knowledge management: a social representations perspective. Communications of the Association for Information Systems **17**(15) (2006). https://doi.org/10.17705/1CAIS.01715

Ven, A.H. van de, Poole, M.S.: Explaining development and change in organizations. The Academy of Management Review **20**(3) (1995)

van Marrewijk, A., Ybema, S., Smits, K., Clegg, S., Pitsis, T.: Clash of the titans: temporal organizing and collaborative dynamics in the panama canal megaproject. Organ. Stud. **37**(12), 1745–1769 (2016) van Nimwegen, C., Bergman, K.: Effects on cognition of the burn after reading principle in ephemeral media applications. Behaviour & Information Technology (2019)

Vázquez-Herrero, J., Direito-Rebollal, S., López-García, X.: Ephemeral Journalism: News Distribution Through Instagram Stories. Social Media + Society, Sage Publishing (2019)

Vera, F., Mehrotra, R.: Temporary flows & ephemeral cities. Room One Thousand, 3 (2015). Retrieved from https://escholarship.org/uc/item/18f9p6np

Vidal-Abarca, M.R., Gómez, R., Sánchez-Montoya, M., Arce, M., Nicolás, N., Suárez, M.: Defining dry rivers as the most extreme type of non-perennial fluvial ecosystems. Sustainability **12**, 7202 (2020). https://doi.org/10.3390/su12177202

Villaespesa, E., Wowkowych, S.: Ephemeral storytelling with social media: snapchat and instagram stories at the brooklyn museum. Sage. Social Media + Society **1**(13)

vom Brocke, J., Winter, R., Hevner, A., Maedche, A.: Special issue editorial – accumulation and evolution of design knowledge in design science research: a journey through time and space. J. Asso. Info. Sys. (2021)

von Briel, F., Recker, J., Davidsson, P.: Not all digital venture ideas are created equal: Implications for venture creation processes. J. Strategic Info. Sys. (2018) https://doi.org/10.1016/j.jsis.2018.06.002

Wakefield, L., Wakefield, R.: Anxiety and ephemeral social media use in negative eWOM creation. J. Interact. Mark. **41**, 44–59 (2018)

Webster, J., Watson, R.: Analyzing the past to prepare for the future: writing a literature review. MIS Q. **26**(2), xiii-xxiii (2002)

Welsh, S.: Ephemerality as data prevention: values for an ethics of ephemeral mobile media. Mobile Media & Communication 1–17. Sage (2020)

Williams, R.: Television: Technology and Cultural Form. Fontana, London (1974)

Xu, B., Chang, P., Welker, C., Bazarova, N., Cosley, D.: Automatic archiving versus default deletion: what snapchat tells us about ephemerality in design. In: CSCW Conf Comput Support Coop Work. Author manuscript; available in PMC 2018 (2018)

Yongguang, Z., et al.: Characteristics and factors controlling the development of ephemeral gullies in cultivated catchments of black soil region, Northeast China. Soil and Tillage Research. **96**(1–2), 28–41 (2007). https://doi.org/10.1016/j.still.2007.02.010

Yoo, Y.: Computing in everyday life: a call for research on experiential computing. MIS Q. **34**(2), 213–231 (2010)

Young, T.G.: Evidence: toward a library definition of ephemera. RBM A Journal of Rare Books Manuscripts and Cultural Heritage **4**(1) (2003). https://doi.org/10.5860/rbm.4.1.214

Zuckerberg, M.: A Privacy-Focused Vision For Social Networking. https://m.facebook.com/nt/screen/?params=%7B%22note_id%22%3A2420600258234172%7D&path=%2Fnotes%2Fnote%2F&refsrc=deprecated Retrieved online 11 October 2021

Zurcher, L.: Social-psychological functions of ephemeral roles: a disaster work crew. Human Organization **27**(4), 281–297. Society for Applied Anthropology (Winter 1968)

Co-design Theory Adoptability: How Organizational Change is Co-created by Design Theorists and Theory Adopters

Jan Pries-Heje[1][✉] [iD] and Richard Baskervillle[2] [iD]

[1] Roskilde University, Roskilde, Denmark
janph@ruc.dk
[2] Georgia State University, Atlanta, USA

Abstract. Descriptive theories tell us how to understand the world better and pre-scriptive theories tell us how to make the world better. Design theories are of the latter kind but usually involves a product or process artifact to create changes as well. Despite a focus on utility, there is little evidence about how design theories become adopted after their development. We know too little about how design theories are applied, adopted, adapted, and emerge and change over time. We present a study of an organizational change design theory that was adopted in 108 different organizations. The results indicate that the theory was adopted As-Is in 25% of the cases. But it was adapted in various ways for use in the remaining organizations. Our analysis of these cases provides a typology of eight categories of adoptability. Among these, organizations most commonly adapted the recom-mended organizational strategy. As a result of these and other findings we show how design theory adoption is a continuous co-creation process between design theorists and design adopters.

Keywords: Design theory · Design logic · Organizational change · IT adoption

1 Introduction

In this paper we build forward from concepts found in design science research (DSR) [1]. DSR is a relatively new interventionalist research paradigm with much in common with action research [2], clinical field work [3], etc. Such research approaches seek to learn by practicing and develop knowledge by solving practical problems. In DSR, interventions usually center designing, building and evaluating an artifact situated in a problem setting. Like other interventionalist research, DSR interventions are driven by theory. Theory for DSR often takes specific forms: *design theory* entails the relationships between generalized requirements and generalized artifact designs [4]; *design principles* express heuristics for designing a class of artifacts [5]. Joan van Aken proposed the use of technological rules as a means of expressing the prescriptive outcomes of management theory, i.e., collectively representing management design theories. Technological rules were first described in Mario Bunge's [6, 7] works on philosophy of science; they are a

© IFIP International Federation for Information Processing 2022
Published by Springer Nature Switzerland AG 2022
A. Elbanna et al. (Eds.): TDIT 2022, IFIP AICT 660, pp. 24–39, 2022.
https://doi.org/10.1007/978-3-031-17968-6_2

means of contrasting scientific knowledge from technological knowledge. Technological rules entail three elements: (1) prescribed actions based on (2) desired outcomes and (3) contingencies. We can think of these rules as technological propositions that proceed from a scientific theory. Technological rules can guide practitioners (such as engineers, accountants, physicians, and project managers) who may not know the theory but do know common practices by which outcomes are known to follow actions when taken under known contingencies.

Adoptability is an ability to start-to-use (i.e., adopt) some new artifact, be it a method, a technology, a framework, etc. Innovation lies not only in the new artifact, but also in the act of starting-to-use. Hence adoptability is created by adaptability. The ability of a design theory to apply persistently across a class of problems and a class of solutions (i.e., artifacts) depends on its accommodation for adoptability of these artifacts. The artifacts must adapt to a range of similar problems in a range of different contexts. Indeed, the change involved in such artifacts may quickly amount to a transformation. The contemporary demand for rapid and transformational change in technical artifacts means that adoptability not only applies to the artifact, but also to the design theory itself. The notion of *design theory adoptability* regards a characteristic liability or tendency for the design theory itself to change in order for it to guide the design of artifacts that adapt to a transformational change in the range of problems and contexts.

With technological rules as a frame, we see there are eight kinds of ways that practitioners adapt technical knowledge. The purpose of this paper is to illustrate how this frame can reveal patterns in adaptation of technical knowledge in practice.

In this paper we report our research into the adoptability of design theory in practical settings. Our choice of design theory to study was an organizational change nexus [8] and we obtained access to 108 documented cases that applied a design theory for choosing organizational change strategy. The organizational change nexus design theory was based on technological rules [9]. We analyzed the achievement of adoptability through the use of a *heuristic operator*. This heuristic operator encodes adoptability into the design theory by adapting the logic present in the design principles.

The paper is organized as follows. First, we discuss design logic and technological rules. In Sect. 3 we present a framework we derived to analyze adoptability. Then in Sect. 4 we present our multi-case study research method, and then in Sect. 5 we present our analysis of adoptability and answer the research question. Finally, we discuss and conclude the paper in Sect. 6 and 7.

2 Design Logic: Analytical Versus Heuristic Technological Rules

Van Aken sought to improve the practical usefulness of the corpus of management research: "academic management research has a serious utilization problem" [9, p. 219]. Organizational research is too often descriptive and historical. There is little direct usefulness of this kind of reflective study, especially for managers confronting newer, more current problems. For management research to have a greater impact on management, it must become more prescriptive and more design-oriented.

A design theory (or a set of design principles) is a generalized or abstract form of design as a design for a class of artifacts [4, 5, 10, 11]. While, some of the seminal work in science of design considered design logic [e.g., 12], the IS research community has instead focused on design theory. The works in design logic often concern electronic circuit logic design, or uses the term less formally to regard the general thinking behind designs for communication [e.g., rhetorical design logic or community design, 13, 14]. As information systems researchers, we use the term design logic for a set of formal principles of reasoning employed by designers for creating a design. Such logic sits in the realm of meta-design because it represents a formal set of principles that may be used across a general class of designs.

Simon's [12] influential definition of a science of design required an imperative logic, one involving not statements of the way things *are*, but statements of the way things *should become*. Imperative logics have serious flaws. For example, systems of imperative logic often have a different purpose: more often associated with ethics than design [15]. As a substitute, Simon introduced declarative logic within a search process. Fundamentally, the designer uses a declarative framework as a means of expression to represent the design solution. Then the design process has only to search through various values for the elements of the framework until a satisfactory design is discovered (satisficing). "Problem-solving systems and design procedures in the real world do not merely assemble problem solutions from components but must search for appropriate assemblies" [12, p. 124].

Consistently with Simon's design logic, van Aken [16] proposed management theory was a type of design theory that consists of "field-tested and grounded technological rules" [9]. This proposal includes two possible outputs: artifacts and interventions. A professional episode includes three kinds of designs. The object-design defines the artifact or intervention. The realization-design is the plan for implementing the artifact or intervention. The process-design is a plan for the design process itself. Designing is a means of developing prescriptive knowledge.

For van Aken, "A technological rule follows the logic of 'if you want to achieve **Y** in situation **Z**, then perform action **X**'. The central element of the rule is action **X**, a general solution concept for a type of field problem" [17, p. 23]. A formal expression of this rule would be,

$$(Z, Y) \rightarrow X$$

In this rule, **x** is the imperative "Do **x**". Imperative logic prescribes the behaviour of human actors. An example of this logic would be the technological rule, "If you want to achieve user acceptance of a new technology in a situation of user alienation, then adopt a co-creative design approach." This technological rule might be stated,

((USER ALIENATION), (USER ACCEPTANCE OF A NEW TECHNOLOGY)) →
ADOPT A CO – CREATIVE DESIGN APPROACH

This rule may seem too tidy. Perhaps co-creation works best in collaborative organizational cultures. If so, **Z** would become "user alienation in a collaborative culture". Exactness in expressing all contingencies that affect the choice of action **X** can be done with multiple rules, each defining different contingencies and/or outcomes. (Such was Simon's [12] notion of searching through a forest of declarative rules.) The alternative to creating a forest of rules with compounded terms is to keep the rules simple but define the process of applying them as a process of adaptation [9].

A process of adapting the rules to specific situations involves establishing a generative function. Pawson and Tilley [18] relate adaptability to *generative causality*. Generative causality means that the exact meaning of the terms in the technological rule is a result of translations by managers, not any natural cause. The meaning is anchored to intention: an outcome sought by such interventions. Technological rules are a generative form of causal relationship.

If adoption of technological rules is a practice involving translation and interpretation, practice must be informed by the underlying theory. In our example above, the underlying theory is a fundamental socio-technical theory. This theory explains how co-creation approaches build acceptance through involvement and commitment among participating users. Such involvement and commitment emerge because participation and co-creation in design decisions empowers users. This participation gives them shared control over their futures. For this reason, technological rules (Bunge's technical knowledge) must be grounded in theory (Bunge's scientific knowledge) [17]. Grounding prevents technological rules from degenerating into an instrumental form of rules-of-thumb. "In engineering and in medicine, grounding of technological rules can be done with the laws of nature and other insights from the natural and the life sciences (as well as from insights developed by these design sciences themselves). In management, grounding can be done with insights from the social sciences" (p. 25). Regardless of how useful technological rules may be in practice, they are not theories in design science until they are grounded in a way that is acceptable to social science.

3 Heuristic Operators and Design Logic

"However, many prescriptions in a design science are of a heuristic nature. They can rather be described as 'if you want to achieve Y in situation Z, then something like action X will help'. 'Something like action X', means that the prescription is to be used as a *design exemplar*. A design exemplar is a general prescription which has to be translated to the specific problem at hand; in solving that problem, one has to design a specific variant of that design exemplar." [9, p. 227].

Distinguishing between algorithmic and heuristic prescriptions opens the design process not only to analytic productions, but also generative productions. Generative productions add creativity and innovation to the process of implementation of technological rules. They incorporate problem-situated knowledge that allow the rules to succeed. Generative productions require the evaluation of "something like" to incorporate creative invention in adapting the prescriptive action X to the exact context at hand. Generative productions are required because, in practice, organizational change cannot always be reduced to an analytical X, Y, Z formula because every organization has its own unique characteristics and contingencies.

We represent this notion of "something like" action X using a heuristic operator ($\sim$) as part of the logical representation of the technological rule. The revised technological rule now represents "if you want to achieve Y in situation Z, then something like action

X will help." Such a rule would be represented by,

$$(Z, Y) \rightarrow \sim X$$

This revised rule represents a design production that contains both analytical and generative elements. The analytical element arises from the core rule,

$$(Z, Y) \rightarrow X$$

The generative element arises in the open adoptability around the action to be taken. This rule allows the designer to invent an adaptation of action X that best fits the designer's situation. This adaptable action, $\sim X$, allows the design to be partly generative. It now requires a different form of reasoning on the part of the designer in deciding how exactly the special form of action X should emerge. But it still retains the core logic of the creator of the design rule: the design theorist. So adoption of the design theory is a co-creation of both design theorist and design theory adopter.

Human organizations are deeply diverse. This diversity in the settings means that action $\sim X$ may be more often the norm than action X itself. For many technological rules, it is possible that the ideal setting for action X arises only rarely, making action $\sim X$ a necessity for most cases. An example of this logic is, "If you want to achieve user acceptance of a new technology in a situation of user alienation, then adopt something like a participative design approach". This technological rule might be stated,

$$((USER\ ALIENATION), (USER\ ACCEPTANCE\ OF\ A\ NEW\ TECHNOLOGY)) \rightarrow$$
$$ADOPT\ SOMETHING\ LIKE\ A\ CO - CREATIVE\ DESIGN\ APPROACH$$

It follows that these diverse human settings make it likely that situation Z is also an idealization that may occur rarely in its exact form. Again, the heuristic operator can be used to represent a adaptable technological rule. "If you want to achieve Y in a situation something like Z, then something like action X will help."

$$(\sim Z, Y) \rightarrow \sim X$$

In the absence of specific deductive logic to help disambiguate $\sim Z$, the determination as to whether the situation at hand is in fact "something like" Z will itself be a generative production. The designer must imagine the relevant ways in which the two situations relate. Indeed, the technological rule can be made fully adaptable. "If you want to achieve something like Y in a situation something like Z, then something like action X will help."

$$(\sim Z, \sim Y) \rightarrow \sim X$$

Without specific deductive logic to help disambiguate $\sim Y$, the determination as to whether the goals at hand are in fact "something like" Y is a generative production. The designer must imagine the relevant ways in which the two sets of goals are similar and the ways that they are different. The heuristic operators offer the designer the latitude for generative productions that are flexible enough to adapt the design logic to the particular setting. In addition to permitting generative productions in a design setting, heuristic operators introduce generality into design logic. For example, the core technological rule, will often arise as a kind of empirical *point solution*:

$$(Z, Y) \rightarrow X$$

A rule such as, "If you want to achieve user acceptance of a new technology in a situation of user alienation, then adopt a co-creative design approach" results from a field experience in which participative design provided a way to overcome user alienation. At that time of its origination, the design logic embodied in the rule provided a quite pointed, specific, practical solution to a quite pointed, specific, practical problem. This point solution is advanced as the general rule above. In this generalization, we translated the point logic (as used in the original setting) into the technological rule (the design logic). However, there are differences. In the point logic, the co-creative design was quite specific. For example, the point logic might have involved assigning users as well as developers to co-creative design teams, user specification review sessions, or prototyping together. In the design rule, these point solutions are expressed more generally as "co-creative design".

The heuristic operator further opens up the generality, suggesting that "something like co-creative design" should operate successfully. This enhanced adoptability enables the designer to generate alternatives to co-creative design that work better in the setting-at-hand. It effectively makes co-creative design an element of some unstated general class of solutions that will need to be re-conceptualized in the future.

Heuristic operators are found in genetic algorithms to incorporate problem-dependent knowledge in order to transform any infeasible solution into a feasible one [19]. Our heuristic operator can be described as a *modal operator*. Modal words and phrases are sentential adverbs. Sentential adverbs modify whole phrases or sentences. Examples of modal words include *necessarily* and *possibly*. In our case, the heuristic operator modifies a phrase like "want to achieve user acceptance of a new technology" to mean "want to *something like* achieve user acceptance of a new technology."

The logic around such modal operators is largely a linguistic topic. Modal logic provides the systematic expression of concepts that are represented in natural language by modal words and phrases. Modal logic operates as a meta-language that characterizes the logical, syntactical, and semantical properties of an object language [20].

Normally the modal expression in the object language is distinct from the associated operator in the meta-language. For example, we might specify a heuristic sign (say, ~) as a symbol in our object language that stands for heuristic. For our metalanguage, we would require a heuristic operator (say, □) as an expression of our metalanguage that stands for the operation that concatenates the heuristic sign with any other expression [20]. However, the scope of this paper is limited to explaining how this particular modal (heuristic) operates within a quite specific object language that is not ours to define [9]. This object language is limited to certain existing expressions of technological rules because of our focus on DSR. It is beyond the scope of this paper to specify a general object language for the universal application of the adoptability modal. Similarly, there is no necessity to develop a universal metalanguage. Simplicity commands that we conflate the notion of a heuristic sign in an object language with its related concatenation operation in a metalanguage, using the tilde as our heuristic operator (~) to imply both the notion *and* the attachment of that notion to a phrase or sentence.

In terms of modal scope, the heuristic operator is broader in scope and one of many possible parents of the narrower-scope modal *exactly*. The expression *something like participative design* will include the possibility of *exactly participative design*. The narrower scope of the modal *exactly* will have other parents of broader scope, such as *at least*, as in *at least a design conference* [21]. Similarly, expressions can be *modal free* (i.e., adoptability free technological rules). Modal free technological rules are those in which the heuristic operator (our modal sign) does not occur at all. Some expressions are *modally closed* (i.e., adoptability closed technological rules). Modally closed technological rules are those in which every occurrence of a phrase within the technological rules is an occurrence within the scope of the heuristic operator (our modal sign) [20].

3.1 Applying the Heuristic Operator

We applied the heuristic operator initially to express our working theory about our expectations for common patterns of adoptability in organizational settings. This working theory involved two working propositions:

Working proposition 1: If the situation (Z) is unadaptable, designers are driven to more analytical mental productions, and this analysis will resolve the solution to the action (X) and the goal (Y) exactly as specified in the unadapted rule.

Working proposition 2: If the situation (~Z) is adaptable, designers will be driven to more generative mental productions and these will tend to adapt the action (~X) and/or the goal (~Y).

If these working propositions hold, common patterns of adoptability should cluster around four of the eight possible rule patterns:

$$(Z, Y) \rightarrow X$$
$$(\sim Z, \sim Y) \rightarrow \sim X$$
$$(\sim Z, \sim Y) \rightarrow X$$
$$(\sim Z, Y) \rightarrow \sim X$$

If the working propositions hold, the other patterns should be rare:

$$(Z, \sim Y) \rightarrow \sim X$$
$$(Z, \sim Y) \rightarrow X$$
$$(Z, Y) \rightarrow \sim X$$
$$(\sim Z, Y) \rightarrow X$$

4 Research Methodology

We examined the validity of the heuristic operator using a qualitative, multiple case study. Our approach involved a "clinical perspective in fieldwork" originally described by Edgar Schein [3]. The fieldwork involves interventions and the findings are validated by the resulting improvements. Our purpose in this fieldwork was to validate the use of adoptability logic to express and test theoretical propositions. Whether the outcome of the fieldwork confirms or disconfirms the propositions is less important than the validity and clarity of the logic used to express the propositions and the results (for our purposes). In the cases at hand, as the reader will see, the fieldwork disconfirms these propositions. But it is the logical clarity with which this result finds expression that satisfies our basic research goals. The ability to reformulate the propositions for further examination may indeed provide better evidence for the strength of the adoptability operation than an alternative result that simply confirmed the theory under test.

In this fieldwork, practicing information systems project managers explored the adoptability in their technological rule settings. The purpose of this fieldwork was to see whether the use of a heuristic operator as a logical modifier for technological rules would lead to insights into the use of technological rules in real project settings.

4.1 The Organizational Change Nexus

The study of organizational change may be the most important management discipline. Academic and practitioner contributions to organizational change have been built on empirical work in a wide variety of organizations and from such different perspectives as psychology, sociology, and business. Examples of this work include descriptive accounts of change, normative models to guide the change process, theoretical models for understanding and analyzing change, typologies of different approaches to organizational change, and empirical studies of the success or failure of change. Most recently IT-related change has come into focus in studies of digital transformation [cf. 22].

The process by which an organization selects an approach to organizational change is often ad hoc or driven by habit, i.e. 'we did this the last time, let us do it again'. Different change approaches each has their advocates and adherents, and there is little comparative research for choosing among such approaches. To deal with this wicked problem Pries-Heje and Baskerville [8] derived an organizational change nexus which can be used to recommend one or more appropriate change approaches among ten prominent organizational change strategies.

The 10 change approaches can be said to follow technological rules in that a specific approach – action X - is recommended, based on a description of the current situation (Z) and the organizational change (Y) wished-for. Hence, the 10 change approaches from Pries-Heje and Baskerville [8] can be expressed as technological rules.

One of the 10 change strategies, for example, is called "commanding" which is well suited for situations (Z) where change is required fast and/or where organizational structures needs to be changed. Another is called "production oriented" which focusses on the flow of value in the organization, identification of bottlenecks, and removal of these bottlenecks (that is the change). Yet another is "business process reengineering" which aims for a total redesign of the organization. The use of this last change strategy requires a solid crisis like continuing major economic losses. This strategy involves the carte blanche designing of the optimal organization that centers on providing value to the customer. The change regards implementing this optimal organization. Two examples of the technological rules are shown in Fig. 1.

If you want to initiate organizational change **in a situation** where you:

    Believe that formal structures needs change

    Where change is needed fast

Then choose a *Commanding* approach where change is driven and dictated by (top) management; one where management takes on the roles as owner, sponsor and change agents.

If you want to initiate organizational change **in a situation** where:

    You believe that target group is very diverse and has large individual differences

    The target group are experts

Then choose an *Optionality* approach where change is driven by the motivation and need of the individual; it is to a large degree optionality.

Fig. 1. Example technological rules from the organizational change nexus.

The organizational change nexus was implemented as:

- An IT artifact that is using design theories to score "fit" for each change strategy
- Questionnaire about the contingencies of the situation in the organization and the wished-for change
- Guidelines for engaging with practice

Together these parts can guide managers in evaluating and choosing which of the ten change strategies that would be most appropriate in an actual organizational setting for a defined organizational change. The IT artifact calculates a *fit* on a scale going up to 100% fit based on contingencies of the situation today and the desired change.

The organizational change nexus was articulated as follows: "… to improve the ability for organizational change managers to rationally select the most appropriate change strategies" [23] and they conclude "We developed a framework that binds together ten well-known organizational change strategies into a prescriptive recommendation for a cohesive and suitable change strategy for a particular organization's unique situation. The change strategies to be prescribed develop from a list-of-fit that indicates the relative suitability of each of the ten strategies to the organization's vision and setting" [23]. While the originators only evaluated the nexus in four companies in the financial sector, they predicted that it would be useful in other IT-organizations and –projects.

That prediction was confirmed in November 2014 when the organizational change nexus was incorporated as an prominent part of the ISO/IEC standard 33014 on software process improvement [24]. This standard has three levels: strategic, tactical and operational. The ten change strategies are included at the strategic level – and mentioned by name – to be used once an organization has identified its business goals and the scope of the organizational change. At this point the nexus can be used for identifying the *overall change strategy*. Hence the inclusion of this meta-level design theory as part of a recognized international standard indicates a very successful use of the nexus.

4.2 Multi Case Study Fieldwork

We have collected data from 108 managers using the organizational change nexus up until March 2022 where 16 mainly project managers applied the nexus. An example is a case from 2022 where the overall change desired is less food-waste in a supermarket chain, and the concrete design artifact is a digital tool called How-Less-Waste that a major part of supermarket chain employees are to adopt. Now the question is how? The owner of the change, a program manager responsible for implementing the change in the 100 of supermarket stores, a change agent, and a representative from the target group of 1000s of employees meet and fill out the nexus questionnaire [8, Figure 3, p. 741]. The manager using the nexus then facilitates a discussion until the group agrees on what the situation is for this organizational change. The agreement is fed into a spreadsheet that uses the 10 design theories to calculate the fit for each of 10 change strategies. In the concrete example the three highest scoring change approaches are exploration (50% fit), production-driven and lean (43.75% fit), and a business process reengineering (BPR) change strategy (40%). Based on these fits the manager now decides to implement the organizational change aiming for less food-waste by first exploring ways to achieve less waste, and then implementing in a big production-oriented scale. However, the manager decides to ignore the third high scoring change strategy BPR. Thus, our perception of this change is that Y is clear and described well by the nexus. Z is clear and the participants can reach agreement on all 32 contingency factors that together describes the situation. But X is adapted in that the recommendation of combining the three change approaches with the best fit is not followed.

The way the 108 managers learned to use the nexus in their home organizations in a 4-semester executive master in project management and organizational change. The second semester focused on organizational change and the organizational change nexus was a mandatory part of the curriculum. Over the years we have collected data from more than 300 applications by the executive master students. For this paper we chose 108 change projects emphasizing IT-related changes such as the example above. All 108 participants chosen were managers at project level or higher in their own organizations. The project managers were asked to do the following:

1. Choose and describe an organizational change in the context of their own organization
2. Indicate agree or disagree to nexus statements. Preferably in a process where all relevant managers (relevant to the change that is) participates
3. Use agreement and disagreement scoring to calculate fit for each of the 10 strategies
4. Plan the organizational change based on the best fitting change strategies
5. Write a report documenting the plan, to what extent the plan was implemented, and write a critical review of the use of the nexus

On average the reports from the 108 change projects chosen were 5 pages long plus an appendix with the scoring (agreements and disagreements).

5   Analysis of the 108 Cases

The reports from the 108 organizational change applications were analyzed using a framework looking as shown in Table 1 with an example of the coding of three organizations (see also the example case on less food-waste in a supermarket chain above).

Table 1. Example coding of 3 out of 108 cases

Case	2. You want to achieve Y	3. … in situation Z,	4… then perform action X	5. Re-articulation	6. Perception after use – we could use
A	Y clear; Better performance of Revenue Information by more effective IT use	Z clear;	X clear; Combining 2–3 strategies. No discussion on how to combine	The organization was changed. Unfortunately too fast (hinting at the commanding strategy) It would have been smart to use the specialist driven strategy more. The organization was filled with specialists	It makes sense to combine these 2–3 strategies
B	Y ambiguous; Unclear. Not described more precisely than "development" which can be anything	Z clear; Teachers at High School teaching different subjects – now also using virtual meetings	X clear; Combining specialist, learning and optionality	"It is also interesting to take a closer look at what strategies does NOT suit the organization, especially if these strategies have been tried without luck"	"The model operationalizes behavior and strategy in relation to each other which makes it really applicable" "A very little investment in time gives management a targeted way to reflect on change"

(continued)

Table 1. (*continued*)

Case	2. You want to achieve Y	3. … in situation Z,	4… then perform action X	5. Re-articulation	6. Perception after use – we could use
C	Y clear; Reorganization causes by digital transformation leading to fewer people in the organization	Z ambiguous; Top management still has not told us why the reorganization and what values it is expected to give	X ambiguous; Optionality (scoring highest) cannot be used for this type of change (reorganization)	"The tool does not take into account feelings and individual personal preferences"	"The model can give an indication … but the model does not take into account local contingencies"

The coding is based on Joan van Aken [17, 25] and his notion of "technological rules" presented earlier. The organizational nexus [8] can be seen as 10 design theories that each aim for a desired change "Y" with some contingent characteristics, i.e. whether the change is tangible or not; The situation today "Z" also having some characteristics i.e. how successful we have been in the past wit hour change projects; And the ten overall change strategies "X".

In Table 1 the design theory elements "Y", "Z" and "X" are coded in column 2–4. At the top of each field it is stated whether any adaptation or translation was taking place. In Case A, for example, no adaptation of the nexus took place. Whereas in case B the scope of the change wished-for was unclear; it was just a direction "development" using virtual meeting apps. And in case C the situation was unclear as management had not communicated why the reorganization (= the change) was necessary, as well as the recommended change strategy – Optionality – that could not be used for a directed reorganization. Thus cases A, B and C are respectively examples of no adaptation at all, very little adaptation, and quite a lot of adaptation.

In Table 1, Column 5 called "Re-articulation" the eventual considerations when making a tactical plan are given, and in column 6 called "Perception after use" we have coded any critical reflection the project manager may have had when using the nexus in their own practice.

There are eight potential codings of the 108 cases:

1. $(Z,Y) \rightarrow X$ (everything follows nexus)
2. $(\sim Z,Y) \rightarrow X$ (the change wished-for adapted to fit nexus)
3. $(Z, \sim Y) \rightarrow X$ (description of situation adapted in relation to nexus)
4. $(Z,Y) \sim \rightarrow X$ (the change strategy adapted e.g. by combining several or taking #2)
5. $(\sim Z, \sim Y) \rightarrow X$ (change AND situation description adapted)
6. $(Z, \sim Y) \sim \rightarrow X$ (situation AND change strategy adapted)
7. $(\sim Z,Y) \sim \rightarrow X$ (change wished-for and change strategy adapted)
8. $(\sim Z, \sim Y) \sim \rightarrow X$ (everything adapted to local conditions)

The waste-less-food example above is here a type 4 in that neither Z or Y changes, but one of the recommended strategies are left out – hence adapting X.

In Table 2 you can see how many of each type we found in our coding

Table 2. Instances of each of 8 types of adoptability found in coding of 108 cases

TYPE	No. of Instances
Type 1: (Z,Y) → X (everything follows nexus)	27
Type 2: (~Z,Y) → X (the change desired adapted to fit nexus)	14
Type 3: (Z, ~ Y) → X (description of situation adapted in relation to nexus)	12
Type 4: (Z,Y) → ~X (the change strategy adapted e.g. by combining several or taking #2)	24
Type 5: (~Z, ~ Y) → X (change AND situation description adapted)	6
Type 6: (Z, ~ Y) → ~X (situation AND change strategy adapted)	12
Type 7: (~Z,Y) → ~X (change desired and change strategy adapted)	5
Type 8: (~Z, ~ Y) → ~X (everything adapted to local conditions)	7

The most common coding in Table 2 was no. 1, which is using the nexus exactly as intended. The least common coding was no. 5, which adapted the change AND the situation, and no. 7, which adapted the change and the strategy recommended. There were respectively 6 and 5 instances in those. Further, adaptations of a single element – types 2. to 4. – were more common than changing two elements (types 5.-7.). In general it was much more common – about 75% – to adapt some element or elements (2.-8.) than not (no. 1.).

6 Discussion

In Fig. 2 we have summarized our work presented until now. At the top of the figure you find the Organizational Change Nexus consisting of three parts. The three parts are the 10 design theories formulated as technological rules (X), a questionnaire posing statements about the context (Y and Z) and some guidelines for how to engage the case practice; an IT artifact that based on the identified context calculates the "fit" for each of the ten design theories. In the middle you have the 108 cases in our fieldwork; in each case a number of top-, middle- and project managers were involved in scoring the fit for the ten change strategies. Then at the bottom, we have the results of our analysis and coding; 25% did no adaption at all, whereas 69% adapted something; and 6% adapted everything – organizational context, change context and change strategy.

As a whole the fieldwork offers results at two levels. The first level regards the outcome in terms of the propositions that were disconfirmed by the data. The second level regards the validity and usefulness of the heuristic operator when used to modify the predicate logic of technological design rules.

6.1 Discussion of the Fieldwork

While the confirmation/disconfirmation was not our primary objective, we must not overlook a brief discussion of these results in terms of their implications for future research. Our fieldwork does not support the working propositions and consequently does not support the working theory. Actually, the most common patterns appeared to be those that we expected to be most rare. The most common pattern involved no adaptability (Type 1 in Table 2). This situation is a common pattern in our data, similar to one in which the action to be taken is adaptable, $(Z,Y) \rightarrow \sim X$.

However, the data suggest that this logic may need to be expanded. The other most-common pattern involved adoptability in the situation (Z). We speculate that the presence of adoptability in Z drives designers to make an analytical treatment of Y and X, $(\sim Z,Y) \rightarrow X$.

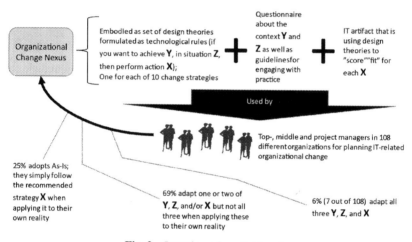

Fig. 2. Overview of our fieldwork

6.2 Discussion of the Heuristic Operator

While our qualitative fieldwork is not an ideal way to prove or disprove theories, it does strongly validate the usefulness of the heuristic operator in design logic. Whether the outcome of the fieldwork confirms or disconfirms the propositions is less important than the validity and clarity of the logic used to express the propositions and the results.

The fieldwork indicates that a heuristic operator permits a clearer understanding and representation of the expected and unexpected variation between the elements of a design logic expression and an instance of the application of this design logic. Our work offers an original contribution in its development of a heuristic operator. Simon's [12] original formulation of the Science of Design proposed the design logic as an expression of a scientific design. He mentions design theory only in passing. The availability of the heuristic operator is an improvement in expressions of design logic that make such logic both more valid and more practical for use in empirical DSR fieldwork.

Our work also extends van Aken's [9] application of Bunge's [6, 7] technological rules as an expression of management design logic. By adding heuristic operators to van Aken's logic, we believe these technological rules provide a more realistic and practical expression of their prescriptive value.

We offer an original contribution by providing means for expressing points within the design process at which a designer must work creatively to make prescriptive design theories and prescriptive design logic fit a design setting at hand. The heuristic operator presents a declaration of the need for such generative productions on the part of those applying a design theory. Heretofore, explicit points of such generative opportunities have had no formal means of expression in design logic or design theories.

The heuristic operator in our work is tightly tied to design logic in the form of technological rules. Future research is needed to explore how adoptability can be more explicitly expressed in other forms of prescriptive design theories in DSR. Our work was successful in critically validating the heuristic operator. It also provided a means for considering design theory propositions. However, we need more research in how adoptability properties, whether of artifacts, theories, or logic, can be evaluated as an outcome of DSR.

Furthermore, in relation to diffusion and adoption of theories in practice the adoptability and the heuristic operator can be seen as a kind of co-creation of adoption between design theorists and practitioners. We know that 3 out of 4 adoptions a given theory – in our case a design theory on how to plan your organizational change – more or less. We haven't seen other papers being that specific about what is being changed – adopted – in theories when "translated" to practice.

7   Conclusion

Our clinical fieldwork explains how the adoption of a design theory on organizational change occurred for 108 different organizations. It is quite unique to have data on how a theory is applied or translated in practice. Through the lens of technological rules and heuristic operators, different kinds of adaptability appear. In our illustrative cases, only in 25% of the more than 100 cases reported here the nexus theory was applied as-is. In 75% of the cases the nexus theory was adapted in one of seven different ways, the most popular adaptation was to accept the description of the situation today (Z), the desired change (Y) but change the action, what one should be doing (X).

This analysis of our fieldwork data represents a considerable improvement in expressions of adaptability in design logic that will also make it more practical for use in future empirical DSR fieldwork. Future DSR research can use this logic to examine explicit adoptability rules for new design theories.

References

1. Hevner, A.R., March, S.T., Park, J., Ram, S.: Design science in information systems research. MIS Q. **28**, 75–105 (2004)
2. Baskerville, R., Wood-Harper, A.T.: Diversity in information systems action research methods. Eur. J. Inf. Syst. **7**, 90–107 (1998)

3. Schein, E.: The Clinical Perspective in Fieldwork. Sage, Newbury Park, Calf (1987)
4. Baskerville, R., Pries-Heje, J.: Explanatory design theory. Bus. Inf. Syst. Eng. **2**, 271–282 (2010)
5. Markus, M.L., Majchrzak, A., Gasser, L.: A design theory for systems that support emergent knowledge processes. MIS Q. **26**, 179–212 (2002)
6. Bunge, M.: Scientific Research I: The Search for System. Springer-Verlag, New York (1967)
7. Bunge, M.: Scientific Research II: The Search for Truth. Springer-Verlag, New York (1967)
8. Pries-Heje, J., Baskerville, R.: The design theory nexus. MIS Q. **32**, 731–755 (2008)
9. van Aken, J.E.: Management research based on the paradigm of the design sciences: the quest for field-tested and grounded technological rules. The J. Manage. Stud. **41**, 219–246 (2004)
10. Gregor, S., Jones, D.: The anatomy of a design theory. J. Assoc. Inf. Syst. **8**, 312–335 (2007)
11. Walls, J.G., Widmeyer, G.R., El Sawy, O.A.: Building an information system design theory for vigilant EIS. Inf. Syst. Res. **3**, 36–59 (1992)
12. Simon, H.A.: The Sciences of the Artificial. MIT Press, Cambridge, Mass (1996)
13. Bryan, S.P.: Cognitive complexity, transformational leadership, and organizational outcomes. Louisiana State University and Agricultural & Mechanical College, United States -- Louisiana (2002)
14. Fritzen, S.A.: Can the design of community-driven development reduce the risk of elite capture? Evidence from Indonesia. World Development **35**, 1359–1375 (2007)
15. Gensler, H.J.: Formal ethics. Cambridge Univ Press (1996)
16. van Aken, J.E.: Valid knowledge for the professional design of large and complex design processes. Des. Stud. **26**, 379–404 (2005)
17. van Aken, J.E.: Management research as a design science: articulating the research products of mode 2 knowledge production in management. Br. J. Manag. **16**, 19–36 (2005)
18. Pawson, R., Tilley, N.: Realistic Evaluation. Sage, London (1997)
19. Chu, P.C., Beasley, J.E.: A genetic algorithm for the multidimensional knapsack problem. Journal of Heuristics **4**, 63–86 (1998)
20. Cocchiarella, N.B., Freund, M.A.: Modal Logic: An Introduction to its Syntax and Semantics. Oxford University Press, New York (2008)
21. Breakstone, M.Y., Cremers, A., Fox, D., Hackl, M.: On the analysis of scope ambiguities in comparative constructions: converging evidence from real-time sentence processing and offline data. Semantics and Linguistic Theory **21**, 712–731 (2011)
22. Vial, G.: Understanding digital transformation: a review and a research agenda. Managing Digital Transformation 13–66 (2021)
23. Pries-Heje, J., Vinter, O.: A framework for selecting change strategies in IT organizations. In: International Conference on Product Focused Software Process Improvement, pp. 408–414. Springer (Year)
24. ISO/IEC_33001: Information technology -- Process assessment -- Concepts and terminology. Geneva, Switzerland. (the first of the ISO/IEC 330xx serie of standards) (2015)
25. van Aken, J.E.: The nature of organizing design: both like and unlike material object design. Working Paper 06.13, Eindhoven Centre for Innovation Studies, Department of Technology Management, Technische Universiteit Eindhoven (2006)

A Service-Dominant Logic Perspective on Information Systems Development as Service Ecosystems of Value Co-creation

Gro Bjerknes and Karlheinz Kautz[✉] ![ORCID]

RMIT University, Melbourne, VIC 3000, Australia
karlheinz.kautz@rmit.edu.au

Abstract. Information Systems Development (ISD) is at the heart of the diffusion of information technologies. It is constantly reshaped by new developments and changing environments. The appearance of extra-organizational platform capabilities and the emerging shift in business and society from a goods-dominant to service-dominant logic (SDL) represent such a development. SDL offers a holistic perspective with an emphasis on value co-creation in service ecosystems that goes beyond the traditional boundaries of organizations. In this capacity, it lends itself to a study of ISD as service ecosystems of value co-creation in such an environment. On this background, we investigate the following research questions: How is value co-creation in ISD projects that transcend traditional organizational settings managed and performed, and how does SDL provide plausible explanations to understand such contemporary ISD? For this purpose, we present a case of ISD in the context of the United Nations Children's Fund (UNICEF) which engaged various groups of actors including Pacific Islander youth in the development of a digital game to raise attention about climate change and use the foundational concepts of SDL to demonstrate how value is co-created by a diverse group of actors in such a setting.

Keywords: Information Systems Development · Service-dominant logic · Service ecosystems · Value co-creation

1 Introduction

Information Systems Development (ISD) is at the heart of the diffusion of information technologies. It is constantly reshaped by new developments and changing environments. The appearance of extra-organizational platform capabilities and the emerging shift in business and society from a goods-dominant to service-dominant logic (SDL) represent such a development (Kazman and Chen 2009) where SDL offers a holistic perspective on value co-creation in service ecosystems that goes beyond the traditional organizational boundaries. In this capacity, it lends itself to a study of ISD as service ecosystems of value co-creation in such an environment. We therefore investigate the following research questions: How is value co-creation in ISD projects that transcend traditional

© IFIP International Federation for Information Processing 2022
Published by Springer Nature Switzerland AG 2022
A. Elbanna et al. (Eds.): TDIT 2022, IFIP AICT 660, pp. 40–57, 2022.
https://doi.org/10.1007/978-3-031-17968-6_3

organizational settings managed and performed, and how does SDL provide plausible explanations to understand such contemporary ISD? To answer these research questions, we studied a case of ISD in the context of a United Nations Children's Fund (UNICEF) initiated project.

The UNICEF is an intergovernmental, non-for-profit organization and program that provides humanitarian and development assistance to children and mothers in developing countries. UNICEF (P), short for UNICEF (Pacific Islands Countries), has recognized social media's value for distributing important information on matters such as health, emergencies, education and climate change (UNICEF (P) 2013). Engaging youth is a focus for UNICEF (P) but the organization has been challenged by Pacific Islander (PI) youth, who were not significantly engaging with content shared on UNICEF (P)'s Facebook (FB) page, to be 'younger and less boring' in using social media. Thus, to explore the abilities of digital technologies to involve youth to influence decision making affecting their lives, UNICEF (P) invited and engaged PI youth in participating in the development of an information system, a FB-based game here called 'Pacific Climate Change Challenge Game' (PC3G) to raise awareness about climate change in that region (Fisher 2012).

The paper is structured as follows: the next section includes as theoretical background a brief introduction into SDL. We then position our research with regard to the existing work on SDL in the ISD literature. Subsequently, we present our research method, describe the setting of our study, provide our analysis, discuss our findings and finish with some conclusions.

2   Theoretical Background

SDL is grounded in the field of service marketing as part of the service paradigm. It draws on multiple theoretical sources such as economic, institutional, and practice theories, along with complexity and systems sciences (Lusch and Vargo 2019).

We use SDL and its foundational concepts with its emphasis on service ecosystems as developed by Lusch and Vargo (2019) over 2 decades to understand value co-creation in ISD projects. SDL is based on the premise that service, as the application of one actor's resources, e.g., knowledge and skills, for the benefit of oneself or another, is the basis of all economic and social exchange, focusing on the two-way dynamics of exchange, that a service is exchanged for a service (Lusch and Vargo 2019).

"[V]alue creation does not just take place through the activities of a single actor (customer or otherwise) or between a firm and its customers but among a whole host of actors. [...] value is not completely individually, or even dyadically, created but, rather it is created through the integration of resources, provided by many sources, including a full range of market-facing, private and public actors. In short, cocreation of value is the purpose of exchange [...]." (Vargo and Lusch 2016, p. 23).

Value is co-created by multiple actors in actor-to-actor networks, which always include a beneficiary, or as Vargo et al. (2008, p. 146) put it "[i]n S-D logic, the roles of producers and consumers are not distinct, meaning that value is always cocreated, jointly and reciprocally, in interactions among providers and beneficiaries through the integration of resources and application of competences." Value is perceived and determined by the beneficiary on the basis the service's value-in-use (Vargo et al. 2008).

The value co-creation process takes place in service ecosystems that are coordinated through actor-generated institutions and institutional arrangements. Vargo and Lusch (2016) understand these concepts, based on institutional theories, in a very broad sense; they consider culture, traditions, customs, norms, formal laws, policies, regulations, informal conventions, and agreements as mechanisms for cooperation and coordination that have an impact on and can hinder or support resource integration and the value cocreation process.

Service ecosystems are complex, emergent, and self-organizing (Vargo and Lusch 2017). They are multi-level in their structure, where higher level structures emerge from lower-level interactions (Lusch and Vargo 2019). These levels are not independent of each other, rather they present different analytical perspectives. Service ecosystems unfold over time as actors reciprocally provide service and co-create value by creating and recreating institutional arrangements to coordinate the service-to-service exchange (Lusch and Vargo 2019).

Fig. 1. The narrative of SDL according to Vargo and Lusch (2016).

Vargo and Lusch (2017) summarize their narrative and framework of SDL in a circular process model comprised of actors in actor-to-actor networks who are involved in resource integration and service exchanges that are enabled and constrained by endogenously generated institutions and institutional arrangements that in turn establish nested and interlocking, self-governed, self-contained, and self-adjusting service ecosystems of value co-creation (see Fig. 1). Each foundational concept in the model can serve as an entry point for analysis.

We will use these key ideas of SDL for the analysis of our empirical data. Before doing so we first position our research in the existing literature on SDL in ISD and then introduce our research method and setting.

3   SDL in the ISD Literature

The concept of service has received IS research attention for many years (Fielt et al. 2013) in areas such as service design, service innovation, and service management (Böhmann et al. 2014). There has been less focus on SDL in the IS field; and only very few studies have investigated ISD from an SDL perspective.

Keith et al. (2009, 2013) present a method for managing ISD projects by conceptualizing ISD activities as services, but do not relate their work to SDL and its foundational concepts. Their study focuses on the adoption process of the method and its effects on scope, cost, and time more than on the development process itself. Babb and Keith (2012) provide a conceptual argument and reconceptualize ISD methods from an SDL and value co-creation perspective to support the selection of adequate ISD methods in the current dynamic and hardly predictable environment of ISD. They argue that agile and hybrid ISD methods are co-creative by nature and are instances of a general shift towards SDL in business and society. The authors underline the importance of a service's value-in-use beyond traditional quality and value measures related to a product's delivery within time and cost constraints. However, they do not provide empirical support for their argument.

Acknowledging SDL as the wider background of their research, and postulating that SDL has significantly affected the way ISD organizations operate and are structured, Öbrand et al. (2019) provide a longitudinal case study of the development, support, and sales of complex integrated IT services in an ISD organization. The focus of their investigation is on how risks emerge in the development of these services. They produce interesting results on the interstitiality of IT risk in such an environment, but they do not apply the key concepts of SDL. Barqawi et al. (2016) used SDL in an action research project to explore a specific activity in an ISD organization, namely release management in a software-as-a-service environment and performed some interventions to enhance service quality based on selected SDL key concepts and premises.

Also positioning their work in the context of SDL, without explicitly applying the underlying concepts, Kazman and Chen (2009) offer a model for the development of crowdsourced, service-oriented information systems derived from analysis of community-based service systems development, open-source software systems, and ultra large-scale systems. Their model takes the form of a set of system characteristics and accompanying development principles with implications for practical application. Kautz et al. (2019) applied the principles, understanding the enactment of the model as an organizational innovation, in a previous study of the PC3G development project and empirically confirmed its usefulness for understanding the process of co-creation in ISD. But, like Kazman and Chen (2009) they did not use the full SDL narrative and its comprehensive theoretical concepts for that analysis. Kautz and Bjerknes (2020) have also investigated ISD as value co-creation based on a perspective that considers value co-creation in service development as a form of innovation (Zwass 2010; Alves et al. 2016) and supplemented that analysis with selected SDL concepts based on Lusch and Nambisan's (2015) work (see below). Bjerknes and Kautz (2019) applied the complete SDL framework; however, their study of agile approaches to ISD is based exclusively on the perspective of project managers and product owners. Lusch and Nambisan (2015) used SDL to gain a broader perspective on service innovation. Their focus is on how digital technology in the form of service platforms can contribute to value co-creation.

The present work is based on these predecessors, but rather than focus on particular concepts or organizing principles, on digital technology or on selected ISD activities or a particular ISD method, the starting point for our analysis is the full set of concepts that characterize SDL according to Vargo and Lusch (2016; Lusch & Vargo 2019).

4   Research Approach and Method

This research is interpretive. Given the limited literature concerning our research topic, our investigation is based on an exploratory, qualitative, single case study (Creswell 2003) of an ISD project, which involves a number of different organizational units and stakeholder groups.

Access to the case organization was provided directly by two key informants. The first informant had been involved in the project as a representative of UNICEF (P) and communications specialist. He was the project sponsor and project co-coordinator at all project stages, we refer to him as the sponsor. He shared email correspondence and all relevant documents and provided reflections on the process. The second key informant also participated during the whole project as a consultant and facilitator. She brought her distinct IS expertise on the interplay between people, processes, information, and IT to the project. The two authors conducted interviews with the key informants and had access to the record of the project debriefing, which the consultant had held with the three developers concerning their respective roles and experience during the project. Given the distributed location of the participants the extensive email trail between the different participants was the main data source. Lee (1994) argues that email communication can provide a rich understanding of what has occurred. Emails included those between the sponsor, the consultant, the three developers, three testers, four adolescent social media facilitators, as well as email correspondence from UNICEF including headquarter (HQ) staff in New York, climate change experts and learning experts from the Commonwealth of Learning (COL) (https://thecommonwealth.org/commonwealth-learning), an organization that provided advice and some funding. These emails contained status information, reflections before, during and after the development and implementation of the game, conceptual feedback, and recollections concerning input into the design of the game, the elements of climate change it was addressing, test results as well as technical feedback. More detail about the different co-creators, their relationship and their location will be provided in the next section.

The empirical data also comprised social media postings by four adolescent social media facilitators including an invitation for input and further feedback on the game. This was launched as a FB album. The data included the initial responses to the request for input and the feedback postings that were received from PI youth. It also encompassed activity data on the page after the game's implementation. Finally, project documentation including the UNICEF (P)'s strategic plan for digital engagement, the COL Terms of Reference for the project, the project brief and the design document produced by the developers outlining the game, as well as its evaluation report were valuable data sources as were further project notes by the sponsor and the consultant.

Our analysis was guided by the SDL framework. Following Miles et al.'s (2014) 'data condensation' strategy we produced a timeline (see Fig. 2) spanning the project period and a case narrative, which is included below in a concentrated form. The narrative builds a conceptual model and provides a sequence of events and serves as a frame of reference for the analysis of the data (Fincham 2002). Our understanding of value co-creation in the service ecosystems of the PC3G development project has come about through an iterative process of interpretation, collaboration, comparison and connecting of prior research and empirical data. During the analysis we regularly discussed our emerging results with the two informants and through their feedback increased the interpretive rigor of our study.

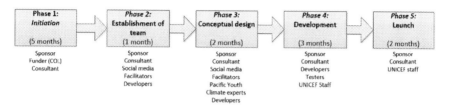

Fig. 2. Timeline, phases, and participants of the PC3G development project.

5   A Case Narrative

With the help of the timeline, we identified five phases of the project, which will be described in more detail: 1 Initiation of the idea and funding; 2 Establishment of the team; 3 Conceptual design of the game; 4 Development of the game; 5 Launch of the game.

5.1   Phase 1 – Initiation of the Idea and Funding

As a starting point, based on PI youth critique of the UNICEF(P)'s web site, the communications specialist at UNICEF (P) proposed a project to the organization. He was concerned that although UNICEF (P) had a strong social media presence and was regularly communicating with their audience via social media, two-way interaction was very limited. His major objective was to ensure that PI youth engaged more with UNICEF. His vision was to engage youth through encouraging them to participate in an ISD project via social media. Given the threats posed to small Pacific Islands from climate change the proposal was to develop a digital game, which would help PI youth to learn about climate change. He put this proposal to COL, which provided modest funding and then approached an IS professor in Melbourne, Australia, known to him from previous collaboration with a request to become a project member as a consultant to help establish, and if necessary, manage a development team. She honorary joined the project in this capacity.

5.2   Phase 2 – Establishment of the Team

The consultant then approached three young research students in her network, who fulfilled the position requirements; these accepted the invitation and were immediately appointed as the developers for a period of 30 working days with an original project runtime of 2 1/2 months. One developer lived in Hong Kong, another in regional Victoria, Australia, and one in Melbourne. The latter two knew each other, but did not know the third developer on beforehand, nor did they meet this developer in person during the project. The sponsor's first email to the development team including the consultant described his vision and what he wanted to achieve, the game's purpose was to create awareness about the impact of climate change. At the same time, he contacted four adolescents from Fiji to be social media facilitators for soliciting and gathering ideas from PI youth about the game. The social media facilitators posted a photo with a message inviting input and set this up as a FB album with text encouraging UNICEF (P) FB fans to contribute to the design of the game. Initial input and comments relating directly to the game came from 16 fans, 15 additional fans hitting the 'like' button of these postings; subsequently many more fans visited the page, provided feedback on the game under development, and eventually subscribed to the page (see descriptions of phases 3–5).

During the same period, the consultant facilitated a process among the three developers and the sponsor to agree on communication protocols between them. The sponsor was happy for the developers to manage the project themselves in terms of the ideas for the game and how the work was undertaken. The developers' first meeting was a telephone conversation about how they would manage the process given they were geographically dispersed. They agreed they would email each other every couple of days to cater for the short timeline for finalising the game. They also planned to use Skype to talk regularly and instant messaging and chat to communicate. Although there was no formal team leader, one student quickly took charge of managing how things would work. At the end of each meeting an email summarizing progress was sent to the sponsor by the informal leader. He reviewed the progress. If he thought there was something that needed to be changed or wanted to provide feedback, he emailed the informal leader, or alternatively called her. Brief notes were taken from these Skype meetings focusing on any requested changes.

5.3 Phase 3 – Conceptual Design of the Game

The first development objective was to reach agreement on what the game would be and its look and feel. One developer researched relevant aspects of climate change, another looked at different approaches to and types of FB games and the third investigated appropriate technologies, tools, and development approaches. As idea development progressed the sponsor became an intermediary sharing these ideas with experts from the funding organization, international climate change experts and UNICEF staff. Further information on climate change in particular was provided on a regular basis by the relevant experts to the sponsor. He provided this feedback including ideas of the involved PI youth provided through the FB page and facilitated by the social media facilitators to the developers.

The requirements of the sponsor and ideas of the key stakeholders, PI youth, and UNICEF (P) staff, guided the developers. The team used the following process: At the beginning the sponsor asked the developers to think about some ideas, then they collected their ideas to see which of these ideas could be combined. This led to three major ideas; each with a particular focus from one developer which reflected what they individually thought the youth and UNICEF (P) should concentrate on. This resulted in the PC3G consisting of three games in one. Each game was quite different in the way that the players would interact; one requires players to identify potential CO_2 emitters; one requires them to understand the climate change threats and initiate action, e.g., to evacuate or rebuild before serious consequences; one highlights the causes of floods and the need for flood mitigation. An important design principle was to ensure that each game was not too complicated. The developers found the page postings very helpful. The responses from the PI youth had suggested that the game needed to be very interactive, interesting and colorful; it should have graphics, be fun and focused on action, something, which promoted to be positive and to make change.

5.4   Phase 4 – Development of the Game

After the developers and the sponsor had agreed on the consolidated game's design, development proper, including detailed design, coding, testing and evaluation could begin. Managing the process "was very challenging because we would not face each other and sit together", one developer commented. The development team took an active role in ensuring input in the form of further information and feedback was managed effectively and encouraged further participation by the sponsor, UNICEF staff, and PI youth. As there was no opportunity to discuss, elaborate and clarify ideas and concerns face to face information and communication had to be very concise. As the team members were working independently and each component of the game was developed separately, several issues arose during this phase. These issues are highlighted in a statement from one developer: "The game came in three different formats, totally different interfaces. The developing process of the three people was quite different. It came as three totally different styles of game, different user interface, different color, a lot of things were different. There was no standard look to the three different games. Fortunately, finally we got this sorted out – the three games now look quite similar".

The sponsor and UNICEF staff reviewed the first version of the consolidated game and provided feedback; this included the colors, fonts and graphics, the text and help provided with the game. The sponsor highlighted that further work was needed on standardization and how the three components linked together to be one game. He also reinforced the need for links to further information be embedded in each game.

Technical testing and evaluation were iterative. The developers conducted technical unit and system testing to uncover programming errors and ensure user interface consistency. Each developer tested the work of the others and provided feedback through their phone and Skype meetings and email. While they tested for programming errors, the game was functionally tested by UNICEF (P) staff that played the game and provided feedback to the sponsor. A technical person within UNICEF also tested the game and provided technical feedback once the team had incorporated the earlier feedback. Further user evaluation similar to user acceptance testing was undertaken by three friends of the developers in China, who were young and used FB. They played the game and provided advice suggesting that the graphics and artwork needed to be still more attractive. They thought players would be encouraged to play longer if the game was even more interesting. Based on further feedback from their peer group and their own evaluations, the social media facilitators also provided feedback along these lines, which they communicated to the sponsor and at times directly to the developers, suggesting the game be more colorful and easier to play. All feedback was considered, further changes made, and the final version of the game was ultimately accepted by the sponsor.

5.5 Phase 5 – Launch of the Game

An email to various international UNICEF groups announced the launch of the game 13 months after its initiation. The game had a favorable reception as many positive comments on what had been achieved were made by UNICEF worldwide, PI youth and FB fans. A media release issued after the launch showed UNICEF's positive assessment of the initiative (UNICEF (P) 2011). Postings on the UNICEF (P) fan page highlighted how successful the game was with requests for the game to be translated into Pacific languages and a request to include it on the Madagascar UNICEF page. The game was further distributed through three other FB sites and put into use. The launch event marked the end of the project.

6 Analysis and Findings

6.1 Actors and Actor-to-Actor Networks

We identified multiple actors in various roles in the actor-to-actor network[1] of what we identified as the PC3G development service ecosystem (*see* subsection 'Service Ecosystems') as project participants. Some took on various roles, others joined the service ecosystem ad hoc on request, while yet others and their roles became less significant or even disappeared throughout the service ecosystem's existence. The actors, their roles, and their locations are listed in Table 1. The actor-to-actor network, the interactions, and collaborations of various intensity between actors in that service ecosystem are depictured as part of Fig. 3. Some actors contributed to co-creation of value with direct, many however without direct relations, interaction, or knowledge of others.

The case analysis shows how the concept of actor transcends the producer-customer (as well as consumer or user) divide in contemporary ISD as some actors, especially those who traditionally would be considered passive customers or future users, become involved in actor-to-actor networks and actively contribute as partners with ideas, requirements, and feedback in the value co-creation process beyond conventional organizational boundaries.

6.2 Resource Integration and Service Exchange

The actors provided resources, knowledge, and skills that were continuously integrated and applied in reciprocal, direct, and indirect service-to-service exchanges that contributed to the ongoing recreation of the service ecosystem. Here we provide some examples; Table 1 summarizes all identified resources and services.

---

[1] Further service ecosystems can be identified consisting of subsets of the listed actors in the actor-to-actor network.

The sponsor's resources consisted of skills to create an initial project vision and plan, social networking talent, access to a network of actors to develop the game, the ability to communicate with diverse actors, and the capability to coordinate diverse actors in project. He applied these resources as services to other actors who reciprocally provided their services to him.

As a service the COL provided the resource of project funding, and in exchange the sponsor's applied skills in form of a well-coordinated and executed project resulted in an outcome that supported the objective of climate education. The climate experts possessed knowledge climate challenges and as a service shared it with the sponsor who as a return service communicated that knowledge to the developers.

The sponsor's service to the developers comprised his support in coordinating and assessing their work, and to filter, prioritize, and communicate the ideas, requirements, and feedback he received from other actors in the ecosystem. The developers provided ISD knowledge and in a direct service-for-service exchange developed the game's functional and technical design and programming as an immediate service to the sponsor. These developer activities also represent an indirect service to other actors, notably UNICEF(P) and the PI youth, as potential beneficiaries of the project.

Table 1. Actors, roles, locations, and their integrated resources and exchanged services.

Actor/role/location	Resources[a]	Service
UNICEF (P) communications specialist/ Sponsor Project co-ordinator Overall decision maker/ Fiji, Pacific Islands	Vision for the game Access to resources Skills/knowledge about coordinating projects, communicating with diverse stakeholders including youth	Coordinated & integrated resources Led & managed project Filtered/prioritised ideas, requirements, feedback Evaluated designs
IS professor/Consultant/Melbourne, Australia	Access to students with ISD skills Knowledge about managing ISD projects Knowledge about ISD	Integrated suitable students in the PC3G development service ecosystem & helped develop rules of engagement & cooperation between sponsor & developers Provided guidance
Three research students/ Developers in the core development team/ Hongkong, Melbourne, & Regional Victoria, Australia	Knowledge about ISD Access to testers	Developed the games Integrated testers into the ecosystem

(continued)

Table 1. (*continued*)

Actor/role/location	Resources[a]	Service
Four Fiji adolescents/ Social media facilitators/ Fiji, Pacific Islands	Access to other PI youth	Engaged other youth, provided a channel for youth opinions, filtered their input, ideas, requirements, feedback
International climate experts/ Providers of climate change expertise/ Globally distributed	Knowledge about climate change challenges & how to meet them	Shared relevant climate change knowledge with sponsor

[a]Digital technologies such as PCs, Internet, and digital means for communication such as email, Skype and FB were a shared resource for all the actors in their various roles.

The social media facilitators' access to the PI youth led to the exchange of a further service that gave the latter a voice on requirements for the design and early versions of the game. These opinions were the resources that the PI youth brought to the situation, and as a service they provided the social media facilitators with input for the game development. This input became a resource for the social media facilitators who applied it with the sponsor and in direct service exchange with the developers.

We noted that digital technologies and resources embodied in the applied ISD approach when used for cooperation and coordination take the form of institutional arrangements.

6.3 Institutions and Institutional Arrangements

Institutions and institutional arrangements are a special kind of resource. Some arrangements existed before the project started and became part of the service ecosystem; others were negotiated by some actors in the beginning while still others emerged over the course of the project during the resource integration and service exchange processes. Here we present some examples.

The sponsor's initial vision and requirements were the foundation for cooperation and coordination in the project. It originated as a cognitive arrangement. Shared with other actors, it became a normative arrangement. The Terms of Reference document, along with the formal contracts between UNICEF (P) and the three developers that included the budget, plan, and expected deliverables were regulative arrangements for the service ecosystem.

The developed communication protocol provided a communication structure that compensated for minimal documentation and helped manage the high flux rate as a normative arrangement. The regular planning meetings and feedback sessions, along with early game versions based on short iterations, were further normative arrangements. The role of social media facilitators, the additional role of facilitator in the development team, and the norms for collaboration determining the division of labor as the team went along were all actor-developed arrangements.

The cooperation and coordination mechanisms and the structural arrangements in the service ecosystem were aligned and consistent with the ISD method which itself was an institutional arrangement, as were the egalitarian management practices, the flat organizational and governance structure where the sponsor and the social media facilitators represented coordination mechanisms between the three developers and PI youth.

Above we identified digital technologies as resources; when used for coordination they are also institutional arrangements that helped overcome project challenges like the distribution of actors over geographical and time zones, limited timelines, the high change rate, and the evolving competencies of the developers.

None of the institutional arrangements hindered service exchange. This indicates that they were well aligned with the actors' roles and different knowledge and skills resulting in value propositions and the co-creation of value for all actors.

6.4 Value and Value Co-creation

Co-created value propositions emerged when some actors were considered by others, or themselves, as potential beneficiaries, and became values when accepted as such by a beneficiary. The co-created value propositions and values were perceived differently by each set of actors. The values comprised different components and came into being through different actor relationships, but all actors experienced an increase in wellbeing through the co-created value.

For the PI youth as one, if not the main, beneficiary of the service ecosystem, the value proposition that they accepted was a game that offered important information about climate change in an attractive, entertaining way. The service exchange interactions were also of value for them, they produced the satisfaction of being listened to and having their feedback taken seriously. The resulting strengthened relationship between PI youth and UNICEF (P) became an accepted value proposition that was co-created.

The gratification of helping others as a value proposition was an accepted value by the consultant, the three developers, UNICEF (P) staff, and the functional testers. The two former also emphasized the value of the relationships they had developed with each other and the sponsor. The developers also accepted the value of the newly gained knowledge, skills, and recognition they received for the services in the ISD activities.

Another value proposition for UNICEF (P/HQ) was the achievement of their objective: proof of concept of their social media strategy to mobilize youth in two-way communication. They and the climate experts possibly also gained value from the furtherance of their mission to spread awareness about climate change. This assumption is unverified, as is the value proposition for the COL.

6.5 Service Ecosystems

The focal point of our analysis was what we call the PC3G development service ecosystem. It was surrounded by the larger UNICEF (P) service ecosystem consisting of numerous actors in various roles such as other non-governmental organisations (NGOs), health care provides, global climate actors, parents, schools, children, communities to just name a few.

This service ecosystem consisted of two further interlocked, partly overlapping, and nested service ecosystems. The first we called 'the requirements and use service ecosystem'. It is associated with requirements gathering and analysis, functional design evaluation, prototype and usability testing, and related feedback. The second we called 'the design and realisation service ecosystem'. It concerns the functional and technical design, technical realisation, technical testing, and related feedback. This service ecosystem had another one embedded which we denoted 'the core development team service ecosystem'. Within the latter another was nested, 'the developer service ecosystem'. These service ecosystems and the actors involved are represented in Fig. 3. Our analysis reveals that the project exhibited the fundamental characteristics of service ecosystems which we illustrate with some examples.

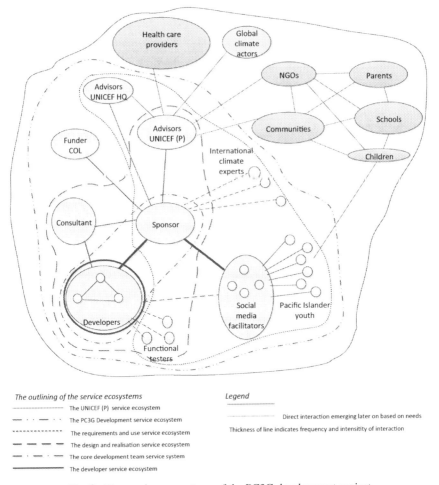

Fig. 3. The service ecosystems of the PC3G development project.

In terms of complexity, despite its manageable number of actors compared to other service ecosystems, the project was simultaneously stable and unstable. The sponsor's initial project vision and plan, his specification of the overall requirements, the developers' formal contract, and the communication protocol, created a relatively stable space within which service exchanges unfolded. However, the project had to deal with instability brought about by the continuous flow of ideas, requirements, change requests, and feedback occasioned by the involvement of diverse actors spread across continents and time zones. The focal ecosystem balanced this complexity with emergent institutional arrangements that divided actors into the identified interlocked service ecosystems.

This emerging organizational form that allowed for a steady yet flexible response to the input coming in short iterations of controllable task size, as well as the regular planning and feedback sessions led to the emergence of a regular rhythm and work pace that afforded stability and flexibility. The organizational structure of the dispersed actors was not planned, nor was the inclusion of certain actors. The PI youth, the UNICEF staff, and the climate experts joined the project voluntarily when called upon and left of their own accord without notice. These are instances of emerging behaviors.

Self-organization unfolded as the project was not led and controlled top-down but managed in an egalitarian manner. The sponsor acted as a facilitating co-ordinator. He set up an environment with short communication paths that fostered task self-assignment, largely autonomous decision-making, and joint responsibility. Self-organization and self-governance were evidenced in the way the social media facilitators solicited and filtered requirements provided by other youth, and how the latter offered ideas. The self-directed entry and exit by PI youth, UNICEF (P/HQ) staff, and the three juvenile testers are other instances of emergent self-organization.

7 Discussion and Conclusion

We have applied SDL because it puts a strong emphasis on the concepts of value and value co-creation that transcend the producer-customer/consumer/user divide (Lusch and Nambisan 2015). The purpose of value is to increase the collective wellbeing of all actors in an ecosystem so that value co-creation becomes a contribution to the wellbeing of others (Vargo and Lusch 2016) as was the case in the PC3G development project.

The concept of value co-creation in service ecosystems therefore warrants further reflections on the relationship between SDL, its foundational concepts and ISD methods. SDL does not prescribe operational principles or methods; it provides foundational concepts and premises. Our analysis shows and reinforces the importance of, and the increased focus on, value and value co-creation in contemporary ISD that has been advocated by agile ISD and project management methods since the early 2000s (Highsmith 2002; Highsmith 2009) – regardless of the application of a particular ISD method and without any relation to SDL.

Kazman and Chen (2009) argue that despite incorporating customer feedback in the development process, the application of agile ISD does not reflect an SDL perspective when customers are treated as self-contained and passive recipients of value, or as part of institutional arrangements where they are replaced by proxies. Babb and Keith (2012) in contrast reason that agile methods are well suited for the co-creation process as put forward in the SDL framework. Bjerknes and Kautz (2019) support this position through their empirical study of agile ISD as service ecosystems in three projects with institutional arrangements that followed the agile principles with a focus on value co-creation with and for customers. We therefore argue that agile ISD methods per se are not incompatible with SDL and affirm that it is not the agile methods as such that support or hinder value co-creation, but rather other institutional arrangements in which they are embedded. In the PC3G development project all characteristics of a supportive service ecosystem were in place, including a methodological approach similar to an agile method that led to accepted value propositions and co-created value for all actors.

Based on SDL's view that all actors in a service ecosystem are partners, Babb and Keith (2012) further argue that co-creation establishes a mode of equality and empowerment under which ISD operates. In this context, co-creation has been related to participatory design (Iversen 2014), here distributed participatory design (DPD) where the actors are geographically dispersed (Lukyanenko et al. 2016).

Our analysis demonstrates how SDL and DPD converge in contemporary ISD despite the different worldviews underlying the two approaches, because the actors were guided by communal, humanistic goals while keeping instrumental considerations in sight. Our research shows that under these circumstances the two approaches are compatible, demonstrating how humanistic and instrumental outcomes can be synergistically connected. In this way, the work contributes to a sociotechnical perspective as foundational to the IS discipline (Sarker et al. 2019). In our case, value was not predominantly co-created for and by employees and workers, but for and by diverse, voluntary actors in the service ecosystems, including research student developers, regional youth, intergovernmental organisations' staff, and subject matter experts.

Further reflecting on the theoretical and practical implications of SDL on ISD leads us to one of SDL's foundational sources: complexity science that has long been recognized as a valuable approach to understanding ISD. Several researchers have applied complexity science and provided organizing principles and suggestions for best practice of the ISD process. For instance, Benbya and McKelvey (2006) do so, but without empirical grounding, while Meso and Jain (2006) and Vidgen and Wang (2009) put forward empirical-based principles for agile ISD. Placed in the larger context of SDL and based on an analysis of large ISD projects Kazman and Chen (2009) offer principles and implications with an emphasis on egalitarian management of open, networked teams for practical application in ISD with distributed actors in crowd-sourced settings.

Our work is based on these predecessors, but rather than using SDL as a backdrop and limiting our work to any particular ISD approach, we use the full set of SDL concepts for our analysis. Our investigation empirically displays how these concepts are interrelated and allow a broad, yet holistic examination of the researched case from the different perspectives embedded in the framework. As such, we show how SDL-based principles and derived implications are advantageous for comprehending and organizing contemporary ISD.

This discussion also warrants a brief remark on SDL's demanding terminology. We found that some concepts, notably those of 'resource' and 'institutional arrangement' expose ambiguity. We also experienced that the current ISD vocabulary is still firmly rooted in a goods-dominant, firm-centric logic. It will take joint efforts to integrate SDL and its language with the constructs of projects, developers, customers, methods, and profits. This is not a straightforward task.

In conclusion, we applied Vargo and Lusch's multi-theorectical SDL framework and conceptualized ISD as service ecosystems of value co-creation. Our study confirms empirically that the framework and its conceptual devices offer a holistic perspective to capture the nature of contemporary ISD. It shows the strength of the service ecosystems metaphor as it grasps how current ISD goes beyond organizational boundaries. Instead of bureaucratic, hierarchical structures, our analysis uncovered an emergent, dynamic network of actors involved and collaborating in ISD.

Despite its particular context, the project shares its dynamic, complex, and emergent nature with other contemporary ISD endeavors (Duggal 2018). While we believe that our contributions based on analytical generalization (Walsham 1995) of a single case study will hold beyond this case, we acknowledge that future research is needed to verify and refine our results.

References

Alves, H., Fernandes, C., Raposo, M.: Value co-creation: concept and contexts of application and study. J. Bus. Res. **69**(5), 1626–1633 (2016). https://doi.org/10.1016/j.jbusres.2015.10.029

Babb, J., Keith, M.: Co-creating value in systems development: a shift towards service-dominant logic. J. Inf. Syst. Appl. Res. **5**(1), 4–15 (2012). http://jisa.org/2012-5/ISSN:1946-1836

Barqawi, N., Syed, K., Mathiassen, L.: Applying service-dominant logic to recurrent release of software: an action research study. J. Bus. Ind. Mark. **31**(7), 928–940 (2016). https://doi.org/10.1108/JBIM-02-2015-0030

Benbya, H., McKelvey, B.: Toward a complexity theory of information systems development. Inf. Technol. People **19**(1), 12–34 (2006). https://doi.org/10.1108/09593840610649952

Bjerknes, G., Kautz, K.: Agile development as service ecosystems. In: Proceedings of the 2019 Australasian Conference on Information Systems, pp. 86–96 (2019). https://acis2019.io/pdfs/ACIS2019_PaperFIN_021.pdf

Böhmann, T., Leimeister, J.M., Möslein, K.: Service systems engineering. Bus. Inf. Syst. Eng. **6**, 73–79 (2014). https://doi.org/10.1007/s12599-014-0314-8

Creswell, J.: Research Design – Qualitative, Quantitative and Mixed Methods Approaches. Sage Publications, Thousand Oaks, CA (2003)

Duggal, J.: The DNA of Strategy Execution: Next Generation Project Management and PMO. Wiley & Sons, Hoboken, NJ (2018)

Fielt, E., Böhmann, T., Korthaus, A., Conger, S., Gable, G.: Service management and engineering in information systems research. J. Strat. Inf. Syst. **22**(1), 46–50 (2013). https://doi.org/10.1016/j.jsis.2013.01.001

Fincham, R.: Narratives of success and failure in systems development. Br. J. Manag. **13**(1), 1–14 (2002). https://doi.org/10.1111/1467-8551.00219

Fisher, J.: Engaging Pacific youth through a Facebook game. ACM Inroads **4**(3), 79–85 (2012). https://doi.org/10.1145/2381083.2381103

Highsmith, J.: Agile Software Development Ecosystems. Addison-Wesley, Boston, MA (2002)

Highsmith, J.: Agile Project Management: Creating Innovative Products, 2nd edn. Addison-Wesley Professional, Boston, MA (2009)

Iversen, O.S.: What is the difference between co-creation and participatory design? Same or Not? (2014). https://www.researchgate.net/post/What_is_the_difference_between_co-creation_and_participatory_design. Accessed 10 Oct 2021

Kazman, R., Chen, H.: The metropolis model a new logic for development of crowdsourced systems. Commun. ACM **52**(7), 76–84 (2009). https://doi.org/10.1145/1538788.1538808

Kautz, K., Bjerknes, G., Fisher, J., Jensen, T.: The process of co-creation in information systems development: a case study of a digital game development project. In: Andersson, B., et al. (eds.) Advances in Information Systems Development: Designing Digitalization. Lecture Notes in Information Systems and Organisation, vol. 34, pp. 187–206. Springer Publishing Company, Berlin, Germany (2019)

Kautz, K., Bjerknes, G.: Information systems development as value co-creation. Commun. Assoc. Inf. Syst. **47**, 1–24 (2020). https://doi.org/10.17705/1CAIS.04701

Keith, M., Demirkan, H., Goul, M.: Service-oriented software development. In: Proceedings of the 2009 AMCIS Conference (2009). https://aisel.aisnet.org/amcis2009/100

Keith, M., Demirkan, H., Goul, M.: Service-oriented methodology for systems development. J. Manag. Inf. Syst. **30**(1), 227–260 (2013). https://doi.org/10.2753/MIS0742-1222300107

Lee, A.S.: Electronic mail as a medium for rich communication: an empirical investigation using hermeneutic interpretation. MIS Q. **18**(2), 143–157 (1994). https://doi.org/10.2307/249762

Lukyanenko, R., Parsons, J., Wiersma, Y.F., Sieber, R., Maddah, M.: Participatory design for user-generated content: understanding the challenges and moving forward. Scandinavian J. Inf. Syst. **28**(1), 37–70 (2016). https://aisel.aisnet.org/sjis/vol28/iss1/2/

Lusch, R.F., Nambisan, S.: Service innovation: a service-dominant logic perspective. MIS Q **39**(1), 155–175 (2015). https://doi.org/10.25300/MISQ/2015/39.1.07

Lusch, R.F., Vargo, S.L.: An overview of service-dominant logic. In: Vargo, S.L., Lusch, R.F. (eds.) The SAGE Handbook of Service-Dominant Logic, pp. 3–21. Sage Publications, London, UK (2019)

Meso, P., Jain, R.: Agile software development: adaptive systems principles and best practices. Inf. Syst. Manag. **23**(3), 19–30 (2006). https://doi.org/10.1201/1078.10580530/46108.23.3.200 60601/93704.3

Miles, M.B., Huberman, M.A., Saldana, J.: Qualitative Data Analysis, 3rd edn. Sage Publications, London, UK (2014)

Öbrand, L., Augustsson, N.P., Mathiassen, L., Holmström, J.: The interstitiality of IT risk: an inquiry into information systems development practices. Inf. Syst. J. **29**(1), 97–118 (2019). https://doi.org/10.1111/isj.12178

Sarker, S., Chatterjee, S., Xiao, X., Elbanna, A.: Sociotechnical axis of cohesion for the IS discipline: its historical legacy and its continued relevance. MIS Q **43**(3), 685–719 (2019). https://doi.org/10.25300/MISQ/2019/13747

UNICEF (P): Pacific Island Countries (2013). Retrieved from http://www.unicef.org/pacificislands/index.html

UNICEF (P): Behind the bytes, Press releases. Retrieved from http://www.unicef.org/pacificislands/media15625.html (December 2014, page no longer available), text available on request from the authors (2011)

Vargo, S.L., Lusch, R.F.: Institutions and axioms: an extension and update of service-dominant logic. J. Acad. Mark. Sci. **44**(1), 5–23 (2016). https://doi.org/10.1007/s11747-015-0456-3

Vargo, S.L., Lusch, R.F.: Service-dominant logic 2025. Int. J. Res. Mark. **34**(1), 46–67 (2017). https://doi.org/10.1016/j.ijresmar.2016.11.001

Vargo, S.L., Maglio, P., Akaka, M.A.: On value and value co-creation: a service systems and service logic perspective. Eur. Manag. J. **26**, 145–152 (2008). https://doi.org/10.1016/j.emj.2008.04.003

Vidgen, R., Wang, X.: Coevolving systems and the organization of agile software development. Inf. Syst. Res. **20**(3), 355–376 (2009). https://doi.org/10.1287/isre.1090.0237

Walsham, G.: Interpretive case studies in IS research: nature and method. Eur. J. Inf. Syst. **4**(2), 74–81 (1995). https://doi.org/10.1057/ejis.1995.9

Zwass, V.: Co-creation: toward a taxonomy and an integrated research perspective. Int. J. Electron. Commer. **15**(1), 11–48 (2010). https://doi.org/10.2753/JEC1086-4415150101

Digital Transformation Progress Model for Supporting Co-creation During a Digital Transformation Initiative

Steven Alter[✉]

University of San Francisco, San Francisco, CA 94117, USA
`alter@usfca.edu`

Abstract. Reflecting the IFIP 8.6 theme of "cocreating for context," this conceptual contribution proposes a model designed to support co-creation within an unfolding context of varying internal and external conditions as a digital transformation (DT) strives to achieve its goals. It proposes a digital transformation progress model (DTPM) that combines a work system perspective with ideas related to DT, including DT initiative, DT success, phases of DT, and tangible and intangible resources for change that affect DT initiatives. The model expresses the combined impact of the favorability of five categories of resources for change at any point in a DT initiative's trajectory. The categories are momentum, capabilities, forces, drivers and impediments of change, and catalysts of change. Potential uses of the DTPM and follow-on research are discussed briefly.

Keywords: Digital transformation · Co-creation · Work system perspective · Resources for change

1 Digital Transformation as Co-creating for Context

"Co-creating for context," the theme of the 2022 IFIP 8.6 conference, emphasizes the increasing diversity, complexity, and uncertainty of context(s) influencing the diffusion of emerging IT. The CFP discusses many possible topics including what is happening "at the precipice of digital transformation." This paper pursues the topic of digital transformation (DT) as a prime example of "co-creating for context."

This conceptual contribution proposes a digital transformation progress model (DTPM) for supporting co-creation as a DT initiative unfolds within a context of time-varying internal and external conditions. Traditional project management approaches emphasizing Gantt chart topics would miss many issues and obstacles that could affect the initiative's trajectory as a co-creation effort within diverse contexts. The DTPM combines project status and momentum information with subjective judgments related to issues and obstacles likely to affect the initiative's current status, future trajectory, and possible outcomes.

The proposed DTPM assumes that DT occurs through change trajectories in IT-enabled mission-critical work systems (WSs). It assumes that the general phenomenon of

© IFIP International Federation for Information Processing 2022
Published by Springer Nature Switzerland AG 2022
A. Elbanna et al. (Eds.): TDIT 2022, IFIP AICT 660, pp. 58–76, 2022.
https://doi.org/10.1007/978-3-031-17968-6_4

DT is not linked to specific emerging technologies such as cloud computing, blockchain, and machine learning. It does not incorporate DT mantras about maintaining visible leadership by top executives, improving digital literacy, and changing corporate culture, nor does it suggest a normative DT process or assume that DT necessarily involves strategic responses to technology-related disruptions in industry or society.

Goal. This paper proposes a model-based approach for supporting or analyzing co-creation as a DT initiative strives to achieve its goals within the unfolding context of varying internal and external conditions.

Organization. Section 2 summarizes the work system perspective because DT calls for significant changes in mission-critical work systems. Section 3 presents definitions and other ideas related to DT. Section 4 explains how the DTPM links the favorability of five categories of resources for change to a DT initiative's likelihood of successful outcomes throughout its evolving trajectory. Section 5 briefly discusses potential uses of the DTPM. Section 6 identifies limitations and follow-on research.

The DTPM was developed through an iterative process incorporating interests and research experiences related to DT, value co-creation, work systems, implementation case studies, and the resource-based view. Many of this paper's ideas are presented without detailed background explanations that would be expected in a full journal article but would exceed this paper's length limitations.

2   Work System Perspective Underlying the DTPM

Brief background summarizing existing coverage of the work system perspective (WSP) [1–3] is needed since the DTPM focuses on initiatives related to mission-critical WSs as defined within that perspective. The WSP has been used in teaching (e.g., [4–6]) and in research articles on various topics, but I am not aware of its use in models for supporting DT.

Definition of Work System. A WS is a system in which human participants *and/or* machines perform work (processes and activities) using information, technology, and other resources to produce specific product/services for internal and/or external customers. WSs may be sociotechnical (human participants perform work with help of machines) or totally automated (machine performs all work). ISs, projects, highly focused supply chains, and totally automated WSs can be viewed and analyzed as WSs.

Definition of Information System. An IS is a WS whose essential activities are devoted to capturing, storing, retrieving, transmitting, deleting, manipulating, and displaying information. ISs may exist to produce their own product/services or may exist to support other WSs. The notion of essential activities is analogous to the idea of deep structure in representation theory [7].

Work System View of an Enterprise. An enterprise (or major business unit or supply chain crossing enterprises) can be viewed a set of WSs whose operation and interactions maintain the enterprise, determine how it obtains and applies resources, and produce product/services for customers and economic results for the enterprise.

Aspects of a Work System That May Change During DT. The nine elements of the work system framework (Fig. 1) are viewed as changeable in the course of DT initiatives. The elements of that framework outline a basic understanding of a WS's form, function, and environment during a period when it is stable enough to retain its identity even though incremental changes may occur. *Processes and activities, participants, information,* and *technologies* are completely within the WS. *Customers* and *product/services* may be partially inside and partially outside because customers often participate in activities within a WS and because product/services take shape within a WS. *Environment, infrastructure,* and *strategies* are viewed as outside of the WS even though they have direct effects within a WS and may be affected by a significant DT initiative. "Elements of the WS framework" will be referred to as "WS elements" even though the last three are partially or totally outside and not controllable by a WS.

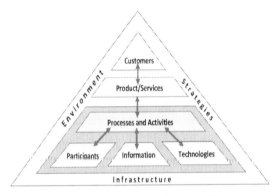

Fig. 1. Work system framework

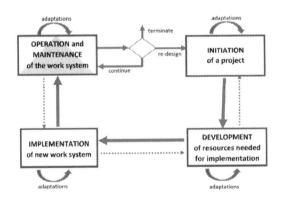

Fig. 2. Work system life cycle model

The WS life cycle model (WSLC – Fig. 2) describes how WSs (including ISs) evolve through iterations of planned change through projects (initiation, development, and implementation phases) and unplanned change (adaptations and workarounds). Significant changes affect multiple elements of the WS framework, not just technologies.

The development phase creates or acquires and then tests software and other resources needed for implementation in the organization. The implementation phase involves changes in work practices. The WSLC's four idealized phases (and their sub-phases) express a waterfall-like approach to identifying things that should happen as a WS evolves iteratively. Key activities and responsibilities remain even if the phases are partially merged in agile approaches and regardless of whether the WS uses homegrown software, commercial application software, or external platforms. Even when development and implementation are partly merged, each iteration determines requirements (at some level of detail), acquires, produces, fixes, tests, and debugs any needed software, decides how to implement WS changes, identifies implementation problems, and trains WS participants.

3   Ideas for Understanding Digital Transformations

The effort to develop a DTPM was motivated by the increasing importance of DT and my unawareness of models that might support DT initiatives more effectively than project management, change management, and IT portfolio management models.

The comprehensive DT literature review in [8] made further review seem redundant. It found 282 DT articles, of which only 28 defined DT. Many definitions had significant shortcomings related to "circularity, unclear concepts, and conflation between the concept and its impacts" (p. 119). [8] defined DT as "a process that aims to improve an entity by triggering significant changes to its properties through combinations of information, computing, communication, and connectivity technologies." (p. 118). Later [8, p. 122] expanded on that definition by noting eight "building blocks of the DT process" in the literature: strategic responses, disruptions, use of digital technologies, structural changes, changes in value creation paths, organizational barriers, negative impacts, and positive impacts. This paper recognizes the relevance of those factors, while proposing a model designed to help managers trying to steer a DT initiative.

3.1   Developing the DT Progress Model

Inspection of current DT-related articles and consultant web sites concluded that a useful model of DT needed to start with a clear definition of DT, should support DT initiatives, and ideally should help researchers visualize DT issues. It should go beyond recycling common assertions about management support, experience, adequate resources, realistic scheduling, disruptions, and emerging technologies. Developing a DT model based on the WSP seemed more straightforward than using institutional theory, technological change, strategy analysis, diffusion of innovation, or other approaches because DT necessarily involves changes in work systems.

My initial attempt to imagine a DTPM applied aspects of the WSP including work system theory (WST) and the work system method (WSM), a related systems analysis method designed to help business professionals visualize WSs and collaborate effectively with IT professionals. The general idea of applying a WS lens to mission-critical WSs seemed plausible but an initial descriptive application of WST and WSM said nothing unique about DT. The next step was trying to describe how DT initiatives call for new extensions or combinations of WS-related understandings in [1–4]. The search for richer conceptualizations touched on empirical studies [9, 10], views of innovation [11], discussions of forces [12, 13], the resource-based view [14], dynamic capabilities [15], a new framework for describing theoretical perspectives [16] and its application to the WSP [17]. Trial and error iterations in developing the new model included some aspects of design science research but did not use DSR explicitly.

3.2 Definitions Related to DT and DT Initiative

The DTPM builds on definitions from WST and on definitions related to DT.

Definition of DT. Enterprises serve their customers through the operation and interactions of numerous WSs. Accordingly, DT is defined as an enterprise-level transformation which IT-related changes enable strategically significant changes in mission-critical WSs. Thus, DT is neither about the diffusion of IT nor about industrial or societal changes inspired or enabled by IT. DT typically focuses on selected mission-critical WSs, not on the entire enterprise, and not on shared IT infrastructure unless infrastructure changes enable significant changes in mission-critical WSs. DT-related changes during DT initiatives are typically directed toward some combination of major business concerns such as operational excellence, profitability, product/services for customers, and/or the customer experience.

Definition of DT Initiative. An identifiable DT initiative involves the initiation, oversight, and management of one or more DT-related projects from inception to completion or abandonment. Applying a project viewpoint to DT initiatives assumes that typical project details such as schedules, dependencies, and resources will be articulated clearly, tracked, and possibly adjusted as conditions change. As with many large projects, DT initiatives may be merged into other projects or may be terminated before achieving their goals.

Time Frame for DT. Viewed in project-like terms, a DT initiative has a start date, a set of milestones that help in tracking progress, and a projected date of completion that may be revised.

DT as an Adjustable Trajectory. The planned trajectory of an ongoing DT effort (including timing, intermediate milestones, intended end points, and human, technical, and financial resources) may be modified during a DT initiative based on its current status and assessments of opportunities, constraints, and other concerns.

Success of a DT Initiative. This is described in two ways, both of which recognize that DT initiatives are large, complex projects whose ambitions and scope may change due to opportunities and/or constraints that were not recognized initially. The first view of success describes the extent to which projects in a DT initiative are completed on schedule and absorb an appropriate amount of human, technical, and financial resources in creating or modifying mission-critical WSs in accordance with original or revised transformational visions. The second view of success focuses on the extent to which new or improved WSs achieve and sustain the transformational vision and eventually are extended. Both views of success call for subjective assessments that may differ between observers.

3.3 Phases of a Digital Transformation

The phases of a DT can be viewed as a 5-phase variation on the WSLC that nonetheless recognizes that iterations and overlaps between phases may occur [11]:

1. **Impetus.** Recognition of enterprise-level challenges that a DT could try to address.
2. **Transformational vision.** The management vision of how those challenges will be addressed and what outcomes will be achieved.
3. **Resource acquisition.** The process of creating, obtaining, improving, and/or channeling resources that are needed for DT implementation.
4. **Implementation.** Making WS changes needed to achieve the transformational vision.
5. **Operation and maintenance.** Operation and support of transformed WSs.

Identifying general phases of DT initiatives distinguishes those initiatives from less specific diffusion of technological innovation or societal change related to innovative technologies. Executing DT initiatives requires that their transformational vision will be translated into projects that acquire and use resources to create or improve mission-critical WSs. A DT initiative without well-defined projects is more like a management exhortation that lacks operational follow-through. The nature and scope of projects within DT initiatives may evolve over time, especially since DT initiatives typically are undertaken in dynamic business contexts where needs and ambitions that launched a DT initiative might be overtaken by events in the surrounding context(s) or might evolve based on experience within the initiative.

3.4 Resources for a Digital Transformation

The idea of "resources for change" has been used in a variety of ways in relation to management, education, law, medicine, social relationships, organizational change, and elsewhere. Many iterations of trying to apply various aspects of the WSP to DT initiatives led to visualizing five types of "resources for change" that contribute to whether and how DT initiatives will achieve their goals. Largely tangible resources for change include (1) momentum toward the transformational vision and (2) capabilities needed to achieve the vision. Intangible resources include (3) forces affecting all or most of a WS, (4) drivers and impediments of change related to specific WS elements, and (5) catalysts affecting the micro-dynamics of DT-related changes. Each type of resource has many different facets that may have positive, neutral, or negative impacts on current and future progress of projects within the DT initiative. The various facets of the five types of resources for change typically are not totally independent. Most managers probably would ignore that issue if the larger categories helped them identify and collaborate around important concerns.

Momentum Toward the Transformational Vision. A specific WS's DT-related momentum is the extent to which its current state and the state of ongoing projects that affect it are consistent with the current schedule and the DT's transformational vision (which both may have been revised). Typical ideas in project management focus on those concerns, which are expressed in project management tools that focus on project status, future milestones, available human, financial, technical, and informational resources, and key dependencies along the critical path to the project's conclusion.

Shared enthusiasm and significant progress toward the goal can be viewed as resources that reinforce shared beliefs that the goal makes sense and is attainable. Conversely, participants in a project that seems adrift may tend to believe that their efforts are pointless and will not pay off for themselves or for the organization.

Capabilities Needed to Achieve the Transformational Vision. DT requires a combination of appropriate software development and implementation capabilities, financial capabilities (adequate budget and financial systems and flexibility) and trustworthy leadership and organizational change capabilities (e.g., dynamic capabilities defined in [15] as "the firm's ability to integrate, build, and reconfigure internal and external competences to address rapidly changing environments"). Low levels of capabilities of any of those types imply that a DT initiative likely requires additional inputs of energy, time, money, personnel, and/or technical resources.

Management responses to inadequate capabilities are often more difficult than simply acquiring additional staffing or funding. For example, inadequate technical capabilities call for bringing new people into the project, which is often difficult because time spent bringing new project participants up to speed is time not spent on completing ongoing tasks [18].

Forces Affecting a Work System as a Whole. The idea of forces and force fields as discussed by Lewin [12] is not common in the IS field even though it has been used to describe a struggle between driving and restraining forces, e.g., in software development firms [19]. Also, Porter's five forces model [13] is used widely to describe business competition. The idea of thinking about forces in relation to the WSP originally came from an extended analogy with physics [16] and was discussed in [17].

Figure 3 identifies five types of forces that may have positive or negative impacts on DT-related changes in a WS.

- **Cohesive forces** tend to hold WSs together, e.g., incentives, goals, controls, alignment. Five alignment arrows within the work system framework (Fig. 1) highlight typical paths for cohesive forces.
- **Innovative forces** aligned with the transformational vision propel the progress of DT initiatives because they support coordination and maintain direction.
- **Disruptive forces** tend to impede DT initiatives by dissipating energy and sometimes degrading WSs significantly. e.g., internal misalignments, discontent, poor management, design flaws. Those issues mirror the idea of entropy from physics, i.e., a generalized type of disruptive force that increases disorder.

- **Inertial forces** impede progress by dissipating energy and resisting planned or unplanned changes in WS operation. Organizational inertia is cited frequently as a key challenge in overcoming resistance to change, e.g., in organizational behavior, general management, and systems dynamics, where the related phenomenon is called policy resistance ([20, pp. 5–12]).
- **Forces at a distance** (analogous to gravity) may propel or impede progress toward DT goals. These forces stem from broad phenomena related to economics, competition, regulation, demographics, and technological change. Such forces may not be apparent to participants in mission-critical WSs that have operated adequately for years but are not aligned with a DT initiative's requirements or goals.

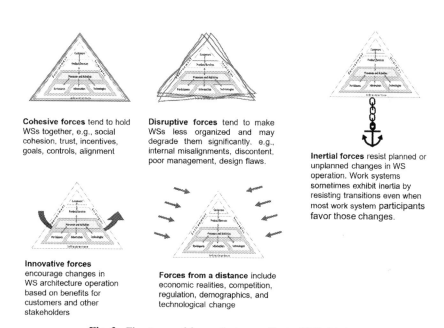

Cohesive forces tend to hold WSs together, e.g., social cohesion, trust, incentives, goals, controls, alignment

Disruptive forces tend to make WSs less organized and may degrade them significantly. e.g., internal misalignments, discontent, poor management, design flaws.

Inertial forces resist planned or unplanned changes in WS operation. Work systems sometimes exhibit inertia by resisting transitions even when most work system participants favor those changes.

Innovative forces encourage changes in WS architecture operation based on benefits for customers and other stakeholders

Forces from a distance include economic realities, competition, regulation, demographics, and technological change

Fig. 3. Five types of forces that may affect a DT initiative

Drivers and Impediments Related to WS Elements. In contrast with forces in Fig. 3 that apply to an entire WS, many drivers or impediments of change are related to individual WS elements [11] and sometimes are reminiscent of some of the factors in UTAUT [21, 22]. Figure 4 shows typical examples of such factors, all of which are expressed so they can be drivers or impediments for DT. For example, low customer satisfaction could be a driver of DT while high customer satisfaction might impede DT by making the need for change less evident. Similarly, the motivation and ambitions of WS participants might have positive or negative impacts depending on how well the DT initiative is aligned with those motivations and ambitions.

Many factors in the IS literature on post-adoption behavior can be viewed as drivers or impediments related to WS elements. The drivers and impediments in Fig. 4 include many factors that go beyond the variables that appear in the most widely cited IS theories (e.g., TAM, UTAUT) that focus mostly on determinants of technology acceptance and use rather than on IT-enabled changes in mission-critical WSs.

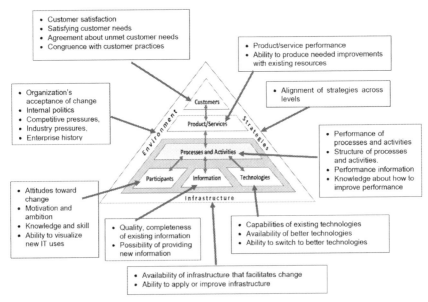

Fig. 4. Drivers and impediments related to elements of the work system framework

Some of the factors in Fig. 4 overlap somewhat with forces in Fig. 3. For example, Fig. 3's *forces from a distance* include competition, and Fig. 4's factors related to the WS element *environment* include competitive pressure. That type of overlap is not surprising since forces that affect an entire WS necessarily involve factors that affect one or more of its elements. For current purposes, thinking separately about forces affecting an entire WS and factors related to specific WS elements is potentially useful for visualizing a DT initiative's status and prognosis.

Catalysts Affecting the Micro-Dynamics of DT. Consideration of micro-dynamics of DT is needed because day-to-day activities often reflect expressed or unexpressed beliefs that may support or resist a DT initiative. Micro-dynamics can be described in terms of three catalysts, *needing, understanding,* and *liking,* that affect the cooperation vs. resistance of WS participants and other stakeholders [11]. The verb forms *needing, understanding,* and *liking* are used instead of psychological terms such as affective or rational because they express ideas more directly in relation to innovation, adoption, and adaptation in organizational settings. Positive perceptions related to *needing, understanding,* and *liking* tend to be positive for DT, although with some exceptions.

- **Needing.** This is the extent to which individuals or groups perceive that they need an innovation for achieving their own goals. Greater perceived need usually leads to greater support of an innovation.

- **Understanding.** This is the extent to which individuals or groups understand how an innovation can (or cannot) be applied and how and why it might (or might not) be beneficial. Greater understanding may or may not be associated with acceptance or rejection of an innovation. The simplest cases are when people accept or reject an innovation because they understand its genuine benefits or shortcomings. In other cases, people who understand an innovation's beneficial impact for an enterprise might reject it due to conflicts with personal or group goals or interests. (Remember the Luddites.) Similarly, people who misunderstand an innovation might accept it because they cannot foresee its negative implications for them or their group.
- **Liking.** This is the extent to which individuals or groups like an innovation. It is easier to implement innovations that are liked. Implementation efforts tend to be more painful and costly in time and effort when innovations are disliked.

Issues related to micro-dynamics may reveal problems that are obstacles to achieving DT benefits. Various forms of resistance ranging from benign neglect to low-level sabotage could determine whether the DT initiative will be embraced and implemented fully, especially when WS participants, managers, and other stakeholders have conflicting perceptions and beliefs about whether a DT initiative will improve work conditions, will require different skills, or might cause layoffs.

3.5 Resource Favorability

Google Scholar found no instances of papers that contained both resource *favorability* and *digital transformation* even though it found some instances of *resource favorability* in relation to mineral resource projects and several other topics.

The DTPM uses *resource favorability* to summarize the extent to which specific resources or groups of resources for change at any point during a DT initiative's trajectory seem likely to contribute positively (or negatively) to likely success for specific WSs. The favorability of those resources can be explained based on examples, described qualitatively based on subjective perceptions, or rated numerically in various ways. Numerical favorability ratings afford aggregation of otherwise incommensurate factors, although meaningful aggregations require careful attention to the relative importance of different resources and to dependencies and other relationships.

Resource favorability is perceived differently for the five different types of resources for change in Fig. 3. Favorability perceptions related to momentum might be based on information in a project scorecard, e.g., progress vs. plan, critical path to completion, and so on. Favorability related to capabilities might be expressed similarly based on likely availability of human and technical resources. Favorability related to forces, WS-specific drivers/impediments, and WS catalysts might be understood most effectively through narrative evidence obtained through surveys, interviews, management meetings, or other information collection. Stories and examples often would be important, e.g., when a DT initiative's momentum might seem favorable until a key vendor loses technical experts, leading to the management challenge of finding and evaluating alternatives quickly. A different approach would express resource favorability using numerical scales that summarize situations without collecting a lot of detailed information.

For current purposes, a favorability rating for the current state of any specific resource is a point on a continuous dimension going from extremely unfavorable to extremely favorable for the successful completion of the DT initiative. Perceptions on that type of scale could be collected by using a slider that makes it unnecessary to focus on numerical distinctions (e.g., 4.6 vs. 5.2 out of 7) that might not matter when aggregating perceptions of multiple individuals. Table 2 will illustrate how the slider could use colors such as red for unfavorable, yellow for neutral, green for favorable, and slider inputs from people providing favorability ratings could be converted to numerical scores. Data about the current or past favorability of different resources could be weighted in a variety of ways and combined numerically.

4   Digital Transformation Progress Model

The proposed DTPM is designed to facilitate efforts to monitor a DT initiative and make decisions that try to maximize its chances of success. Those decisions should consider positive and negative aspects of the five types of resources for change that often are relevant to the continuing progress of a DT initiative. Throughout the DT initiative, the relevant information ranges from largely objective (e.g., the degree of completion of a specific step in a project or the availability of specific IT resources) through highly subjective (e.g., the level of anger and resistance among stakeholders who might be affected adversely). It could also include the level of threat from external factors such as likely changes in governmental regulations or likely product announcements by competitors. In effect, a DTPM should relate a plethora of diverse information to possible outcomes of the DT initiative based on the current situation at any point during the initiative's lifecycle.

The DTPM is based on the favorability of resources for change. Figure 5 represents the DTPM as it might be applied to an entire DT initiative or might be applied separately to mission-critical WSs considered individually. Figure 5 represents the following verbal statement of the model:

> *The favorability of five categories of resources for change for WSs targeted by the DT initiative contribute individually and in combination to the likelihood of the initiative's eventual degree of completion and business success. The categories are momentum, capabilities, forces affecting the WSs, drivers and impediments related to WS elements, and catalysts of change. Each category includes resources for change whose state can be described at any time during a DT initiative and can be compared to an ideal state relative to the progress of the DT initiative. The state and favorability of important resources for change typically vary over time as the DT initiative unfolds due to adjustment in projects within the DT initiative and ongoing changes in the targeted WSs and in the surrounding environment.*

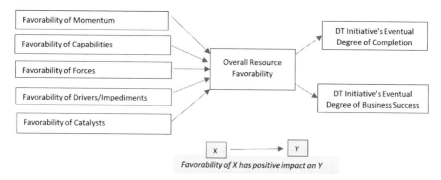

Fig. 5. Digital transformation progress model

Factors that contribute to the five categories of resources for change are not shown in Fig. 5 because each category involves many factors mentioned earlier.

A subjective understanding of how and why the DT initiative is in good shape or has significant challenges typically should be more useful to executive and managers than a point prediction of the probability of success or a numerical probability distribution for a given level of goal achievement. Executives and managers who already have access to typical project management tools would not look to the DTPM to provide the same information. A more likely use of the DTPM is as a basis for sense making and discussion leading to further off-line discussion and executive action if needed, i.e., action beyond typical project management decisions such as modification of short-term plans based on current status, dependencies, available resources, and the current critical path to completion.

4.1 Comparison with UTAUT

The widely cited UTAUT (the Unified Theory of Acceptance and Use of Technology) [21, 22] provides a useful point of comparison even though technology acceptance and use differs greatly from DT. A diagrammatic representation of conclusions from a recent meta-analysis of research related to UTAUT [22, p. 39] said that use behavior is affected directly or indirectly (via behavioral intention) by:

- seven independent variables from UTAUT2 (performance expectancy, effort expectancy, social influence, price value, hedonic motivation, facilitating conditions, habit)
- four extensions (technology compatibility, user education, personal innovativeness, and costs of technology
- effects of four types of moderating variables (individual characteristics, national culture, type of technology, and controls).

Those variables are related to some but not all aspects of the DTPM's five types of resources for change. Several of those variables address momentum and capabilities, the two DTPM types of resources for change that are directly related to project management. Since UTAUT variables operate primarily at an individual level, they do not addresses forces that affect WSs as a whole. On the other hand, some UTAUT variables touch on topics that the DTPM expresses differently in its other categories.

An additional point for comparison concerns usage. The extensive meta-analysis in [22] shows that UTAUT is designed for testing the validity of hypothesized relationships between specific variables and technology use, a question primarily of interest to academic researchers. In contrast, the DTPM is designed to support DT initiatives that involve much more than whether specific technologies will be used.

5 Potential Uses of the DT Progress Model

The concepts built into the DTPM provide an organized way to visualize a DT initiative, to anticipate and identify issues as a DT initiative unfolds, and to evaluate approaches for dealing with those issues. The DTPM assumes that DT achieves goals by creating or changing mission-critical WSs and that the likelihood of success is related to the favorability of five categories of resources for change.

The DTPM affords three potential types of use that will be discussed next. The first is as a framework for visualizing aspects of an ongoing DT initiative. The second is as an organizing principle for narrative DT project reports. The third is as an organizing principle for quantitative DT project reports that combine favorability ratings that would be tailored to situation-specific conditions and would be collected and combined based on user preferences.

5.1 DTPM as a Framework for Visualizing Aspects of an Ongoing DT Initiative

When viewed as a framework outlining a mental model, the DTPM encourages executives to think about the DT as an integrated enterprise initiative that can be divided into a set of projects directed at creating or improving mission-critical WSs. The current status of each project is a starting point for considering favorable and unfavorable aspects of five categories of issues that may call for executive decisions and action.

5.2 DTPM as an Organizing Principle for Narrative DT Project Reports

Table 1 shows a hypothetical example of the type of information in a DTSM-based executive summary for an ongoing DT initiative. Table 1 assumes that the DT initiative involves two mission-critical work systems (WS1 and WS2) and that a brief summary statement might mention several issues for each category of resource favorability for each WS. Additional information would be available as backup.

Table 1. Imagined narrative summary from an executive information system for an imagined DT initiative involving two mission-critical work systems (WS1 and WS2)

WS	Category	Summary of major observations
WS1	Momentum	• Project is several weeks ahead of schedule • Given excellent progress and high commitment, probably should not redeploy anyone until the milestone that will be completed in one month
	Capabilities	• Two technical experts left to join a competitor. We need to replace them quickly to make sure that technical design is done properly • The timing is bad because the technical experts were in the middle of producing a revision of the underlying architecture
	Forces	• A database startup firm has produced a new product that might help us expedite programming. Evaluation requires several weeks of research, which seems worth the possible one week slip in the schedule
	Drivers and impediments for WS elements	• Some customers have noticed that our interactions with them are not nearly as frequent or friendly as interactions from our main competitor • Most work system participants are quite satisfied with the existing software
	Catalysts	• Spirits are generally fine
WS2	Momentum	• Major strike at a supplier of a supplier. No immediate resolution. This could be a very serious problem due to dependency on our supplier • Otherwise the project is moving as expected
	Capabilities	• Adequate resources, could use several other change agents but these can be filled in later

(continued)

Table 1. (*continued*)

WS	Category	Summary of major observations
	Forces	• Inertia is turning into a big deal. Many staff members have little appetite for this type of project, especially since a significant software upgrade last year proved more difficult than expected • Discontent is running high, partly because of disagreements between three key managers
	Drivers and impediments for WS elements	• Most WS participants believe that the existing information is quite sufficient for performing their responsibilities well • Customers also seem reasonably satisfied with our product/services. Their main concern is cost
	Catalysts	• Many long-time supervisors are quite disgruntled about the scope of change that will be required in their work practices. Many say that these changes were dumped on them with no warning or discussion

5.3 DTPM as an Organizing Principle for Quantitative DT Project Reports

Table 2 illustrates one of many possible formats for a numerically oriented favorability report showing favorability ratings for the five categories of resources for change. It uses sliding scales to represent a continuum of possibilities from very unfavorable to very favorable for different issues. That type of report could help executives visualize the current state and direction of change for a DT initiative and could encourage them to inquire further about specific issues. Table 2 presents two types of information: 1) The left side shows the most recent three weeks of favorability ratings related to the five categories of resources. 2) The right side shows current favorability ratings for selected resources for change within each category. Many versions of this type of report and other reports based on the same kinds of information could be produced. For example, using the blue slider to illustrate progress across 3 weeks is just an illustrative example. Some executives might prefer 2 week or 4 week histories. Nothing is sacred about the different types of resources that are listed for each category. Executives involved in specific DT initiatives might be more interested in other types of resources for each category and might prefer other formats for reporting.

Table 2. Imagined quantitative summary from a project management system – including current favorability for types of resources and changes over 3 weeks for resource categories)

Category and 3 week history of category favorability	Resources (within the category)	Resource Favorability (current)
Momentum	Projected completion date	
	Progress in last two weeks	
	Cost vs. budget	
Capabilities	Staff availability	
	Technical capabilities	
	Vendor availability	
	Dynamic capabilities	
Forces	Cohesive forces	
	Disruptive forces	
	Innovative forces	
	Inertia	
	Forces from a distance	
Drivers and impediments for WS elements	Customers	
	Product/services	
	Processes and activities	
	Participants	
	Information	
	Technologies	
Catalysts	Understanding	
	Liking	
	Needing	

6 Conclusion

The DTSM represents a new way to visualize digital transformation, a major area of practice and research. Its diverse facets include many business and societal issues that extend beyond traditional technology acceptance and use research topics. The new app-roach treats DT as a strategic initiative focusing on IT-enabled creation or improvement of mission-critical WSs. The DTSM incorporates many ideas that executives and man-agers should consider as DT initiatives unfold and that IS researchers might incorporate into research related to both IT adoption and DT.

The DTSM fits within the conference theme of "co-creating for context" because DT is a major IT-related type of co-creation involving rich interactions between local, corporate, and broader economic contexts. The DTSM's five categories of resource favorability cover that spectrum selectively, with momentum and capabilities focusing on project issues while forces, drivers and impediments, and catalysts of change focusing on internal and external issues related to the WSs being created or improved.

This conceptual contribution does not provide empirical verification of its intended value and is limited to defining, combining, and illustrating its central ideas. Also, the overall approach was developed in a highly iterative way that did not follow an established methodology such as design science research because a simple iterative approach based on personal knowledge and experience seemed adequate for proposing a unique model. A full journal paper would explain the central ideas more fully, but would still leave a number of questions in the following areas:

Assumptions About DT. The literature review in [8] demonstrated the substantial difficulty in defining DT. The DTSM is based on definitions of DT and DT initiative that focus more on IT-enabled organizational change than on the idea of disruption or the use of emerging technologies. Some researchers probably would not prefer that approach, especially if they are concerned about differentiating DT from IT-enabled organizational change (e.g., [23]).

Completeness of the DTSM. The DTSM organizes many ideas that are relevant to DT, but surely might be specified in more detailed way, perhaps making it more like the results of the meta-analysis of UTAUT research mentioned earlier [22, p. 39]. That level of detail was the product of many research efforts by many researchers. The DTSM might be specified in more detail in the future, but it is not obvious that a more detailed presentation would actually be more useful, as implied by a comment by Wittgenstein [24] cited in closing a paper [25] about the elusive definition of information: "Is it even always an advantage to replace an indistinct picture by a sharp one? Isn't the indistinct one often exactly what we need?".

Usability of the DTSM. This paper mentioned the DTSM's potential for organizing mental models and for generating two types of reports that might support DT initiatives. Testing those proposed uses might lead to insights about how to use the existing DTSM effectively and how to improve it.

Follow-on Research. Case studies, survey research, or even careful coding of a sample of existing DT case studies might validate the idea that the favorability of multiple resources for change can be linked to the success of DT initiatives. Action research and action design research might demonstrate the extent to which executives can use these ideas. Study of project management tools might find ways to add DTPM-related information to existing approaches for large, consequential projects. More direct evidence of the DTSM's value requires research projects involving researchers and organizations willing to try using the DTSM while pursuing DT initiatives.

References

1. Alter, S.: The Work System Method: Connecting People, Processes, and IT for Business Results. Work System Press, Larkspur, CA (2006)
2. Alter, S.: Defining information systems as work systems: implications for the IS field. Eur. J. Inf. Syst. **17**(5), 448–469 (2008)
3. Alter, S.: Work system theory: overview of core concepts, extensions, and challenges for the future. J. Assoc. Inf. Syst. **14**(2), 72–121 (2013)
4. Truex, D., Alter, S., Long, C.: Systems analysis for everyone else: empowering business professionals through a systems analysis method that fits their needs. In: Proceedings of the European Conference on Information Systems (2010)
5. Petkov, D., Petkova, O., Sewchurran, K., Andrew, T., Misra, R.: The work system method as an approach for teaching and researching information systems. In: Information Systems Theory, pp. 413–424. Springer, New York, NY (2012)
6. Bolloju, N., et al.: Improving scrum user stories and product backlog using work system snapshots. In: Proceedings of the American Conference on Information Systems (2017)
7. Burton-Jones, A., Recker, J., Indulska, M., Green, P., Weber, R.: Assessing representation theory with a framework for pursuing success and failure. MIS Q. **41**(4), 1307–1333 (2017)
8. Vial, G.: Understanding digital transformation: a review and a research agenda. J. Strat. Inf. Syst. **28**(2), 118–144 (2019)
9. Davison, R.M., Wong, L.H., Alter, S., Ou, C.: Adopted globally but unusable locally: what workarounds reveal about adoption, resistance, compliance, and non-compliance. In: Proceedings of the European Conference on Information Systems (2019)
10. Laumer, S., Alter, S., Maier, C.: A systems perspective on is user satisfaction in digitalized organizations: conclusions from five case studies. In: Proceedings of the DIGIT Workshop Prior to International Conference on Information Systems (2019)
11. Alter, S.: A systems model of IT innovation, adoption, and adaptation. In: Proceedings of the European Conference on Information Systems (2018)
12. Lewin, K.: Field Model in Social Science: Selected Theoretical Papers. Harper, New York (1951)
13. Porter, M.E.: The five competitive forces that shape strategy. Harv. Bus. Rev. **86**(1), 78–137 (2008)
14. Barney, J., Wright, M., Ketchen, D.J., Jr.: The resource-based view of the firm: ten years after 1991. J. Manage. **27**(6), 625–641 (2001)
15. Teece, D.J., Pisano, G., Shuen, A.: Dynamic capabilities and strategic management. Strateg. Manage. J. **18**(7), 509–533 (1997)
16. Alter, S.: Framework for describing a theoretical perspective: application to the Bunge-Wand-Weber ontology and general systems theory. In: Proceedings of the Australian Conference on Information Systems (2021)
17. Alter, S.: A framework for describing theoretical perspectives: overview and application to the work system perspective. In: Hawaii International Conference on System Sciences (2022)
18. Brooks, F.P., Jr.: The Mythical Man-Month: Essays on Software Engineering. Pearson Education (1995)
19. Capatina, A., Bleoju, G., Matos, F., Vairinhos, V.: Leveraging intellectual capital through Lewin's Force Field Analysis: the case of software development companies. J. Innov. Knowl. **2**(3), 125–133 (2017)
20. Sterman, J.D.: Business Dynamics: Systems Thinking and Modeling for a Complex World. Irwin McGraw-Hill, Boston (2000)
21. Venkatesh, V., Morris, M.G., Davis, G.B., Davis, F.D.: User acceptance of information technology: toward a unified view. MIS Q. **27**(3), 425–478 (2003)

22. Blut, M., Chong, A.Y.L., Tsigna, Z., Venkatesh, V.: Meta-analysis of the unified theory of acceptance and use of technology (UTAUT): challenging its validity and charting a research agenda in the Red Ocean. J. Assoc. Inf. Syst. **23**(1), 13–95 (2022). https://doi.org/10.17705/1jais.00719
23. Wessel, L., Baiyere, A., Ologeanu-Taddei, R., Cha, J., Blegind-Jensen, T.: Unpacking the difference between digital transformation and IT-enabled organizational transformation. J. Assoc. Inf. Syst. **22**(1), 102–129 (2021)
24. Wittgenstein, L.: Philosophical Investigations. Macmillan, New York (1953)
25. Boell, S., Cecez-Kecmanovic, D.: What is 'Information' beyond a definition? In: Proceedings of International Conference on Information Systems (2015)

Co-creation in Design, Implementation and Use

Co-creating a Digital Symptom Tracker: An App as a Boundary Object in the Context of Pediatric Care

Anna Sigridur Islind[1]([✉]) [iD], Helena Vallo Hult[2,3] [iD], Karin Rydenman[3] [iD], and Per Wekell[3,4] [iD]

[1] Department of Computer Science, Reykjavik University, Reykjavik, Iceland
islind@ru.is
[2] School of Business, Economics and IT, University West, Trollhattan, Sweden
[3] NU Hospital Group, Trollhattan, Sweden
[4] University of Gothenburg, Gothenburg, Sweden

Abstract. The rise of digital health has provided new opportunities for patients to be more actively involved in their health and wellbeing. Despite the increased use of mobile health apps, there is still a lack of research on patient self-monitoring, and few studies have focused on children with chronic diseases and their parents. In this study, we draw from a case of the design of a mobile application – a symptom tracker – to continuously monitor children with periodic fever and the theoretical concept of boundary objects, to understand the role of digital artifacts in current healthcare practice. The research approach is qualitative, building on interview data with parents and experiences from the co-design process involving researchers, physicians, and other key stakeholders. The aim of the paper is to contribute with a better understanding of how an app for tracking children's fever (a symptom tracker) can support the pediatricians as well as the parents and their children during the treatment process. The research question is: *In what ways can a symptom tracker increase stakeholder involvement and how may this affect their relationship boundaries and collaborations?* Our findings suggest that the symptom tracker can be seen as a boundary object that binds the children, parents, and pediatricians treating them by connecting the app to the context of both the patients and healthcare practice. We argue that such an object (symptom tracker) can function as external support and, thereby, an essential part of the treatment process.

Keywords: Boundary object · Co-creation · Children · Information systems · Medical apps · Mobile health · Self-monitoring · Digital symptom tracker · IT design and diffusion · Pediatric care

1 Introduction

The increased use of consumer health technologies and wearables, such as mobile health apps for self-care and symptom trackers, brings significant change to healthcare practice

Published by Springer Nature Switzerland AG 2022
A. Elbanna et al. (Eds.): TDIT 2022, IFIP AICT 660, pp. 79–93, 2022.
https://doi.org/10.1007/978-3-031-17968-6_5

[1–3]. Increased patient engagement and patient-generated health data (PGHD) enable patients to be more engaged and understand and manage their health due to the transparency and access to data [4]. However, it is also shifting how work is performed, as the work conducted exclusively by health professionals in the past is now also conducted by patients [5–8]. Patient self-monitoring can be initiated by the healthcare provider or by the patients themselves and refer to technologies such as health apps that patients can use to measure and analyze their health data (e.g., heart rate, blood pressure and blood sugar levels in combination with dietary habits, exercise, sleep patterns, stress etc.). The utilization of digital care is often described as part of the solution to challenges facing modern healthcare, related to an aging population, chronic disease management and subsequent pressure on healthcare providers to prioritize and decide on how to make use of limited resources. The push for digital care also includes democratization of healthcare processes, intended to provide equal care and the patients' right to gain and access information and be more proactive in their health and wellbeing [9, 10]. Despite the potential, however, actual use of patient self-monitoring within clinical practice remains limited, partly due to issues related to safety, reliability, and security of using consumer wearables in health care and that patients rarely are involved in the design process [1, 11, 12]. There is still a lack of research on patient self-monitoring in general, and few studies have focused on children with chronic diseases and their parents.

In this paper, we focus on self-monitoring initiated by healthcare, more specifically on the design of an app for collecting subjective data over an extended period to continuously follow children with a prolonged state of fever. Prior research has shown that monitoring the fever episodes closely has benefits such as improved patient quality of life, alongside more precise and personalized disease management. A symptom tracker can be used to gather data on the periodic fever episodes, which can help in understanding the regularity and severity of the illness, increase engagement, and promote patient empowerment while enhancing adherence to treatment [6, 13]. The overall project goal is to contribute with insights that can help improve and innovate healthcare practice in the real-world context of pediatric care while also addressing the need for more research on app design and development within the scope of Information systems (IS) and health information technology (HIT) research. The project as a whole, highlights the importance of a data-driven approach to systematically collecting data over an extended period to forward clinical practice and research on complex, chronic topics such as periodic fever, which is under-researched to date. Empirically we draw from a case of designing a mobile application – a symptom tracker – to monitor children with periodic fever continuously. The study is theoretically informed by the concept of boundary objects, first introduced by Star and Griesemer (1989), and regarded as a valuable perspective for understanding the role of digital artifacts in current healthcare practice [14, 15]. More specifically, the paper aims to examine how an app for tracking children's fever (a symptom tracker) can support the pediatricians as well as the parents and their children during the treatment process, and how this may affect the relationship boundaries between patients and healthcare professionals, and how their collaboration can be strengthened. The research question is: *In what ways can a symptom tracker increase stakeholder involvement and how may this affect their relationship boundaries and collaboration?*

The remaining part of the paper is structured as follows: first, we outline related research and introduce the theoretical background and the concept of boundary objects; we then describe research methods (study background, data collection, and analysis); followed by the research findings and analysis; finally, we discuss the results in relation to the boundary object literature, and end with a conclusion and outlook for future work.

2 Related Research

Over the past years, researchers across disciplines have studied the datafication of health-care and self-care practices, enabled by the increase in mobile apps, both designed, developed and delivered by healthcare as well as brought in by patients [4, 16, 17]. Within the IS field, health information technology (HIT) research has shifted from an initial interest in health care as a new context for evaluating traditional IT artifacts to an increased interest in a broader range of topics such as consumer health care applications and wearables. This suggests that the IS field's HIT research focus is diversifying, with, for instance, the impact of health IT and analytics on patient behaviors and outcomes as an emerging theme [18, 19]. In this paper, we build on and contribute to the growing body of literature on data work, datafication and data-driven healthcare by examining the role of mobile health and medical apps for self-monitoring in specific.

The design, development and use of digital artifacts (such as m-health apps) both increase and change the data flow into healthcare, which, in turn, requires new forms of data work, e.g., data collaboration, translation work with data and increased flow of data into healthcare settings as well as patients' lives [2, 4, 20]. Patient-generated health data (PGHD) encompasses data produced and collected by patients (or those seeking healthcare) and brought into healthcare to enhance the quality of care and pinpoint the problem at hand. PGHD includes both objective health data collected from wearables, such as blood pressure and weight, as well as subjective self-assessments such as sleeping habits and pain assessment. The collection of PGHD and engagement in self-monitoring through data can reinforce the behaviors that prove to be of good value through visualizations of that data [4, 14]. Data is made available to the care provider, who can follow if the values deviate from the normal. The purpose of self-monitoring is to strengthen the patient's self-care, control over their health, and security experience while also leading to better use of health care resources. The possibility of detecting periods of deterioration at an early stage means that unnecessary and costly visits to emergency rooms and admissions can be avoided. However, prior research highlights that to fulfill the positive outcomes of mHealth apps, such as improved patient quality of life, alongside more precise and personalized disease management, they need to be linked to clinical practice and adapted to the context of both patients and healthcare [21, 22].

A review of the literature shows that self-monitoring may improve patient symptoms and lead to medication changes and that patients typically perceive self-monitoring tools as helpful in improving communication with health care providers [23]. Still, despite the potential and documented benefits, both patients and healthcare professionals tend to be reluctant to use such technologies [1, 11, 12]. Prior research on related topics such as shared decision making (SDM) and patient-centered communication point to an agreement on the patient's right to be involved and take an active role in decisions concerning their health, although health professionals' intentions to engage in shared decision-making are still uncertain [24]. Research in this area has also, to a large extent, focused on observable behaviors to compare and understand differences in content and outcomes while overlooking interactional and contextual dimensions, such as social relationships and the situated nature of human sense-making [25]. Dadgar and Joshi [11] emphasize the need for patient involvement in designing digital artifacts for self-monitoring, particularly identifying and supporting values important for patients, rather than focusing merely on lowering costs and improving clinical outcomes. The fundamentals of co-design entail that the relevant stakeholders have a voice in the design processes that will ultimately affect their lives [26, 27]. Recent examples from healthcare have likewise shown that including tertiary stakeholders, such as parents, in co-design can lead to digital technology that will both be relevant and useful [28, 29].

Furthermore, patients' use of medical apps and online health information can impact consultations positively as well as negatively. The COVID-19 pandemic has accelerated the trend towards digital and remote healthcare delivery, introducing novel challenges and uncertainties. One area of concern regards the relationship and communication between the patient and healthcare professionals, where more research is needed to capture social and contextual dimensions in practice [25]. Studies have shown that patients' online health information-seeking can improve the patient-physician relationship and change the traditional structure of that relationship, in which patients rely on healthcare professionals as sole providers of medical information [30]. Both patients and healthcare professionals can experience feelings of anxiety in response to insecurities around, for instance, the quality of health data and information and the inability of the professionals to provide answers to questions. However, the professionals can also take on a guiding role to facilitate data interpretation, feeling more valued by the patients. They can also learn from and together with the patients as the new forms of data work also seem to increase patients' reliance on professional knowledge and expertise [31, 32].

3 Theory

According to the literature, an object becomes a boundary object when it serves as a device for transformation, translation, and negotiation at the practice boundaries [33–42]. What is needed in such a process is a form of a representation, for instance, in terms of a model or in terms of a physical object, which can serve as a boundary object that binds two partners together in order to support knowledge sharing and co-creation of meaning [29, 43, 44]. However, boundary objects can only facilitate parts of the communication surrounding—for example, a symptom tracker can only function as just that, a symptom tracker—and as such, the object itself cannot replace communication and collaboration [14, 45].

To dig deeper into the pre-existing understanding of the effects of a technical system on the social system and vice versa, such as the impact of a symptom tracker on healthcare practice (and vice versa), the theoretical lens of boundary objects can be useful. The following text will, therefore, further explore the socio-technical interplay and the meaning of the technology (i.e., the digital symptom trackers) for the practices involved (the healthcare professionals' work, the parents' role, the childrens' agency) which it is being designed and developed for and will later be operated alongside.

Boundary objects are often technological artifacts but can also be physical objects that bind professions or stakeholders, such as drawings or prototypes [34, 46], repositories, standardized forms or workflow matrices [39]. Boundary objects can also be on a more abstract level, such as processes, methods [47], metaphors [48], or narratives [35]. Boundary objects have been studied in various contexts where different kinds of artifacts have been conveyed as boundary objects. These include studies within museums [41], using engineering drawings as boundary objects [36, 49], aircraft maintenance requests [50], human genome mapping [51], robots in educational settings [52], digital platforms in healthcare settings [42] and medical patient records [53] as boundary objects. Grand challenges have been studied as boundary objects within human genome mapping, where it is argued that they allow for the involvement of different communities that change over time, even though the true consensus is often lacking when it comes to grand challenges [51]. Seeing them as boundary objects still allows for collaboration and cooperation in situations (such as human genome mapping) where there is a struggle to sustain initiatives over a long time frame [51]. In that case, the challenge itself was the boundary object whereas we would like to argue that the challenge of prolonged periodic fever in children, and the large scale obsticles that logging symptoms of periodic fever brings, can in a similar way be seen as way to cross and bridge boundaries but we would like to extend the view and clarify that we seee the digital symptom tracker as the boundary object.

While the term boundary objects can be used for various artifacts, it usually applies to somewhat stable artifacts. Ewenstein and Whyte [54] argue for the notion of making a distinction between closed and open boundary objects. Their arguments show the importance of closed boundary objects as stable and structured representations of expert knowledge. Closed boundary objects are, therefore, well-structured and concrete boundary objects that span well-defined boundaries of expert practices [54], and these have been emphasized as having a large capacity as mediators in the relation between groups [37]. Most research on boundary objects draws on closed boundary objects in accordance with [54]. In contrast, open boundary objects are ill-structured, open-ended boundary objects that raise questions and stimulate a dialog instead of being well-structured and finished solutions. These open boundary objects can be seen as helpful for evolving and raising questions about some aspects of the design process while also strategically stabilizing other aspects of the design [54]. Therefore, open boundary objects are more present as an integrated part of the design process [42, 44]. Moreover, open boundary objects can be of two specific sorts: designated boundary objects or boundary objects-in-use [44]. Designated boundary objects are, from the very beginning, designed to function as boundary objects, whereas boundary objects-in-use happen to become boundary objects during either the design process or implementation process [14, 44]. Boundary objects can also be both; both designated boundary objects but also function as a boundary object-in-use, utilizing both states make it a stronger boundary object.

Emergent boundary objects are boundary objects that have not yet been stabilized or gained final meaning, according to Dalsgaard, Halskov and Basballe [55]. In accordance with Ewenstein and Whyte [54], they can also be seen as open boundary objects. The literature on boundary objects in general addresses boundary objects as something that is negotiated and interpreted differently by the different communities of practice involved. However, the boundary object itself is generally not transformed during the design process, while emergent boundary objects and open boundary objects are often derived from complex, wicked problems and begin in design concepts that continuously change and evolve during the design process [54, 55]. Open boundary objects can be especially applicable as a concept where non-artifacts are seen as boundary objects [41, 56]. The distinction made by [54] between open and closed boundary objects has grounds in Leigh Star's (2010) distinctions "between the 'ill-structured' use of boundary objects between social worlds and more specific 'tailored uses' within those worlds" [56, 57]. What we wanted to arrive at, from our theoretical outline, is that open and emergent boundary objects that are ill-structured and somewhat designated but have not yet become boundary objects-in-use, are our primary focus in this paper.

4   Research Methods

In this paper, we report on an ongoing project and the combined experiences from the co-design process involving researchers, Swedish pediatricians (physicians specializing in medical care for children), parents and other key stakeholders. In our design phase, we wanted a broader perspective and therefore did not limit participants only to parents to children with periodic fever but instead draw on interviews with 100 parents that have contributed to our co-design process.

The research approach is qualitative, intending to capture insights into the needs and views of the parents and health professionals and the nature of the structured support that a mobile application (symptom tracker) can provide. All interviews were read several times, collaboratively coded, and analyzed through content analysis [58], and validated with pediatricians. As mentioned above, the design approach is co-design, and the project considers all stakeholders involved in the co-design process. In contrast, this paper focuses on the views of the parents (based on the interview data) and implications when co-designing for continuous monitoring of children.

4.1   Research Context

The focus of this study is on self-monitoring initiated by healthcare, more specifically on the design of an app for collecting subjective data over an extended period to continuously follow children with a prolonged state of fever (PFAPA, Periodic Fever, Aphthous Stomatitis, Pharyngitis, and Cervical Adenitis). The research setting is in Swedish public healthcare, at one of the larger non-university hospital groups, consisting of three hospitals and around 5,000 employees that provide healthcare and medical services for 270,000 inhabitants. The overall objective within the larger project is to enable digital documentation of symptoms of periodic fever and to research onset, regularity, the severity of illness, and environmental causes that could be at play in the episodes. Furthermore, through the digital symptom tracker, we aim to increase the engagement of parents and find new patterns through visualizations of the data.

PFAPA syndrome is the most common autoinflammatory disorder among children in many parts of the world. It typically has an onset under the age of five and is a common and important differential diagnosis among preschool children that experience recurrent fevers. The fever episodes usually last 3–6 days and typically recur regularly with an interval of 3–6 weeks. Between the fever episodes, the child is typically symptom-free with normalized inflammatory variables and grows normally [59, 60]. Awareness and recognition of PFAPA are crucial to providing adequate treatment and avoiding mis-diagnosis. Therefore, a symptom tracker is considered helpful for tracking the disease progression, characterizing the fever episodes, and getting an overview of their regular-ity. However, it can be challenging for the parents to document and report symptoms in a structured manner, especially using an analog tracker (e.g., a paper-based symp-tom journal). A user-friendly and co-designed app can therefore be a valuable tool in diagnosing as well as in assessing the symptoms over time.

The app will be used in Sweden to support parents of children with PFAPA to systematically and continuously digitally log and track symptoms [61]. The multidisci-plinary research team consists of researchers and designers with pediatrics and health informatics expertise.

4.2   Data Collection and Analysis

The research approach is qualitative, and the data collection for this phase was conducted through semi-structured interviews with parents [62], combined with experiences and observations from the co-design process, emphasizing the design phase, including work-ing meetings and project documentation (document analysis). In this paper we report our findings from the initial part of the design process. We wanted a broader perspective on parents' needs and views of using a mobile application in this phase, as the app will be used both for children with periodic fevers and for healthy controls. Therefore, the participants are not limited only to parents to children with periodic fever. The interviews were semi-structured around topics, where each main topic had subtopics. The goal of the user interviews is to determine what sort of interface would suit the parents best and what kind of interface would best suit the medical staff, as well as what data and infor-mation would be relevant for them in the application. We plan to continue by specifically include parents to children with PFAPA, and their pediatricians in the co-design process in the next phase of the project. Data collection activities are specified in Fig. 1.

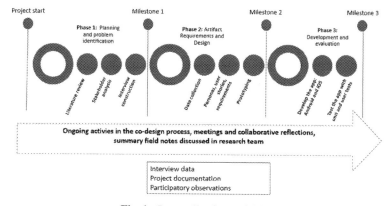

Fig. 1. Data collection activities

All interviews were read several times, collaboratively coded, and analyzed through content analysis [58] and validated with pediatricians. The analysis was conducted using an interpretive and iterative approach to find common themes and patterns in the empirical material and theoretically informed by the boundary object literature, explicitly looking for occurrences where the participants described aspects related to communication, collaboration and interaction. As mentioned above, the design approach is co-design, and the project considers all stakeholders involved in the co-design process. In this paper, the focus is on the views of the parents (based on the interview data) and implications when co-designing for continuous monitoring of children.

5 Findings

In the following text, we summarize the findings from the parents, and healthcare professionals, focusing on how the app can facilitate reflections, increase compliance and engagement, and strengthen collaboration and communication between and among the parents and their children and the health professionals.

5.1 Asynchronous Communication to Create a Bridge

Several parents reported that they wanted to communicate directly and securely with their pediatrician within the app. The messages, or chat, would have to be asynchronous, as the parents are aware that they might want to send a message to their pediatrician in the middle of the night. Still, they do however not expect their pediatrician to answer them. They do mind that the messages are only delivered in the morning since they want the messages within the app only because they are afraid to forget to send the message if they are unable to do it when they come to think of it due to extended sleep deprivation. On that note, one parent described: "*Sometimes, when my child is sick, I wake up, and it might be days since I got a good night's sleep. Those nights, it would be good to be able to send a message just there and then, not because I want a reply there and then, but because I really don't want to forget to send the pediatrician a message if something has drastically changed.*" Sending messages in an asynchronous format would be helpful to reduce the risk of the parents forgetting to send them.

The parents said that they: "*...really want it to be easy, simple and quick to write down my child's symptoms*" and also stressed the importance of choosing the day: "*I need to be able to choose which day I am writing down symptoms for, just so that I do it correctly.*" Moreover, they stressed that they would like to be able to ask a healthcare professional a question: "*it is important to me to be able to do that, and I also want to be able to see answers from a healthcare professional.*" The healthcare professionals also discussed the need for a messaging service: "*I want to be able to see messages from parents, and similarly, I want to be able to respond to parents' messages.*"

5.2 Notifications to Increase Compliance

Parents also highlighted a need for support in terms of timely reminders, as they knew from experience that even though they had the ambition and willingness to register symptoms regularly, it is easy to forget, especially when being sleep deprived, and the primary focus is on taking care of one's child that is ill. Regarding notifications, one parent uttered: *"Oh, yes. That and just that would help me enormously."* A third parent offered the opinion that notifications might even help with the systematics in the registration: *"It is good to have something that helps you remember the important things, and it would help to register the symptoms every day at the same time systematically."* Yet another parent expressed that it could help during stressful times: *"I might forget, when my child is sick I am sometimes going on very little sleep, but if I would get a notification, then I would still register. So, notifications would help me."* The parents would gain from having notifications implemented within the app.

They also discussed the need for reminders to fill out the symptom tracker: *"I would like to be reminded to fill in the diary, and I also want to be able to look at symptoms from older dates."* Moreover, they discussed the need to personalize the time of the reminders: *"If I could choose when the reminders would appear, that would be just amazing. I am probably not like everyone else; my routine is messed up, and I would like to set the time when the reminders should appear myself. I am tired sometimes when I get notifications in other apps, and then I have zero energy to fill them out and end up ignoring them. If I could choose the time of when the notification should appear on my screen, then I would definitely make an effort to fill it out."*

5.3 Visualizations to Trigger Reflection

Regarding how the information registered in the app could be presented, one parent suggested: *"Maybe some kind of graph that shows a clear and simple pattern in the information. Perhaps we should try to fill in more information than symptoms to see if there is any correlation between external factors and changes in the body. That would be really good,"* while another parent said: *"Just simple. The only thing that matters is that I can see a trend for a specific time period. Everything needs to work fast and efficiently; I rarely have time that I can afford to waste when I have a sick child."* One parent also offered the view that the visualizations might help with reflection: *"If I could see how it is over time, then I could also see when it is better because sometimes it might be better for a longer time as well, but it is difficult to know without seeing it visually."* From these quotes, it is apparent that visualizations are a crucial part of an app for monitoring periodic fever.

The healthcare professionals stressed that they would like a simple overview: *"What we need is to be able to see an overview of many patients at once in an accessible way and also be able to see specific entries of a child's symptoms on a specific date and be able to look up a specific child so that I can see information about a child that I have under observation."* Moreover, when analyzing the needs of the healthcare professionals and the parents combined, there are undoubtedly important aspects that overlap, which is illustrated here by a quote from a parent: *"I want to get a good overview of a child's symptoms from day to day"* which is echoed by the healthcare professionals. Also: *"I would like to be able to see a graph of symptoms from previous months,"* a comment from the parents and healthcare professionals. Moreover, both stakeholder groups identified that they would like it to be: *"very clear whether a child has had PFPFA syndrome on a particular day; it really needs to be crystal clear."*

5.4 Overview to Encourage Engagement

Several parents discussed that an app could help with overview. One parent commented: "*It would be an easy way to track the information and to have an overview of the information too. Everything is always there then; there is no way to search a paper.*" Another parent shared a similar opinion: "*App, yes, definitely. More work to write it, and I would lose the paper and forget it at home when I would go to the doctor with my child.*" Regarding the notion of having margins set within the app with a specific fever margin that could indicate to the parents when to contact a healthcare professional, one parent said that it might be good to have: "*It might be good to have, just to be one the safe side if there are any uncertainties and so on, but I am rarely uncertain*" While another parent said: "*It might be ok, but I do know it so well myself, from years of experience.*" Yet another parent also thought that others might need it, but not them due to experience: "*It might not be so bad to include for inexperienced people, but I do not need it, I know it.*" These quotes make it clear that the parents are the experts, they know their children, and they have insights that they rely on wholeheartedly. From that, we conclude that the parents are essential stakeholders in a design process where the aim is to aid their care for their children; they have vast experience.

6 Discussion

In this paper, we explore how an app can support parents and their children during the treatment process and how this may affect the boundaries between parents and healthcare professionals. In this specific context, the children cannot care for themselves, and the app that connects the parents and the pediatricians, therefore, becomes a central entity. We argue that the digital symptom tracker can function as a boundary object and, thereby, an essential part of the treatment process.

As stated earlier, an object becomes a boundary object when it serves as a device for transformation, translation, and negotiation at boundaries. More specifically, a boundary object is an artifact with different roles for different groups that might have boundaries between them. As such, a boundary object can allow groups to unite and form a functional relationship, and boundary objects are instances that enable groups that do not share pre-existing consensus, boundaries or professions to consolidate, find common ground and work together [41, 56, 63–66]. In our case, we illustrate four specific parts of the app that are essential, which have boundary-crossing activities connected to them. First, we show that asynchronous communication can create a bridge between the parents and the pediatricians. Secondly, notifications can increase compliance in the treatment process, which is in line with [12, 19], who found that increased collection of PGHD and engagement in self-monitoring is fruitful. Thirdly, our findings show that visualizations can trigger reflection. Those findings correspond with the importance of linking personalized disease management to clinical practice and co-create it in context, as highlighted in prior research [21, 22]. Finally, we show that providing an overview in the app can encourage engagement, which is illustrative of how an object becomes a boundary object when it serves as a device for transformation, translation, and negotiation at the practice boundaries [33–42].

In this paper, we show the nature of the structured support that a mobile application (symptom tracker) can provide. The app and its elements can be seen as a shared object. In such a process, what is needed is a representation, like a model or a physical object, which can serve as a boundary object that binds two partners together to support knowledge sharing and co-creation of meaning [29, 43, 44]. Based on that, we argue that a symptom tracker serves as a boundary object to coordinate and communicate [56]. Boundary objects are the links in the communication processes where different perspectives are to be negotiated and discussed into a co-created meaning and consensus. In layman's terms, boundary objects play an important role as shortcuts to communication and serve as playgrounds for knowledge sharing among different communities of practice [63, 67, 68]. However, boundary objects can only facilitate *parts* of the communication surrounding the boundary object and cannot be seen as a tool that can function as any replacement [69]. The object itself cannot replace communication and collaboration. We are aware that a symptom tracker cannot, and should not, replace the close collaboration between the parents and the pediatricians in the care of the child. In the literature, boundary objects are often technological artifacts but can also be other types of artifacts. In our case, we use open and emergent boundary objects as the app is still under development.

Awareness and recognition of PFAPA are vital for providing the patient with adequate treatment and avoiding misdiagnosis. The diagnosis is mainly based on the patient's medical history and symptoms, but no specific test or clinical process exists to confirm or deny the diagnosis. Instead, it is necessary to follow the course of the disease over time [59, 60]. Therefore, a symptom tracker is considered a valuable tool for following the process, characterizing the fever episodes, and getting an overview of their regularity. However, it can be challenging for the parents to document and report symptoms in a structured manner when the symptom tracker is on paper. In line with prior research, our findings highlight that to fulfill positive outcomes of mHealth apps, such as improved patient quality of life, alongside more precise and personalized disease management, they need to be linked to clinical practice and adapted to the context of both patients and healthcare [21, 22]. A symptom tracker can be used as a way to gather patient-generated health data, which can help patients organize details and activities of the illness, increase engagement, and promote patient empowerment while enhancing adherence to treatment [6, 13]. Data work and datafication in healthcare extend the longstanding interest related to electronic health records (EHR), where research efforts have typically focused on large-scale, national standards and strategic infrastructural changes [18, 70], to emerging technologies developed outside of healthcare, such as internet of things, wearable technology, fitness, wellness, preventive care, home care and rehabilitation, where the partnership between individuals and healthcare providers is important, and toward other types of information systems that can assist in different aspects of healthcare, such as collaboration and learning [28]. Our findings confirm and extend prior research regarding self-monitoring and changes to the role of patients, and the influence of this change on the healthcare professionals [2, 6].

To sum up, our findings show a need for structured support to be able to build a shared view of what the difficulties of the treatment process entail. Our analysis further suggests that an app for tracking the periodic fever of children can play an essential role in providing such structure and increasing compliance and engagement. The parents are critical stakeholders in the co-creation process due to their vast experience caring for their children. As illustrated in our findings, the parents are the experts. They know their children and have instincts that they rely on wholeheartedly. In all, the pediatricians, together with the parents, have enabled the co-creation of a symptom tracker as a boundary object in pediatric care.

7 Conclusion

In this paper, we draw on a project that has the unique value of being the first symptom tracker to follow children with periodic fever in Nordic countries. There is limited research on what sets of fever episodes on how frequently they occur. Moreover, there is little documentation at the moment for tracking these aspects further to revolutionize the knowledge on what sets of these episodes for children. The children diagnosed with periodic fever usually stay home more. Their parents are sleepless, but there is another documented aspect; the children diagnosed with periodic fever (PFAPA symptom) are generally healthier otherwise than other children their age. Developing an app for parents of children with periodic fever to document their symptoms would be revolutionary in the effort of furthering the understanding of periodic fever for children. Furthermore, the data from the app is shared with pediatricians so that they can monitor their symptoms. On a theoretical level, our paper contributes with a deeper understanding of how the co-created symptom tracker can function as a boundary object that binds the children, parents, and pediatricians treating them together.

References

1. Piwek, L., Ellis, D.A., Andrews, S., Joinson, A.: The rise of consumer health wearables: promises and barriers. PLoS Med. **13**(2), e1001953 (2016)
2. Vallo Hult, H., Hansson, A., Svensson, L., Gellerstedt, M.: Flipped healthcare for better or worse. Health Informatics J. **25**(3), 587–597 (2019)
3. Óskarsdóttir, M., Islind, A.S., August, E., Arnardóttir, E.S., Patou, F., Maier, A.: Importance of getting enough sleep and daily activity data to assess variability: longitudinal observaational study. JMIR Form. Res. (2022)
4. Islind, A.S., Lindroth, T., Lundin, J., Steineck, G.: Shift in translations: data work with patient-generated health data in clinical practice. Health Informatics J. **25**(3), 577–586 (2019)
5. Gui, X., Chen, Y.: Making healthcare infrastructure work: unpacking the infrastructuring work of individuals. In: Proc. Proceedings of CHI 2019, Glasgow, Scotland, UK2019, pp. 1–14 (2019)
6. Islind, A.S., Vallo Hult, H., Johansson, V., Angenete, E., Gellerstedt, M.: Invisible work meets visible work: infrastructuring from the perspective of patients and healthcare professionals. Proc. HICSS, January 5–8 (2021)
7. Norström, L., Islind, A.S., Vallo Hult, H.: Balancing the social media seesaw in public sector: a sociomaterial perspective. IRIS Selected Papers of the Information Systems Research Seminar in Scandinavia (8) (2017)
8. Vallo Hult, H., Islind, A.S., Norström, L.: Reconfiguring professionalism in digital work. Systems, Signs and Actions **12**, 1–17 (2021)
9. Romanow, D., Cho, S., Straub, D.: Editor's comments: riding the wave: past trends and future directions for health IT research, MIS Quarterly **36**(3), III-A18 (2012)

10. Gellerstedt, M.: The digitalization of health care paves the way for improved quality of life? J. Syst. Cybern. Inf. **14**(5), 1–10 (2016)
11. Dadgar, M., Joshi, K.D.: The role of information and communication technology in self-management of chronic diseases: an empirical investigation through value sensitive design. J. Assoc. Inf. Syst. **19**(2), 2 (2018)
12. Vallo Hult, H.: Digital Work: Coping with Contradictions in Changing Healthcare. University West (2021)
13. Islind, A.S., et al.: Individualized blended care for patients with colorectal cancer: the patient's view on informational support. Support. Care Cancer **29**(6), 3061–3067 (2020). https://doi.org/10.1007/s00520-020-05810-5
14. Islind, A.S.: Platformization: Co-Designing Digital Platforms in Practice. University West (2018)
15. Terlouw, G., Kuipers, D., Veldmeijer, L., van't Veer, J., Prins, J., Pierie, J.-P.: Boundary objects as dialogical learning accelerators for social change in design for health: systematic review. JMIR Hum. Factors **9**(1), e31167 (2022)
16. Erikainen, S., Pickersgill, M., Cunningham-Burley, S., Chan, S.: Patienthood and participation in the digital era. Digit. Health **5**, 2055207619845546 (2019)
17. Lupton, D.: The digitally engaged patient: self-monitoring and self-care in the digital health era. Soc. Theory Health **11**(3), 256–270 (2013)
18. Davidson, E., Baird, A., Prince, K.: Opening the envelope of health care information systems research. Inf. Organ. **28**(3), 140–151 (2018)
19. https://www.misqresearchcurations.org/blog/2018/6/20/health-information-technology
20. Bossen, C., Pine, K.H., Cabitza, F., Ellingsen, G., Piras, E.M.: Data work in healthcare: an Introduction. Health Informatics J. **25**(3), 465–474 (2019)
21. Peyroteo, M., Ferreira, I.A., Elvas, L.B., Ferreira, J.C., Lapão, L.V.: Remote monitoring systems for patients with chronic diseases in primary health care: systematic review. JMIR Mhealth Uhealth **9**(12), e28285 (2021)
22. Gilani, S.M., Tanvy, A., Pasha, M.F., Thanzami, V.: Professional and peer social support-oriented mhealth app: a platform for adolescents with depressive symptomatology. In: Proc. Hawaii International Conference on System Sciences (HICSS) (2022)
23. Lancaster, K., et al.: The Use and Effects of Electronic Health Tools for Patient Self-Monitoring and Reporting of Outcomes Following Medication Use: Systematic Review. J. Med. Internet. Res. **20**(12), e294 (2018)
24. Légaré, F., et al.: Interventions for increasing the use of shared decision making by healthcare professionals. Cochrane Database Syst. Rev. (7) (2018)
25. van Dael, J., Gillespie, A., Neves, A.L., Darzi, A.: Patient–clinician communication research for 21st century health care. Br. J. Gen. Pract. **72**(715), 52–53 (2022)
26. Joshi, S.G., Bratteteig, T.: Designing for prolonged mastery. On involving old people in participatory design. Scand. J. Inf. Syst. **28**(1) (2016)
27. Kensing, F., Greenbaum, J.: Heritage: Having a Say': 'Routledge International Handbook of Participatory Design (Routledge), pp. 41–56 (2012)
28. Vallo Hult, H., Islind, A.S., Master Östlund, C., Holmgren, D., Wekell, P.: Sociotechnical co-design with general pediatricians: ripple effects through collaboration in action. Proc. AMCIS, Salt Lake City, UT, USA (2020)
29. Islind, A.S., Lundh Snis, U.: From co-design to co-care: designing a collaborative practice in care. Systems, Signs and Actions **11**(1), 1–24 (2018)
30. Tan, S.S.L., Goonawardene, N.: Internet health information seeking and the patient-physician relationship: a systematic review. J. Med. Internet Res. **19**(1), e9 (2017)
31. Ahluwalia, S., Murray, E., Stevenson, F., Kerr, C., Burns, J.: 'A heartbeat moment': qualitative study of GP views of patients bringing health information from the internet to a consultation. Br. J. Gen. Pract. **60**(571), 88–94 (2010)

32. Van Den Broek, E., Sergeeva, A., Huysman, M.: "Every little thing makes us think of cancer": how patient access to medical records influences role relations (2018)
33. Bartel, C.A., Garud, R.: Narrative knowledge in action: adaptive abduction as a mechanism for knowledge creation and exchange in organizations. The Blackwell Handbook of Organizational Learning and Knowledge Management 324–342 (2003)
34. Bechky, B.A.: Sharing meaning across occupational communities: the transformation of understanding on a production floor. Organ. Sci. **14**(3), 312–330 (2003)
35. Boland, R.J., Tenkasi, R.V.: Perspective making and perspective taking in communities of knowing. Organ. Sci. **6**(4), 350–372 (1995)
36. Carlile, P.R.: A pragmatic view of knowledge and boundaries: boundary objects in new product development. Organ. Sci. **13**(4), 442–455 (2002)
37. Carlile, P.R.: Transferring, translating, and transforming: an integrative framework for managing knowledge across boundaries. Organ. Sci. **15**(5), 555–568 (2004)
38. Levina, N.: Collaborating on multiparty information systems development projects: a collective reflection-in-action view. Inf. Syst. Res. **16**(2), 109–130 (2005)
39. Nicolini, D., Mengis, J., Swan, J.: Understanding the role of objects in cross-disciplinary collaboration. Organ. Sci. **23**(3), 612–629 (2012)
40. Pawlowski, S.D., Robey, D.: Bridging user organizations: knowledge brokering and the work of information technology professionals. MIS Q.: Manag. Inf. Syst. **28**(4), 645–672 (2004)
41. Star, S.L., Griesemer, J.R.: Institutional ecology, 'translations' and boundary objects: amateurs and professionals in Berkeley's museum of vertebrate zoology, 1907–39. Soc. Stud. Sci. **19**, 387–420 (1989)
42. Islind, A.S., Lindroth, T., Lundin, J., Steineck, G.: Co-designing a digital platform with boundary objects: bringing together heterogeneous users in healthcare. Health Technol. **9**(4), 425–438 (2019). https://doi.org/10.1007/s12553-019-00332-5
43. Boland Jr, R.J., Tenkasi, R.V.J.O.s.: Perspective making and perspective taking in communities of knowing. Organ. Sci. **6**(4), 350–372 (1995)
44. Islind, A.S., Lundh Snis, U.: Learning in home care: a digital artifact as a designated boundary object-in-use. J. Workplace Learn. **29**(7/8), 577–587 (2017)
45. Akkerman, S.F., Bakker, A.: Boundary crossing and boundary objects. Rev. Educ. Res. **81**(2), 132–169 (2011)
46. Pawlowski, S.D., Robey, D.: Bridging user organizations: knowledge brokering and the work of information technology professionals. MIS Quarterly, 645–672 (2004)
47. Swan, J., Bresnen, M., Newell, S., Robertson, M.: The object of knowledge: the role of objects in biomedical innovation. Hum. Relat. **60**(12), 1809–1837 (2007)
48. Koskinen, K.U.: Metaphoric boundary objects as co-ordinating mechanisms in the knowledge sharing of innovation processes. Eur. J. Innov. Manag. **8**(3), 323–335 (2005)
49. Henderson, K.: Flexibile sketches and inflexible data bases: visual communication, conscription devices, and boundary objects in design engineering. Sci. Technol. Human Values **16**, 448–473 (1991)
50. Lutters, W.G., Ackerman, M.S.: Achieving safety: a field study of boundary objects in aircraft technical support. Book Achieving Safety: A Field Study of Boundary Objects in Aircraft Technical Support, pp. 266–275 (2002)
51. Winter, S.J., Butler, B.S.: Creating bigger problems: grand challenges as boundary objects and the legitimacy of the information systems field. J. Inf. Technol. **26**(2), 99–108 (2011)
52. Malinverni, L., Valero, C., Schaper, M.M., de la Cruz, I.G.: Educational robotics as a boundary object: towards a research agenda. Int. J. Child-Comput. Interact. **29**, 100305 (2021)
53. Berg, M., Bowker, G.: The multiple bodies of the medical record. Sociol. Q. **38**(3), 513–537 (1997)
54. Ewenstein, B., Whyte, J.: Knowledge practices in design: the role of visual representations as epistemic objects', Organ. Stud. (2009)

55. Dalsgaard, P., Halskov, K., Basballe, D.A.: Emergent boundary objects and boundary zones in collaborative design research projects. In: Book Emergent Boundary Objects and Boundary Zones in Collaborative Design Research Projects (ACM), pp. 745–754 (2014)

56. Star, S.L.: This is not a boundary object: Reflections on the origin of a concept. Sci. Technol. Human Values **35**(5), 601–617 (2010)

57. Nandhakumar, J., Panourgias, N.S., Scarbrough, H.: From knowing it to "getting it": envisioning practices in computer games development. Inf. Syst. Res. **24**(4), 933–955 (2013)

58. Graneheim, U.H., Lundman, B.: Qualitative content analysis in nursing research: concepts, procedures and measures to achieve trustworthiness. Nurse Educ. Today **24**(2), 105–112 (2004)

59. Wekell, P., Karlsson, A., Berg, S., Fasth, A.: Review of autoinflammatory diseases, with a special focus on periodic fever, aphthous stomatitis, pharyngitis and cervical adenitis syndrome. Acta Paediatr. **105**(10), 1140–1151 (2016)

60. Rydenman, K., Berg, S., Karlsson-Bengtsson, A., Fasth, A., Wekell, P.: PFAPA-syndrom– en viktig differential-diagnos hos barn med återkommande feberepisoder [PFAPA syndrome – An important differential diagnosis in children with recurrent fever], Lakartidningen, 116:FP9U (2019)

61. Vallo Hult, H., Islind, A.S., Wekell, P., Rydenman, K.: Decreased memory bias via a mobile application: a symptom tracker to monitor children's periodic fever. Stud. Health Technol. Inform. (2022)

62. Myers, M.D.: Qualitative Research in Business and Management. SAGE (2013)

63. Wenger, E.: Communities of practice and social learning systems. Organization **7**(2), 225–246 (2000)

64. Kimbler, K.: App store strategies for service providers. In: Book App Store Strategies for Service Providers, pp. 1–5. IEEE (2010)

65. Kimble, C., Grenier, C., Goglio-Primard, K.: Innovation and knowledge sharing across professional boundaries: political interplay between boundary objects and brokers. Int. J. Inf. Manage. **30**(5), 437–444 (2010)

66. Fischer, G.: External and shareable artifacts as opportunities for social creativity in communities of interest. In: Book External and Shareable Artifacts as Opportunities for Social Creativity in Communities of Interest, Citeseer, (2001)

67. Brown, J.S., Druguid, P.: Organizational learning and communities-of-practice: towards a unified view of working, learning and innovation. Organ. Sci. **2**, 40–57 (1991)

68. Cook, S.D.N., Brown, J.S.: Bridging epistemologies: the generative dance between organizational knowledge and organizational knowing. Organ. Sci. **10**(4), 381–400 (1999)

69. Akkerman, S.F., Bakker, A.: Learning at the boundary: an introduction. Int. J. Educ. Res. **50**(1), 1–5 (2011)

70. Fitzpatrick, G., Ellingsen, G.: A review of 25 years of CSCW research in healthcare: contributions, challenges and future agendas. Computer Supported Cooperative Work: CSCW: An International Journal **22**(4–6), 609–665 (2013)

The DECENT Toolkit to Support Design of User Engagement of Mobile Health Technologies from a Practice Theory Perspective

Tochukwu Ikwunne(✉) 🆔, Lucy Hederman 🆔, and P. J. Wall 🆔

ADAPT Centre, Trinity College Dublin, Dublin, Ireland
ikwunnet@tcd.ie

Abstract. User engagement is critical for the successful adoption and use of mobile health apps, but it is also influenced by a variety of factors that are not always easily accessible or quantified by designers in practice. The goal of this paper is to facilitate the application of activity theory and the communicative ecological framework to uncover various socio-cultural contexts for user engagement designs using the Design Process Engagement Enhancement System (DECENT) toolkit. The DECENT toolkit is an innovative theory-based design tool and associated method that includes socio-cultural filtration and a socio-cultural checklist that are augmented in the phases of the user-centered design model. This paper presents a set of consolidating concepts to guide future design practice which broaden designers' knowledge of mobile health app designs for user engagement. Finally, to fully explain and design for user engagement in mobile health, an integrated approach incorporating a variety of technological and socio-cultural factors is presented.

Keywords: User engagement · Socio-cultural filtration · Socio-cultural contexts · Mobile health

1 Introduction

Effective user engagement is a universal goal in the design of content, products, systems, services and apps, and every designer strives to engage users [1]. Inadequate engagement may be caused by an imbalance in the integration of appropriate theoretical content and features that maintain user interest [2, 3]. Ikwunne et al. [4, 5] conducted a systematic review of the user engagement design process and discovered a lack of consideration for socio-cultural contexts in the design of mobile health (mHealth) interventions. The systematic review recommended that such socio-cultural contexts be considered and addressed systematically by identifying a design process for engaging users in mHealth interventions [5]. In this paper, we frame user engagement as a context-dependent, individual-specific psychological state that emerges from two-way interaction with an object, such as an app [6–8]. This is important as although the effectiveness of mHealth

© IFIP International Federation for Information Processing 2022
Published by Springer Nature Switzerland AG 2022
A. Elbanna et al. (Eds.): TDIT 2022, IFIP AICT 660, pp. 94–104, 2022.
https://doi.org/10.1007/978-3-031-17968-6_6

initiatives depends to a large extent on user engagement [9, 10], many such interventions frequently do not include user-engaging attributes [11].

In our globalized economy new products are frequently developed for international markets. Because user characteristics and needs differ significantly across regions [12], product development for global markets requires organizations to design products with these differences in user characteristics and needs in mind. According to Shen et al. [13, p.7] "*Successful interface metaphors should be developed or adapted through cultural requirements by or regarding, representatives of the culture for which they are intended*". Culture is defined as the similar patterns of thinking, feeling, and acting of people who belong to the same group but are different in these patterns from other groups [14]. This notion of acting is largely based on unwritten rules and habits passed down from generation to generation [15].

Thus, culture, politics and society must be considered when designing and developing technology. According to Honold [16], the approach to learning how to use a new mobile phone may vary depending on national culture. According to Honold's findings, German users prefer a user manual, whereas Italians prefer learning by doing. Furthermore, while the salesperson is an important source of information for Chinese users, for Indian users, the entire family is involved in the knowledge acquisition process. Honold's research shows that culture influences patterns of user-product interaction and engagement, implying that designers should account for these differences in knowledge acquisition approaches. However, determining the nature of this impact may be difficult in the absence of theory and a deeper understanding of how users actually actually engage with technologies [17]. This emphasizes the importance of theoretical models that provide a framework for assessing users' socio-cultural contexts for user engagement designs. Also, design guidelines are needed for user engagement design practice.

This paper introduces the Design Process Engagement Enhancement System (DECENT) toolkit which is specifically designed to bridge these socio-cultural and theory-practice gaps. Our DECENT toolkit may be seen as a novel theory-based design toolkit and associated method that includes socio-cultural filtration and a socio-cultural checklist that is supplemented by the user-centered design model's phases. This toolkit and methodology addresses the research question - how can we develop a useful tool capable of supporting the design process for user engagement?

The contributions of this paper are twofold: firstly, the DECENT toolkit is presented as an innovative design tool and method to assist designers in leveraging activity theory (AT) and communicative ecological framework (CEF) for user engagement design of health apps; and secondly, the toolkit will better-assisting designers in imagining user engagement issues, as well as assessing the conceptual importance of the three components of the DECENT toolkit -personas, capture and postcards, and communication delight.

2 Related Work

Designing mHealth apps for user engagement necessitates first understanding existing theories and then applying this knowledge in design practice. This section provides a brief outline of our analytical framework, starting with a discussion on user engagement theories in general before moving on to a more specific discussion of AT and the CEF.

2.1 User Engagement Theories

The theories of user engagement have been extensively researched [1]. Ikwunne et al. [18] provide an overview of the disciplinary foundations, descriptions, and conceptualizations of engagement as they relate to each of the eight theories and models. The eight theoretical perspectives that focus on engagement were identified as Flow Theory [19], Motivation Theory [20], O'Brien and Tom's Model of Engagement [21], Sidner et al.'s Model of Engagement [22], Technology Acceptance Model [23], Unified Theory of Acceptance and Use of IT [24], Short et al.'s Model of User Engagement [25] and Ludden et al.'s 'PERMA' Framework [26].

The summary indicates that theoretical conceptions of engagement can be separated into several categories, including academic, cognitive, intellectual, institutional, emotional, behavioral, social, and psychological. These distinctions are made to aid a particular type of sociocultural context-dependent analysis and design, rather than to provide objective knowledge of engagement as a universal neurophysiological or social reality. These reasons point to the ontological perspectives on engagement that have been brought to bear. As well as the choice of using activity theory and the CEF as appropriate models used in this paper for uncovering users' socio-cultural contexts for user engagement designs.

2.2 Activity Theory and the Communicative Ecological Framework

Activity theory and the CEF are widely recognised as practice theories used as organizing principles for understanding the socio-cultural complexity of users. For example, Engeström's [27] model of AT, derived from psychology, information systems design, human-computer interactions, organizational learning, and cultural studies emerged as a result of the socio-cultural perspective. It investigates the complexities of human-environment interactions by identifying activity system units, how they are related, their various voices, their history, flaws, and changes [28]. The subject, object, and community are the elements of an activity system, and the artifacts used in context-determining activities are tools, rules, and divisions of labour.

While AT can explain why an individual user interacts with mHealth artifacts in daily communication, the Altheide [29] model of CEF provides a rich description of how each individual interacts with mHealth artifacts in broader socio-cultural contexts. These theories are used to inform the development of DECENT tools. Thus, AT and CEF are used as a lens or organizing principle to uncover a user group's socio-cultural contexts for user engagement designs.

Section 3.2 describes how we use the AT model to inform the design of personas. As an example, we explained how AT provided a comprehensive set of tools for comprehending individual user complexities that inform components of the DECENT framework. Also, Sect. 3.2 explains how the AT model is used to guide the design of the capture & postcards tools. The two examples show that while AT can explain why users engage with mHealth, it lacks the vocabulary to investigate what causes specific users to engage with mHealth apps through their daily communication in broader socio-cultural contexts. However, applying AT to mHealth app engagement does not provide insight into how users' engagement with mHealth apps is structured in social contexts. To address this limitation, CEF is used to provide a rich description of how mHealth is structured in a social context by integrating three layers of interpretation (technical, social, and discursive). Section 3.2 further describes the use of CEF to inform the design of the communication delight tool, with examples of how CEF provided a comprehensive understanding of socio-cultural contexts of user engagement with mHealth apps that inform components of DECENT framework.

3   Research Methodology

This study used a design science research methodology (DSRM) [30, 31] to provide a process model to create DECENT tools. The steps included in the model are:

1. Problem Identification and Motivation – The problem is that many mHealth apps lack engaging attributes, necessitating the development of a framework to support the design process for user engagement.
2. Solution Objectives – DECENT is developed to support the design process for user engagement with mHealth apps.
3. Design and Development – Tools such as personas, capture & postcards, and communication delight as DECENT framework components are created using activity theory and communicative ecological framework as theoretical models. The details of how these tools were designed are explained in Sect. 3.2.
4. Demonstration – The next stage of the research will be to consult with developers and end-users of mHealth apps that use artifacts to see if the artifact can solve the identified problem.
5. Evaluation – interviews and focused group discussions will be conducted to determine the efficacy and efficiency of DECENT in solving the identified problem.
6. Communication – The description of three components of the DECENT framework including their design and purpose is described in this paper. The evaluation of the DECENT framework and other components will be described in a future paper.

The following section depicts all of DECENT's components as well as how socio-cultural filtration and a socio-cultural checklist of the DECENT framework are augmented in the phases of the user-centered design model.

3.1   The DECENT Framework

The DECENT framework is a process-oriented user-centered design process that takes a socio-cultural approach. It emphasizes aesthetic, socio-cultural, and contextual values and has a critical understanding of the importance of design in socio-cultural contexts. The DECENT framework has six phases, and it is adapted from a user-centered framework, as shown in Fig. 1. Phase1: Socio-cultural filtration – This phase involves a collection of sets of tools to understand users' socio-cultural contexts. Phase 1 consists of six tools: (1) contextual inquiry, (2) personas, (3) capture cards and postcards, (4) self-built guide, (5) communication delight, and (6) ethics. Other phases of DECENT include analysis of needs assessment of users, design solution, socio-cultural checklist, evaluation, and implementation.

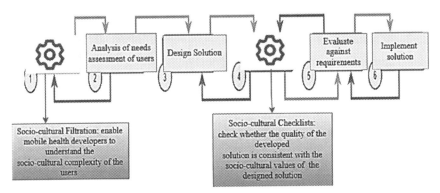

Fig. 1. The DECENT framework as adapted from the User-Centered Design framework as extended by our method.

The presented socio-cultural filtration and socio-cultural checklist in Fig. 1 fit nicely into the first and second phases of already existing user-centered design framework. The socio-cultural filtration phase focuses on enabling mHealth designers to understand the user's socio-cultural contexts; this is the input to the first phase of user-centered design, the "analysis of user needs assessment," which focuses on understanding the user's needs and values.

The second addition to the user-centred design framework is a checklist following the "design" phase. This checklist checks that the socio-cultural aspects identified as a result of the first, socio-cultural filtration, phase have been addressed by the solution.

Moreover, AT and CEF provide a holistic context for informing DECENT tools in phase 1 of the DECENT framework. The next section describes how the AT model informed the development of personas, capture, and postcards. The use of CEF to inform the design of the communication delight tool is described in Sect. 3.2. The AT inspired tools explore individualized contexts, while the CEF ones explore socio-cultural contexts in Phase 1 of DECENT. Phases 1 and 4 are built on top of the existing phases of UCD.

3.2   Designing the DECENT Tools for Capturing Users' Socio-cultural Contexts

The first phase of the DECENT framework consists of a collection of tools for capturing users' socio-cultural contexts. The following sections provide three examples of how AT and CEF are used as organizing principles to inform the design of DECENT tools such as personas, capture & postcards, and communication delight.

The AT Model to Inform the Design of Personas. AT serves as an analytical lens for understanding and describing the process of achieving the goal of creating effective personas. Figure 2 shows a persona tool which is a realisation of the application of AT to aid developers to achieve their goals of creating an effective persona. Personas are used as a tool to represent a specific group of people based on their interests and behavior (Fig. 2).

Collecting insights about the users' socio-cultural backgrounds, frustrations, and goals will aid in developing a broad understanding of the users. Personas are created

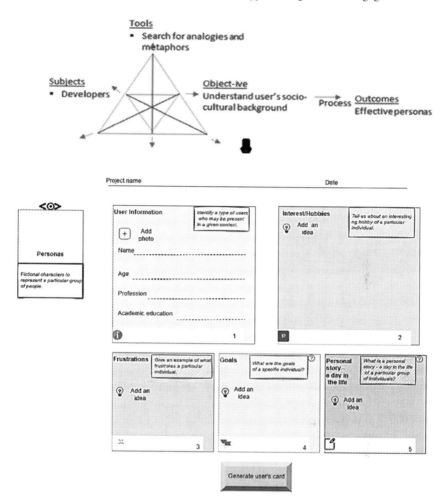

Fig. 2. Examples of creating personas tools from the lens of AT.

by combining trend observations [32]. Improved communication about the target users within the design team and with other stakeholders is one of the widely described benefits of personas in the literature [33–35]. Personas, according to Chapman and Milham [36], still lack a solid empirical foundation. A name and a picture are chosen to represent the fictional representative in a persona, and the persona is described in narrative form, according to Miaskiewicz and Kozar [37]. The activity theory model provides a holistic context with which to design personas. The tool can be used to collect information, interest and frustrations, occupation, goals, and personal stories in a day of the life of the individual.

AT Model to Inform the Design of Capture and Postcards Tools. Figure 3 depicts how AT can be used as a lens to inform the design of capture and postcards tools which aids in understanding how users engage or disengage with mHealth products.

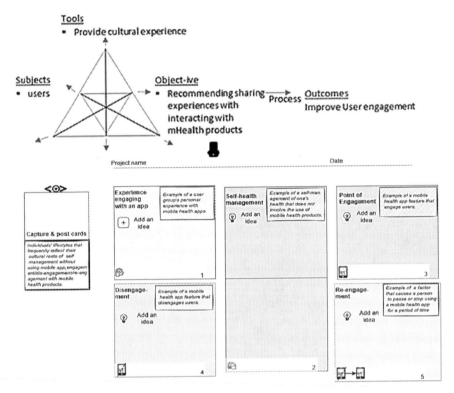

Fig. 3. Examples of creating capture and postcard tools from the lens of AT.

The capture and postcards tool are designed based on the use of AT that serves as an organizing principle to understand the socio-cultural complexity of users interacting with mHealth products (Fig. 3). Users are described as "innovators" based on the AT model because they are actively involved in co-creating their user engagement designs with the designers. They share more information with developers about different points of engagement/disengagement with mHealth products that they have previously used to improve user engagement. The AT model provides a context with which to design the capture and postcards tool.

The capture and postcards tool are intended to motivate users to provide various points of engagement when interacting with mobile apps. Capture and postcard capture special moments of users engaging with mHealth products, as well as different stages of points of engagement/disengagement, to uncover insights about users' lifestyles, which are often reflected in their inherent cultural roots while engaging with mHealth products for user engagement designs.

The two examples in Sects. 3.2 show that while AT can explain why users engage with mHealth, it lacks the vocabulary to investigate what causes specific users to engage with mHealth apps through or their daily communication in broader socio-cultural contexts. As a result, applying AT to mHealth app engagement does not provide insight into how users' engagement with mHealth apps is structured in social contexts. To address

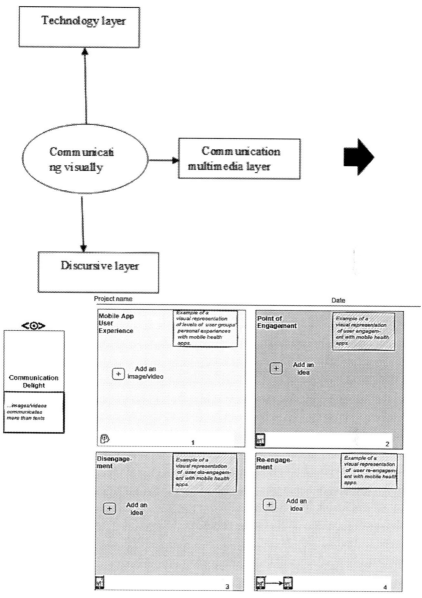

Fig. 4. Example of creating communication delight tool from the lens of communicative ecology framework.

this limitation, CEF is used to provide a rich description of how mHealth is structured in a social context by integrating three layers of interpretation (technical, social, and discursive). Example is shown in the next section of how CEF provided a holistic content of socio-cultural contexts of user complexities that inform components of DECENT framework.

CEF Model to Inform the Design of Communication Delight Tool. Figure 4 shows how CEF can be used to understand and describe how users should share their ideas in form of images communicate between two or more cultures. The idea of communicative ecology emerged as a reaction to issues those studies attempting to identify a causal relationship between discrete technologies and social impacts overlook variables critical to the successful implementation and adoption of technologies in situ [38]. The three layers of CEF, according to Foth and Hearn [39], are as follows: The technology and media layer describes the methods used to communicate between different people and groups, and it includes all communication devices, distribution systems (digital or analog), and the technical systems that enable them (e.g software). The discursive layer is ideational and focuses on the actual communication content, such as stories, understandings, beliefs, and symbols that define – in this case – design culture and user engagement design practices. The people layer describes the various people and groups involved, as well as their social relationships and the social institutions and structures that connect them. The CEF serves as a framework to inform the design of the communication delight tool. Communication delight, inspired by previous work done to share ideas and facilitate communication in the form of images between two or more cultures [40], allows designers and users to share ideas and communicate via images and visual diagrams.

Our interactions with software developers on ways to uncover the socio-cultural background of users sparked the idea of using visual images to communicate between two or more cultures. Thus, communication delight is used as a DECENT tool to enable mobile health users to communicate with designers or other users by interacting with them using images rather than words to share their experiences with mobile health products. Language barriers may no longer irritate the user as a result.

4   Conclusion

This paper presents the outcome of early phases of a Design Science approach to the design of the DECENT toolkit, a bespoke and innovative theory-based design tool and associated method to support the design of mobile health apps. We described the Phase 1 components of the DECENT framework and focused on the theories that informed them, their design, and their purpose. Future iterations of this work will further describe the components, develop, refine, and test our DECENT framework in a specific application of mHealth interventions in Sierra Leone. This will be framed by our use of AT and CEF to evaluate whether the outcome resulting from the DECENT toolkit has impacted user engagement in this case either positively or negatively.

Acknowledgments. This research was conducted with the financial support of Science Foundation Ireland under Grant Agreement No. Grant 18/CRT/6222 at the ADAPT SFI Research Centre at Trinity College Dublin. The ADAPT SFI Centre for Digital Content Technology is funded by Science Foundation Ireland through the SFI Research Centres Programme and is co-funded under the European Regional Development Fund (ERDF) through Grant #13/RC/2106_P2.

References

1. Doherty, K., Doherty, G.: Engagement in HCI: conception, theory, and measurement. ACM Comput. Surv. (CSUR) **51**(5), 1–39 (2018)
2. Hingle, M., Patrick, H.: There are thousands of apps for that: navigating mobile technology for nutrition education and behavior. J. Nutr. Educ. Behav. **48**(3), 213–218 (2016)
3. Tang, J., Abraham, C., Stamp, E., Greaves, C.: How can weight-loss app designers best engage and support users? A qualitative investigation. Br. J. Health. Psychol. **20**(1), 151–171 (2015)
4. Ikwunne, T., Hederman, L., Wall, P.J.: Design processes for user engagement with mobile health: a systematic review. Int. J. Adv. Comput. Sci. Appl. **13**(2), 291–303 (2022)
5. Ikwunne, T., Hederman, L., Wall, P.J.: Understanding user engagement in information and communications technology for development: an exploratory study. In: Stephanidis, C., Marcus, A., Rosenzweig, E., Rau, P.-L.P., Moallem, A., Rauterberg, M. (eds.) HCII 2020. LNCS, vol. 12423, pp. 710–721. Springer, Cham (2020). https://doi.org/10.1007/978-3-030-60114-0_46
6. Brodie, R.J., Hollebeek, L.D., Jurić, B., Ilić, A.: Customer engagement: conceptual domain, fundamental propositions, and implications for research. J. Serv. Res. **14**(3), 252–271 (2011)
7. Brodie, R.J., Ilic, A., Juric, B., Hollebeek, L.: Consumer engagement in a virtual brand community: an exploratory analysis. J. Bus. Res. **66**(1), 105–114 (2013)
8. Hollebeek, L.: Exploring customer brand engagement: definition and themes. J. Strateg. Mark. **19**(7), 555–573 (2011)
9. Böhm, A.K., Jensen, M.L., Sørensen, M.R., Stargardt, T.: Real-world evidence of user engagement with mobile health for diabetes management: longitudinal observational study. JMIR Mhealth Uhealth **8**(11), e22212 (2020)
10. Grady, A., Yoong, S., Sutherland, R., Lee, H., Nathan, N., Wolfenden, L.: Improving the public health impact of eHealth and mHealth interventions. Australian and New Zealand Journal of Public Health **42**(2), 118–119 (2018). https://doi.org/10.1111/1753-6405.12771
11. Machado, G.C., et al.: Smartphone apps for the self-management of low back pain: a systematic review. Best Pract. Res. Clin. Rheumatol. **30**(6), 1098–1109 (2016)
12. Ono, M.M.: Emergent strategies for designing new products facing cultural diversity, within the globalisation context. In: 2nd conference on innovative research in management, Stockholm (2002)
13. Shen, S.T., Woolley, M., Prior, S.: Towards culture-centred design. Interact. Comput. **18**(4), 820–852 (2006)
14. Hofstede, G.: Cultures and Organizations: Software of the Mind. McGraw-Hill, New York (1991)
15. De Angeli, A., Kyriakoullis, L.: Globalisation vs. localisation in e-commerce: cultural-aware interaction design. In: Proceedings of the working conference on Advanced visual interfaces, pp. 250–253 (2006)
16. Honold, P.: Learning how to use a cellular phone: comparison between German and Chinese users. Tech. Commun. **46**(2), 196–205 (1999)
17. Sonderegger, A., Sauer, J.: The influence of socio-cultural background and product value in usability testing. Appl. Ergon. **44**(3), 341–349 (2013)
18. Ikwunne, T., Hederman, L., Wall, P.J.: Theoretical perspectives towards culture-centered user engagement design for mobile health in the global south. In: Future Technologies Conference (2022)
19. Cowley, B., Charles, D., Black, M., Hickey, R.: Toward an understanding of flow in video games. Comput. Entertain. (CIE) **6**(2), 1–27 (2008)
20. Seddon, K., Skinner, N.C., Postlethwaite, K.C.: Creating a model to examine motivation for sustained engagement in online communities. Educ. Inf. Technol. **13**(1), 17–34 (2008)

21. O'Brien, H.L., Toms, E.G.: What is user engagement? A conceptual framework for defining user engagement with technology. J. Am. Soc. Inform. Sci. Technol. **59**(6), 938–955 (2008)
22. Sidner, C.L., Lee, C., Kidd, C.D., Lesh, N., Rich, C.: Explorations in engagement for humans and robots. Artif. Intell. **166**(1–2), 140–164 (2005)
23. Davis, F.D.: A technology acceptance model for empirically testing new end-user information systems: theory and results. Doctoral dissertation, Massachusetts Institute of Technology (1985)
24. Venkatesh, M., Davis, D.: User acceptance of information technology: Toward a unified view. MIS Quarterly **27**(3), 425 (2003). https://doi.org/10.2307/30036540
25. Short, C., Rebar, A., Plotnikoff, R., Vandelanotte, C.: Designing engaging online behaviour change interventions: a proposed model of user engagement (2015)
26. Ludden, G.D., Van Rompay, T.J., Kelders, S.M., van Gemert-Pijnen, J.E.: How to increase reach and adherence of web-based interventions: a design research viewpoint. J. Med. Internet Res. **17**(7), e4201 (2015)
27. Engeström, Y., Miettinen, R., Punamäki, R., (eds.): Perspectives on Activity Theory. Cambridge University Press, Cambridge (1999)
28. Frambach, J.M., Driessen, E.W., van der Vleuten, C.P.M.: Using activity theory to study cultural complexity in medical education. Perspect. Med. Educ. **3**(3), 190–203 (2014). https://doi.org/10.1007/s40037-014-0114-3
29. Altheide, D.L.: An ecology of communication: toward a mapping of the effective environment. Sociol. Q. **35**(4), 665–683 (1994)
30. Bichler, M.: Design science in information systems research. Wirtschaftsinformatik **48**(2), 133–135 (2006). https://doi.org/10.1007/s11576-006-0028-8
31. Peffers, K., Tuunanen, T., Rothenberger, M.A., Chatterjee, S.: A design science research methodology for information systems research. J. Manag. Inf. Syst. **24**(3), 45–77 (2007)
32. Roussou, M., Katifori, A., Pujol, L., Vayanou, M., Rennick-Egglestone, S.J.: A life of their own: museum visitor personas penetrating the design lifecycle of a mobile experience. In: CHI'13 Extended Abstracts on Human Factors in Computing Systems, pp. 547–552 (2013)
33. Cooper, A., Reimann, R.M.: About Face 2.0. Wiley Publishing, Indianapolis (2002)
34. Grudin, J., Pruitt, J.: Personas, participatory design and product development: an infrastructure for engagement. In: Proceedings of the Participatory Design Conference, pp. 144e161. ACM Press (2002)
35. Ma, J., LeRouge, C.: Introducing user profiles and personas into information systems development. In: Proceedings of the Americas Conference on Information Systems. AIS (2007)
36. Chapman, C.N., Milham, R.P.: The personas' new clothes: methodological and practical arguments against a popular method. Proc. Hum. Factors Ergon. Soc. Annu. Meet. **50**(5), 634–636 (2006). https://doi.org/10.1177/154193120605000503
37. Miaskiewicz, T., Kozar, K.A.: Personas and user-centered design: how can personas benefit product design processes? Des. Stud. **32**(5), 417–430 (2011)
38. Dourish, P.: What we talk about when we talk about context. Pers. Ubiquit. Comput. **8**(1), 19–30 (2004)
39. Foth, M., Hearn, G.: Networked individualism of urban residents: discovering the communicative ecology in inner-city apartment buildings. Inf. Commun. Soc. **10**(5), 749–772 (2007)
40. Lee, D.Y.: Interaction of cultures through Design'Cross-Cultural Design (CCD) learning model: the development and implementation of CCD design education in South Korean higher education. Doctoral dissertation, University of London, Goldsmiths (2016)

Good Morning Chatbot, Do I Have Any Meetings Today? Investigating Trust in AI Chatbots in a Digital Workplace

Lorentsa Gkinko[(✉)] [iD] and Amany Elbanna [iD]

Royal Holloway University of London, Egham, UK
Lorentsa.Gkinko.2015@live.rhul.ac.uk, Amany.Elbanna@rhul.ac.uk

Abstract. The adoption and implementation of Conversational AI applications such as AI chatbots in the workplace is rapidly growing. The success of integrating AI chatbots into organisations critically depends on employees' use since AI technology evolves through machine learning and analysis of use data. Since trust is a key aspect that determines technology continuous use, this research questions: How employees experience trust in Conversational AI and how it impacts its continuous use? To answer the research question, we conducted qualitative inductive research using rich empirical data from a large international organisation. The findings highlight that employees developed three forms of trust, namely, emotional, cognitive and organisational trust. The theoretical and practical implications of the findings are discussed.

Keywords: Artificial intelligence · Conversational AI · Trust · Workplace of the future

1 Introduction

Conversational Artificial Intelligence (AI) in the workplace is becoming increasingly important in organisations for the digitalisation of work processes. It is estimated that the market size of AI-enabled chatbots will reach $2.4 billion by 2028 [1]. Its adoption and implementation was accelerated as a result of the COVID-19 pandemic [2, 3]. It is suggested that the volume of interactions handled by Conversational AI including text-based chatbots, and voice assistants has increased during Covid-19 by as much as 250% in many industries [4]. Conversational AI represents a novel and distinctive class of smart information systems (IS) that differs from previously studied traditional enterprise systems [5]. They exhibit conversational abilities which allows users to explore data and services using natural language either via text or voice [6, 7]. It also exhibits anthropomorphic features that triggers users emotions [8]. This is in addition to its underlying machine learning technology that allows it to evolve with continuous use to better fit its organisational context and use patterns.

Conversational AI could be externally-facing serving customers or internally-facing serving employees. It could be text-based known as AI chatbot or AI-enabled chatbot or

© IFIP International Federation for Information Processing 2022
Published by Springer Nature Switzerland AG 2022
A. Elbanna et al. (Eds.): TDIT 2022, IFIP AICT 660, pp. 105–117, 2022.
https://doi.org/10.1007/978-3-031-17968-6_7

voice-based known as digital assistant or digital human. This study focuses on internally facing AI chatbot that is text-based. The use of internally-facing AI chatbot is an important development in enterprise systems [9]. It is considered a way to tackle employees' applications overload and provide them with a friendly interface to access and integrate corporate information from different sources based on employees' needs [8, 10]. It could promote employees' productivity [11] by taking over repetitive tasks and simplifying processes which could lead to employees' satisfaction.

Despite the key importance of use in the evolving performance of AI chatbots and the organisational growing investment in this technology, research on employees' actual use of AI chatbots in their organisational context is still in its infancy [12, 13]. This is particularly the case in AI applications where scholars argue that organisations achieve significant performance improvements when humans and machines work together [14]. Trust plays a key role in the formation of this partnership [15, 16]. Scholars agree that trust in technology is a fundamental construct and primary predictor of its use and continuous use [17, 18]. Therefore, Employees' trust in Conversational AI could affect not only its initial acceptance but most importantly its continuous use. Hence, it could enable or hinder the integration of the technology into the organisation [15, 19, 20].

Against this backdrop, this study examines employees experience of trust in their actual use of AI chatbots in their workplace. It is guided by the research question of: How employees experience trust in AI chatbots and how this impacts its use? To answer the research question, we collected rich qualitative data from a global organisation and followed an inductive approach to the data analysis. Our results provide insights to the foundation of employees' trust of the AI chatbot. They show that employees develop cognitive and emotional trust towards the AI chatbot, which is complemented by organisational trust. The findings reveal that cognitive-based trust, such as transparency mechanisms, enhances trust but is not adequate for the AI chatbot's continuous use and employees' engagement. Instead, emotional-based trust engages employees and could support its continuous use. This research theoretically contributes to the technology trust literature through examining employees' trust in new class of AI technology. It draws the attention to the elements of experiential trust and their reinforcing role on AI continuous use. Furthermore, it extends the IS studies on trust to the new technology of AI and highlights the role fo trust in the collaboration between employees and Conversational AI. It also add a qualitative experiential perspective to this largely quantitative body of literature.

The remainder of this paper is structured into five sections: Section two reviews the existing literature on Conversational AI and trust in technology. Next, we describe our research methodology and data analysis. Subsequently, we present the research findings and conclude by discussing the contributions, implications, and limitations of our study.

2   Literature Review

2.1   Conversational AI

Conversational AI refers to a new mode of interaction with information systems where the user and the system interact in a human-like conversation using natural language while the system utilizes machine learning to improve its conversational and information retrieval and integration capability. Example of voice-based conversational AI systems include Alexa, Apple's Siri, Google Assistant. To realise the value of Conversational AI, organisations need to consider not only technical and organisational aspects but also use patterns and users' involvement [21, 22]. Employees' trust in Conversational AI could affect its acceptance and use and as a consequence, could hinder or enable the integration of the technology into the organisation [15, 19, 20]. Furthermore, the use is impacted by the expectations users have of the interaction are based on their mental model of how they believe the system works and are a driving factor for satisfaction when using information systems [23].

The adoption and use of AI chatbots has been studied mainly from a customer point of view to increase their satisfaction, engagement, and trust [24]. Moreover, productivity was found to be the main motivation for customers to use AI chatbots [25]. The effect of Conversational AI influences consumers' purchase intention [26, 27]. On the other side, customer's attitude toward the brand influences the likelihood to use and recommend the AI chatbot [28].

In addition to identifying the elements that affect customer satisfaction, research finds that the design elements of conversational AI play important role in users' trust and perceptions. For example, studies uncover that strengthening the hedonic quality in AI chatbot strengthens their human likeness and thereby their overall user experience [29]. Also, studies find that the use of human-like language or name are sufficient to increase perception of the AI chatbot as being human-like and plays a role in customer's satisfaction [30].

However, the design elements of the AI applications rely on the context of the application domain to perform different tasks. For example, researchers have classified the design elements into mechanical AI, which is ideal for service standardisation, thinking AI for service personalisation, and feeling AI for service relationalisation through social, emotional, communicative, and interactive tasks [22]. Research finds that Conversational AI that acts and reacts empathetically can be used to improve interactions and deepen trust and as a result, this can also generate greater acquisition and retention rates among customers [22]. Therefore, scholars argue that Conversational AIs design should focuse on the relation with the users attempting to build bonds with them, whether customers and employees in order to increase trust, enhance collaboration, and meet employees' needs for social and relational support in the digital workplace [31]. In addition, anthropomorphic features have been found to have a greater influence from the functional AI chatbot design features into users' perceptions [32].

Research has highlighted the importance of design in IS as it could have implications on users' perceptions of technologies and their encounters [33]. The characteristics of AI chatbots can be defined based on the two main design dimensions of function and form. The functional design elements of AI chatbots are characterized by their natural language processing and their ability to learn and adapt. The design elements of form -the aesthetic and behavioural elements of the AI chatbots- include the conversational interaction, social presence and embodiment as illustrated in Table 1.

The AI chatbot's tangible and intangible characteristics elicit positive aesthetic and affective responses [34]. However, stronger humanisation of AI chatbots, through the design element of form, does not necessarily result in higher user enjoyment [32]. Instead of influencing the hedonic share of technology acceptance, anthropomorphic design features have the strongest and most significant effect on utilitarian aspects of chatbot acceptance and trust [15, 32, 33].

Anthropomorphism (i.e., human likeness) which is embedded in the AI chatbot's design elements of form, defines the degree to which an intelligent agent like an AI chatbot is displayed with human characteristics, which in turn, increases users' trust in computer agents and influences adoption [35]. Anthropomorphic features may lead to the development of social and emotional bonds with the AI technology [32].

Table 1. Characteristics of AI chatbots adapted from [8]

Design dimension	AI Chatbot characteristic	Definition	References
Function	Natural language processing	The ability of an AI chatbot to communicate with natural language	[36, 37]
	Learning agent	The ability of an AI chatbot to learn from a user's input	[38, 39]
Form	Conversational interaction	Interactive two-way communication: user-driven (reactive) or chatbot-driven (proactive or autonomous)	[40, 41]
	Social presence	The feeling of virtual togetherness or "being with another"	[33, 42, 43]
	Embodiment	AI chatbots could have virtual or physical representation or could be disembodied	[30, 44]

Research investigating employees' use of AI chatbots in their workplace is nascent. There is little understanding of employees' trust of this new technology in their work context.

2.2 Trust in Technology

IS research has studied trust in various contexts such as e-commerce, recommendation systems and e-government [45]. It has been argued that trust affects technology acceptance and use [46]. It has been also treated as a significant element of human and computer partnership [17, 47, 48]. Trust has been conceptualized as a multidimensional construct comprising of dimensions of trusting beliefs namely, integrity, competence, and benevolence [49]. Each of these dimensions provides a particular perceptual perspective from which an individual contemplates the potential trustee namely; competence which is the ability to effectively perform, benevolence, acting in the user's interest, and integrity, meaning that the technology adheres to principles like promise-keeping and honesty [50]. Previous IS studies examined the role of trust in technology adoption intentions mainly from a quantitative point of view [51]. They found that the social influence and facilitating conditions, defined as "the degree to which an individual believes that an organisational and technical infrastructure exists to support the use of the system" [52, p. 453] were the main the strongest predictors of trust in the personal use of IoT in a medical context to address issues of personal data disclosure [52]. Similarly, trust was found to be the most significant factor predicting the customers' intention to adopt mobile banking [53]. While, trust in AI chatbots has been mostly studied from a customer perspective [18, 20, 54] and in healthcare [55–57].

The success of integrating a technology such as AI into organisations critically depends on employees' trust in the technology [46]. Research found that access to knowledge, transparency, explainability, certification, as well as self-imposed standards and guidelines to be important factors that increase overall trust in AI [58].

However, little is known about employees' actual use of AI chatbots in organisations even though employees play a key role in the chatbot usage [8].

Trust has also been conceptualised as being both cognitive, based on rational thinking and emotional based on affect [59]. According to McAllister [59], people develop social connections that provide support and comfort, denoting irrational factors as emotion-driven trust that complement cognitive trust which is based on perceptions of trustee reliance and competence. Specifically, the role of anthropomorphism has been highlighted for emotional trust and invite users to assign human qualities to their interaction with it. Affect-based trust relies on the emotional ties and personal ties with the individuals that act as a foundation for trust, while cognitive reasoning based on performance-relevant cognitions such as transparency, reliability, the specific tasks of the technology and personalisation and persuasion tactics for the context of AI is the basis of the cognitive-based trust [15, 60]. The form of AI representation and its level of machine intelligence influence the development of trust [15, 60]. The cognition-based trust positively influences affect-based trust [15, 60] and each one complements the other [59]. Furthermore, trusting beliefs, the trustor's perceptions that the trustee has attributes that are beneficial to the trustor, alone are inadequate to explain trusting decisions because these decisions involve both reasoning and irrational factors, such as emotions and mood [61]. In the context of AI chatbots, research finds that employees might experience mixed emotions from their use of AI chatbots and that positive emotions might counterbalance the negative, resulting in the continuous use of AI chatbots [8].

3   Methodology

The study adopted an interpretive case study approach in order to understand employees' experiences with the AI chatbot and how trust is formed. The interpretive approach was selected as it explores how and why a phenomenon behaves in a particular manner [48]. It is in line with the view that reality and the knowledge are socially constructed between researchers and respondents. It examines employees experiential trust of using AI chatbots in the workplace that can be understood through the meanings that participants assign to them.

3.1 Case Description

The global organisation Omilia, which is anonymized for confidentiality purposes, developed an AI chatbot in 2019 for the internal use of its employees to be self-sufficient and experience a seamless working environment. Initially, the AI chatbot was developed to provide IT support services, but later evolved from its initial use with additional services such as translation in multiple languages and dictionary for internal terms and acronyms and sentiment analysis. The AI chatbot was developed based on the Microsoft Bot Framework utilizing the Azure Cloud Services. The utilisation of the cognitive services helps the AI chatbot to continuously learn based on users' input.

3.2 Data Collection

This study is part of a wider research programme investigating AI chatbots use in organisations. The data collection took place from December 2019–April 2022 and was based on semi-structured interviews, participant observations and document reviews. We conducted 46 semi-structured go-along interviews [62, 63] including two email communications with 2 directors, 1 project manager and 2 developers and 41 users. Users were selected randomly from different organisational levels and teams who agreed to participate in the interviews on the basis of confidentiality and were based in different locations globally. All interviews were tape recorded and transcribed verbatim. The focus of these interviews was on understanding employees' perceptions and experiences of use within the organisation. The interviews addressed themes relevant to the research topic, including people's experiences and challenges on their use of the AI chatbot in their daily work. Moreover, observations of use took place and the users shared screen shots with the researcher. All the data and the organisation's name and location have been anonymized to maintain confidentiality.

3.3 Data Analysis

The data was analysed inductively by using thematic analysis approach to identify patterns within data [64]. Inductive approach was deemed as suitable for the exploratory nature of the study [65], particularly when the phenomenon is new. During the initial stage of the analysis, we proceeded with a preliminary exploration of the data by identifying elements that conveyed trust and began with an open coding, followed by axial coding. During this phase, the identification of codes was approached by both data and theory for the emotional and cognitive elements of trust [66]. The codes were later distilled into the aggregate dimensions.

4 Research Findings

This section presents the main components of trust and how employees' formed perceptions about trust in the AI chatbot. It also shows that employees' trust in the AI chatbot is both emotionally and cognitively driven by the technology while it is also influenced by their trust in the organisation and their colleagues.

4.1 Emotional Trust

Our findings indicate that users experience Emotional-based trust. This originates from the AI chatbot's design elements, namely the tangibility, anthropomorphism and closeness. The visual presence of the AI chatbot allows users to build a personal relationship and refer to the AI chatbot by its name as the following quote shows.

> *"It's cute, that little thing [pointing to the AI chatbot icon on the screen], I think [organisationally-given name of chatbot] is kind of cute" Int35*

Anthropomorphism refers to the human-likeness, the perception of a technology as having human qualities. This AI chatbot characteristic invited users to share responsibility for the outcomes and not to directly "blame the bot", trusting that it is not the chatbot's fault. The following quote eloquently summarises this point:

> *"So, I mean, it might be wrong to say it has become dumb, it might be that I didn't come up with the right questions that the chatbot could answer." Int 5*

4.2 Cognitive Trust

Reliability is critical to technology trustworthiness. When the behaviour of the AI chatbot meets the expectations of the users, it infuses cognitive trust in further use. Specifically, this is also the case when the AI chatbot provides the sources of the information:

> *"It's not mistrusting, because the chatbot doesn't answer. It provides me the source of the information (in addition to the answer), and sometimes it simply answers. If it says I have this entitlement, I believe it." Int 36*

Even though sometimes transparency is related to how the AI chatbot achieves its results, users' trust displays a confidence percentage in the outcomes. The user below highlights that the percentage that the AI chatbot provided was a very specific number and this helped them to trust its result, without necessarily knowing how it arrived to it:

> *"It gives you a percentage. It ranges from 0% which is negative to 100% which is positive. I just did some analysis and it told me 75.27%, very specific number I'm not sure how it arrived there, but yeah. I just said, it's basically, it checked Skype profile so, that is where it gave me this. I'm not sure what it checks, what emotion I have on the skype profile, but it gave me 78.32% positive, so there's something negative, I'm not sure what, but anyways, yeah. Int 5*

4.3 Organisational Trust

Another form of trust that was evident in the data is trust in the organisation and trust in colleagues. Users rely on the AI chatbot because of a colleague recommendation or because it's an "internal tool", implying that they trust the organisation and in return the AI chatbot. This is illustrated in the following quote:

"I turn to the bot when I was advised to use it. I rely on what they (the colleagues) say that 'use this' and I do, and then I use whatever comes out of it, or when I'm total clueless then I just give it a try. I take it as an official tool that we are allowed to use." Int 6

Since the AI chatbot operates on the organisation Intranet, users feel comfortable with using it, mentioning that the information is secure. The user bellow, illustrates this view:

"When I use it here for work and it's on the intranet and all the information is secure, I feel comfortable using it." Int 7

5   Discussion

This study focuses on the use of Conversational AI and in particular AI chatbots by employees in the workplace. It aims to answer the question of how employees experience trust in an AI chatbot and how it impacts its use. The research follows an inductive approach. The study shows that trust, apart from being cognitive factor, is also influenced by emotions [49]. The findings show that users trust in the AI chatbot is not only emotional and cognitive but it is also impacted by the organisational setting and environment.

Employees' trust in the AI chatbots is cognitively established through the functional and form characteristics of the technology. In line with previous research, anthropomorphic design features influence trust [48]. Specifically, the findings demonstrate that the AI chatbot's social characteristics and the way it engages users, play an important role in the development of emotional trust. The social cues of the AI chatbot enhance emotional trust, even when cognitive trust is negatively impacted by receiving erroneous outcomes. Cognitive trust emerges primarily from the accuracy of the results it provides. Users were confident to use the AI chatbot for a new query due to successful previous positive encounters in the past, which led to increased trust. Unlike previous studies arguing that initial trust levels drop as a result of experience [15], our case study findings indicate that users' trust is advancing with their use as they get engaged with the AI chatbot and create a personal relationship with it. The closeness of the AI chatbot affects its emotional trust. This confirms that the virtual appearance and ways of interaction influences the likability and trust [15]. Also, users' understanding that they play a role in training the AI chatbot has infused emotional trust.

Employees' cognitive and emotional trust in the AI chatbot is complemented by their trust in the organisation and their colleagues. Users' engagement with the interactive AI chatbot allows for continuous use due to its learning capabilities. Their commitment is enhanced not only by the correct results it provides, since they could also be erroneous, but mostly by the social cues of the AI chatbot, which create a personal interaction with it and are represented by the design dimension of form. In addition, the interactive character of the AI chatbot, as it has been designed, provides agency to the users in many ways such as reporting mistakes, providing feedback, correcting results, which contribute to greater organisational commitment and users feel they play an active role on the AI chatbot's improvement.

6 Contribution, Limitations and Further Research

Our study has theoretical and practical implications. The study mainly contributes to the nascent research on AI technology use in the workplace and in particular AI chatbots. It also contributes to previous literature on the role of trust in technology use, by qualitatively exploring the elements that shape user's trust in AI chatbots at the workplace. It highlights the important aspect of the context in which the AI chatbot is applied and draws the attention to the complementarity of the organisational context in supporting the cognitive and emotional-based trust in the AI chatbot technology. It draws the attention to the key role of emotional trust in AI chatbots and the role the design characteristics and decision play in this regard. By using a qualitative interpretive approach, we gained an in-depth understanding to processes and social action that is not exposed through more formalized means, such as questionnaire surveys [67, 68]. The use of AI chatbots was examined in a natural setting to identify connections and allow for contextual exploration of the research phenomenon, which led to the uncovering of a new form of trust, namely the organisational trust and would have not been possible to identify by following a quantitative approach. Interpretive information systems research maintains that the social world is not given but constructed through actors' perceptions and actions [68, 69] In our research, this provides the key to understanding how employees experience trust in Conversational AI and how it impacts its continuous use.

Our research findings inform practitioners about the AI chatbot use. It shows that its continuous use is influenced by employees' trust in the technology and their organisation. To succeed in their AI chatbot implementation, practitioners should consider ways to infuse employees' cognitive and emotional trust in the AI chatbot in addition to building trust in the organisation.

References

1. Grand View Research: Chatbot market size worth $2,485.7 million by 2028 | CAGR: 24.9%. Retrieved 14 Nov 2021. from https://www.grandviewresearch.com/press-release/global-chatbot-market (2021)
2. Iansiti, M., Richards, G.: Coronavirus Is Widening the Corporate Digital Divide. Harvard Business Review, 2–5. Retrieved from https://hbr.org/2020/03/coronavirus-is-widening-the-corporate-digital-divide (2020)
3. Sundareswaran, V.: Chatbots are on the rise. This approach accounts for their risks. *weforum.org.* Retrieved 13 Oct 2021, from https://www.weforum.org/agenda/2021/06/chatbots-are-on-the-rise-this-approach-accounts-for-their-risks/ (2021)
4. Comes, S., Schatsky, D., Chauhan, R.: Conversational AI. *Deloitte.* Retrieved 28 Mar 2022, from https://www2.deloitte.com/us/en/insights/focus/signals-for-strategists/the-future-of-conversational-ai.html?id=us:2sm:3tw:4di_gl:5eng:6di (2021)
5. Elbanna, A., Dwivedi, Y., Bunker, D., Wastell, D.: The search for smartness in working, living and organising: beyond the 'technomagic': editorial for special issue of information systems frontiers. Inform. Syst. Frontiers **22**(2), 275–280 (2020). https://doi.org/10.1007/S10796-020-10013-8/TABLES/1
6. Dale, R.: The return of the chatbots. Nat. Lang. Eng. **22**(5), 811–817 (2016). https://doi.org/10.1017/S1351324916000243

7. Følstad, A., Brandtzaeg, P.B.: Chatbots and the new world of HCI. Interactions **24**(4), 38–42 (2017). https://doi.org/10.1145/3085558

8. Gkinko, L., Elbanna, A.:. Hope, tolerance and empathy: employees' emotions when using an AI-enabled chatbot in a digitalised workplace. Inform. Technol. People 0959–3845 (2022). https://doi.org/10.1108/ITP-04-2021-0328

9. Gkinko, L., Elbanna, A.: Chatbots at work: a taxonomy of the use of chatbots in the workplace. In: Dennehy, D., Griva, A., Pouloudi, N., Dwivedi, Y.K., Pappas, I., Mäntymäki, M. (eds.) I3E 2021. LNCS, vol. 12896, pp. 29–39. Springer, Cham (2021). https://doi.org/10.1007/978-3-030-85447-8_3

10. Sun, Y., Li, S., Yu, L.: The dark sides of AI personal assistant: effects of service failure on user continuance intention. Electron. Mark. **32**, 17–39 (2021). https://doi.org/10.1007/s12525-021-00483-2

11. Kimani, E., Rowan, K., McDuff, D., Czerwinski, M., Mark, G.: A conversational agent in support of productivity and wellbeing at work. In: 2019 8th International Conference on Affective Computing and Intelligent Interaction (ACII), pp. 332–338. IEEE (2019). https://doi.org/10.1109/ACII.2019.8925488

12. Gkinko, L., Elbanna, A.: AI in the workplace: exploring emotions on chatbot use in IT services. In: Dennehy, M., Griva, D., Pouloudi, A., Dwivedi, N., Pappas, Y. K., Mäntymäki, I. (eds.) Responsible AI and Analytics for an Ethical and Inclusive Digitized Society, I3E 2021, pp. 18–28. Springer Nature Switzerland, Cham (2021)

13. Wang, X., Lin, X., Shao, B.: Artificial intelligence changes the way we work: a close look at innovating with Chatbots. J. Assoc. Inform. Sci. Technol. (2022). https://doi.org/10.1002/asi.24621

14. James Wilson, H., Daugherty, P.R.: Collaborative intelligence: humans and AI are joining forces. Harv. Bus. Rev. **96**(4), 114–123 (2018)

15. Glikson, E., Woolley, A.W.: Human trust in artificial intelligence: review of empirical research. Acad. Manag. Ann. **14**(2), 627–660 (2020). https://doi.org/10.5465/annals.2018.0057

16. Maedche, A., et al.: AI-based digital assistants. Bus. Inf. Syst. Eng. **61**(4), 535–544 (2019). https://doi.org/10.1007/s12599-019-00600-8

17. Li, X., Hess, T.J., Valacich, J.S.: Why do we trust new technology? a study of initial trust formation with organizational information systems. J. Strat. Inf. Syst. **17**(1), 39–71 (2008). https://doi.org/10.1016/j.jsis.2008.01.001

18. Følstad, A., Nordheim, C.B., Bjørkli, C.A.: What makes users trust a chatbot for customer service? an exploratory interview study. In: Bodrunova, S.S. (ed.) INSCI 2018. LNCS, vol. 11193, pp. 194–208. Springer, Cham (2018). https://doi.org/10.1007/978-3-030-01437-7_16

19. Liu, D., Weistroffer, H.R.: Statistically significant! but is trust of practical significance? J. Comput. Inform. Syst. **62**(2), 247–258 (2020). https://doi.org/10.1080/08874417.2020.1783723

20. Zierau, N., Hausch, M., Bruhin, O., Söllner, M.:. Towards developing trust-supporting design features for AI-based chatbots in customer service. In: International Conference on Information Systems, ICIS 2020 - Making Digital Inclusive: Blending the Local and the Global (2021)

21. Bavaresco, R., et al.: Conversational agents in business: a systematic literature review and future research directions. Comput. Sci. Rev. **36**, 100239 (2020). https://doi.org/10.1016/j.cosrev.2020.100239

22. Huang, M.H., Rust, R.T.: Engaged to a robot? the role of AI in service. J. Serv. Res. **24**(1), 30–41 (2021). https://doi.org/10.1177/1094670520902266

23. Grimes, G.M., Schuetzler, R.M., Giboney, J.S.: Mental models and expectation violations in conversational AI interactions. Decis. Support Syst. **144**, 113515 (2021). https://doi.org/10.1016/j.dss.2021.113515

24. Rapp, A., Curti, L., Boldi, A.: The human side of human-chatbot interaction: a systematic literature review of ten years of research on text-based chatbots. Int. J. Hum. Comput. Stud. **151**, 102630 (2021). https://doi.org/10.1016/J.IJHCS.2021.102630

25. Brandtzaeg, P.B., Følstad, A.: Why people use chatbots. In: International Conference on Internet Science, pp. 377–392. Springer, Cham (2017)

26. Song, M., Xing, X., Duan, Y., Cohen, J., Mou, J.: Will artificial intelligence replace human customer service? the impact of communication quality and privacy risks on adoption intention. J. Retail. Consum. Serv. **66**, 102900 (2022). https://doi.org/10.1016/j.jretconser.2021. 102900

27. Qin, M., Zhu, W., Zhao, S., Zhao, Y.: Is artificial intelligence better than manpower? the effects of different types of online customer services on customer purchase intentions. Sustainability **14**(7), 3974 (2022). https://doi.org/10.3390/su14073974

28. Zarouali, B., Van Den Broeck, E., Walrave, M., Poels, K.: Predicting consumer responses to a chatbot on facebook. Cyberpsychol. Behav. Soc. Netw. **21**(8), 491–497 (2018). https://doi. org/10.1089/cyber.2017.0518

29. Smestad, T.L., Volden, F.: Chatbot personalities matters. In: Bodrunova, S.S., et al. (eds.) INSCI 2018. LNCS, vol. 11551, pp. 170–181. Springer, Cham (2019). https://doi.org/10. 1007/978-3-030-17705-8_15

30. Araujo, T.: Living up to the chatbot hype: The influence of anthropomorphic design cues and communicative agency framing on conversational agent and company perceptions. Comput. Hum. Behav. **85**, 183–189 (2018). https://doi.org/10.1016/j.chb.2018.03.051

31. Patel, S., Chiu, Y.-T., Khan, M.S., Bernard, J.-G., Ekandjo, T.A.T.: Conversational agents in organisations. J. Glob. Inf. Manag. **29**(6), 1–25 (2021). https://doi.org/10.4018/jgim.202 11101.oa53

32. Rietz, T., Benke, I., Maedche, A.:. The impact of anthropomorphic and functional chatbot design features in enterprise collaboration systems on user acceptance. In: Proceedings of the 14th International Conference on Wirtschaftsinformatik, pp. 1656–1670. Siegen, Germany (2019). Retrieved from http://ksri.kit.edu

33. Qiu, L., Benbasat, I.: Evaluating anthropomorphic product recommendation agents: a social relationship perspective to designing information systems. J. Manag. Inf. Syst. **25**(4), 145–182 (2009). https://doi.org/10.2753/MIS0742-1222250405

34. Naderi, E., Naderi, I., Balakrishnan, B.: Product design matters, but is it enough? consumers' responses to product design and environment congruence. J. Product Brand Manag. **29**(7), 939–954 (2020). https://doi.org/10.1108/JPBM-08-2018-1975

35. Sheehan, B., Jin, H.S., Gottlieb, U.: Customer service chatbots: anthropomorphism and adoption. J. Bus. Res. **115**, 14–24 (2020). https://doi.org/10.1016/j.jbusres.2020.04.030

36. Meyer von Wolff, R., Hobert, S., Schumann, M.: How may i help you? – state of the art and open research questions for chatbots at the digital workplace. In: Proceedings of the 52nd Hawaii International Conference on System Sciences, pp. 95–104. HICSS 2019 (2019). https://doi.org/10.24251/hicss.2019.013

37. Lebeuf, C., Zagalsky, A., Foucault, M., Storey, M.A.: Defining and classifying software bots: A faceted taxonomy. In: Proceedings - 2019 IEEE/ACM 1st International Workshop on Bots in Software Engineering, BotSE 2019, pp. 1–6 (2019). https://doi.org/10.1109/BotSE.2019. 00008

38. Benbya, H., Davenport, T.H., Pachidi, S.: Artificial intelligence in organizations: current state and future opportunities. MIS Q. Executive **19**(4), ix–xxi (2020)

39. Quesada, J.F., Martín Mateos, F.J., López-Soto, T. (eds.): FETLT 2016. LNCS (LNAI), vol. 10341. Springer, Cham (2017). https://doi.org/10.1007/978-3-319-69365-1

40. Gnewuch, U., Morana, S., Maedche, A.: Towards designing cooperative and social conversational agents for customer service. In: ICIS 2017: Transforming Society with Digital Innovation (2018). Retrieved from http://ksri.kit.edu

41. Chaves, A.P., Gerosa, M.A.: How Should My Chatbot Interact? A Survey on Social Character-istics in Human–Chatbot Interaction Design. Int. J. Hum.–Comput. Interact. **37**(8), 729–758 (2020). https://doi.org/10.1080/10447318.2020.1841438

42. Toader, D.-C., Boca, G., Toader, R., Măcelaru, M., Toader, C., Ighian, D., Rădulescu, A.T.: The effect of social presence and chatbot errors on trust. Sustainability **12**(1), 256 (2019). https://doi.org/10.3390/su12010256

43. Biocca, F., Harms, C., Burgoon, J.K.: Toward a more robust theory and measure of social presence: review and suggested criteria. In Presence: Teleoperators Virtual Environ. **12**, 456–480 (2003). https://doi.org/10.1162/105474603322761270

44. Diederich, S., Brendel, A.B., Kolbe, L.: On conversational agents in information systems research: analyzing the past to guide future work. In: Proceedings of the International Conference on Wirtschaftsinformatik, pp. 1550–1564 (2019)

45. Christophe, M., Elie-Dit-Cosaque, C.M., Straub, D.W.: Opening the black box of system usage: User adaptation to disruptive IT. Eur. J. Inf. Syst. **20**(5), 589–607 (2011). https://doi.org/10.1057/ejis.2010.23

46. Müller, L., Mattke, J., Maier, C., Weitzel, T., Graser, H.: Chatbot acceptance: A latent profile analysis on individuals' trust in conversational agents. In: SIGMIS-CPR 2019 - Proceedings of the 2019 Computers and People Research Conference, pp. 35–42. ACM (2019). https://doi.org/10.1145/3322385.3322392

47. Mcknight, D.H., Carter, M., Thatcher, J.B., Clay, P.F.: Trust in a specific technology: an investigation of its components and measures. ACM Trans. Manag. Inf. Syst. **2**(2), 25 (2011). https://doi.org/10.1145/1985347.1985353

48. Komiak, S.Y.X., Benbasat, I.: The effects of personalization and familiarity on trust and adoption of recommendation agents. MIS Q.: Manage. Inform. Syst. **30**(4), 941–960 (2006). https://doi.org/10.2307/25148760

49. Hoff, K.A., Bashir, M.: Trust in automation: Integrating empirical evidence on factors that influence trust. Hum. Factors **57**(3), 407–434 (2015). https://doi.org/10.1177/0018720814547570

50. Wang, W., Qiu, L., Kim, D., Benbasat, I.: Effects of rational and social appeals of online recommendation agents on cognition- and affect-based trust. Decis. Support Syst. **86**, 48–60 (2016). https://doi.org/10.1016/j.dss.2016.03.007

51. Elbanna, A.: The validity of the improvisation argument in the implementation of rigid tech-nology: the case of ERP systems. J. Inf. Technol. **21**, 165–175 (2006). https://doi.org/10.1057/palgrave.jit.2000069

52. Arfi, W.B., Nasr, I.B., Kondrateva, G., Hikkerova, L.: The role of trust in intention to use the IoT in eHealth: application of the modified UTAUT in a consumer context. Technol. Forecast. Soc. Chang. **167**, 120688 (2021). https://doi.org/10.1016/J.TECHFORE.2021.120688

53. Alalwan, A.A., Dwivedi, Y.K., Rana, N.P.: Factors influencing adoption of mobile banking by Jordanian bank customers: extending UTAUT2 with trust. Int. J. Inf. Manage. **37**(3), 99–110 (2017). https://doi.org/10.1016/j.ijinfomgt.2017.01.002

54. Nordheim, C.B., Følstad, A., Bjørkli, C.A.: An initial model of trust in chatbots for customer service - findings from a questionnaire study. Interact. Comput. **31**(3), 317–335 (2019). https://doi.org/10.1093/iwc/iwz022

55. Powell, J.: Trust me, i'm a chatbot: how artificial intelligence in health care fails the turing test. J. Med. Internet Res. **21**(10), e16222 (2019). https://doi.org/10.2196/16222

56. Nadarzynski, T., Miles, O., Cowie, A., Ridge, D.: Acceptability of artificial intelli-gence (AI)-led chatbot services in healthcare: a mixed-methods study. Digital Health **5**, 2055207619871808 (2019). https://doi.org/10.1177/2055207619871808

57. Amiri, P., Karahanna, E.: Chatbot use cases in the Covid-19 public health response. J. Am. Med. Inform. Assoc. **29**(5), 1000–1010 (2022). https://doi.org/10.1093/jamia/ocac014

58. Bedué, P., Fritzsche, A.: Can we trust AI? an empirical investigation of trust requirements and guide to successful AI adoption. J. Enterp. Manage. **35**(2), 530–549 (2021). https://doi.org/10.1108/JEIM-06-2020-0233

59. McAllister, D.J.: Affect- and cognition-based trust as foundations for interpersonal cooperation in organizations. Acad. Manag. J. **38**(1), 24–59 (1995). https://doi.org/10.5465/256727

60. Radziwill, N.M., Benton, M.C.: Evaluating Quality of Chatbots and Intelligent Conversational Agents (2017). Retrieved from http://arxiv.org/abs/1704.04579

61. Lewis, J.D., Weigert, A.: Trust as a social reality. Soc. Forces **63**(4), 967–985 (1985). https://doi.org/10.1093/sf/63.4.967

62. Myers, M.: Qualitative Research in Business & Management. Sage Publications (2013)

63. Creswell, J.W., Poth, C.N.: Qualitative Inquiry and Research Design: Choosing Among Five Approaches. Sage Publications (2017)

64. Carpiano, R.M.: Come take a walk with me: the "Go-Along" interview as a novel method for studying the implications of place for health and well-being. Health Place **15**(1), 263–272 (2009). https://doi.org/10.1016/j.healthplace.2008.05.003

65. Boyatzis, R.: Transforming Qualitative Information: Thematic Analysis and Code Development. Sage (1998)

66. Gioia, D.A., Corley, K.G., Hamilton, A.L.: Seeking qualitative rigor in inductive research: notes on the Gioia methodology. Organ. Res. Methods **16**(1), 15–31 (2013). https://doi.org/10.1177/1094428112452151

67. Creswell, W.J., Creswell, J.D.: Research Design: Qualitative, Quantitative and Mixed Methods Approaches, 5th edn. SAGE Publications Inc. (2018).

68. Klein, H.K., Myers, M.D.: A Classification scheme for interpretive research in information systems. In: Qualitative Research in IS: issues and trends. IGI Global (2001). https://doi.org/10.4018/9781930708068.ch009

69. Orlikowski, W.J., Baroudi, J.J.: Studying information technology in organizations: research approaches and assumptions. Inf. Syst. Res. **2**(1), 1–28 (1991). https://doi.org/10.1287/isre.2.1.1

AI/Human Augmentation: A Study on Chatbot – Human Agent Handovers

Polyxeni Vassilakopoulou[1]([✉]) [iD] and Ilias O. Pappas[1,2] [iD]

[1] Department of Information Systems, University of Agder, Universitetsveien 25, 4630 Kristiansand, Norway
{polyxenv,ilias.pappas}@uia.no
[2] Department of Computer Science, Norwegian University of Science and Technology, Sem Saelandsvei 9, 7491 Trondheim, Norway

Abstract. The combination of chatbots with live chats supported by human agents creates a new type of man-machine coordination problem. Prior research on chatbot interactions has focused mostly on the interaction between end users and chatbots and there is limited research on the interaction between human chat agents and chatbots. This study aims to fill this gap contributing to the body of research on coordinating humans and artificial conversational agents by addressing the Research Question: How can the handover between chatbots and chat employees be handled to ensure good user experience? The study aims to contribute to the emerging discipline of Human-Centered AI providing insights on how to create AI-enabled systems that amplify and augment human abilities while preserving human control by identifying key aspects that need to be considered when integrating chatbots in live chat workflows.

Keywords: Chatbots · Live chats · Workflow optimization · Human-AI coordination · Automation · Augmentation · Digital public services

1 Introduction

Chatbots are increasingly being used for the delivery of public services, with a focus on citizen inquiries and information [1]. Chatbots are digital conversational agents that can interact with different user groups using natural language, at any time of the day, every day. They enable 'rich' and expressive digital interactions convincingly simulating how a human would behave in a conversation [2]. They can automate communication tasks that used to be performed by human agents. Yet, a chatbot can't replace a real human for all inquiries. It is common practice to have chatbots lead to live chat agents for a human to human chat when the dialogue cannot be completed due to complex inquiries or other difficulties in communication. A chatbot with a live chat takeover is a combined solution for handling customer inquiries efficiently: a chatbot undertakes the most straightforward part of the conversation and a human agent is taking over if it is not possible for a bot to complete it. This can happen when the conversation requires understanding nuanced messages or addressing complex issues.

In service design it is important to consider the totality of interactions focusing at whole relationships and going beyond digital automation [3]. The combination of chatbots with live chats (i.e. chatting with human agents) provides such a holistic approach but remains under-researched. Prior research on chatbot interactions focused mostly on the interaction between end users and chatbots. For instance, it is known that when users are stressed, human agents are better in expressing the necessary empathy to help deal with the situation [4]. Recent research points to the required characteristics and to the pitfalls that must be avoided to ensure good interaction with end users [5, 6]. Nevertheless, there is limited research on the interaction between human chat agents and chatbots. Chatbots are gradually becoming "co-workers" within customer service units, they handle simple inquiries allowing human chat agents to focus on complex cases. This study aims to fill this gap contributing to the body of research on coordinating humans and digital conversational agents by taking a "co-worker" perspective. To this end, we propose the following Research Question (RQ):

RQ: How can handovers between chatbots and chat employees be streamlined?

To address the RQ we aim to examine what happens when citizens first interact with a chatbot and then are transferred to a human agent. While chatbots can free humans for other activities, the partnership of humans with chatbots will require refactoring communications to use the relative strengths and address the weaknesses of both machines and humans [7, 8]. Creating Artificial Intelligence (AI) that allows both a high level of automation and a high level of human control is a key aim of human-centered AI [9]. Human-centered AI is the emerging discipline for AI-enabled systems that amplify and augment human abilities while preserving human control and ensuring ethically aligned design.

In this paper we present the research design and early conceptualizations for an inquiry on chatbot - human agent coordination within public service delivery in Norway. The Norwegian government promotes the responsible use of Artificial Intelligence (AI) in public administration aiming to lead the way in developing human-friendly and trustworthy solution [10]. Chatbots are key citizen-facing AI applications. The management of handovers between chatbots and humans is important for ensuring the quality of service for citizens and the quality of work experience for workers handling the live chats.

The remainder of the paper is structured as follows. First, the conceptual background is laid out; then, an overview of the method is provided. Next, initial findings are presented. The paper is concluded by pointing to aimed contributions and directions for the continuation of research.

2   Conceptual Background

A chatbot is a virtual cooperation arrangement, where at least two sides communicate based on an initial inquiry from a user. The end user receiving answers to inquiries through a chatbot is a human end in the communication but also, human agents that are handed over conversations from chatbots are part of the "human end". To understand the unfolding of chatbot-human chat agent coordination, we need to examine actual practices and the sociotechnical arrangements established.

Overall, chatbots have a number of significant strengths for service organizations but at the same time have significant limitations. This is why there is a growing interest for combined solutions of chatbot service delivery with a live chat takeover for handling customer inquiries efficiently. The table that follows (Table 1) provides an overview of strengths and weaknesses of chatbots and live chats.

Table 1. Chats performed by chatbots *vs* human chat agents: strengths and weaknesses

Channel	Strengths	Weaknesses
Chat with chatbot	Real-time responses 24/7 Easily scaled-up for demand surges Answers common/standard questions Can point to information available on web pages Can accommodate the needs of special user groups (e.g., with hearing problems)	Lacks empathy - can lead to frustration Cannot handle complex or unusual inquiries
Chat with human agent	Enables a wide scope of problem-solving Empathy Supports relationship-building, flexible human customer service	Subject to office hours Cannot be scaled-up easily to handle demand surges Cognitive limitations especially under time pressure

The advantages show that chatbots can be good as the first line of customer support. They can instantly answer simple queries that have predefined or predictive patterns. But they might lack the ability to think and adapt complex questions where the customers might need answers they can rely on. Furthermore, empathy and relationship building are best with human agents. Computer systems can respond to users' emotions (e.g., frustration) [11], however human agents are better in expressing empathy to help deal with emotionally loaded situations [4]. It is possible to balance using both chatbots and human agents, first to handle simple queries with bots and then transfer more complex queries to human agents. The key question that remains is what is the best time to handover the interaction with the citizen from the chatbot to the human agent and what information needs to be shared to facilitate this handover. The chatbot needs to be able to handover the interaction at the right moment, while including all the relevant information that will help the human agent process the chat.

3   Method

To address our RQ, this study proposes performing both qualitative and quantitative data collection across three different public organisations that use chatbots for service delivery. Traditional user-oriented research methods will be employed including interviews, participatory evaluation sessions and also, digital ethnographies. Chat interactions can be captured via timestamps (beginning-end), count of conversation turns, missed messages (the ones that the chatbot was unable to process), chat outcome (e.g., turned to human agent, clicked link to web content etc.), type of device and browser used.

We propose this research design because it can help us identify broad, statistically derived patterns and also develop rich accounts of the underlying mechanisms driving such patterns. The design involves a multistep process through which we will collect multiple types of data (digital traces of conversations, interview data, process mapping) and carry out multiple analyses (qualitative coding, computational operationalization of variables, statistical modeling, and visualizations). We aim to inductively identify constructs and relationships between constructs using iterative interactions with the data corpus and emergent theory informed by relevant literature.

4   Triggering Chatbot – Human Chat Agent Handovers

The first step in our research is to identify the triggers for handovers to human chat agents. These triggers belong to two main areas: a) *sensemaking* issues (i.e., situations where the chatbot cannot understand the citizen requests or the citizen cannot understand the chatbot responses) and b) *AI service limitations* (due to atypical (new) requests, complex requests or requests that are beyond the service area designated for the bot). Figure 1 provides a conceptual overview of these two main areas.

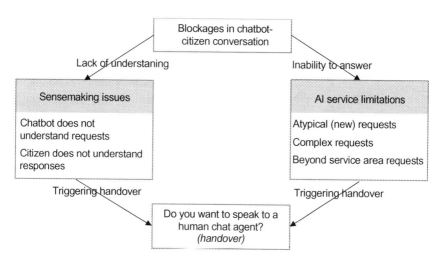

Fig. 1. A conceptual overview of handover triggers.

To enrich our understanding, a qualitative inquiry on identified triggers will be performed developing insights related to the timing of handovers and the information to be shared.

5 Conclusion and Future Research

Chatbots are an exemplary consumer-oriented artificial intelligence application. There are significant opportunities for enhancing their interplay with human chat agents and for streamlining chatbot-human chat agent handovers to achieve human augmentation and not mere automation in service delivery. This study aims to contribute to the design of citizen service chatbots. In prior research handovers from autonomous systems to human agents have been mainly studied in the field of autonomous vehicles [12]. This study can generate knowledge both related to citizens' and to workers' perspectives identifying key aspects that need to be considered when integrating chatbots in live chat workflows. However, it should be noted that as the study will be performed in the context of public organizations one of the limitations is that it will be specific to such organizations and the particularities of service delivery by private organizations will not be covered. The suggested work can contribute to research on AI and autonomous agents as part of big data analytics ecosystems for successful digital transformation [13]. Improving the handover between chatbots and human agents, can increase the range of use cases for chatbots, enhance empathy when needed and support the development of stronger relations, thus offering a significantly improved overall experience to citizens.

References

1. Mehr, H.: Artificial Intelligence for Citizen Services and Government. Ash Center for Democratic Governance and Innovation. Harvard Kennedy School, Cambridge, MA (2017)
2. Androutsopoulou, A., Karacapilidis, N., Loukis, E., Charalabidis, Y.: Transforming the communication between citizens and government through AI-guided chatbots. Gov. Inf. Q. **36**, 358–367 (2019)
3. Vassilakopoulou, P., Grisot, M., Aanestad, M.: Enabling electronic interactions between patients and healthcare providers: a service design perspective. Scandinavian J. Inform. Syst. **28**, 71–90 (2016)
4. Guzmán, I., Pathania, A.: Chatbots in customer service. Accenture Technical Report (2016). www.accenture.com/t00010101T000000__w__/br-pt/_acnmedia/PDF-45/Accenture-Chatbots-Customer-Service.pdf
5. Amershi, S., et al.: Guidelines for human-AI interaction. In: Proceedings of the 2019 CHI Conference on Human Factors in Computing Systems, p. 3. ACM (2019)
6. Følstad, A., Nordheim, C.B., Bjørkli, C.: What makes users trust a chatbot for customer service? An exploratory interview study. In: Bodrunova, S.S. (ed.) INSCI 2018. LNCS, vol. 11193, pp. 194–208. Springer, Cham (2018). https://doi.org/10.1007/978-3-030-01437-7_16
7. Gartner: Gartner Says By 2020, Artificial Intelligence Will Create More Jobs Than It Eliminates (2017). www.gartner.com/en/newsroom/press-releases/2017-12-13-gartner-says-by-2020-artificial-intelligence-will-create-more-jobs-than-it-eliminates
8. Vassilakopoulou, P., Haug, A., Salvesen, L.M., Pappas, I.O.: Developing Human/AI interactions for chat-based customer services: lessons learned from the Norwegian Government. Eur. J. Inform. Syst. **33**, 1–13 (2022)

9. Shneiderman, B.: Human-centered artificial intelligence: reliable, safe & trustworthy. Int. J. Human-Comput. Interact. **36**, 495–504 (2020)
10. Norwegian Ministry of Local Government and Modernisation: National Strategy for Artificial Intelligence (2020). www.regjeringen.no/contentassets/1febbbb2c4fd4b7d92c67ddd353 b6ae8/en-gb/pdfs/ki-strategi_en.pdf
11. Hone, K.: Empathic agents to reduce user frustration: the effects of varying agent characteristics. Interact. Comput. **18**, 227–245 (2006)
12. Hancock, P.: Some pitfalls in the promises of automated and autonomous vehicles. Ergonomics **62**, 479–495 (2019)
13. Pappas, I.O., Mikalef, P., Giannakos, M.N., Krogstie, J., Lekakos, G.: Big data and business analytics ecosystems: paving the way towards digital transformation and sustainable societies. IseB **16**(3), 479–491 (2018). https://doi.org/10.1007/s10257-018-0377-z

Co-creating Through Robotic Process Automation – The Role of Consultants in a Public Sector Automation Journey

Björn Johansson$^{(\boxtimes)}$ ⓘ and Fredrik Söderström ⓘ

Department of Management and Engineering, Linköping University, 581 83 Linköping, Sweden
{bjorn.se.johansson,fredrik.soderstrom}@liu.se

Abstract. This short paper reports on an ongoing study related to automation journeys in public sector organizations. From interviews with Robotic Process Automation (RPA) consultants, we highlight and discuss the specific capability of "making technology work" by referring to and using a core capability framework. The capability of making technology work, which we see as needing attention from both suppliers and customers if the adoption of the automation technology should be successful. We argue that this capability becomes a crucial capability; from the start of the journey and after arriving at the destination, if successful, co-creation should happen and be continuously a fact.

Keywords: Robotic Process Automation · RPA · Co-creation · IS capabilities

1 Introduction

This paper discusses the role of consultants' when a public sector organization develops automation by using Robotic Process Automation (RPA) technology. RPA can be described as front-end automation of business processes where software robots mimic the behaviour of human system interaction (Lacity and Willcocks 2016). Therefore, RPA is often described as a technology that should be driven by business departments themselves rather than the IT-department (Aguirre and Rodriguez 2017). RPA basically means integration using the user interface/front-end, indicating that this solution could be described as *Lightweight IT* instead of traditional advanced back-office integration, i.e. *Heavyweight IT* (Bygstad 2017). Accordingly, this type of development could be seen as an endeavour that potentially starts from the perspective that civil servants in a public sector business departments want to further develop their business by using RPA technology to automate business processes (Söderström et al. 2021; Uskenbayeva et al. 2019). It could be that the civil servants see a need or a possibility for the business department to improve and streamline its business through this type of digitalization. Therefore, a request might be made to the IT department, and for different reasons, the IT department might be a bit resistant. This resistance could result from civil servants searching for an option to improve operations by themselves and then identifying RPA

A. Elbanna et al. (Eds.): TDIT 2022, IFIP AICT 660, pp. 124–129, 2022.
https://doi.org/10.1007/978-3-031-17968-6_9

as a potential solution. The result could be that the business department contacts an RPA supplier (Toll and Söderström 2020). After doing this, it becomes a question of what competencies the civil servants need and what competencies the RPA consultant needs to provide. All this results in the following research question addressed: What do the stakeholders in this RPA development endeavour need to do? This question then addresses what competencies or capabilities each stakeholder (Civil servants and RPA consultants) need to have and how the interaction between these stakeholders needs to be conducted for co-creation to happen in this context. In this short paper, we introduce the question and the topic by presenting theoretical grounding in the next section, followed by a research method section and a discussion section in which we discuss the capability of making technology work, before the final section that presents concluding remarks and forthcoming research.

2 Theoretical Grounding

This research has as a starting point the core capability framework by Feeny and Will-cocks (1998). From that, the discussion around the role of the stakeholders (RPA consultants and civil servants) and what competence and capability are needed to have successful co-creation related to RPA is highlighted. The first thing that needs to be clarified is what co-creation means in this context. RPA co-creation could be described as the development of business processes that comes from the interaction between a provider/supplier of RPA and the actual usage of the RPA. This requires collaboration between the two parties, and they must understand each other clearly. For instance, this could be related to middlemen's work (Mahnke et al. 2008) in an outsourcing relationship or the role of consultancy (Bessant and Rush 1995) in technology transfer. For public organizations that start to use RPA software, developing RPA technology further is probably not part of their competencies and hence not a core competency. Therefore, it can also be claimed that in most cases, organizations need to be aware of this need for knowledge transfer and actively procure this competence from the supplier. Accordingly, co-creation occurs when implementing and using the software, which can be described as a service as business logic or service logic (Grönross and Ravald 2011). This also stipulates that the user organization needs some form of capability or capabilities for this business logic to become successful. One of the questions addressed in this paper is what kind of competencies the suppler of RPA sees as needed in the user organizations. We use a framework developed by Feeny-Willcocks to explore this, which consists of three internal intersecting areas and includes nine core IS capabilities as presented and defined shortly in Table 1 below.

Table 1. Core IS capabilities defined Feeny and Willcocks (1998)

#	Core IS capabilities	Definition
1	Leadership	Integrating IT effort with business purpose and activity
2	Business systems thinking	Ensuring that IT capabilities are envisioned in every business process
3	Relationship building	Facilitates the broader dialogue, establishing understanding, trust and cooperation amongst business users and IT specialists
4	Designing technical architecture	Creating the coherent blueprint for a technical platform that responds to present and future business needs
5	Making technology work	Rapidly troubleshoot problems disowned by others across the technical supply chain and identify how to address business needs that cannot be appropriately satisfied by standard technical approaches
6	Informed buying	Analyse the external market for IT/e-business services; select a sourcing strategy to meet business needs and technology issues; lead the tendering, contracting, and service management processes
7	Contract facilitation	Ensure the success of existing contracts for IT services
8	Contract monitoring	Holding suppliers to account against both existing service contracts and the developing performance standards of the services market
9	Vendor development	Identifying the potential added value of IT/e-business service suppliers

3   Research Method

The research partly described in this paper builds on a qualitative interpretive case study (e.g. Walsham 1995) performed among two consultancy firms (suppliers) with expert knowledge and competence in automation and RPA. The aim is to determine what capabilities these suppliers think a potential customer needs to have about automation technology. As presented in the theoretical grounding, we see the IS core capabilities framework by Feeny and Willcocks (1998) as a suitable approach to further explore this area. The framework was used as a guide for interviews and analysis. Accordingly, in this paper, we present our thoughts about the capability of making technology work from a supplier perspective when a customer adopts RPA.

Data collection consisted of eight (8) semi-structured interviews with representatives from two (2) consultancy firms specializing in automation and RPA. All respondents

Table 2. Interviews

#	Date	Role	Supplier	Duration
1	2020–06-01	Manager	S1	45 min
2	2020–06-04	Head of business area	S1	55 min
3	2020–06-04	Business analyst	S1	60 min
4	2020–06-15	Senior project manager	S2	90 min
5	2020–10-14	Developer	S2	70 min
6	2020–10-14	Developer	S2	60 min
7	2020–11-25	Business analyst, technical lead	S1	90 min
8	2021–05-31	Senior project manager	S2	60 min

were actively involved in projects concerning automation and RPA. Respondents' roles ranged from management, project manager, developers, business analyst and technical lead. A detailed overview of interviews is shown in Table 2 above. The two supplier firms were of similar size and categorized as SMEs. Both firms specialize in developing and delivering solutions and services in automation and RPA to customers in the private and public sectors. Accordingly, these firms have a similar service offering to their customers, consisting of consultancy and support regarding business/process automation as part of digital transformation. The interviews were recorded, transcribed, and analysed based on the described Core IS Capability framework (Feeny and Willcocks 1998). Questions asked during the interviews followed an interview guide covering service offerings, solutions, work practices, lessons learned, and recurring challenges. We slightly adjusted the original framework by Feeny and Willcocks (1998) during this study to increase its applicability in the focused research context. We justify this change because we believe that the initial framework was influenced by the original context of outsourcing IT services.

4   Discussion

During RPA automation, the technological platform is implemented and deployed within the adopting organization, as in other types of automation. The RPA platform thus becomes part of the organization's current internal technological infrastructure. Accordingly, there are differences between customer and external service providers regarding the continuous delivery of technology services and infrastructure. Also, while major outsourcing contracts involve significant financial investments, RPA implementations have a lower financial entry. Based on these motives, in the current research stage presented in this short paper, we have chosen to delimit the discussion by focusing on capability five, "making technology work". This capability refers to how there is in-house knowledge and competence to rapidly react, troubleshoot and solve technological problems (Feeny and Willcocks 1998). According to Kirchmer and Franz (2019), RPA is a digital enabler applied or discussed in many organizations as a potential technology addressing business needs. However, Kirchmer and Franz (2019) also claim that many organizations struggle to realize the full potential of RPA, referring to statistics that state that 30–50% of RPA initiatives fail.

Thus, Kirchmer and Franz (2019) conclude that there is a need for approaches that support identifying processes to automate, improve those business processes considering the end-to-end process context and sustain the results through appropriate governance and hybrid workforce management. Moreover, Juntunen (2018) states that to develop, implement, and maintain RPA successfully, there is a need for internal RPA competence. There is a need to complement existing in-house technical competencies, skills, and knowledge with support from external partners' technical resources. The capability of "making technology work is, according to Kasraian et al. (2016), a crucial capability in the operation phase of RPA. Empirical data from suppliers confirm this need for technological knowledge transfer from supplier to the customer and knowledge development concerning RPA (e.g. Senior Project Manager, S2). The sense of what technical knowledge and competence of RPA is needed to be developed and maintained in-house seems to be no different from other technologies. Thus, the IT-support function still needs to solve emerging technical issues during phases such as implementation, maintenance and support and further development of an RPA solution. We, therefore, argue the capability of making RPA technology work includes high levels of competence regarding the technological architecture and solution, i.e. the RPA platform, as well as the processes and operations of the organization. This competence should include how the organization operates in the current and how the organization can be developed in the future and therefore has a strong relation to and is dependent on the former capability of business systems thinking. Knowing the importance of knowledge transfer and training demands is also necessary when procuring RPA related services. Hence, this relates to the possibility of having co-creation between supplier and customer in the case of RPA adoption. The adopting organization must understand what is needed to have the technology work, while the provider must understand what they need to provide for successful co-creation through RPA. This is not only required for the initial stage; it is also related to ongoing processes to manage, maintain, and develop the RPA solution.

5 Concluding Remarks and Forthcoming Research

In this short paper, we describe the potential of using the core capability framework to highlight what is needed to focus on for parties when the adoption of RPA takes place. The focus was directed to the capability of making technology work, which we see as needing attention from both suppliers and customers if the adoption of the automation technology should be successful. By highlighting the need to have a close relationship within this endeavour, it can be concluded that this is a key to having successful co-creation. The next step would be to explore other ongoing relationships between suppliers and customers in their automation journey. This will enable the development of clear advice to give both suppliers and customers on how to start the journey and how to be able to enjoy the final destination.

Acknowledgements. The research presented in this paper was funded by AFA Insurance; an insurance company owned by Sweden's labour market parties.

References

Aguirre, S., Rodriguez, A.: Automation of a business process using robotic process automation (RPA): a case study. In: Figueroa-García, J.C., López-Santana, E.R., Villa-Ramírez, J.L., Ferro-Escobar, R. (eds.) WEA 2017. CCIS, vol. 742, pp. 65–71. Springer, Cham (2017). https://doi.org/10.1007/978-3-319-66963-2_7

Bessant, J., Rush, H.: Building bridges for innovation: the role of consultants in technology transfer. Res. Policy **24**, 97–114 (1995)

Bygstad, B.: Generative innovation: a comparison of lightweight and heavyweight IT. J. Inf. Technol. **32**, 180–193 (2017)

Feeny, D.F., Willcocks, L.P.: Core IS capabilities for exploiting information technology. Sloan Manage. Rev. **39**, 9–21 (1998)

Grönross, C., Ravald, A.: Service as business logic: implications for value creation and marketing. J. Serv. Manage. **22**, 5–22 (2011)

Juntunen, K.: Influence of contextual factors on the adoption process of Robotic process automation (RPA): Case study at Stora Enso Finance Delivery (2018)

Kasraian, L., Sammon, D., Grace, A.: Understanding core IS capabilities throughout the IS/IT service co-production lifecycle. J. Decis. Syst. **25**, 290–301 (2016)

Kirchmer, M., Franz, P.: Value-driven robotic process automation (RPA). In: Shishkov, B. (ed.) BMSD 2019. LNBIP, vol. 356, pp. 31–46. Springer, Cham (2019). https://doi.org/10.1007/978-3-030-24854-3_3

Lacity, M.C., Willcocks, L.P.: A new approach to automating services. MIT Sloan Manag. Rev. **58**, 41–49 (2016)

Mahnke, V., Wareham, J., Bjorn-Andersen, N.: Offshore middlemen: transnational intermediation in technology sourcing. J. Inf. Technol. **23**, 18–30 (2008)

Söderström, F., Johansson, B., Toll, D.: Automation as migration? – Identifying factors influencing adoption of RPA in local government. In: European Conference of Information Systems (ECIS 2021) (2021)

Toll, D., Söderström, F.: What is this' RPA'they are selling? In: EGOV-CeDEM-ePart-*, pp.365–370 (2020)

Uskenbayeva, R., Kalpeyeva, Z., Satybaldiyeva, R., Moldagulova, A., Kassymova, A.: Applying of RPA in administrative processes of public administration. In: 2019 IEEE 21st Conference on Business Informatics (CBI), pp. 9–12. IEEE (2019)

Walsham, G.: Interpretive case studies in IS research: nature and method. Eur. J. Inf. Syst. **4**, 74–81 (1995)

Is Inner Source the Next Stage in the Agile Revolution?

Lorraine Morgan[1]([envelope]), Rob Gleasure[2], and Abayomi Baiyere[2]

[1] National University of Ireland Galway, Galway, Ireland
`lorraine.morgan@nuigalway.ie`
[2] Copenhagen Business School, Frederiksberg, Denmark
`rg.digi@cbs.dk, aba.digi@cbs.ki`

Abstract. Modern business leaders know it is important to be able to work fast, adapt to change, and build on existing solutions. This is especially true of digital business, where the high rate of change creates a continuous stream of new problems and new opportunities. Many have called for business leaders to adopt more 'agile' structures and processes that embrace change, transparency, and employee empowerment. Now a new complementary approach called 'inner source' is emerging to help address this. Inner source does not only embrace speed and change; it also lays out techniques for globally distributed agile teams to systematically store and reuse solutions in a shared, organization-wide repository. This paper explores this new management concept – where it came from, what it means – and illustrates its value in large organizations. Building on a number of illustrative cases, we explain how certain business leaders have brought the principles and practices of inner source to their respective organizations.

Keywords: Inner source · Agile · Adoption

1 Introduction

The last 20 years or more has seen the emergence of a number of agile systems development (ASD) methods, such as XP [1] and Scrum [2] for example. Use of these methods is highly prevalent across the community and have helped businesses work fast and adapt to change. Yet the emphasis on 'good enough' improvements and ongoing discovery has hindered agile approaches' capacity to build on existing solutions. Indeed, it may have actually been a step backwards. Conboy and Morgan (2011) argued that an agile environment needs to incorporate open innovation principles that enables a culture of collaboration and knowledge-sharing with other teams and business units [3]. To address this, business leaders are now implementing Inner Source, which is defined as the adoption of open source best practices and tools by professionals interacting inside an organization [4, 5]. Just like agile, inner source began as a set of systems development methods. Yet just like agile, inner source is spreading to other forms of business leadership. While the initial focus of Inner Source was on sharing code, this approach also features a high degree of open innovation, a phenomenon that focuses on tearing

© IFIP International Federation for Information Processing 2022
Published by Springer Nature Switzerland AG 2022
A. Elbanna et al. (Eds.): TDIT 2022, IFIP AICT 660, pp. 130–136, 2022.
https://doi.org/10.1007/978-3-031-17968-6_10

down and collaborating across silo boundaries [6, 7]. Moreover, Inner Source involves changing the philosophy of working, creating communities of empowered developers spread across different countries to work transparently on co-creation activities, resulting in improved productivity and innovation [8–10]. The overall objective of this research is to explore how and why the adoption of inner source practices and principles benefit large organizations. In the case descriptions that follow, we present a juxtaposition of Inner Source with agile across different adoption points in time.

2 Research Design

This research is part of an ongoing 12-year study on inner source and hence our research model is longitudinal in nature. For this paper, we adopted a comparative case study approach and focused on five organizations that adopted inner source (see Table 1) as they have contrasting histories and business models. For example, some emerged in the digital era (Zalando, Paypal) rather than moving from older established industries (Philips Healthcare, Bosch, Ericsson), some focus primarily on physical goods (Zalando, Philips Healthcare) rather than digital offerings (Paypal, Ericsson), and some have a more global focus (Philips Healthcare, Paypal) rather than targeting a specific region (Zalando). Philips Healthcare were one of the first companies to implement inner source and a well-known champion of this approach. In 2011 we performed an immersive study of the company, which included eight interviews with senior project managers and software developers. From 2016 to 2021, we further collected data through a number of interviews with project managers, software team leaders and software developers involved in inner source implementations in Bosch, Paypal, Ericsson and Zalando. Given that one of the authors has been working with these organizations on a number of inner source research projects over the past 12 years and is a member of the Inner Source Commons, a community comprising 1500 inner source practitioners from 500 companies, we also drew heavily on ethnographic methods such as participant observations in Ericsson and Zalando to better understand how and why the adoption of Inner Source values and technologies helped these businesses build on existing solutions. In line with the longitudinal nature of our study, we analyzed data periodically over the period 2011 to 2021. For our coding we focused on identifying and analyzing distinct stages of inner source adoption, as well as the benefits and challenges associated with the approach.

Table 1. Data sources

Company	Industry	Data sources
Philips Healthcare	Health	8 interviews (International Partnership Project Manager, Director of Software Services, Software Team Leaders

(*continued*)

Table 1. (*continued*)

Company	Industry	Data sources
Bosch	Technology & services	4 interviews (Software Team Leaders, Software Engineers) Participant observations
Paypal	Financial services	3 interviews (Head of Open Source, Technology Leader)
Ericsson	Telecommunications	3 interviews (Program Manager, Software Engineering Manager Participant Observation
Zalando	Fashion	2 interviews (Inner Source Manager Participant observations

3   Case Studies

3.1   Pre-agile and 'Big Bang' Adoption of Inner Source at Philips Healthcare

Philips Healthcare are one of the best-known early adopters of Inner Source, which they introduced in 2007 - five years before beginning their agile transformation in 2012. The inner source initiative at Philips Healthcare started with a component suite built around the DICOM (Digital Imaging and Communication in Medicine) standard, a popular medical-imaging system. Philips Healthcare traditionally relied on top down development approach, in which a central platform development group developed components and separate product groups integrated them into different solutions. This ensured the firm could build on existing solutions. However, the top-down reuse of software components also created bottlenecks and jarred with the growing need for fast, responsive, client-facing innovation. The initial focus of the inner source initiative at Philips Healthcare was on software, encouraging open collaboration, distributed ownership of the source code, and frequent release and integration of software components. The company deployed CollabNet Enterprise Edition as the enabling infrastructure for this transformation. Yet leadership quickly realized these new practices could act as a broader catalyst to change how the company was managed. Their focus therefore shifted to facilitating the sharing of knowledge and expertise across functionally and geographically distributed teams, providing easy access to all the information of the product line, improving communication and cooperation among teams, and creating a sense of shared ownership and control of the product line. This inner source approach gave teams the freedom to work closely with individual clients and develop/adapt new solutions quickly, while simultaneously reducing re-work and increasing transparency, cooperation, and peer learning across the organization. Executives felt an increase in both horizontal and vertical transparency and cooperation, as newfound visibility allowed individuals and teams to build a profile that rewarded their day-to-day efforts. Philips Healthcare credit the introduction of inner source as not only enabling new product launches and substantially reducing the time to market, but for changing the culture of the organization towards cumulative learning and innovation.

3.2 Pre-agile and Incremental Adoption of Inner Source at Bosch

Bosch were also early adopters of inner source, introducing it before they made the move to agile. However, the manner in which Bosch moved to inner source was different. It began as an 'experiment' in 2009 for a small number of teams and several years passed before inner source spread across the company. As with Philips Healthcare, the initial focus of introducing inner source at Bosch was the quality and efficiency of software development. Specifically, Bosch wanted to address the narrowing of relationships that occurred because of their distributed organization of business units across locations and time zones. Yet as with Philips Healthcare, management recognized this change had more profound implications. The early success of inner source created an appetite for new norms in Bosch, which leaders used to drive cultural change and a move towards openness, transparency, self-organization, self-determination and meritocracy. It also laid foundations for the organization-wide agile transformation in 2015. Gains in productivity, reduced lead times, and improved collaboration have coincided with higher reports of employee happiness and personal growth, which has also boosted employee retention. Bosch established an infrastructure by migrating to a single collaboration platform called Bitbucket for employees to collaborate across boundaries. Use of inner source has spread across functions and roles in the organization and the number of users on the inner source platform at the time of writing has increased to 10,000 from countries all over the world. Use of this platform has led to many success stories within Bosch, including the recent Bosch AI-powered Virtual Visor which won the CES 2020 Innovation Award in Las Vegas. This visor replaces traditional sun visors in cars with a transparent liquid crystal display that adapts to areas of sun glare without limiting visibility. The combination of agile and inner source approaches allowed Bosch to build increasingly sophisticated technological components, without compromising the focus on observed user experience and feedback.

3.3 Parallel Incremental Adoption of Agile and Inner Source at Ericsson

Unlike the previous companies, Ericsson performed the inner source and agile transformation in parallel. The rapid growth and evolution of new technologies and standards (3G, 4G and 5G) for mobile networks since the 1990s had strained Ericsson's organizational and communications structures. Management felt this strain was likely to increase due to future technologies such as the Internet of Things. They began developing a cloud-based platform and related set of services with the intention of supporting agile feature-specific development teams. In 2013, Ericsson realized that inner source approaches would complement their new agile philosophy by encouraging collaboration and learning across teams, rather than only within them. As with Philips Healthcare and Bosch, while much of the initial inner source discussion at Ericsson was about introducing new tools to support systems development. However, the broader effects were once again felt across the organization. Specifically, management credit the adoption of inner source with stimulating a change towards a more 'open' culture that reduces territoriality and encourages individuals to extend and improve upon each other's work. Building on the establishment of a flexible community portal, Ericsson introduced new governance structures. They also introduced new core teams tasked with building internal and external communities around key extensible components. Documented benefits included an increase in cross-unit collaboration, the production of higher quality robust components, and faster and more effective customer support.

3.4 Parallel Incremental Adoption of Agile and Inner Source at Paypal

Paypal also introduced inner source and agile in parallel, though their path to implementing it was different. The company underwent a major agile transformation in 2013, launched as a 'big bang' change across over 300 cross-functional delivery teams. Management were satisfied this change had improved the speed of development and the ability to respond to user needs. However, they felt it had done little to address silos of knowledge and collaboration in the organization. These silos were often fueled by historic tensions between backend and frontend developers, as well as between competing specialists who were convinced they needed to maintain sole ownership of components to ensure quality. Contrasting with their 'big bang' move to agile, Paypal decided to introduce inner source in 2015 over multiple stages. They first identified key services and set up shared repositories. They then allocated specific individuals working on those services the role of 'Trusted Committer'. These individuals would oversee shared resources to ensure common standards were maintained. Further, this Trusted Committer role changed hands every two weeks. Management noted sharp quantifiable gains in efficiency among participating teams after six months. These quantifiable gains fed into a growing appetite to expand and improve on shared resources. Individuals and teams became more likely to mentor others, as they knew everyone's contributions would become a common asset. Collaboration also improved between frontend and backend teams, as each learned more about interdependencies in their work and established new trust relationships and overall better individual performance.

3.5 Post-agile Adoption of Inner Source at Zalando

Zalando was founded in 2008 but has grown rapidly since then (at the time of writing the company has more than 2,000 employees from 77 nations, spread out across over 200 delivery teams across Europe). Zalando were an agile company from their inception, which had allowed them to expand into new areas and work with closely with customers to discover new solutions. However, the rapid growth had created organizational partitions that senior management felt were harming both the culture and practical cohesion of the company. Zalando therefore felt they could use inner source as a catalyst for building a more collaborative and united culture. Key to this was to align development activities in a way that encouraged conversation across teams, built around a shared customer-orientation – a challenge they addressed by introducing new inner source tools and governance structures. The company started using Github Enterprise, a collaboration platform that brought all developers together on a single platform, enabling them to build and share software easily and effectively, helping to eliminate dependencies and ensure teams were not waiting on each other to complete critical pieces of work. This platform also provides teams with the opportunity to talk about their work and accept feedback from those outside the team. Furthermore, core team was put in place to oversee the inner source initiative, providing various tools and guidelines around inner source practices that teams could adopt. The company also has an API Portal that provides a central repository of approximately 600 APIs and one where API specifications of all deployed services can be found. Management at Zalando credit the adoption of inner source with a reduction in re-work and siloing, an increase in product awareness, and a reduction in time to market. The benefits are not limited to cumulative outputs. Zalando also credit inner source with improvements in employee mobility and onboarding, as individuals on one team are more willing and able to contribute to components developed by other teams, due to added familiarity in both the components themselves and how those teams manage the development process.

4 Conclusion

This research presents some findings from a range of companies to show why and how inner source was adopted. As is evident, inner source helps establish an open source culture, providing companies with many benefits including improved job satisfaction and overall performance, increased productivity and innovation and reduced time to market. Providing the infrastructure and tools necessary as well as introducing new roles or core teams to build communities are some of the key requisites for adoption (something also described in more detail by Stol et al. (2014)). Overall, we believe that inner source is a complimentary value add to agile, providing companies with the capability to build on existing solutions whilst not conflicting with their ability to work fast and adapt to change. Nonetheless, while we have seen a significant interest from practitioners over the past number of years, research on Inner Source in the Information Systems domain is relatively sparse. Hence, further studies are needed.

Acknowledgement. This work was supported with the financial support of the Science Foundation Ireland grant 13/RC/2094_2.

References

1. Beck, K.: Extreme Programming Explained: Embrace Change. Addison-Wesley, Reading, Mass (2000)
2. Schwaber, K., Beedle, M.: Agile Software Development with SCRUM. Prentice Hall (2002)
3. Conboy, K., Morgan, L.: Beyond the customer: opening the agile systems development process. Inf. Softw. Technol. **53**, 535–542 (2011)
4. Morgan, L., Gleasure, R., Baiyere, A.: Share and share alike: how inner source can help create new digital platforms. Calif. Manage. Rev. **64**(1), 90–112 (2021)
5. Stol, K.-J., Avgeriou, P., Babar, M.A., Lucas, Y., Fitzgerald, B.: Key factors for adopting inner source. ACM Trans. Softw. Eng. Methodol. **23**(2), 2 (2014)
6. Morgan, L., Feller, J., Finnegan, P.: Exploring inner source as a form of intraorganisational open innovation. In: Proceedings of the European Conference on Information Systems (2011)
7. Campraro, M., Riehle, D.: Inner source definition, benefits, and challenges. ACM Comput. Surv. **49**(4), 1–36 (2017)
8. Riehle, D.: Agile Feature Teams vs. Inner Source (2018). Available at: https://dirkriehle.com/2018/09/25/agile-feature-teams-vs-inner-source/

9. Cooper, D., Stol, K.-J.: The InnerSource Approach to Innovation and Software Development. O'Reilly Media Inc. (2018)
10. Carroll, N., Morgan, L., Conboy, K.: Examining the impact of adopting inner source software practices. In: Proceedings of the 14th International Symposium on Open Collaboration, Paris (2018)

Open Source Software Governance: Towards a Link to the Business World

Hazar Y. Hmoud[1]([✉]), Zainah Qasem[2], Dao's Hajawi[3], and Jumana Ziad Al. Zoubi[4]

[1] The School of Business, Department of Management Information Systems,
The University of Jordan, Amman, Jordan
h.hmoud@ju.edu.jo

[2] The School of Business Department of Marketing, The University of Jordan, Amman, Jordan
z.qasem@ju.edu.jo

[3] The School of Business, Department of Marketing, The University of Jordan, Amman, Jordan
d.hajawi@ju.edu.jo

[4] The School of Business, Department of Public Administration, University of Jordan, Amman, Jordan
j.zoubi@ju.edu.jo

Abstract. In this article, we argue that the lack of theoretical definition in the literature related to open-source governance opens the floor for multiple possibilities to define it. Therefore, the existence of a baseline to refer to a robust governance solution is deemed crucial. We posit that defining vertical product domains as a benchmark to measure governance solutions robustness helps in theory advancement in governance literature. The creation of vertical product domains is the output of successful open-source projects due to the transformation of open sourcing. We develop a conceptual understanding to precisely define the vertical domains in open-source projects and future agenda for open source governance theory advancement.

Keywords: Open-source software · Vertical domains · Governance

1 Introduction

Since the early years of the twenty-first century, Open-source software (OSS) supporters have called to liberate developers by allowing them to run, copy, distribute, study, and improve software codes (Stallman 2002). Open-source software (OSS) is the source code used and distributed under open source licenses (Raymond 1998; O'Mahony 2003; de Laat 2007). These licenses are restrictive and permissive ones.

For the restrictive licensing, the software shall remain open sourced. All decentralized collaborations (technical and non-technical) between the heterogenous software developers inside and outside the organization's boundaries are combined to create and reshare software codes. Researchers found that such software is a general software such as an operating system that can be implemented across the different industries (Fitzgerald 2006). Therefore, governance in this case works as an input to trigger participants'

© IFIP International Federation for Information Processing 2022
Published by Springer Nature Switzerland AG 2022
A. Elbanna et al. (Eds.): TDIT 2022, IFIP AICT 660, pp. 137–141, 2022.
https://doi.org/10.1007/978-3-031-17968-6_11

motivations to participate (Crowston et al. 2012); not only do the intrinsic and extrinsic motivations for participants determine their participation attitude, but also the governance solution used (in terms of license type for example) (Lerner and Tirole 2005b) will also determine if such a project is an "itch worth scratching" (Raymond 1999a).

However, for the permissive licensing, the license of the modified software can be changed and the software may be privatized. Accordingly, companies that participate in the development of the OSS under permissive licensing may be negatively affected; their contributions may be privatized by other competitors. As a result, governance is becoming even more critical than before to protect participants' intellectual property whom are unwilling to forfeit their intellectual property for nothing (O'Mahony 2003). Therefore, Governance should take a new theoretical direction with the introduction of permissive licenses because interested individual customers or commercial firms (simply, the market) can consequently interfere with changing the project license and the technical future. This means that Governance is currently affected by market variables.

Literature reviews have focused on Governance as a solution to sustain motivations rather than paying attention to the market effect on these solutions. In this paper, we are redirecting the theoretical attention from the process of developing a general OSS software that can be used across the different industries and governing its participants motivations and collaboration styles toward the process of developing a software that is directed by a market and is implemented across a niche or a specific market; this is referred to as a vertical domain software (Fitzgerald 2006). The long-term implication of accomplishing the article aims to move the open-source theory from enriching the literature about different governance solutions to providing practical solutions supported by theory and implemented in an open-source environment.

The finding of this theoretical paper will help in suggesting aspects for OSS vertical domain as well as providing a governance research agenda for each aspect.

2 Literature Review

Open-source software (OSS) is the source code used and distributed under OSS licenses (Raymond 1998; O'Mahony 2003; de Laat 2007). It confirms the central role played by the decentralized collaboration between the heterogeneous software developers inside and outside the organization's boundaries while keeping the same spirit of intellectual rights that immensely differs from the proprietary software property rights.

Studying OSS governance is challenging for researchers because governance definition in the literature is divergent. Researchers neither agreed upon a robust definition nor common characteristics to deal with Governance. This divergence makes it hard for researchers to identify variables for governance measurement. It is believed in this article that we need to shift our focus from traditional Governance to a robust governance solution, solutions that are effective in fulfilling the projects' output. This is true as "Link to the business world" is the core inner value for OSS. OSS is valued only when linked to business regardless of profits being generated or not.

Traditional governance concepts focus on discussing social values, for example (Kassen 2022). Trust and reputation are the fundamental social values governing OSS communities (Lerner and Tirole 2002a). Moreover, authority and control are discussed in leadership and decision-making necessary to ensure effective participation from contributors (Di Tullio and Staples 2013, Ferraz and Santos 2022). In addition, ownership and licensing are another crucial discussion for OSS governance under which the shifting from restrictive to permissive licensing was explored and discussed (Hmoud et al. 2016, O'Mahony, and Karp 2022).

However, the robust governance solutions, as suggested by Fitzgerald (2006), need to stimulate OSS projects in vertical domains either by the creation of OSS with complex business requirements that goes beyond the conventional wisdom of the participants and find their way through the different industry sectors or through the engagement in OSS projects that require more specialized knowledge in a specific industry sector.

3 Research Agenda

3.1 Vertical Domains in Terms of Domain-Specific Applications

Vertical domains include domain-specific applications (Riepula 2011). Those applications can be described according to Yoo et al. (2010) where a novel product software can be developed and gains its power from the heterogeneity of its actors. Instead of developing a general software, it is argued to build a comprehensive vertical domain software that can serve the heterogenous needs of a certain industry or market. This can be implemented by sharing the core software that can be general enough to attract different customers and satisfy their incremental and customizable needs. These needs are transferred into different software requirements and features that are developed as layers of software complementarities. And the final project is undoubtedly complex! It is complex in its requirements, features, compatibility, development, and maintenance.

To do so, heterogenous actors need to be shaped into networks that appraise the role of exchanging resources out of the boundaries of the common hierarchies and markets (Malone et al. 1994). Organizations need to attract actors to design and develop a novel product outside the closed premises where the organization is placed. Moreover, knowledge shared between the heterogenous actors needs to be related to design hierarchies that produce an unexpected product with brilliant components that all fit together in different layers of software technologies. It is believed that governing a complex novel software needs to focus on:

- How the different contributions in OSS projects can be combined to produce one complex project that is effective than creating different projects solely?
- What processes can be used to mine the information generated by the different contributors to produce the needed knowledge? How conflicts over different knowledge and systems development processes can be managed?
- What are the challenges of finding the robust social arrangements that could be addressed by the participants? And how the productivity of the open source project would affect their incentives to collaborate?
- How to measure the effect of the market (contributors that are individual customers or employees in commercial firms) on the open source governance?

3.2 Vertical Domains in Terms of Sector Oriented Projects.

Vertical domains include mission-critical applications (Poba-Nzaou et al. 2014). The emphasis of this article is on the vertical domains that are more oriented toward a specific mission, such as ERP in higher education and healthcare sectors. The OSS projects aim to pool the contributors' resources to reduce the cost and increase the performance and control (Dolphin 2014), as well as share risks, which are achieved through appropriate governance mechanisms. Reducing the cost refers to investing through capacity building, knowledge sharing, and human resources development. Increasing the performance results from sharing resources, skills, and experiences. In terms of control, mission critical OSS projects are considered a solution for the build-buy dilemma when adopting information technology by providing the organization more control over the software in terms of maintenance, customizations, and support.

As their requirements are specific, vertical OSS products are designed and maintained by knowledgeable and experienced developers in that area. This also may require developers to be paid to contribute to the OSS project.

- Based on the above discussion, the following governance questions are suggested:
- What are the formal and defined coordination mechanisms used?
- How OSS communities govern the public and private tensions between contributors?
- What are the rules governing the collaboration between contributors?
- How are monitoring and sanction going to be practiced I these new settings?

4 Conclusion

This paper suggested the vertical domains perspective of OSS projects would fit as a benchmark to measure governance robustness for OSS projects. Such perspecruive is argued to contribute to theory advancement for OSS governance literature as new direction for governance research questions are suggested.

References

Benlian, A., Hess, T.: Opportunities and risks of software-as-a-service: findings from a survey of IT executives. Decis. Support Syst. **52**(1), 232–246 (2011)

Crowston, K., Wei, K., Howison, J., Wiggins, A.: Free/Libre open-source software development: What we know and what we do not know. ACM Comput. Surv. (CSUR) **44**(2), 1–35 (2008)

De Laat, P.B.: Governance of open source software: state of the art. J. Manage. Gov. **11**(2), 165–177 (2007)

Di Tullio, D., Staples, D.S.: The governance and control of open source software projects. J. Manag. Inf. Syst. **30**(3), 49–80 (2013)

Ferraz, I.N., Santos, C.D.D.: Transformation of free and open source software development projects: governance between the cathedral and bazaar. Revista de Administração de Empresas, 62 (2022)

Fitzgerald, B.: The transformation of open source software. MIS Q. 587–598 (2006)

Henri, F., Pudelko, B.: Understanding and analysing activity and learning in virtual communities. J. Comput. Assist. Learn. **19**(4), 474–487 (2003)

Hmoud, H.Y.: The 'private-collective' innovation model under permissive licensing: a case study of OpenNebula open source software (Doctoral dissertation, University of Nottingham) (2018)

Kassen, M.: Open data governance in Sweden: government data transparency in the context of social democracy. In: Open Data Governance and Its Actors. SNGET, pp. 97–132. Springer, Cham (2022). https://doi.org/10.1007/978-3-030-92065-4_5

Lerner, J., Tirole, J.: The scope of open source licensing. J Law Econ Organ **21**(1), 20–56 (2005)

Markus, M.L.: The governance of free/open source software projects: monolithic, multidimensional, or configurational? J. Manage. Governance **11**(2), 151–163 (2007)

O'Mahony, S.: Guarding the commons: how community managed software projects protect their work. Res. Policy **32**(7), 1179–1198 (2003)

O'Mahony, S., Karp, R.: From proprietary to collective governance: How do platform participation strategies evolve? Strateg. Manag. J. **43**(3), 530–562 (2022)

Poba-Nzaou, P., Uwizeyemungu, S., Raymond, L., Paré, G.: Motivations underlying the adoption of ERP systems in healthcare organizations: insights from online stories. Inf. Syst. Front. **16**(4), 591–605 (2012). https://doi.org/10.1007/s10796-012-9361-1

Raymond, E.: The Cathedral and the Bazaar: Musings on Linux and Open Source by an Accidental Revolutionary, USA, O'Reilly Media, Inc (1999a)

Raymond, E. . The Magic Cauldron (1999b). http://www.catb.org/esr/writings/magic-cauldron/magic-cauldron.html#toc1 2014]. Accessed 10 Apr 2022

Riepula, M.: Sharing source code with clients: a hybrid business and development model. IEEE Softw. **28**(4), 36–41 (2011)

Rolandsson, B., Bergquist, M., Ljungberg, J.: Open source in the firm: opening up professional practices of software development. Res. Policy **40**(4), 576–587 (2011)

Stallman, R.:Free software, free society: Selected essays of Richard M. Stallman. Lulu. Com (2022)

Yoo, Y., Henfridsson, O., Lyytinen, K.: Research commentary—the new organizing logic of digital innovation: an agenda for information systems research. Inf. Syst. Res. **21**(4), 724–735 (2010)

IS Use and Impact in Context

Setting Goals in a Digital Transformation of Environmental Assessment: A Case Study

Ashna Mahmood Zada[✉] ⓘ, Peter Axel Nielsen ⓘ, and John Stouby Persson ⓘ

Department of Computer Science, Aalborg University, Selma, Lagerlöfsvej 300, 9220 Aalborg, Denmark
amza@cs.aau.dk

Abstract. Since The Sustainable Development Goals (SDGs) emerged in 2015, they have become a guide for managing present sustainability challenges. However, we have limited knowledge about inter-organizational goal setting for digital transformations towards sustainable development. Recognizing this shortcoming, we report an in-depth case study of an inter-organizational digital transformation and the challenges of setting goals towards promoting progress on SDGs in environmental assessments. An environmental assessment is an obligatory procedure securing environmental concerns are considered before a decision is made, either for individual projects or public plans and programs. From analyzing the activities in environmental assessments, we outline their distinct digitalization goals and the stakeholders' associated experiences. These findings extend preliminary research on what drives digital transformation in environmental assessment and highlight environmentally responsible activities where information systems can make a difference. The paper discusses how these findings show a further need for research on the digital transformation of environmental assessment.

Keywords: Digital transformation · Environmental assessment · Inter-organization · Case-study

1 Introduction

Digital transformation and sustainability stand as leading trends shaping our society. The sustainable development goals (SDGs) have set a common agenda and have been accepted as shared sustainability goals since their adaptation in 2015. The SDGs contain longer-term and more diverse goals (e.g., climate action, economic growth, responsible consumption, and production) meant to encourage organizations towards sustainable development. Yet, there are unutilized opportunities for digitalization to aid a transformation towards sustainable development [3, 8, 19]. The call to tackle societal challenges in the IS domain often reiterates that solutions call for holistic, transdisciplinary, and interdisciplinary attempts to which different disciplines, including Information Systems (IS), must contribute [18, 39]. However, too few studies on environmental sustainability include the IS perspective, despite evidence pointing towards a positive relationship between digitalization and sustainability [11, 27].

© IFIP International Federation for Information Processing 2022
Published by Springer Nature Switzerland AG 2022
A. Elbanna et al. (Eds.): TDIT 2022, IFIP AICT 660, pp. 145–162, 2022.
https://doi.org/10.1007/978-3-031-17968-6_12

On its own, implementing or adopting a digital technology does not correspond to digital transformation [36]. Instead, digital transformation is the leverage of technology in a specific context that necessitates changes in the organizational and societal structure, which opens for innovative ways to create value in this emerging and ever-changing environment [1, 5]. While, digital transformation impacts value creation and value capture, it has also taken a stance as a pervasive influence, where digital products become more the rule than the exception [19]. As digital transformation changes most areas of society [28, 33, 35], the role of digital technologies in digital transformation encompasses paradoxes and uncalled-for burdens [39, 41]. Thus, the process of digital transformation within IS research is still not well understood [12, 32, 37]. More specifically research indicate that paradoxical externalities [14] may emerge from complex digital transformations, however, we still lack an understanding of how to navigate complex digital transformation, distinctly how to navigate different stakeholders digitalization goals in digital transformations towards sustainable development/advancing SDGs. Motivated by this observation, we report an attempt to coherently explain this shortcoming with an in-depth case study of setting digitalization goals in an inter-organizational digital transformation of environmental assessments (i.e., EAs) in Denmark towards the SDGs, by addressing the research question: How can we understand the digitalization goals of different stakeholders in a digital transformation of environmental assessment (EA)?

An environmental assessments (EA) is obligatory when building a new bridge or raising 150 m high wind turbines according to two EU Directives known as 'Environmental Impact Assessment' and 'Strategic Environmental Assessment'. EA is a procedure securing those environmental concerns are considered before a decision is made, either for individual projects or public plans and programs. The EA procedure implies the process of identifying, predicting, evaluating, and mitigating the potential environmental effects of a proposed plan, program, or project, which is documented in a public EA report. The benefits of an EA process lie in supporting better decision-making by considering how a prospective activity can be optimized to minimize or simply avoid negative effects on the environment. Other benefits include actualizing public participation, increasing protections for human health, reducing risks of environmental harm and contributing to sustainable development, paving the way towards the SDGs [20]. Accordingly, the case is an opportunity to improve our understanding of digital transformation tackling the societal challenges of EA and sustainability.

2   Related Research

The research question opens for two types of related research: digital transformation and the sustainable development goals.

2.1   Digital Transformation

Digital transformation is understood to initiate a broad variety of changes in all areas of human society [30, 35, 37]. This understanding warrants three observations, which indicate that digital transformation is not only organization-centric but also social and technological [30]. The distinction between the three perspectives lies in the digital transformation goals. Goals from an organizational perspective may be to discover new business models or alter value creation paths through innovation [15]. Goals from a social perspective may be to improve individuals' quality of life through increased social welfare, collaboration, autonomy in users, and quality of service [15, 37]. Finally, from a technological perspective, digital technologies may become a goal in itself, representing value creation and survival in the new digital reality [30]. It is, however, difficult to draw a clear line between these perspectives because of their interdependence.

Digital technologies have become omnipresent and play a growing role in our lives, making digital transformation the main challenge confronting organizations [33]. Despite its complexity, the growing expectations from the promise of digital transformation motivates organizations to pursue digital transformations. Unsurprisingly, many organizations pursuing digital transformation do not reach their goal and consequently miss out on the expected benefits [28, 36, 42]. The inability to reach digitalization goals indicates that while we may have an advanced understanding of specific aspects of digital transformation, we still have a void in our understanding, and if not addressed, we will continue to build weak assumptions on how digital transformation can be managed and sustained [37].

Digital transformation increases the complexity of the environment in which organizations function and affords more information, communication, and connectivity, as digital technologies enable new collaboration among diversified actors. These affordances also create dependencies among actors whose interests may not always align [2, 37], which points towards how digital transformation may impact inter-organizational collaborations. Digital transformation drives increased collaboration among organizations. However, we need to know more about inter-organizational activities and experiences when embarking on collaborative digital transformation efforts in practice [25, 44]. Inter-organizational collaborations cross organizational borders, which means stakeholders are loosely coupled. Identifying these stakeholders and exploring their perspectives in terms of their interests and goals [4] can be essential steps in establishing a successful digital transformation. This highlights how organizations, which already are considered complex systems due to the multiplicity of groups within them, only become more complex with the addition of external groups. These groups refer to the stakeholders within and outside the organization – those who have a 'stake' in its activities [40]. In our study, SDGs is a key societal stake in the digital transformation of EA.

2.2 Sustainable Development Goals

By the end of the 20th century, the concept of sustainable development became one of the most vital thoughts for society [27]. The concept of being "green" impacts all segments of society and drives us towards sustainable development. However, considering the sustainable development-related research, the exact role of digitalization toward sustainability is unclear, especially in Central Europe [16]. An encompassing definition of sustainability is "development that meets the needs of the present without compromising the ability of future generations to meet their own needs" [20, 26]. Related to this definition is the triple bottom line of economic, social and environmental dimensions, which points to the sustainability concept's complexity and uncertain interdependencies [26].

A set of universal goals (i.e., The Sustainable Development Goals - SDGs) for sustainability emerged in 2015, to meet the urgent environmental, political and economic challenges facing our world. The SDGs became a reference point for global policy-making processes and represented a paradigm shift in which development is considered in every aspect of society [21]. In this regard, much aspiration has been assigned to the relations between the SDGs and EAs and the relevance of integrating SDGs in EAs is widely acknowledged [3]. EAs and their process for identifying, predicting, evaluating, and mitigating the potential environmental effects of a proposed plan, program, or project can play a key role in achieving SDGs. Integrating SDGs in EA means bringing SDGs into the core of formalized decision-making on policies, plans and projects. Further, EA can provide a systematic framework for understanding the effects of decisions on SDGs [3].

With the overall growing awareness of economic, political and environmental concerns, sustainability has become a necessity. As a result, Green has emerged as a new subfield in the IS discipline. Green IS has become an accomplished field with the responsibility and potential for IS scholars to contribute to reducing and mitigating the effects of many environmental problems. While notable achievements have been made in shaping Green IS as a subfield in the IS discipline, the emergence of Green IS, is still by far too slow, given the magnitude of the problem, indicating how Green IS can do more [39]. With digital technologies gaining a prominent position in our everyday lives, their vital role in enhancing and promoting a sustainable future has not gone unnoticed. Still, the IS perspective on sustainability is often at the margin of academic and public discussions [3, 34].

The strategic roles of IS (automation, information and transformation) can lead the society towards sustainability. However, the literature concerning sustainability shows that an IT-enabled transformation towards sustainability is just beginning and cannot happen too fast [27, 38]. Thus, current literature leads to an arising question, how do we integrate sustainability strategically during a digital transformation. As exhibited in this section, current research claims that sustainability has become part of the agenda and that digital transformation offers endless opportunities. Correspondingly digital transformation has gone from being a technological opportunity to a pure necessity for managing the needs and expectations of the world's growing population [23]. However, the limited research focusing on the interrelations between digitalization and sustainability is a definite research gap.

3   Research Approach

We address the research question on understanding the digitalization goals of different stakeholders in a digital transformation by investigating the unusual case of EA in Denmark. The case study approach is appropriate to address the nature and complexity of setting goals in its inter-organizational context – a contemporary phenomenon in its real-life setting [2, 45]. Additionally, the case study approach is especially suitable for inquiry in which research and theory are at their early and formative stages [2]. The unusual case [17], an on-going inter-organizational digital transformation of EA in Denmark, is one of the first initiatives towards digitally transforming the way society accesses and communicates information during environmental assessment processes. This case of digital transformation is an initiative that transcends organizational borders and societal interests, which affects both public- and private organizations. Consequently, our case differs from what we commonly know from digital transformation literature. Obtaining in-depth insights from this case can be important for similar inter-organizations and the IS community to advance knowledge of digitalization goals within the EA domain.

3.1 The Case

The digitalization of Danish EAs was initiated in October 2020 as a partnership between 15 public and private organizations creating an inter-organization of different stakeholders organized in an innovation project called DREAMS, www.dreamsproject.dk. According to the project charter, the overall goal is: "to promote progress on SDGs by digitally transforming the way society accesses and communicates information about environmental impacts of projects and plans in order to enable the best decisions towards green transition in a transparent and inclusive democratic process". To achieve this goal two solutions were proposed (i.e., CAUSA and baseline). CAUSA is the more novel tool, which is expected to provide the involved stakeholders with an overview of how similar activities in a specific geography were assessed, including impacts and mitigation measures. Additionally, CAUSA will include interlinkages to the SDGs. Whereas the open-access baseline tool is expected to provide an overview of environmental data. Prior to the DREAMS project, the involved stakeholders had access to different digitalized solutions (i.e., both internal and public solutions). Whilst the existing solutions affords the stakeholders in several ways, they also come with challenges. More specifically, the current practice has drawbacks as highly manual (e.g., sharing of word documents, XL-files and PDFs with attachments between different actors), time-consuming (e.g., searching for heterogenous data) causing inefficient EA processes.

Accordingly, the relevance of the digitalization of EA is supported and positively perceived across stakeholders invested in the DREAMS project (i.e., consultants, developers, authorities, and civil society). EAs occur on the basis of two EU Directives and known as 'Environmental Impact Assessment' and 'Strategic Environmental Assessment'). The EA procedure implies the process of identifying, predicting, evaluating, and mitigating the potential environmental effects of a proposed plan, program or project, which is documented in a public EA-report.

EA reports must be produced before a decision that may significantly affect the environment [31]. An EA procedure occurs when a developer seeks to carry out a certain type of project or plan. Normally it is recommended that the EA process begin as soon as possible so the developer can consider the analysis of their proposed plans (e.g., incorporate mitigation measures into their plans, which will reduce, control or eliminate a project's adverse effects). An EA process's benefits lie in its potential for supporting better decision-making by considering how a prospective project or plan can be optimized to minimize or avoid negative effects on the environment. Other benefits include public participation, protections for human health, reducing risks of environmental harm and contributing to sustainable development, paving the way towards the SDGs. In realizing these benefits, the EA must consider cumulative environmental effects, their significance, public comments, mitigation measures, changes to a project caused by the environment, its purpose, and alternative means of carrying it out. These considerations include different actors (i.e., developers, consultants, governmental agencies, regional authorities and civil society). Accordingly, the different actors contribute to distinct activities. A developer is responsible for preparing a project description, a draft concerning scoping, ensuring that competent experts (e.g., consultants) develop environmental impact assessment (i.e., EIA). The developer is also responsible for modifying the EA project and EIA draft based on the citizens' or governmental agencies' input. Governmental agencies and regional authorities' responsibilities include appointing affected authorities, conducting hearings with affected authorities and the public, processing the received EIA, and preparing a draft concerning verdict regarding approval. Once again, these agencies are responsible for having a hearing with affected authorities and the public to decide the verdict and make it publicly known. Thus, an EA is a comprehensive social effort to identify, predict and evaluate potential environmental effects of a proposed project or plan prior to undertaking the action. The digital transformation of EAs in Denmark is interesting because: 1) it is one of the first initiatives towards transforming the way society accesses and communicates information during EA processes, and 2) Denmark is one of the most digitalized countries, making Denmark a likely frontrunner.

3.2 Data Collection and Data Analysis

The research was conducted as part of the larger innovation project, DREAMS. We collected empirical data for this case study through qualitative interviews and participant observation [29]. The participant observations covered several workshops in which different stakeholders, each representing a different function during the EA procedure, discussed the problem area. The workshops were conducted and led by the DREAMS project, consequently resulting in secondary data obtained through observations. The stakeholders mainly discussed two questions: (1) which challenges and problems do you experience in relation to your current environmental assessments practice and (2) how do you see digitalization can best alleviate the challenges and problems and help to develop the good EA process and report.

The interviews were semi-structured and followed an interview guide with a point of departure in current work practices, visions for digitalization and perception of DREAMS project's objectives. The guide included questions such as: "What could be a good digitalization goal for the upcoming year" and "What challenges do you experience in your current work practice?" and "How do you see the DREAMS project impact your work practice?". Consequently, the interview guide was a means of encouragement for the participants to give a detailed description of goals, the problem area including experienced challenges. The intention was to interview key stakeholders, and these were selected in detail based on consultations with an expert from the DREAMS project and our observations during stakeholder workshops. Overall, the making of an EA report involves different actors, each contributing with different input (i.e., developers who builds e.g., highways, bridges, tubes, wind turbines, consultants who has the responsibility of writing an EA report, agencies and authorities who consults on prospective EA projects or plans and civil society who discusses prospective EA projects or plans). Accordingly, we interviewed two key stakeholders from each stakeholder group to ensure that the empirical data was inclusive. The qualitative interviews cover 10 encounters, each consisting of less or more than one-hour durations (see, Table 1). All encounters were documented through audio recordings, observation notes and interview summaries.

Table 1. Data collection

Stakeholder type	Organization	Duration
Consultant	NIRAS	46:47
Consultant	COWI	31:56
Governmental agencies	Danish energy agency	47:06
Governmental agencies	The danish environmental protection agency	35:66
Regional authorities	Municipality of Aarhus	1:19:18
Regional authorities	Municipality of Esbjerg	59:13
Developer	The danish road Directorate	44:40
Developer	BaneDK	42:57
Civil society	The Danish society for Nature conservation	16:35
Civil society	DinGeo	14:25

Soft System Methodology was used to thematize and systematize the analysis of digitalization goals. The Soft System Methodology grounded analysis first led to a list of desired goals expressed by stakeholders, to create an overview of the diverse views and interest of change in the DREAMS project. From this, a brief list of relevant human activity systems was created, and for these root definitions were formulated [9, 10]. The most central of these human activity systems and the by far most reemerged became the system to materialization of EAs illustrated in Fig. 1. Thus, the activities documented in Fig. 1 are elicited from the collected data. An EA operates as an administrative document, explaining why the making and the activities in the conceptual model layout a practice that is already settled on a legal basis. The activities in Fig. 1 are thus expected to remain unchanged in the digital transformation. However, this constancy of activities does not prevent the actors in the problem situation from being supported differently.

4 Findings

This section reports the findings from our analyses. The conceptual model of activities for making an EA and the logical dependencies between these activities is shown in Fig. 1. As Fig. 1 emphasizes some activities more than others are highly dependent on each other and occur simultaneously. Figure 1 comprises the most necessary and most minimal set of activities during the making of EA projects and reports. Accordingly, the eight activities include tracing early activities in the EA process to the collaboration between actors to approve or reject an environmental assessment project.

In the following, we account for each activity as outlined in Fig. 1 and each stakeholder's goals for digitalization. These goals for how the practice ought to be are explicitly formed in the specific activity and emphasize how goals for the digital transformation

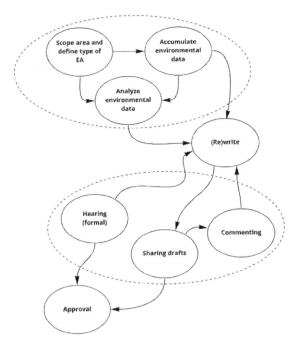

Fig. 1. Activities in making EA projects and plans documented in EA reports

are embedded in said activity. The goals are formed by the experiences stakeholders have faced in each activity. Accordingly, our analysis accounts for the space where digitalization and experiences meet, while still acknowledging that goal setting also can involve other concerns (e.g., ownership, responsibility, and accountability for meeting digital transformation objectives).

4.1   Scoping, Accumulating, and Analyzing

Scoping, accumulating, and analyzing is a pre-requisite when initiating a prospective EA project. These activities are highly influenced by developers, consultants, governmental agencies, and regional authorities. These stakeholders each influence the activities differently, consequently making them relevant in different ways during these activities. The developers are the first instance since they often present a prospective EA project. Accordingly, a developer will have to be part of scoping the project (e.g., what is being built, working methods, information regarding areas to be used, both permanently and temporary). However, scoping happens in close collaboration with consultants and is often not done by developers themselves in practice. But, as Fig. 2 outlines, this is not easy and rather time consuming because data are scattered and not always uploaded, making it difficult to initiate a new EA project.

   The prospective project provided by a developer is then put in supply and won by a consultant based on different factors (e.g., economics, time, and quality). The consultant's primary role is to ensure that the prospective EA project can be realized,

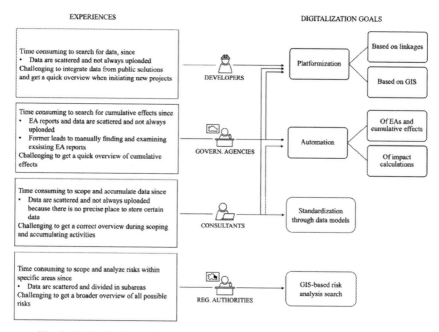

Fig. 2. Digitalization goals for scoping, accumulating, and analyzing activities

which emphasizes iterative collaboration between developers and consultants. Whether or not an EA project can be realized is based on the scoping, accumulation, and analysis of data. If data uncover something that would hinder the realization of a prospective EA, the project will be adapted accordingly. However, scoping, and accumulating data is not a straightforward process and is time consuming, because data are scattered and not always uploaded making it difficult to get a correct overview.

The affected governmental agency's primary function when receiving an application (e.g., concerning a project or a plan from a developer) is to get an overview of the cumulative effects the prospective EA project or plan can have besides the ones already identified. The search for cumulative effects takes place through public platforms, internal GIS solutions and/or looking through existing EAs reports with similar scope to get an overview of already identified cumulative effects. However, getting a quick overview of possible cumulative effects is time consuming as data are scattered and not always uploaded. Like the governmental agencies, the regional authorities receive an application for a prospective EA project or plan. However, their role is primarily to scope and analyze the risks within specific areas, so that possible problems can be allocated as early as possible and a discussion of how these can be minimized. However, as an EA project or plan contain multiple subareas, getting a broader view can be difficult. What reoccurs in the experiences of the different stakeholders is how these activities are described as time consuming because data are scattered, which makes it difficult to get an overview. While the reoccurrence in experiences indicates a common problem (e.g., lack of overview of data), the digitalization goals point towards some consensus and different perceptions of how this problem can be sorted.

The digitalization goal with the most support is platformization. While developers, governmental agencies, and consultants share the same perception of the goal (e.g., platformization), there are some differences between their views. Developers and governmental agencies indicate the platformization should be based on GIS as this will ease the process of realizing what is relevant to assess. Consultants specify that platformization based on linkages will aid the access to data, which supports valid arguments and similar EAs reports who states the same, leading to a correct overview of existing data. In addition, there was a similar perception of digitalization goals between governmental agencies and consultants (e.g., automation). However, there is a difference in understanding what exactly should be automated. While these mentioned goals have backing from several stakeholders, other goals were only declared by one stakeholder. Consultants experience that not all data is uploaded, indicating doubt about where specific data should be uploaded. According to the consultants, the solution would be standardization through data models, emphasizing that all data should have a unique identifier used across organizations involved in EA reports. As a result of challenges when scoping and analyzing risks, regional authorities point towards a GIS-based risk analysis search. According to regional authorities, this digitalization goal should ease getting a broader overview of possible risks when assessing a prospective EA project.

4.2 (Re)write

(Re)writing an EA report is not a standardized practice, as no formal requirement is legally dictated, the law only states that an EA report must be written by a competent person (e.g., often consultants), stressing how consultants are extremely relevant for this activity. An EA report is a legal document that must be approved and stored in either regional or state archives. Consequently, an EA report is based on documentation (e.g., sums up seven out of eight activities in writing supplemented by visualizations), and the progression of outlining and writing an EA report occurs sequentially. Working sequentially might make the process of writing an EA report easier for the consultants. Still, it is problematic when confronted with adjustments from governmental agencies, civil society and regional authorities late in the process. As the initiators behind a prospective EA project, the developers do not directly write the EA report but oversee the consultants' work, which leads to continuous adjustments to decrease the number of adjustments in the final reporting phase. Besides writing the EA report, the responsibilities of consultants also include informing developers whenever a reason for changes to an EA project occurs (e.g., the project is hindered). Accordingly, there is a close collaboration between consultants and developers. However, it is difficult for developers to see the progression in an EA report. While the consultants' experiences indicate that the sequential approach hinders quicker correct decision making, developers express how the iterative process hinders a transparent view of changes. The regional authorities express the problem of being the last instance to view the EA report. Both consultants, developers and regional authorities point towards the same problem and share the goal of minimizing these problems. Consultants, developers and regional authorities see the benefits of having a more iterative collaboration between actors and believe this can be supported through a collaborative content-management system.

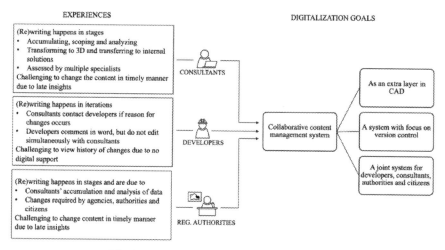

Fig. 3. Digitalization goals for (re)write activity

As outlined in Fig. 3, a notable distinction between the digitalization goals expressed by developers, regional authorities and consultants is the focus on the content-management system in the more traditional sense as opposed to visualization. The developers and regional authorities describe their digitalization goals more traditionally. While developers see it as a tool for more collaboration, focusing on version control to increase transparency, the regional authorities perceive the digitalization to increase collaboration between developers, consultants, authorities, and citizens. Contrary, the consultants focus on a visual collaboration tool, which should add an extra layer in already utilized CAD programs. According to consultants having this extra layer in CAD might make it possible to monitor actions across organizations, consequently increasing the pace for decision making and even helping predict adjustments in a more timely manner. This digitalization goal is rather different from the current collaboration between consultants and other specialists, which happens much more sequentially, leading to impractical work.

4.3   Sharing, Commenting, and Hearing

Sharing, commenting, and hearing activities are essential for the quality of an EA report. These activities are highly influenced by governmental agencies, consultants, regional authorities, and the civil society. While the consultants are responsible for changing an EA report when required, governmental agencies, regional authorities and civil society share the responsibility of pointing towards adjustments. Accordingly, an EA report is often reviewed several times before the content is satisfactory. While several rounds of reviews increase the quality of a prospective EA report, they also come with challenges for the stakeholders. During these rounds of reviews governmental agencies provide adjustments in a commenting sheet, which is divided in general and specific comments. This commenting sheet is shared amongst subspecialist so that the comments can be forwarded collectively to the responsible consultants and developers. Consequently, when receiving the modified EA report, it is a challenge for governmental agencies to distinguish between old and new content. In addition, governmental agencies addressed how citizens tend to draw their ideas for modifications by hand to supplement their comments. While the ideas are good, they are not always easy to interpret. This difficulty makes it challenging for consultants to incorporate them, consequently becoming a weak point during hearings addressing why and which ideas and adjustments were taken into account.

Meanwhile, consultants face another challenge connected to the process of sharing and commenting, which takes place sequentially. However, this challenge does not involve comments from governmental agencies and regional authorities but rather the sharing and commenting processes between internal and external collaborators writing the EA report. An EA report is roughly equivalent to a document based on data and different environmental knowledge. The issue of having a sequential approach is that subspecialists attached to an EA project do not have an early discussion on what can be realized based on their prospective knowledge. Like the consultants, regional authorities experience challenges in becoming aware of adjustments. Regional authorities additionally share how comments can be difficult to distinguish between since these originate from multiple places. While the governmental agencies, consultants, and regional authorities express their challenges in terms of the review round, civil society deals with challenges of a different character. Citizens tend to be faced with two challenges: 1) having difficulties understanding larger and more complex EA reports and

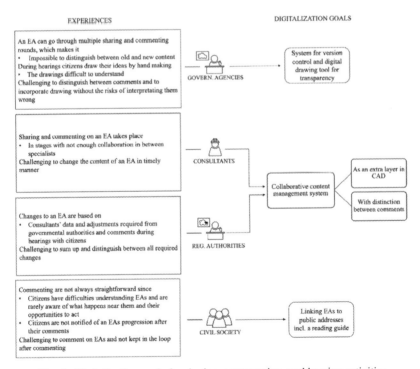

Fig. 4. Digitalization goals for sharing, commenting, and hearing activities

knowing what opportunities they have to influence an EA project, making it difficult to comment and 2) if commenting on an EA report, citizens tend to be kept out of the process that follows, making them unable to get insight into how their comments are being addressed.

Since the consultants and regional authorities share similar challenges during specifically sharing and commenting activities, they also share similar views of digitalization goals (cf. Fig. 4) being a collaborative content management system with some differences in between. Governmental agencies and civil society's dissimilar challenges are also reflected in their very different digitalization goals. What was especially surprising was that the governmental agencies even made a digitalization goal for citizens (e.g., digital drawing tool, which includes an overview of the area of concern) based on their observations during hearings. As a means for easier distinction in old and new content during the multiple commenting rounds, governmental agencies envisioned a system for version control and are already working towards this goal internally in the organization. Meanwhile, the civil society's digitalization goal is different. Their challenge lies in understanding the content of EA reports, their opportunities to influence an EA project and what is happening near them. The citizens' challenges are reflected in the expressed digitalization goals. However, what was surprising was that the consultants mentioned how the citizens' digitalization goal is partially realized as digitalized EA reports linked to public addresses exists. This can point towards a lack of transparency between stakeholders relevant for making EA reports and the civil society.

4.4 Approval

The last activity of an EA process is deciding whether a prospective EA project is approved and can be initiated. Relevant for this activity is especially the affected governmental agencies and regional authorities, as they are the last instance assessing the prospective EA project, concluding its approval or rejection. The decision regarding an EA project's approval or rejection must be published. As mentioned, an EA report tends to go through multiple rounds of commenting and sharing. Regardless of an EA project's origin (i.e., initiated by the Danish parliament or from a private developer) the EA project follows these same procedures (e.g., the eight activities outlined in Fig. 1). However, a difference is that while an EA project initiated by the Danish parliament has been adopted by legislation, EA projects initiated by private developers are dependent on several paragraph approvals (i.e., §20 in the Nature Conservation Act).

Usually, hearings are physical. However, due to the COVID-19 pandemic, hearings were virtual. Both governmental agencies and regional authorities agree that virtually performing hearings has advantages and disadvantages. The most emphasized advantages were the ease for citizens to participate in the hearings from the comfort of their homes and, consequently, the change in participant demographic for these hearings. The most emphasized disadvantages were that the alternation between physical and virtual hearings complicates summing up comments. Accordingly, the digitalization goals expressed by the governmental agencies and regional authorities share similarities as they stem from similar experiences and challenges and have a common wish for a digital hearing portal.

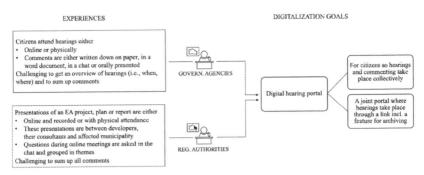

Fig. 5. Digitalization goals for approval activity

5 Discussion and Conclusion

This research aims to advance knowledge on how different stakeholders' digitalization goals can be understood in a digital transformation of environmental assessment. With an unusual case of digitally transforming Danish EAs, we analyzed the stakeholders' experiences using Soft System Methodology [9, 10] to develop a conceptual model of necessary activities for making EA projects and reports (see Fig. 1). Next, we tied the stakeholders' different experiences from the eight identified activities to their digitalization goals. As a result, our findings (see Figs. 2–5) uncovered more nuanced and specific digitalization goals for EAs, as these relate to the specific stakeholders' activities during an EA process. Our findings distinguish four overarching digitalization goals across these stakeholders (i.e., platformization, collaborative content management system, automatization, and digital hearing portal). We explain the stakeholder's different descriptions of the same digitalization goals with their different experiences from the EA activities.

Our findings expand current IS literature on digital transformation by explaining stakeholders' digitalization goals (i.e., through experiences and relating these to specific activities). To the best of our knowledge, existing research concerning digital transformation has not explicitly related digitalization goals to the stakeholder' experiences from a specific activity. Existing research divides digitalization goals into three perspectives (i.e., organizational, social and technology) and identifies goals as strategic roles of information technology (i.e., automate, informate-up, informate-down and transform) [30, 37]. We do not reject the relevance of dividing digital transformation goals into three perspectives (i.e., organizational, social and technological), nor the identified goals (i.e., automate, informate-up, informate-down and transform) [30, 37] as these goals relates to our identified goals (i.e., platformization, collaborative content management system, automatization and digital hearing portal). However, we critique how existing research focuses on abstract and broad sweeping digitalization goals with the risk of digital transformations detached from stakeholders' activities and experiences. The no-win situation being undergoing a digital transformation (i.e., utilizing resources, time, finances) only to realize that affected stakeholders do not see the purpose of the digital transformation and consequently will not contribute to the transformation nor use the implemented digital technologies.

IS literature widely recognizes that digital transformations should begin with a vision and then determine a coherent goal to be achieved [7, 13, 22, 28]. Still, an inability to reach digitalization goals is not uncommon [28, 36, 42]. Existing literature emphasizes that the chance of superior outcomes rises when stakeholders have a shared understanding of goals [6]. While literature unfolds challenges of setting goals during digital transformation [7], there is very little research on achieving shared goal setting in digital transformations [25].

The literature suggests that two variables should be considered: the company size and its activities [44]. Thus, we propose managing digitalization goals by attending to who the goals are for, what experiences they are grounded in, for key activities of EA, and other areas undergoing digital transformation. Setting goals in this way is particularly important for inter-organizations where stakeholders are more loosely coupled, making it more difficult to recognize a common drive for a prospective digital transformation. However, managing stakeholders' diverse but legitimate goals in an inter-organization should be recognized as a key challenge in inter-organizational digital transformation. Approaching goal setting by mapping them to different stakeholders, experiences and activities allows stakeholders to participate in and see the goalsetting process. This participation can enhance goal commitment, help confirm that the goals are not irrational, improve stakeholders' understanding of the goals, and help them achieve the goal [24]. We stress that goals cannot simply be assigned effectively throughout an organization and much less in inter-organizational collaboration about digital transformation.

IS researchers concerned with digital transformation or Green IS have not previously investigated digitalization goals within EA processes, despite its importance for reducing and mitigating the effects of environmental problems. EAs should interest IS researchers wanting to address the calls for IS research on environmental sustainability [11, 26]. While digital transformation and sustainability receive growing attention from IS researchers, limited research has investigated digital transformation and sustainability together [8, 16]. The specification of nuanced digitalization goals for EAs furthers the current understanding of the interplay between sustainability and digitalization, which is currently addressed as a positive relationship [11, 26]. This study's findings thus nuance digitalization goals for EAs as an orientation towards the SDGs and thus further our understanding of digital technologies for the SDGs achievement. Correspondingly, these findings provide preliminary research on what goals drives digital transformation in EA and highlight environmentally responsible activities where IS can make a difference.

In conclusion, our research expands previous studies on the interplay between digital transformation and sustainability, deepening the discourse on initiating inter-organizational digital transformations in practice. Additionally, this study unfolds how establishing a fit between transformational objectives and the diverse digitalization goals of stakeholders should be recognized as one of the main challenges in digital transformations. We acknowledge that addressing an unusual case provides limitations in terms of transferability. However, to further this research we recommend two directions for future research. First, we recommend examining how the proposed goals and experiences can inform other domains, by studying related cases. Second, we suggest a specific focus on the *interplay* between digital transformation and SDGs.

Acknowledgement. This project has received funding from Innovation Fund Denmark -0177-00021B DREAMS. We would like to thank the different stakeholders involved in the DREAMS project, especially Lone Kørnøv and Ivar Lyhne for their constructive comments. In closing, a special thanks to all interviewees for sharing their experiences and knowledge, which provided invaluable insights for this research.

References

1. Baiyere, A., Salmela, H., Tapanainen, T.: Digital transformation and the new logics of business process management. Eur. J. Inf. Syst. **29**(3), 238–259 (2020)
2. Benbasat, I., Goldstein, D.K., Mead, M.: The case research: strategy in studies of information systems. MIS Q. **11**(3), 369–386 (1987)
3. Boess, R.E., Kørnøv, L., Lyhne, I., Partidário, R.M.: Integrating SDGs in environmental assessment: Unfolding SDG functions in emerging practices. Environ. Impact Assess. Rev. **90**(February), 106632 (2021)
4. Boonstra, A., de Vries, J.: Managing stakeholders around inter-organizational systems: a diagnostic approach. J. Strat. Inf. Syst. **17**(3), 190–201 (2008)
5. Bordeleau, F.-È., Santa-Eulalia, L.A.D., Mosconi, E.: Digital transformation framework: creating sensing, smart, sustainable and social (Ŝ4) organisations. In: Hawaii International Conference on System Sciences (2021)
6. Brown, N., Brown, I.: From digital business strategy to digital transformation - how? - a systematic literature review. In: Proceedings of ACM SAICSIT conference (SAICSIT '19). ACM, Skukuza, pp. 1–8 (2019)
7. Bucy, M., Finlayson, A., Kelly, G., Moye, C.: The how of Transformation. McKinsey & Company (2016)
8. Castro, G., González Fernández, M.C., Uruburu Colsa, Á.: Unleashing the convergence amid digitalization and sustainability towards pursuing the sustainable development goals (SDGs): a holistic review. J. Clean. Product. **280**, 122204 (2021)
9. Checkland, P.: Systems Thinking, Systems Practice. John Wiley & Sons Ltd, Baffins Lane, Chichester (1981)
10. Checkland, P., Scholes, J.: Soft Systems Methodology in Action. John Wiley & Sons Ltd, Chichester, West Sussex (1990)
11. Camodeca, R., Almici, A.: Digital transformation and convergence toward the 2030 agenda's sustainability development goals: Evidence from Italian listed firms. Sustainability (Switzerland), **13**(21), 11831 (2021)
12. Carroll, N.: Theorizing on the normalization of digital transformations. In: Proceedings of the 28th European Conference on Information Systems (ECIS), An Online AIS Conference, 15–17 June (2020)
13. Chanias, S., Myers, M.D., Hess, T.: Digital transformation strategy making in pre-digital organizations: the case of a financial services provider. J. Strat. Inf. Syst. **28**(1), 17–33 (2019)
14. Dwivedi, K.Y., et al.: Climate change and COP26: are digital technologies and information management part of the problem or the solution? an editorial reflection and call to action. Int. J. Inf. Manag. **63**(102456) (2022). ISSN 0268-4012
15. Ebert, C., Duarte, C.H.C.: Digital transformation. IEEE Softw. **35**(4), 16–21 (2018)
16. Esses, D., Csete, M.S., Németh, B.: Sustainability and digital transformation in the visegrad group of central European countries. Sustainability (Switzerland), **13**(11), 5833 (2021)
17. Flyvbjerg, B.: Five misunderstandings about case-study research. Qual. Inq. **12**(2), 219–245 (2006)

18. Gholami, R., Watson, T.R., Hasan, H., Molla, A., Bjørn-Andersen, N.: Information systems solutions for environmental sustainability: how can we do more?'. J. Assoc. Inf. Syst. **17**(8SpecialIssue), pp. 521–536 (2016)

19. Hausberg, J.P., Liere-Netheler, K., Vogelsang, K., Packmohr, S., Pakura, S.: Research streams on digital transformation from a holistic business perspective: a systematic literature review and citation network analysis. J. Bus. Econ. **89**(8), 931–963 (2019)

20. Hilali, W., Manouar, A.: Towards a sustainable world through a SMART digital transformation. In: ACM International Conference Proceeding Series, Part F1481 (2019)

21. Kørnøv, L., Lyhne, I., Davila, J.G.: Linking the UN SDGs and environmental assessment: towards a conceptual framework. Environ. Impact Assess. Rev. **85**, 106463 (2020)

22. Krey, M.: Digital transformation in swiss hospitals: a reference modeling approach. In: Yang, X.-S., Sherratt, R.S., Dey, N., Joshi, A. (eds.) ICICT 2020. AISC, vol. 1183, pp. 12–27. Springer, Singapore (2021). https://doi.org/10.1007/978-981-15-5856-6_2

23. Kraus, S., Durst, S., Ferreira, J.J., Veiga, P., Kailer, N., Weinmann, A.: Digital transformation in business and management research: An overview of the current status quo. Int. J. Inf. Manag. **63**,102466 (2022). ISSN 0268–4012

24. Lunenburg, F.C.: Goal-setting theory of motivation. Int. J. Manag. Administr. **15**(1), 1–6 (2011)

25. Matt, C., Hess, T., Benlian, A.: Digital transformation strategies. Bus. Inf. Syst. Eng. **57**(5), 339–343 (2015). https://doi.org/10.1007/s12599-015-0401-5

26. Melville, N.P.: Information systems innovation for environmental sustainability. MIS Q. Manag. Inf. Syst. **34**(1), 1–21 (2010)

27. Obradović, V., Todorović, M., Bushuyev, S.: Sustainability and agility in project management: contradictory or complementary? Int. Sci. Tech. Conf. Comput. Sci. Inf. Technol. **2**, 160–164 (2018)

28. Peppard, J.: Tool to map your next digital initiative. Harward Bus. Rev. 1–5 (2020)

29. Patton, M.Q.: Qualitative Research & Evaluation Methods, 4th edn. SAGE Publications Inc, Thousand Oaks, California (2002)

30. Reis, J., Amorim, M., Melão, N., Matos, P.: Digital transformation: a literature review and guidelines for future research. Adv. Intell. Syst. Comput. **745**, 411–421 (2018)

31. Retsinformation. https://www.retsinformation.dk/eli/ft/201512L00147. Accessed 18 Mar 2022

32. Rowe, F.: Being critical is good, but better with philosophy! From digital transformation and values to the future of IS research. Eur. J. Inf. Syst. **27**(3), 380–393 (2018)

33. Schneider, S., Kokshagina, O.: Digital transformation: what we have learned (thus far) and what is next. Creativity Innov. Manag. **30**(2), 384–411 (2021)

34. Sparviero, S., Ragnedda, M.: Towards digital sustainability: the long journey to the sustainable development goals 2030. Digit. Policy Regul. Gov. **23**(3), 216–228 (2021)

35. Stolterman, E., Fors, A.C.: Information technology and the good life. In: Kaplan, B., Truex, D.P., Wastell, D., Wood-Harper, A.T., DeGross, J.I. (eds.) Information Systems Research. IIFIP, vol. 143, pp. 687–692. Springer, Boston, MA (2004). https://doi.org/10.1007/1-4020-8095-6_45

36. Tabrizi, B., Lam, E., Girard, K., Irvin, V.: Digital transformation is not about technology. Harv. Bus. Rev. 2–7 (2019)

37. Vial, G.: Understanding digital transformation: a review and a research agenda. J. Strat. Inf. Syst. **28**(2), 118–144 (2019)

38. Vidmar, D., Pucihar, A.: Systematic Literature Review: Effects of Digital Technology on Business Models and Sustainability. In: Doucek, P., Basl, J., Tjoa, A.M., Raffai, M., Pavlicek, A., Detter, K. (eds.) CONFENIS 2019. LNBIP, vol. 375, pp. 12–23. Springer, Cham (2019). https://doi.org/10.1007/978-3-030-37632-1_2

39. Vom Brocke, J., Watson, T.R., Dwyer, C., Melville, N.: Green information systems: directives for the IS discipline. Commun. Assoc. Inf. Syst. **33**(1), 509–520 (2013)
40. Wang, W., Liu, W., Mingers, J.: A systemic method for stakeholder identification using soft systems methodology. Elsevier B.V. and Association of European Operational Research Societies (2014)
41. Wessel, L., Baiyere, A., Ologeanu-Taddei, R., Cha, J., Jensen, B., T.: Unpacking the difference between digital transformation and it-enabled organizational transformation. J. Assoc. Inf. Syst. **22**(1), 102–129 (2021)
42. Westerman, G., Davenport, T.H.: Why so many high-profile digital transformations fail. Harvard Bus. Rev. 2–6 (2018)
43. Wimelius, H., Mathiassen, L., Holmström, J.: A paradoxical perspective on technology renewal in digital transformation. Inf. Syst. J. **31**(1), 198–225 (2021)
44. Zaoui, F., Souissi, N.: Roadmap for digital transformation: a literature review. Procedia Comput. Sci. **175**, 621–628 (2020)
45. Yin, R.K.: Case Study Research: Design And Methods (Applied Social Research Methods), 5th edn. Sage publications, Thousand Oaks, CA (2013)

Reviewing Transfer and Diffusion of Climate Technology in Households: Towards a Greener IT Future

Jan Pries-Heje[✉], Magnus Rotvit Perlt Hansen, and Jeffrey Andrew Christensen

Department of People and Technology, Roskilde University, Roskilde, Denmark
{janph,magnuha,jeffreyac}@ruc.dk

Abstract. As the gravity of the impact of climate change on everyday life grows ever more relevant, green technology involving sustainability are also garnering more attention, and, in turn, more sophisticated IT solutions are needed. In this paper we review existing literature on the diffusion and transfer of technology in households in order to strengthen and prepare the future adoption of more IT-oriented sustainability solutions of green IT. We find that a large portion of household studies have taken place in the farming and agricultural sector of developing countries. We find that a large portion of the studies propose implications from a government policy perspective. We also find that a large portion of studies confirm factors influencing the diffusion and adoption coming from diffusion theory. Another significant portion takes a socio-cultural approach perspective. Finally, we find that collaboration, co-creation and participation seem to be effective in furthering the transfer and diffusion of sustainable and green technology in households. We discuss the implications of these different approaches when tackling the diffusion of green IT and propose taking a pluralist and design-oriented perspective since no single perspective or approach so far has resulted in large-scale technology transfer or diffusion to households.

Keywords: Green IT · Climate technologies · Households · Diffusion · Adoption · Technology transfer · Socio-cultural · Participatory · Co-creation · Policy

1 Introduction

Both the climate crisis and the pandemic crisis have shown that both change from the top of society to the bottom of society as well as on various societal institutional levels are in dire need of a change of the technologies that consume energy as well as the practices that support this consumption into "climate technologies". Climate technologies are defined by the United Nations Framework Convention on Climate Change (UNFCCC) as technologies that help us reduce greenhouse gas emissions, and with direct relation to sustainable development goals from the UN (Ban 2016). In 2010 they established the so-called technology mechanism to help countries with technology transfer in both a policy

© IFIP International Federation for Information Processing 2022
Published by Springer Nature Switzerland AG 2022
A. Elbanna et al. (Eds.): TDIT 2022, IFIP AICT 660, pp. 163–176, 2022.
https://doi.org/10.1007/978-3-031-17968-6_13

arm and implementation arm. Probably the most well-known part of the mechanism is the conference of the parties – COP held in UK in 2021.

The types of climate technologies include 'hard' as well as 'soft' types. Those designated as 'hard' are renewable low-end technologies such as "wind energy, solar power and hydropower" but also includes "drought-resistant crops, early warning systems and sea walls". Hard technologies also include so-called 'Green information technology' (Green IT) either embedded or as add-ons that support maintenance, monitoring and management. A windmill for example includes chips that interface with dashboards in control centers to ensure that the windmill runs smoothly according to the general weather as well as the energy market. Green IT refers to "environmentally sound IT", including "dimensions of environmental sustainability, the economics of energy efficiency, and the total cost of ownership…" (Murugesan 2008). Green IT can be understood as higher-level information technology that utilizes, platformizes and visualizes low-level climate technologies, such as interfacing with solar panels, smart meters, water consumption surveillance etc. For this very reason the adoption of green IT requires the adoption of several low-end climate technologies as well as hardware and software that can capture data input and output. UNFCCC also includes 'soft' climate technologies, such as "energy-efficient practices or training", e.g. by changing practices in households, that is necessary for green IT to be utilized to its fullest potential (UNFCCC 2021). Various suggestions for how to attain this have been studied: from the diffusion of load shifting household appliances (Paetz et al. 2013) to smart meter implementation with the intention of close energy consumption monitoring to invoke energy-efficient practices (Dalén and Krämer 2017).

Despite an abundance of studies on climate technology adoption in households, we still need more knowledge on approaching the transfer of soft energy-efficient practices leading to stronger green IT adoption. Hence, this study investigates the research question of *"Which approaches to technology adoption in households can be used to further the future adoption of energy-efficient green IT practices in households?"*.

The path to combining green IT, diffusion and adoption, and households is a narrowly travelled road. As a result, technology adoption in households is the foreground focus as this seems to be the most general and fruitful approach to adopting next-level technology such as green IT. We investigate the research question through a structured literature review with the goal of bringing about a future agenda of sustainable and energy-efficient practices of the future, green, everyday household.

The remainder of the paper is structured as follows: First, we explain our method of our structured literature review. Then we outline our results into four main sections, each section shortly explaining the theoretical foundation for the basis of the reviewed results. Based on the results, we finally conclude our research question and discuss the main findings in terms of potential for research in the future.

2   Method

As our research question is focused on a "which" and "what" question, we selected an inductive approach to discover the various strands of literature of diffusion and transfer of technology in households. Similar to Wolfswinkel et al (2013) we took a grounded theory approach of 5 overall steps: 1) defining the scope, 2) search the literature, 3) decide on the sample to be analyzed, 4) analyze literature and 5) presenting the findings.

Our aim of running queries was for them to remain manageable. For example, "behavior" is not the only keyword that describes actions and performances of members in a household; a similar keyword is "practice". While "household" synonyms could also include "family" and "home" we found that the inclusion of these would make the number of results unwieldly and so we decided on only using "household". "Technology", "information technology", and "information systems" were all synonyms and for the process of adoption we used ""adoption", "use", "change". We used the query "TITLE-ABS-KEY (("information technology" OR "technology" OR "information systems") AND (diffusion OR diffuse OR diffusing OR transfer OR transferring) AND ("household") AND ("behaviour" OR "behavior" OR "use" OR "using" OR "practice" OR "practicing" OR "practising" OR "practise")). Initially we included "Green IT" in the query but the query changed very little and we decided to omit this for the sake of simplicity. We further restricted the query to the years 2000–2022 and the overall research areas to business, energy, computer science, psychology and social sciences. We started our search with one initial query on "households, diffusion and transfer of technology" and found relevant literature based on this and identified different versions of central keywords. We chose Scopus as a single database as this historically contains the broadest range of results.

Initial results from Scopus added up to a total of initial 97 results. All abstracts of the initial results pool were read and assessed for inclusion and divided into six different categories.

Table 1. The initial categories and placement of results. Some results fit into more than one category.

#	Category	Description of category	Results
1	Diffusion of Innovations	Based on DoI, adoption and technology transfer theory	29
2	Socio-Cultural	Focus on socio-cultural dimension	10
3	Macro policy	Based on a macro-level societal point of view	17
4	Participatory & co-creation	Focus on participation and/or co-creation as methods/techniques	9
5	Other/minor) category or Not relevant	E.g. very technology specific or simply not relevant for us	12 + 24

Based on Table 1 we then identified explicit inclusion criteria and used these as the means to arrive at a more manageable number of net results. After the initial categorization, the included papers would be read thoroughly and more strict inclusion criteria would be introduced, so both titles and abstracts had to explicitly mention the main keywords, and if so, we would assess whether the paper fitted into an existing category or we should create a new one.

Next step was to code the results through open coding based on the publication outlet, type of publication (theoretical, practical, experimental), methods used, domain, technology type, household definition, and theoretical strands. Next, we axially coded the papers by comparing them to one another based on the dimensions from the axial coding, and finally we selectively coded the papers based on our findings.

The final review ended up identifying current research and knowledge on what influences how households transfer and diffuses new technology in order to find potential for the future of green IT adoption.

3 Findings

Our findings covered 4 overall groups of papers based on their fundamental approach to household technology transfer. 17 related to macro policy suggestions, 29 related to Diffusion of Innovation theory, 10 related to taking a socio-cultural approach, and 9 related to taking a more participatory approach that would also draw on the method of co-creation.

3.1 Diffusion and Transfer Seen from a Macro Policy Level

We found 17 results that all belonged on the "macro policy level". The macro policy level indicates general policies and regulations decided on and implemented by political decision makers and leaders that are then followed or executed by lower "layers" of other policy makers or those receiving or handling technologies and practices for households. We identified additional abstraction layers that made up the macro policy level: "global"; "national"; and "municipal". For all of the macro layers various actions and legislations have been proposed, yet one major finding indicated that for the policies to be effective in enabling diffusion and transfer of technology on the household level, general income for households needs to be increased and pricing of sustainable energy technologies need to be lowered (Alam et al. 2003) to create the possibility of choice (Reddy et al. 2009). Furthermore, the different initiatives taken on the various layers need to be aligned (Dong et al. 2007; Jin et al. 2006; Martiskainen et al. 2018), indicating a strong interdependency between the policies and initiatives and communication between decision-makers and housing managers and communities rather than a centralized or decentralized composition (Habibis et al. 2014). Finally, technology and price have also been indicated to not be enough (Youtie et al. 2007) because:"… the different existing markets, institutions, consumer behaviors and cultural aspects need to be taken into account since in the end the energy has to be used by the people." (Oldenberg et al. 2015, p. 1).

Global Policy Layer

The global layer resides on a strategic and visionary level and did not only include decision and legislation. The 17 sustainability goals of the United Nations is an example of such visions. Another example from our findings includes establishing global networks of energy access innovation centers to increase awareness and potential for similar ideas

(Nathwani and Kammen 2019). Another example where legislation and policy potentially can be established through agreement is through such semi-global institutions as the EU: in a recent report Energy Efficiency Directives ("German Retrofit Policy in Context" 2013) the problem of purely national market-led energy policies is made clear, as there is no concrete agreement on how to organize and define subsidies between EU countries.

National Policy Layer

The national layer is the current enabler but also the current problem as nations currently all legislate differently, leading to various degrees of openness or closedness towards establishing new potential markets and from here potential business models for innovative companies and households to take advantage of.

It includes creating policies for energy efficiency impact of the actual buildings for its occupants to take advantage of the potential for green energy use. A study found that the physical and materiality of the buildings very consistently predicted the energy use, though the largest discrepancy factor involved the type of inhabitants in the households (Zhao et al. 2018). The national layer provides opportunities for establishing large-scale rollouts through funding and resource deployment that are then creating opportunities for households to latch onto, either through subsidies or special tariffs. One example includes how the overall limitations of cost were reduced for buying and establishing a network of household appliances through IoT in the transition to more environmentally friendly devices (Strielkowski et al. 2019). Furthermore, the potential of energy efficacy has been shown to be done through government actively promoting cleaner fuels and consumption as well as setting up policies of investment between the services, construction and equipment industrial sectors (Yang et al. 2015).

Not all literature results point to only investment and promotion, though, and there are also indications of a need to include social influence and beliefs, effort expectancy and price-value beliefs to make households transition to new technologies such as rooftops providing solar energy (Aggarwal et al. 2020; Martiskainen et al. 2018).

Municipal Policy Layer

The municipal layer contains the potential for establishing local communities, incentives, initiatives and awareness that directly link the households to a relatable local whole. Within the municipal layer of green policies resides the notion of *urban development and design* which includes a "master plan" (Oldenberg et al. 2015) for strategies on decarbonization through stronger public transportation, transitioning to electric vehicles while also minimising road congestion, and also establishing scenarios for local development on neighbourhood and community level in regards to assessing carbon footprints and energy optimization. A central result, given these initiatives, is that such technologies as solar photovoltaic technology and its diffusion requires very different pathways based on the geographical locations of the users of the households with a clear spatial difference between suburbs and inner cities, as well as dwelling type (Newton and Newman 2013). The differences of dwelling types were also found to be of great importance for the local policies in the diffusion of photovoltaic rooftop panels where a change in policy to enable installations in community condominiums from increased by 80% (Schiera et al. 2019).

Other examples on the community level includes the establishment of community-run Energy Cafes in the UK that resulted in various forms of advocacy and engagement with energy technologies on a household level (Martiskainen et al. 2018).

Final Thoughts on Macro Policy Level
There is a need for alignment through the various macro policy layers all the way down to the households where the layers depend on one another. Successful transfer and diffusion of green technology in households can only happen by combining subsidy reduction of prices, establishing demand-side markets and innovation of technology but also through matching with community-driven awareness, trust and beliefs.

3.2   The Importance of Including Factors from Diffusion of Innovations Theory

With a majority of the results using and drawing on, and confirming, Roger's (2010) diffusion of innovations theory, one of the identified papers phrased it very well: "The diffusion of innovation theory remains a valid and relevant framework in studying adoption…"
- Nyairo et al. (2021, p. 57).

Originally Rogers defined diffusion as "the process in which an innovation is communicated through certain channels over time among the members of a social system" (Rogers 2010, p. 5). Innovation here is defined as the perception of newness of a thought, an idea or a technology. In our case we would define the innovation to include both soft and hard climate technologies.

Rogers' (2010) define five things that will make an innovation diffuse faster, namely having a relative advantage, being more compatible, being less complex, having observable advantages, and offering trialability. The adopters of innovations are also placed into five overall groups: (1) Innovators, (2) Early adopters, (3) Early majority, (4) Late majority and (5) Laggards. The first two groups are more open to new ideas and willing to try out technologies whereas the latter 3 become gradually more content with waiting on the technology to mature.

How to shape Climate Technologies in the Household for Stronger Diffusion
Relative advantage and compatibility are aspects of an innovation that strongly influence the intention of a household to adopt new climate technologies (Kapoor and Dwivedi 2020). An example of these two characteristics is for example connection speed of the technologies to WiFi and the internet in general, as well as the general level of trust in IoE (Internet of Everything) applications (Strielkowski et al. 2019). Furthermore, Rizzo et al. (2018) find that performance and sustainability of Green IT "… have a significant impact on household adoption intention". In a study of conservation of water and energy, the main cited adoption reason was the overall cost saving (Hustvedt et al. 2013) and barriers of initial costs (Alam et al. 2003).

While cost and cost savings do seem to play an important role they should not stand alone. Youtie et al. (2007) also found that reducing the cost of technology alone is not enough to raise demand and increase diffusion. Finally, Franceschinis et al. (2017) used psychological constructs from Rogers' theory as a set of criteria and suggested that also beliefs and attitudes of individual consumers play a crucial role in the diffusion.

Household Adopter Groups

Households willing to adopt new green IT have a desire to be at the forefront of technological development as innovators and early adopters (Fischer 2008). This specific type of adopters would also explain why adoption may be less robust, as innovators and early adopters often will try out innovations and then fall back to prior behavior more easily (Jeliffe et al. 2018). In the case of Jeliffe et al. (2018) it was the farming practice of saving seeds that, over time, would undermine the use of a specific high-yield variety of groundnut. Another reason for the lack of robustness was found by Choragudi (2016) who found that many alternatives would also decrease adoption.

Additional Nuances of Household Diffusion and Adoption Behavior

Broughel (2019) put up an interesting distinction, namely between voluntary and involuntary (forced) adoption. Voluntary adoption is when the adopter him or herself decides whether to adopt or not. Whereas involuntary adoption is when someone such as management makes it mandatory (forces) to adopt and use something. Keil et al. (2017) found that adoption behavior of a household may also be dependent on the (social) networks that the household belongs to. Thus, you will more likely adopt something if someone you trust and relate to can persuade you. Klingler (2017) found that the individual electricity consumption behavior were often neglected. In fact, behavior can be so different and have a major impact to whether a climate technology is diffused or not that it can be seen as a contingent problem for which we need contingency theory (Donaldson 2001). This contingency was also elaborated on by Newton and Newman (2013) through the vast differences of households between and within types of cities, as the infrastructures and regulations vary differently from city to city. Finally, Jensen et al. (2015) found that the impact of a climate technology in a household depends on three things: (1) the impact of a device within a household, (2) the diffusion of devices to other households and the number of adopters, and (3) the diffusion of the induced behavioral change beyond these households.

Central Findings From Diffusion Of Innovations Studies

From diffusion of innovations theory, we identify that cost savings and initial cost of acquiring climate technologies can be viewed as a central factor to adoption. Existing behavior and practices were also found to be a challenge as it can be too easy to fall back on these, and finally that too many alternatives and reliance on voluntary adoption might even hinder the choice to adopt climate technologies.

Assumptions include the household as a central unit, an actor viewed as a black box which ultimately also leads to limitations when the dynamics within and between households, as well as other electronic devices, are also factored in.

4   Taking a Socio-cultural Perspective

Where diffusion of innovations favors the innovation, and somewhat uncritically at that, the change in behavior and practices are treated as the outcome of an explicit, cognitive decision of change made by the individual, and as such, not the household that consists of more than one individual. A socio-cultural perspective differs from the diffusion of innovations theory primarily in what is foregrounded and what is backgrounded. The socio-cultural approach provides a sociological, psychological, or anthropological model for investigating the particularities of social practices, discourses, norms, and moral orders. Grounded in social constructivism, perspectives such as these tend to treat technological systems and their devices as the end products of historical construction and thus socially shaped. In giving space to articulate processes of social construction, historical materialism, or even capitalism, the socio-cultural approach often takes a critical perspective on technology and development and on human behavior that is deeply embedded in: *"social situations, institutional context and cultural norms"* (Shove 2010, p. 1276). The socio-cultural approach thus addresses these issues by instead treating change as an outcome of social practices in which any given object is embedded.

The 10 results categorized here varied significantly depending on the case in question and whether the socio-cultural was an approach, a perspective, or an observational method of unit of analysis. For example, Haque et al. (2021) make the argument that: *"adopting a socio-cultural perspective is a crucial, but often overlooked, aspect of scholarly and policy analyses of, and strategies for, energy transitions in the global South."* (Haque et al. 2021). This study shows that energy transitions and technology transfer often will benefit low-income households, more typically referred to as the 'urban poor'. These households can ultimately held become ascribed with accountability because of their systemic failure of energy technology adoption, and without contextual consideration of their socially situated position and limited capital.

Displaying another variation of the socio-cultural approach, (Jagadish and Dwivedi 2018) conduct a study of cooking practices in rural India as a contribution to the study of sustainable energy alternatives. In this approach, a method referred to as 'consensus study' is utilized with the aim to deconstruct cultural domains related to cooking. Here we see how socio-cultural forces and practices become foregrounded as the units of analysis that are taken to influence the uptake and use of cooking technology, in this case by rural households in India. The study treats 'the social' or 'cultural' as a separate domain of reality, and as abstract models or schemas that are treated as resources for cognition: *"people reason using cultural models, defined as cognitive domains/schemas that are intersubjectively shared by a social group."* (Jagadish and Dwivedi 2018).

The socio-cultural approach can be criticized of situating the 'essence' of a technology within social groups or cultures and lead to a form of determinism. For example, the version of 'praxis' called upon by Haque et al. (2021) carries with it an understanding of temporality as a linear flow of conflicts that are carried forward into the future as they simultaneously pass into history.

5   Co-creating Diffusion and Adoption

In contrast, but like the socio-cultural approach, nine of the papers made use of what we have called 'participatory' or 'co-creative' approaches. For instance, Martiskainen et al. (2018) show how energy can be conceived as a site of political engagement and public participation by studying what they refer to as a 'grassroot innovation' – the case of the community-run energy café in the UK. While said to be less explicitly political than the community participation of the 1970s, the community-run energy café is nevertheless shown to work as a practical, economic, and political device through which the public can gather around financial issues or mundane concerns, such as for example energy bills. As such, this 'grassroot innovation' comes to perform 'energy' itself as a political and social matter, but unlike the socio-cultural approach 'energy' is not treated here as a 'social' or 'mental' construction that resides in the heads of any given social group or culture but in the practical activities, behaviors, and material arrangements that bring people together around a shared issue. Here 'energy' is not merely about the 'idea' of energy but involves coffee too.

One study by Zhang et al. (2016) addressed the issue of food sustainability by increasing agricultural yields through a method referred to as "the Science and Technology Backyard (STB) platform". The study was something of a reversal of the more commonsensical model of scientific diffusion where something called 'science' is first thought of as performed, constructed, or cooked-up in a laboratory and then transferred to such sites of production where it may become useful, such as aquacultural warehouses or agricultural settings, The study showed how a radical, participatory approach can be accomplished by involving: *"agricultural scientists living in villages among farmers, advancing participatory innovation and technology transfer"* (Zhang et al. 2016). In contrast to the socio-cultural approach that brings 'the village' into science then, this study brought 'science' to the village.

The literature on co-creation and participation shows a pragmatist approach that involves the target audience. It contrasts the previous literature in that it foregrounds the households themselves as both innovators, creators, practitioners and decision-makers themselves. The limitations of the approach is the scalability as it also involves third-party members in the facilitation, progression and production of the new climate technological innovation.

6 Discussion and Conclusion

We have now shown that technology diffusion and transfer in households is a domain of great variety, importance, as well as a rather comprehensive process. The literature review revealed that many factors and approaches are needed to accomplish transfer and diffusion, all the way from the macro level of governance and legislation to the minute level of involving each household in a more participatory approach. While the macro level can be considered a gatekeeper of factors, including the importance of finding ways to limit the number of choices available, keeping both costs down as well as cost savings, we also found that additional aspects from diffusion of innovations theory are important as well. Here the specific relative advantages of the climate technologies, as well as the compatibility of existing hardware, and a homogeneous relation to the beliefs, values and attitudes of the adopters require alignment. Finally, there is a great risk of mainly identifying innovators and early adopters which may lead to higher number of discontinuances over time. As a result, future focus needs to be on complementing the legislation and technology with approaches that foregrounds the households as a social practice and detailed unit of individuals instead. One way to do so is to take a socio-cultural approach in order to better detail out the capabilities of those engaged in the household and how existing climate technologies could integrate with new technologies as well as the practices of the household. Finally, we also found results that pointed in the direction of direct engagement with the households for stronger sustainability where the households themselves learned about the fit between technology and themselves in a more pragmatist approach to technology transfer.

All the approaches had their own limitations which is why we conclude that there is a need for a more pluralist point of view to support future technology transfer and diffusion of climate technologies in households. The macro level requires a bottom-up understanding as well as firm regulations to ensure the limited but useful choices. Diffusion of innovations theory did not adequately cover the specific shape of the technologies nor focused on the specific structures and interactions of the household as a social system. Whereas the findings on macro level and diffusion of innovations theory could be viewed as "technologically deterministic" in the sense of a real bias towards foregrounding technology as positive, the alternative socio-cultural approach could equally be criticized for adding a scope of practical determinism that fails to include the specific nature of the climate technologies in the foreground, leading to failed attempts to properly propagate the technology transfer in a broad sense. The material or technical dimensions, also known as 'interobjectivity' (Latour 1996), becomes backgrounded in order to give space to the attitudes, beliefs, or social constructs that are treated as shared patterns of cultural or social 'intersubjectivity' (Jagadish and Dwivedi 2018).

For example, the sociologist Elisabeth Shove critiques dominant models of energy policy and governance for failing to recognize that human behavior is deeply embedded in: *"social situations, institutional context and cultural norms"* (Shove 2010, p. 1276). The socio-cultural approach thus addresses these issues by instead treating change as an outcome of social practices in which any given object is embedded.

Our final finding, the co-creation and participatory approach, struck a balance between the previous issues, yet could be criticized for being impractical on a large industrial scale, which is very much needed for this specific type of technology. The findings of Zhang et al. (2016) show the similarity to the idea of science and technology as 'immutable mobiles' (Latour 1986, 1987) that draw visualization and cognition together in material devices and artifacts that can be transported or transferred to the places they may be best put to use. The participatory politics of Marres (2016) are no doubt greatly inspired by her mentor Latour and the philosophy of 'association' that he contrasts to such 'sociology' as that of Shove (2010) and the socio-cultural approaches. Approaches such as these also tend to be grounded in pragmatist philosophy or versions of social constructionism that attend less to the 'social' and more to the 'material' dimensions of a given case. For example, (Martiskainen et al. 2018) draw on the device sociology of Marres (Marres 2013, 2016) and her concern with green experiments as devices of political and material participation. In her work, material devices such as green eco-homes, environmental teapots, and smart meters come to take the stage as material-semiotic actors that also participate in social, political, and ethical activity.

Much of the knowledge acquired through this review can be very useful for tackling the future challenges of adopting more information heavy technology, such as green IT. However, compared to diffusing and transferring technology to household there will most likely be even more to change than simply having households adopt. Technology transfer to households of green IT will most likely be an even larger challenge than what we have seen in past studies on technology diffusion. Behavioral changes are inherently and initially individual and will need to be reinforced by serving up information in an easily digestible manner while also providing the household as a social system a platform for interconnecting other unknown green IT solutions. The process will require more knowledge on the household level as a specific unit of analysis rather than the black box it has been presented as so far because more IT would have to be specifically addressing the physical as well as normative, cognitive and social dimensions of the households. One example that comes to mind is a household that both consumes power, water, gas while producing electricity from solar panels. Combining these into a larger information system certainly requires approaches that lend themselves to continuously assist the household towards a wanted "target behavior" by gathering data and providing suggestions for new practices. Opportunity through context also matters, as situations such as dwelling type should also be factored in. Being owner-occupied, an investment property, or a rental property might affect the interests of the stakeholders involved to improve and change energy-efficient practices.

Based on the target audience we see implications for opportunities as well as caveats that need to be either considered or cleared first and foremost. Designers of climate technologies will need to consider which type of household are the recipients, what the barriers are and how easily it is to penetrate the legislative level or if the solutions proposed are aligned with these. Household theorists must not forget that households make up very complex dynamics that one cannot take for granted. For academics who study households we see that there are many interesting approaches to understanding the dynamics of the household, yet the caveat is that there may be a bias in either swaying towards the technological determinism (i.e. all technology is good) or towards the determinism of the praxis of the household (leading to the drowning of the household technology). There is also an overall issue with specific prescriptive actions and techniques for improving the overall transfer and diffusion that the mere socio-cultural understanding does not cover completely, nor does the participatory approach address these shortcomings.

References

Aggarwal, A.K., Syed, A.A., Garg, S.: Diffusion of residential RT solar – is lack of funds the real issue? Int. J. Energy Sect. Manage. **14**(2), 316–334 (2020). https://doi.org/10.1108/IJESM-02-2019-0004

Alam, M., Rahman, A., Eusuf, M.: Diffusion potential of renewable energy technology for sustainable development: Bangladeshi experience. Energy Sustain. Dev. **7**(2), 88–96 (2003). https://doi.org/10.1016/S0973-0826(08)60358-0

Ban, K.: Sustainable development goals. News Survey **37**(02), 18–19 (2016)

Hazra, S., Bhukta, A. (eds.): Sustainable Development Goals. SDGS, Springer, Cham (2020). https://doi.org/10.1007/978-3-030-42488-6

Choragudi, S.: India revamps green energy sector: What lies for domestic biogas technology? Int. J. Glob. Energy Issues **39**(6), 413–431 (2016). https://doi.org/10.1504/IJGEI.2016.079371

Dalén, A., Krämer, J.: Towards a user-centered feedback design for smart meter interfaces to support efficient energy-use choices. Bus. Inf. Syst. Eng. **59**(5), 361–373 (2017)

Donaldson, L.: The Contingency Theory of Organizations: Sage (2001)

Dong, S.K., et al.: Farmer and professional attitudes to the large-scale ban on livestock grazing of grasslands in China. Environ. Conserv. **34**(3), 246–254 (2007). https://doi.org/10.1017/S03 76892907004213

Ebers Broughel, A.: On the ground in sunny Mexico: a case study of consumer perceptions and willingness to pay for solar-powered devices. World Dev. Perspect. **15**, 1 (2019). https://doi. org/10.1016/j.wdp.2019.100130

Fischer, C.: Who uses innovative energy technologies, when and why? the case of fuel cell MicroCHP in households. Int. J. Environ. Technol. Manage. **9**(2–3), 236–258 (2008). https:// doi.org/10.1504/IJETM.2008.019036

Franceschinis, C., Thiene, M., Scarpa, R., Rose, J., Moretto, M., Cavalli, R.: Adoption of renewable heating systems: an empirical test of the diffusion of innovation theory. Energy **125**, 313–326 (2017). https://doi.org/10.1016/j.energy.2017.02.060

Galvin, R., Sunikka-Blank, M.: German retrofit policy in context. In: Green Energy and Technology, vol. 148, pp. 29–46 (2013). https://doi.org/10.1007/978-1-4471-5367-2_3

Habibis, D., Phillips, R., Phibbs, P., Verdouw, J.: Progressing tenancy management reform on remote Indigenous communities. AHURI Final Report (223), 1–103 (2014). https://www.sco pus.com/inward/record.uri?eid=2-s2.0-84905373098&partnerID=40&md5=96725306f5ae d54daa3201a007974d82

Haque, A.N., Lemanski, C., de Groot, J.: Why do low-income urban dwellers reject energy technologies? exploring the socio-cultural acceptance of solar adoption in Mumbai and cape town. Energy Res. Soc. Sci. **74**, 101954 (2021). https://doi.org/10.1016/j.erss.2021.101954

Hustvedt, G., Ahn, M., Emmel, J.: The adoption of sustainable laundry technologies by US consumers. Int. J. Consum. Stud. **37**(3), 291–298 (2013). https://doi.org/10.1111/ijcs.12007

Jagadish, A., Dwivedi, P.: In the hearth, on the mind: cultural consensus on fuelwood and cookstoves in the middle Himalayas of India. Energy Res. Soc. Sci. **37**, 44 51 (2018). https://doi org/10.1016/j.erss.2017.09.017

Jelliffe, J.L., Bravo-Ureta, B.E., Deom, C.M., Okello, D.K.: Adoption of high-yielding groundnut varieties: the sustainability of a farmer-led multiplication-dissemination program in Eastern Uganda. Sustainability (Switzerland), **10**(5), 1597 (2018). https://doi.org/10.3390/su10051597

Jensen, T., Holtz, G., Chappin, E.J.L.: Agent-based assessment framework for behavior-changing feedback devices: spreading of devices and heating behavior. Technol. Forecast. Soc. Chang. **98**, 105–119 (2015). https://doi.org/10.1016/j.techfore.2015.06.006

Jin, Y., Ma, X., Chen, X., Cheng, Y., Baris, E., Ezzati, M.: Exposure to indoor air pollution from household energy use in rural China: the interactions of technology, behavior, and knowledge in health risk management. Soc. Sci. Med. **62**(12), 3161–3176 (2006). https://doi.org/10.1016/ j.socscimed.2005.11.029

Kapoor, K.K., Dwivedi, Y.K.: Sustainable consumption from the consumer's perspective: antecedents of solar innovation adoption. Resour. Conserv. Recycl. **152**, 104501 (2020). https:// doi.org/10.1016/j.resconrec.2019.104501

Keil, A., D'souza, A., McDonald, A.: Zero-tillage is a proven technology for sustainable wheat intensification in the Eastern Indo-Gangetic Plains: what determines farmer awareness and adoption? Food Secur. **9**(4), 723–743 (2017). https://doi.org/10.1007/s12571-017-0707-x

Klingler, A.L.: Self-consumption with PV + battery systems: a market diffusion model considering individual consumer behaviour and preferences. Appl. Energy **205**, 1560–1570 (2017). https:// doi.org/10.1016/j.apenergy.2017.08.159

Latour, B.: Visualization and cognition. Knowl. Soc. **6**(6), 1–40 (1986)

Latour, B.: Opening one eye while closing the other a note on some religious paintings. Soc. Rev. **35**(S1), 15–38 (1987)

Latour, B.: On interobjectivity. Mind Cult. Act. **3**(4), 228–245 (1996)

Marres, N.: Why political ontology must be experimentalized: on eco-show homes as devices of participation. Soc. Stud. Sci. **43**(3), 417–443 (2013)

Marres, N.: Material Participation: Technology, the Environment and Everyday Publics: Springer (2016)

Martiskainen, M., Heiskanen, E., Speciale, G.: Community energy initiatives to alleviate fuel poverty: the material politics of energy cafés. Local Environ. **23**(1), 20–35 (2018). https://doi.org/10.1080/13549839.2017.1382459

Murugesan, S.: Harnessing green IT: principles and practices. IT Profess. **10**(1), 24–33 (2008)

Nathwani, J., Kammen, D.M.: Affordable energy for humanity: a global movement to support universal clean energy access. Proc. IEEE **107**(9), 1780–1789 (2019). https://doi.org/10.1109/JPROC.2019.2918758

Newton, P., Newman, P.: The geography of solar photovoltaics (pv) and a new low carbon urban transition theory. Sustain. (Switzerland) **5**(6), 2537–2556 (2013). https://doi.org/10.3390/su5062537

Nyairo, N.M., Pfeiffer, L.J., Russell, M.: Smallholder farmers' perceptions of agricultural extension in adoption of new technologies in Kakamega county. Kenya. Int. J. Agri. Extension **9**(1), 57–68 (2021). https://doi.org/10.33687/ijae.009.01.3510

Oldenberg, O., Murshed, S.M., Kremers, E., Mainzer, K., Koch, A.: Model-based analysis of urban energy systems (on the basis of a city's energy master plan). Emer. Complex. Organ. **17**(2) (2015). 10.emerg/10.17357.03a4747a4b28258c105148d3775522a1

Paetz, A.-G., Kaschub, T., Jochem, P., Fichtner, W.: Load-shifting potentials in households including electric mobility-a comparison of user behaviour with modelling results. In: Paper presented at the 2013 10th International Conference on the European Energy Market (EEM), pp. 1–7 (2013)

Reddy, B.S., Balachandra, P., Nathan, H.S.K.: Universalization of access to modern energy services in Indian households-economic and policy analysis. Energy Policy **37**(11), 4645–4657 (2009). https://doi.org/10.1016/j.enpol.2009.06.021

Rizzo, C., Piper, L., Irene Prete, M., Pino, G., Guido, G.: Exploring the perceived image of energy efficiency measures in residential buildings: evidence from Apulia, Italy. J. Clean. Prod. **197**, 349–355 (2018). https://doi.org/10.1016/j.jclepro.2018.06.149

Rogers, E.M.: Diffusion of innovations: Simon and Schuster (2010)

Schiera, D.S., Minuto, F.D., Bottaccioli, L., Borchiellini, R., Lanzini, A.: Analysis of rooftop photovoltaics diffusion in energy community buildings by a novel GIS- and agent-based modeling co-simulation platform. IEEE Access **7**, 93404–93432 (2019). https://doi.org/10.1109/ACCESS.2019.2927446

Shove, E.: Beyond the ABC: climate change policy and theories of social change. Environ Plan A **42**(6), 1273–1285 (2010)

Strielkowski, W., Streimikiene, D., Fomina, A., Semenova, E.: Internet of energy (IoE) and high-renewables electricity system market design. Energies, **12**(24), 4970 (2019). https://doi.org/10.3390/en12244790

UNFCCC. What is technology development and transfer? (2021). https://unfccc.int/topics/climate-technology/the-big-picture/what-is-technology-development-and-transfer

Wolfswinkel, J.F., Furtmueller, E., Wilderom, C.P.: Using grounded theory as a method for rigorously reviewing literature. Eur. J. Inf. Syst. **22**(1), 45–55 (2013)

Yang, Z., Dong, W., Xiu, J., Dai, R., Chou, J.: Structural path analysis of fossil fuel based CO2 emissions: a case study for China. PLoS One, **10**(9), e0135727 (2015) https://doi.org/10.1371/journal.pone.0135727

Youtie, J., Shapira, P., Laudeman, G.: Supply, demand and ICT-based services: a local level perspective. Telecommun. Policy **31**(6–7), 347–358 (2007). https://doi.org/10.1016/j.telpol.2007.05.005

Zhang, W., et al.: Closing yield gaps in China by empowering smallholder farmers. Nature **537**(7622), 671–674 (2016). https://doi.org/10.1038/nature19368

Zhao, D., McCoy, A.P., Agee, P., Mo, Y., Reichard, G., Paige, F.: Time effects of green buildings on energy use for low-income households: a longitudinal study in the United States. Sustain. Cities Soc. **40**, 559–568 (2018). https://doi.org/10.1016/j.scs.2018.05.011

IT Diffusion in the Society: The Expansion of Smart Cities and Their Impact on the Sustainable Development

Kristina Nagode[(✉)] [iD] and Anton Manfreda[iD]

School of Economics and Business, University of Ljubljana, 1000 Ljubljana, Slovenia
{kristina.nagode,anton.manfreda}@ef.uni-lj.si

Abstract. The spread of information technology is now visible at every turn, considering organizations, individuals, and society as a whole. Organizations, aside from the current problems associated with the Covid-19 pandemic, highlight digitalization as one of their main priorities. However, technology and digitalization do not only apply to organizations, but also to the lives of individuals and communities. After all, many places today are faced with major challenges arising from global environmental shifts, rapid urbanization, and ageing infrastructure. On the other hand, digitalization may bring new opportunities and is already establishing the concept of smart cities and communities. At the organizational level, the goals of digitalization are more or less clear, however, the question arises about the goals at the level of society. Climate changes are certainly one of the areas that society cannot ignore. Smart cities and communities can make a significant contribution in this area; however, goals must be set appropriately. Many studies focus on the importance of smart city development, but there is a lack of research linking smart city development (including society as a whole) with quality of life, sustainable development, and a green future. At the same time, adopting digital solutions is becoming increasingly difficult due to rapidly evolving innovations and the difficulty of managing the complexity of intertwining technologies. Therefore, the purpose of this paper is to shed light on the intertwining of these aspects and highlight the factors that can ensure sustainable development in smart communities.

Keywords: Smart cities · Smart society · Digitalization · Sustainability

1 Introduction

Digitalization and the spread of information technology (IT) are affecting many areas. Organizations are focusing on digitalization as one of their priority activities. However, digitalization is not relevant for organizations only. The affordability of IT and consequently its diffusion in society has an impact on the lives of individuals and communities.

In recent years, many places have been facing problems and challenges that are arising from rapid urbanization and ageing infrastructure that is not able to cope with these

A. Elbanna et al. (Eds.): TDIT 2022, IFIP AICT 660, pp. 177–187, 2022.
https://doi.org/10.1007/978-3-031-17968-6_14

challenges. By the predictions, the proportion of people living in urban environments will rise to up to 70% by 2050 [1], making (newly) urbanized regions very impactful on a global level. That said, it is crucial for them to develop in a sustainable manner, to ensure that the natural and social resources are preserved, while at the same time encouraging economic growth and providing a good quality of life for their residents [2].

Digitalization and IT diffusion in society have presented new opportunities and solutions for these issues, resulting in several smart cities and smart community-related initiatives. They are providing digital solutions for efficiently managing mobility, living, environment, citizens, government, economy, architecture, and technology in urban environments [3]. A smart city must be co-integrated into the local community [4], providing good economic, and social living conditions for its residents [5]. The primary understanding of the smart city concept was focused only on the technological perspective, claiming a city smart, depending on the level of integrated IT into its system, whereas the focus nowadays is for a smart city to be sustainable. Digitalization serves merely as a tool to achieve a better life for its residents and achieve sustainable development [6].

However, the question arises whether the goals in several smart cities and communities are properly set. Smart cities and communities can make a significant contribution to climate change and sustainable development; however, these challenges and priorities are often only on the paper agenda of decision-makers. Conceptualization of smart cities has already been well and systematically researched [7, 8]; however, it is still under researched how the use of digital technologies can help in achieving greater sustainability of the smart city concept. Therefore, the purpose of this research is to explore the effects of IT diffusion in smart cities and communities on their sustainability; to identify and examine factors important for the development of smart cities, smart communities, and smart society as a whole, that provide adequate quality of life for individuals, while ensuring sustainable development and green future.

2   Literature Review

2.1   Digitalization and Its Impact on Society

The digitization initiatives started many years ago; yet, it became more predominant in the last years and will also have a significant effect in the future [9]. Digitalization is not influencing organizations merely, but also individuals, organizations, communities, and many other areas. The concept of digitalization is currently used daily and is defined as the use of digital technology to significantly improve organizational performance [10] by integrating digital technologies and business processes inside the organization [11]. Therefore, digital transformation refers to implementing significant changes in the key organizational areas, such as business processes, business models, strategy, and organizational structures [12].

Digitalization is also associated with the usage of modern digital technology that is enabling important business improvements and is influencing consumer lifestyle as well [13]. It is important to add that both, business models and consumer lifestyles as well, are going through substantial changes that are different from the established behaviors in the past [14].

Modern and affordable technologies are thus affecting organizations; yet, at the same time, it is claimed that digital transformation is mostly a "buzzword hinting at the change in the scope and direction of digital government," while "researchers aim to understand how and why these initiatives succeed or fail" [15]. Buzzword or not, it is impossible to neglect the initiatives in the organizations. Nevertheless, digital technologies are presenting a massive potential for innovation and improving performance in organizations and everyday life [16].

2.2 The Smart City Concept

A Smart City is a complex phenomenon, that has been previously defined by many researchers, but does not have a unified definition yet. Taking in account a few aspects from the Informational Systems perspective, it can be described as a city, developed by utilizing a set of advanced IT [17] to manage city's resources efficiently [17], while improving economic, and social living conditions for its residents [5]. While technology is a promising and helpful tool for making a city smart, merely its implementation is not sufficient to bring its benefits to society. According to the best practices from around the world, a Smart City must be co-integrated into the local community [4]. Furthermore, investment in IT infrastructure, as well as human and social capital with a wise management of natural resources through participatory governance in a Smart City fuel sustainable economic growth and a high quality of life [18].

The existing research on the topic can be divided into the following themes: Smart Mobility, Smart Living, Smart Environment, Smart Citizens, Smart Government, Smart Economy, and Smart Architecture and Technologies [3]. Smart environment theme refers to taking care of natural and cultural resources by using IT [19], considering air pollution, forest quality, water quality, green spaces, weather, emission monitoring, waste management, and energy efficiency [3]. Smart living refers to achieving a greater quality of life using IT [19], considering public safety, healthcare, smart education, smart tourism, and smart buildings [3]. Since social and environmental resources are at the center of Smart Cities, it is important to explore the role of IT in helping a Smart City become more sustainable by preserving its resources. Previous research discussing sustainability of Smart Cities has focused on energy efficiency, waste management, quality of water, green spaces, and air pollution [3]. However, there is still a lack of understanding, how the diffusion of IT in a city environment can promote sustainable development.

A Smart City consists of multiple stakeholders, that are included in the sustainable development of a Smart City, namely academia and research institutions, local and regional administrations, energy suppliers, investors, IT sector representatives, citizens, government, property developers, non-profit organizations, planners, policy makers, experts and scientists, political institutions, and media. Their engagement is important for the success of implementation of smart projects [20].

2.3 The Link Between Sustainability and Smart Cities

Sustainability is denoted as quality of a system, while the idea of a sustainable development is a pragmatic and anthropocentric one, with a primary focus on the people and their well-being. The sustainability concept at the beginning mostly revolved around environmental challenges, with a focal point on the idea of limited natural resources, that need to be conserved. The main aspects considered were climate change, clean energy, sustainable transport, sustainable consumption and production, conservation and management of natural resources, and public health. Gradually, the social and economic aspects were being discussed as well, from the perspective of demography and migration, global poverty, and sustainable development challenges [21].

Since urban environments are expanding rapidly and increasingly more people are moving to cities, with half of the world's population already living in them [2], their role in making the world more sustainable is crucial [21]. In more recent definitions, Smart Cities are defined as cities that are run efficiently, intelligently and are at the same time also sustainable [22], with the aim to provide good quality of life for their residents as well as to ensure economic growth and preserve natural and social resources for future generations [2]. Digitalization should be considered as a tool to achieve sustainable development and improve the life of citizens, moreover it provides the greatest benefits when it brings useful solutions for the life of the citizens [6].

3   Research Methodology

Firstly, a bibliometric study was conducted following the approach by [23]. The aim was to present potential differences between the understanding of smart cities between different research fields information and library science field and a cluster of fields exploring sustainability (including meteorology atmospheric sciences, environmental sciences ecology, forestry, oceanography, biodiversity conservation, plant sciences, and marine freshwater biology). The intention behind the study was furthermore to present how various fields approach the sustainability concept in research and to provide a connection between them since they are supposed to follow a unified goal. Since there are no unified definitions of sustainability and smart city concepts, we decided to analyze what are the most used author keywords related to both concepts in the field of information and library science and in the field of 'sustainability.' Data was collected in January 2022 through the Web of Science by the keyword "smart city", analyzed with the VOSviewer software. The search criteria in the Web of Science included only articles with a publication date between 2017 and 2021. Keywords "smart city" and "smart cities" were excluded in the analysis since they are correlated to all the other keywords. Figure 1 includes the keywords from the information and library science area of research and the second graph from the meteorology atmospheric sciences, environmental sciences ecology, forestry, oceanography, biodiversity conservation, plant sciences, marine freshwater biology area of research.

Secondly, to test some influential factors in the interplay between the smart city, sustainability, and green future we have done some preliminary research on the proposed research idea. A web-based questionnaire was prepared and randomly disseminated among different volunteers in different regions. The purpose of preliminary testing was to obtain additional insights into the view on the smart city concept together with emphasizing sustainability related issues.

The questionnaire was, composed of several items measuring the interest in modern technologies, familiarity with the smart city concept, attitude toward different control and measurement sensors, security and privacy issues related to smart cities and several environmental issues within smart cities. Moreover, the elements of smart mobility and smart healthcare were designed into even greater detail. To ensure a shared understanding of the research concepts, a short definition was provided with each indicator. All variables were measured on a 5-point Likert scale.

Data was collected between 2020 and 2021. Overall, 2,947 individuals participated; however, 1,640 responses were included in the analysis, since they responded with all the needed data. The profile of the respondents is presented in Table 1.

Table 1. Profile of the respondents

Demographic characteristics		Share (%)
Gender	Male	37.0
	Female	63.0
Education	Primary	0.4
	Secondary	54.4
	Tertiary - graduate	36.8
	Tertiary - PhD	8.4
Type of settlement	Urban settlement	62.4
	Suburban areas	19.9
	Smaller compact settlement	13.2
	Scattered houses	4.5
Country	Slovenia	38.7
	Croatia	46.0
	Other	15.3
Country - other	Bosnia and Herzegovina	24.9
	North Macedonia	19.2
	Portugal	8.2
	UK	6.3
	Serbia	3.8
	Other	< 2.0

Most respondents are situated in Central Europe; however, there were several respondents obtained from other regions as well, while some respondents did not provide their country of residence.

4   Preliminary Results and Future Research Opportunities

4.1   Bibliometric Study of Sustainability in Smart Cities

In information and library science, sustainability is viewed from five different perspectives, including the following clusters of keywords (see Fig. 1): (1) information and communication technology (ICT), quality of life, (2) information management, (3) e-governance, (4) social media, technology, smart governance, and (5) public value, governance, citizen participation, sustainable development goals (SDG). Quality of life in the explored research field is viewed from three perspectives: (1) privacy, ICT, (2) information management, and (3) sustainability.

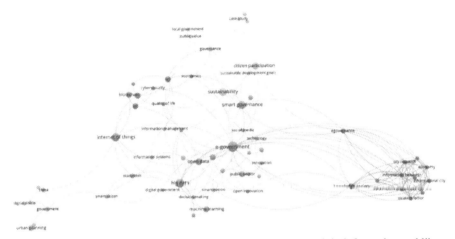

Fig. 1. Bibliometric study of author keywords of smart city research in information and library research.

The keywords that are only used in the information and library research field are quality of life, information management, e-governance, social media, public value, governance, and sustainable development goals. Smart governance in sustainability research of smart cities is indirectly correlated to sustainability through the sustainable city keyword.

In sustainability research, sustainability has been researched from a broader perspective, including the following clusters of keywords (see Fig. 2): (1) energy, blockchain, air quality, (2) citizen participation, ICT, urban development, sharing economy, circular economy, cities, (3) smart mobility, urban governance, internet of things (IoT), (4) big data, privacy, infrastructure, urbanization, India, (5) artificial intelligence (AI), innovation, technology, and (6) machine learning, and (7) sustainable city, sustainable urban development. Sustainable city in the explored research field is viewed from three aspects: (1) urban planning, cities, (2) urban privacy, sustainable urban development, climate change, smart sustainable city, and (3) smart governance, sustainable development. Sustainable urban development is viewed from two perspectives: (1) green city, climate change, sustainable city, and (2) sustainable development.

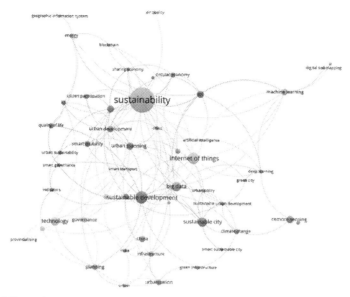

Fig. 2. Bibliometric study of author keywords of smart city research in sustainability research.

The keywords that are only used in the sustainability research field are energy, blockchain, air quality, sustainable city, sustainable urban development, urban development, sharing economy, circular economy, cities, smart mobility, urban governance, IoT, big data, privacy, infrastructure, urbanization, India, AI, innovation, and machine learning.

The only keywords that are used in all the research fields included are citizen participation, ICT, and technology. From the bibliometric study, it is evident that there are big discrepancies between the understanding of sustainability of smart cities. For a successful implementation of sustainable development goals in cities and in society, there is a need for the development of a unified model of smart sustainable communities.

4.2 The Interplay Between Smart City and Sustainability

The concept of a smart city influences individuals and their style of living. The latter is already influenced by the diffusion of technology and digitalization in society. Since individuals are generally reluctant to change, we examined the main concerns related to smart cities. We divided the sample into several groups, namely separately looking at individuals that are more enthusiastic regarding the technology, individuals that live in urban areas and individuals from rural areas only.

As evident from Table 2, the main concerns are related to data privacy, security issues and the use of individual preferences by third parties. Surprisingly, these concerns almost do not differ between the groups.

On the other side, while looking at the potential benefits that smart cities may present, we were focusing mostly on environmental issues (see Fig. 3).

Table 2. Concerns related to smart cities

Concerns related to smart cities	All	Tech. Enth		Urban areas		Rural areas	
	avg	avg	(N)	avg	(N)	avg	(N)
Data privacy	4.1	4.1	(451)	4.1	(906)	4.2	(256)
Security issues	3.9	3.9	(451)	3.9	(903)	4.0	(257)
The use of preferences by other parties	3.9	3.8	(450)	3.9	(904)	3.8	(257)
Historical records of activities	3.5	3.5	(451)	3.5	(906)	3.5	(257)
Transparency and consideration of interests	3.4	3.3	(450)	3.4	(906)	3.4	(257)
Transparency of services	3.3	3.3	(451)	3.3	(904)	3.2	(256)
Complexity of services	3.3	3.1	(451)	3.3	(905)	3.3	(257)
Implementing 5G networks	3.0	2.7	(450)	3.0	(905)	3.0	(257)

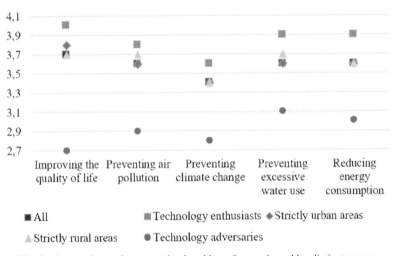

Fig. 3. Smart city environmental-related benefits as viewed by distinct groups.

The axis in Fig. 3 is not fully presented to better highlight the differences. There are almost no differences between individuals living in rural or urban areas; however, there are quite significant differences between individuals that are more technology enthusiastic and individuals that are reluctant towards technology.

Lastly, we examined the view on the smart city concept between individuals that are more sustainability-oriented and once that are not. More specifically, agreement with the elements that should be included in the smart city was compared between both groups. As shown in Fig. 3, individuals that live by sustainable principles perceive different smart initiatives as more important compared to others by placing smart waste disposal as the most important.

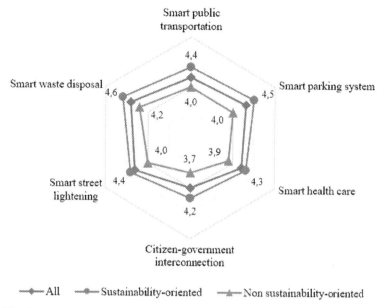

Fig. 4. Smart city elements that should be included as viewed by distinct groups.

We also found significant differences in the preparedness towards installing different sensors among sustainability-oriented individuals and others. More specifically, individuals that live by sustainable principles are more likely to use sensors in their households to monitor waste production to optimize trash collection routes (average value 3.8) and support installing noise monitoring sensors in public streets (average value 3.7) compared to non-sustainability-oriented individuals (average value 3.1 and 2.9).

The above preliminary results support the fact that future research is needed to examine factors important for the development of smart cities and smart communities concerning the adequate quality of life for individuals and ensuring sustainable development and a green future. After all, the preliminary results indicate that the concept of the smart city is perceived differently between individuals with different sustainability orientation. Different perceptions may consequently lead to a different understanding of the smart city concept. Therefore, it is vital to set properly the definition of the concept together with main goals and activities that would lead society towards a green future while maintaining a sufficient level of well-being.

4.3   Limitations and Future Research

A limitation of the research is that the research is constrained by the sample, which is not accurately reflecting the characteristics of the wider society. However, as stated above, the purpose of the initial phase was to receive additional insights and examine key factors related to both smart cities, well-being, and environmental issues in various regions.

The future research will focus on further development of the key factors important for the improvement of smart cities, smart communities, and smart society, that incorporate adequate quality of life, sustainable development, and a green future. Therefore, future research will examine the interplay between sustainable development and green future in relation to smart city, smart community, and smart society as viewed through the lens of key stakeholders important in this interplay. Moreover, future research should also propose proper business models that will ensure this sustainable development. Lastly, the advancement in this area will hardly be achieved without knowing the barriers and main obstacles in the society; thus, exploring opportunities and barriers of digital technologies and various technological factors for supporting sustainable development of smart society in even greater detail is also crucial.

5 Conclusion

The study showed that there are differences in understanding sustainability of smart cities between the information systems field and the sustainability related fields. The preliminary study results indicate end users are concerned about data privacy, security issues, and the use of individual preferences by third parties. The main perceived benefits of smart cities on sustainability from end users are improvement of quality of life, prevention of excessive water use and reduction in energy consumption. Moreover, individuals that live by sustainable principles perceive different smart initiatives as more important compared to others placing smart waste disposal as the most important. They are also more prepared to install and use digital technology solutions to manage the sustainability of a city.

The rapid growth of population and fast urbanization is currently affecting not only the quality of living in several urban areas but also in suburbs and in many vacated areas on the other side. Moreover, several urban areas are facing older existing infrastructure; and therefore, are not able to handle this rapid urbanization. However, modern technology, IT diffusion in society and digitalization itself may provide various solutions that can solve many problems with urbanization on one side and vacated areas on the other side.

Several studies are focusing on the importance of smart city development, but the research linking not only smart city development but also society with quality of life, sustainable development and a green future is lacking. IT and digitalization of society can significantly help in solving modern issues, yet they both can cause even additional problems if not effectively managed and implemented. Due to climate changes, which cannot be overlooked anymore, it is important to emphasize factors that are leading society towards a green future and maintaining a sufficient level of well-being at the same time. However, the latter is not as obvious as it sounds.

References

1. O'Dwyer, E., Pan, I., Acha, S., Shah, N.: Smart energy systems for sustainable smart cities: Current developments, trends and future directions. Appl. Energy **237**, 581–597 (2019)
2. United Nations: 68% of the world population projected to live in urban areas by 2050 (2018)
3. Ismagilova, E., Hughes, L., Dwivedi, Y.K., Raman, K.R.: Smart cities: advances in research—an information systems perspective. Int. J. Inf. Manage. **47**, 88–100 (2019)
4. Manfreda, A., Ljubi, K., Groznik, A.: Autonomous vehicles in the smart city era: an empirical study of adoption factors important for millennials. Int. J. Inf. Manage. **58**, 102050 (2021)

5. Hashem, I.A.T., et al.: The role of big data in smart city. Int. J. Inf. Manage. **36**(5), 748–758 (2016)
6. Schaffers, H., Ratti, C., Komninos, N.: Special issue on smart applications for smart cities–new approaches to innovation: guest editors' introduction. J. Theor. Appl. Electr. Commer. Res. **7**(3), 2–6 (2012)
7. Duygan, M., Fischer, M., Pärli, R., Ingold, K.: Where do smart cities grow? the spatial and socio-economic configurations of smart city development. Sustain. Cities Soc. **77**, 103578 (2022)
8. Zhao, F., Fashola, O.I., Olarewaju, T.I., Onwumere, I.: Smart city research: a holistic and state-of-the-art literature review. Cities **119**, 103406 (2021)
9. Gerth, A.B., Peppard, J.: The dynamics of CIO derailment: how CIOs come undone and how to avoid it. Bus. Horiz. **59**(1), 61–70 (2016)
10. Westerman, G., Calméjane, C., Bonnet, D., Ferraris, P., McAfee, A.: Digital transformation: a roadmap for billion-dollar organizations. MIT Center Digit. Bus. Capgemini Consult. **1**, 1–68 (2011)
11. Liu, D.Y., Chen, S.W., Chou, T.C.: Resource fit in digital transformation: Lessons learned from the CBC Bank global e-banking project. Manag. Decis. (2011)
12. Wischnevsky, J.D., Damanpour, F.: Organizational transformation and performance: an examination of three perspectives. J. Manag. Issues **18**(1), 104–128 (2006)
13. Reis, J., Amorim, M., Melão, N., Matos, P.: Digital transformation: a literature review and guidelines for future research. In: Rocha, Á., Adeli, H., Reis, L.P., Costanzo, S. (eds.) World-CIST'18 2018. AISC, vol. 745, pp. 411–421. Springer, Cham (2018). https://doi.org/10.1007/978-3-319-77703-0_41
14. Loebbecke, C., Picot, A.: Reflections on societal and business model transformation arising from digitization and big data analytics: a research agenda. J. Strateg. Inf. Syst. **24**(3), 149–157 (2015)
15. Mergel, I., Edelmann, N., Haug, N.: Defining digital transformation: results from expert interviews. Gov. Inf. Q. **36**(4), 101385 (2019)
16. Vial, G.: Understanding digital transformation: a review and a research agenda. J. Strateg. Inf. Syst. **28**(2), 118–144 (2019)
17. Peng, G.C.A., Nunes, M.B., Zheng, L.: Impacts of low citizen awareness and usage in smart city services: the case of London's smart parking system. IseB **15**(4), 845–876 (2016). https://doi.org/10.1007/s10257-016-0333-8
18. Praharaj, S., Han, H.: Cutting through the clutter of smart city definitions: a reading into the smart city perceptions in India. City Cult. Soc. **18**, 100289 (2019)
19. Al-Nasrawi, S., Adams, C., El-Zaart, A.: A conceptual multidimensional model for assessing smart sustainable cities. J. Inf. Syst. Technol. Manag. **12**, 541–558 (2015)
20. Jayasena, N., Mallawaarachchi, H., Waidyasekara, K.: Stakeholder analysis for smart city development project: an extensive literature review. In: International Conference on Built Environment and Engineering, p. 06012. EDP Sciences, (Year) (2018)
21. Ahern, J.: From fail-safe to safe-to-fail: Sustainability and resilience in the new urban world. Landsc. Urban Plan. **100**(4), 341–343 (2011)
22. Huang, K., Zhang, X.-S., Wang, X.-F.: Block-level message-locked encryption with polynomial commitment for IoT data. J. Inf. Sci. Eng. **33**(4) (2017)
23. Leung, X.Y., Sun, J., Bai, B.: Bibliometrics of social media research: a co-citation and co-word analysis. Int. J. Hosp. Manag. **66**, 35–45 (2017)

A Negotiated Public Value for Digital Entrepreneurship: A Case Study of Bahrain

Noora H. Alghatam$^{(\boxtimes)}$

University of Bahrain, Sakheer, Bahrain
nhalghatam@uob.edu.bh

Abstract. This paper explores the emergent public value that is negotiated by members of the entrepreneurial ecosystem that include the public sector, private sector and digital entrepreneurs as they work to set up a community for start-ups. The paper employs the theoretical lens of 'public value' [34] to explore the various forms of public value for different stakeholders involved in the entrepreneurial ecosystem certain notions of public value are negotiated. The paper focuses on the case study of Bahrain's national digital entrepreneurship initiative and particularly on how the Startup Bahrain platform was developed. The analysis focuses on the nature of public and private sector collaboration and how this involves an emergent set of public value within national ICT initiatives. The paper highlights the nature of stakeholder's environment and perspectives of public value, the digital platform as contributing to public value, and the entrepreneurial community's negotiated public value.

Keywords: Public value · Digital entrepreneurship · Digital business ecosystems · Public-private sector collaboration

1 Introduction

Many governments across the globe are investing in information and communication technologies to reach socioeconomic goals. One area that has sparked interest in recent years is the role of the state in facilitating digital entrepreneurship by bringing together various stakeholders and offering support to the entrepreneurial ecosystem. Digital entrepreneurship refers to ICTs being employed by businesses to offer digital products and services, or the introduction of an online channel for delivery of products and services by existing businesses. Discourses on digital entrepreneurship often present digital technologies as carrying the potential to improve the performance of businesses and enables them to scale in size and enter new markets. This has led to the formation of policies, institutional structures and technology initiatives to support digital entrepreneurship in various countries. This often entails public and private sector partnerships that offer joint funding schemes, mentoring and government services. The private sector also has introduced various accelerators, co-working space providers and IT and management services to support this field.

© IFIP International Federation for Information Processing 2022
Published by Springer Nature Switzerland AG 2022
A. Elbanna et al. (Eds.): TDIT 2022, IFIP AICT 660, pp. 188–203, 2022.
https://doi.org/10.1007/978-3-031-17968-6_15

This paper explores the negotiated public value that emerges as interactions take place between the public sector, private sector and digital entrepreneurs during their collaboration to set up a community and platform for digital entrepreneurs. We employ [34]'s concept of 'public value' to explore the different public value perspectives from the vantage point of various stakeholders and the emergence of a negotiated public value for the community of digital entrepreneurs. The paper is based on the case study of the national digital entrepreneurship initiative in Bahrain, and specifically the set up and management of the Startup Bahrain platform, over the period of 2006–2018. In this paper, we unpack the role of public and private sector collaboration and explore how public values are played out in such national ICT initiatives. The paper highlights the stakeholder's environment and perspectives of public value, the digital platform as contributing to public value, and the negotiated public value as negotiated by the entrepreneurial community.

This paper begins with a literature review on national ICT initiatives and socioeconomic development as well as public and private sector collaboration in ICT initiatives. The paper then presents the theoretical concept of public value. The third section is an overview of the research methodology using a qualitative research approach. The paper then presents the case study of Start-up Bahrain in terms of the broader sociocultural context that includes the institutional structures, policies and significant milestones to develop the community and platform of digital start-ups. The analysis presents the various public value perspectives by various stakeholders over the course of the initiative from planning to implementation, followed by the negotiated public value for digital entrepreneurship by the community of entrepreneurs themselves. The final sections are a discussion and conclusion about the case and the role of public value negotiation in such national ICT initiatives.

2   Literature Review

2.1   National ICT Initiatives for Entrepreneurial Ecosystems

Many national ICT policies and strategies are centred on the notion of ICTs as a means for administrative reform, efficiency and socioeconomic development. This has led to numerous ICT initiatives run by the public sector such as e-government, e-healthcare programs and smart city projects, to name a few. In recent years, many nations have focussed their attention on the potential that entrepreneurial ecosystems can potentially have on socioeconomic growth and have developed policies and institutional structures to support this. The interest of countries in supporting entrepreneurs and small businesses in the adoption of ICTs is driven by a conceptualization that they carry potential to improve business's performance and contribute to the overall economic activity and growth of nations [10, 11]. Other wider goals that drive such national initiatives associated with ICTs and entrepreneurship is that ICT adoption by the business sector is seen to help businesses grow and create job opportunities as well as enhance innovations and skills in nations [35]. Academic studies have shown diverse results and outcomes that have emerged from such national ICT initiatives that focus on entrepreneurship, even though there are so many positive aspirations linked to them [27, 36]. For this reason, there have been calls to explore such national ICT initiatives as socially embedded and to focus on how these processes of implementation and outcomes are shaped by various factors in the social context [26]. For instance, the influence of the social context and particularly the role of social networks was emphasized in [5]'s study of digital entrepreneurs in China. Similarly, [26]'s work on digital entrepreneurs in Latin America highlights the significance of hybrid networks in shaping their activities.

2.2 Public and Private Sector Collaboration and ICT Initiatives

Such large-scale national ICT initiatives often entail the enrollment of the private sector. This theme has been addressed extensively in many studies that explore the nature and processes of public and private sector collaboration as part of national ICT initiatives such as e-government [19, 21–24]. One specific theme that these studies focus on is the role of new public management and best practice approaches in how these national ICT projects are implemented [12, 13, 15]. The collaboration between the public and private sector has also been conceptualized from a post-NPM perspective that focuses on centralization and a holistic approach, more than decentralization in past project [17, 30].

The national ICT initiatives and projects that are planned and implemented by such intersectoral partnerships come in different formats such as projects for national infrastructure development for smart cities [28] and national platforms for the development of digital entrepreneurial ecosystems as presented in the case study of China [16]. One way, these intersectoral collaborations are played out, is the involvement of accelerators from the private sector that operate alongside public sectors agencies and incubators [20]. Such public and private sector collaboration to support digital entrepreneurship is evident in case studies in Africa [18]. The processes involved in such initiatives are illustrated in [16]'s work on the digital entrepreneurial ecosystems in Zhongguancun in China employs the meta-organization lens to explore the interaction of various actors in terms of the division of labor and integration of efforts. Given that public and private sector actors come with different practices and values this research paper addresses the following research question:

What is the negotiated public value that emerges from intersectoral collaboration during the implementation of a community and platform for Startups?

3 Theoretical Framework: Public Value

Many academics have focussed on studies that explore the processes of public value negotiation and its outcomes in ICT initiatives and projects in the public sector [12, 15]. The concept of public value is defined in different ways such as a performance measure, narrative, a theory for networked community governance and paradigm for the public sector [2, 6]. Public value refers to the value associated with public services and initiatives that take into account the citizen's medium and long-term goals that are beyond notions of efficiency and effectiveness as articulated in new public management [12]. The public value concept often entails many different aims as diverse actors are involved and these need to be balanced out [25].

One way that public value can be explored and understood is a framework presented by [7] which is the strategic triangle of public value which includes the three elements of: authorizing environment, operational capacity and public value outcomes. The concept of public value involves an authorizing environment (or a stakeholder environment) that includes different perspectives and interests of various stakeholders that are part of these project or initiatives. There is also the aspect of operational capacity which enables public sector organizations to reach better performance measures and enhance public value for society. For example, ICTs and digitization of public sector processes can be conceptualized as a means to support public sector organizations and fulfil public value aspirations [15].

Even though the public sector places effort in planning and implementing projects and services, it is the citizens who frame public value as they consume services and engage with the public sector [1]. At one level, citizens place value on aspects the fulfil personal aspirations and benefits. On another level, citizens value aspects of the public sector that generate value for society at large for the medium and long term. This encompasses visions for society as a whole such as care for the environment and social development [1].

There have been many dimensions of public value that have been explored in studies of the public sector [34]. Yet there are relatively few studies that have explored the role of ICTs in processes and outcomes of public value [8, 12]. For example, [15] explore how the social context can shape the role of ICTs in supporting operational capacity to fulfil enhanced public value. One way is through the provision of open data by the public sector and open source to enable innovations. This is often supported by public sector digital platforms that enable citizens and application developers to contribute solutions and resources on the platform [9, 22].

4   Methodology

This paper is based on a qualitative approach and focuses on the case study of the national ICT initiative in Bahrain to develop digital entrepreneurship and particularly the community and digital platform for Startups. The aim was to explore a case study with actors that have different roles and experiences [38]. The data collection included a combination of reviewing secondary data, semi-structured interviews and focus groups. The adoption of a semi-structured interview approach was useful to explore multi-actors case studies that are complex and entail many details [37]. The processes began with a pilot that included the collection of secondary data from new articles, websites and reports. The pilot also included interviews with a manager from a public sector incubator and a researcher from a think tank. The interviews at that stage focussed on understanding important milestones of the initiative and some sociocultural issues faced by digital entrepreneurs.

This was subsequently followed by interviews with public and private sector managers and employees of organizations that were involved in supporting the initiative. These semi-structured interviewed were conducted in the public sector and private sector organizations' site. There were 17 interviews conducted that were one hour to one and half hour long in duration. The data collection process was iterative as there were periods were secondary data and the literature were reviewed to guide further cycles of interviews. The main objective of the interview was to highlight planning, collaboration, implementation and objectives of the initiative. The criteria for selecting participants in the interview process was mainly if they had a managerial role or advisory position in an organization that played an active role developing digital entrepreneurship in the country. For example, some of these organizations included semi-government funding agencies, accelerators, incubators and public sector organizations. At a later stage, the data collection process focused on the community of digital entrepreneurs. There were four focus group events organized to collect data, which were held in the national university campus. The focus groups involved 5–8 digital entrepreneurs. The criteria for selecting focus group members were mainly if they were founders of digital start-ups that offered services and products online through a website or application.

The data analysis phase was an iterative process between reviewing primary and secondary data such as official documents, website, reports and news articles and literature on digital entrepreneurship. One of the main goals was identifying important milestones in the trajectory of the national initiatives in terms of significant policies and regulations and institutional structures created. There was also an interest in identifying the role of key actors and various periods of collaboration between them to setup the community and platform.

The process of data analysis involved three stages for coding of data. First, there were descriptive codes developed which simplify semi-structured interviews into general themes [32]. The focus was on key activities and milestones such as collaboration projects and regulatory changes. At the second stage, the data was analysed based on theoretical constructs such as institutional theory and public value outcomes. The third stage involved emergent pattern codes that builds on earlier coding to highlight themes and patterns. For example, there were themes related to socioeconomic development and scalability as outcomes for the community.

5   Case Study: Digital Entrepreneurship in Bahrain

This section presents the case study of the national ICT initiative for digital entrepreneurship in Bahrain. The section presents three main themes: an overview the Economic Vision 2030 and becoming an ICT innovation hub, relevant institutional structures and the Startup Bahrain's community and digital platform.

5.1   Economic Vision 2030 and Becoming an ICT Innovation Hub

An important dimension of digital entrepreneurship in Bahrain is the Economic Vision 2030 that underpins the initiative. The Economic Vision was announced in 2008 and articulates the most important aims to reach enhanced economic development levels. The policy includes numerous areas of focus by the government and the most relevant to our case of digital entrepreneurship is the theme of high-quality policies which include public and private sector partnerships and outsourcing. This reinforced the drive for sectors to partner in various national projects such as education and healthcare and most recently in creating an environment that support digital entrepreneurship development and growth. Another important aspect of the Economic Vision was the economic theme of diversification of income. This meant an emphasis on high potential markets and opportunities such as the ICT industry. One of the associated aims with this vision is becoming an ICT and innovation hub in the GCC region that can offer facilities, infrastructure and an overall conducive environment for businesses to set up branches in Bahrain [29] and especially in the fintech sector [31, 34]. There are currently numerous IT companies being hosted in the country, many of which are founded by digital entrepreneurs. By creating such a conducive environment for ICT related businesses, Bahrain aims to capitalize on its skilled ICT workforce, which is relatively high in comparison to the region. Supporting the initiation and growth of start-up's also has the potential to create job opportunities and improve investment levels.

Institutional Structures Supporting Digital Entrepreneurship
Bahrain has invested efforts and financial capital to set up various institutional structures, infrastructure developments and regulatory changes to support digital entrepreneurship. One important overarching concept is Team Bahrain which represents a governance model that is based on concepts of agile government that is based on public and private sector partnerships to reach developmental goals.

As such, we find various government agencies such as the Economic Development Board, the Ministry of Industry, Tourism and Commerce, the funding and education agency Tamkeen working together with other private sector accelerators, financial institutions, and IT service providers to support digital entrepreneurship. The aim is to create an environment that encourages international startups to be based in the country and to assist local startups to develop their initiatives and scale. Many of these start-ups have benefited from training, access to capital and the opportunity to use co-working spaces [4; 3]. There have also been many regulatory developments over the past 4 years to support digital entrepreneurship such as bankruptcy laws and the virtual commercial registration service (Sijili) where start-ups can begin their activities without the need for a physical location and address.

5.2   Start-Up Bahrain as a Community and Digital Platform

All these efforts to support digital entrepreneurs culminated to the set up of a formal community and digital platform entitled Startup Bahrain, which focussed on providing entrepreneurs a network and means to gain resources to build capacities and grow. A major actor in this initiative was the Economic Development Board (EDB), which developed the concept and platform and rolled it out in 2017. The EDB realized that there was a gap to be filled in the business environment after a study conducted about high potential startups, which were businesses that are often ICT-based and could scale into other regions and offer their products and services online. These businesses needed information, networking and other resources that were focused on their sector and that was how the idea of the Startup Community and platform came about.

The community and platform involved enrolling different public and private sector teams to organize events, hackathons and to support entrepreneurs. The initiative was set up with the goal of having the EDB as the initiator of the community and then over time as the startups gain momentum and scale, they would take over the managerial aspects of the community and platform.

The set up of Startup Bahrain involved the creation of a leadership that included representatives of the public and private sector and digital entrepreneurs who were active early on in supporting the entrepreneurial community. The of this team would identify needs of the digital entrepreneurs, collect feedback and communicate it to the public sector.

The EDB also played an important role in developing the digital platform Startup Bahrain that was planned and implemented in consultation with the private sector as well. The platform consisted of a web presence that included information, a database about startups and resources from the private sector that entrepreneurs could benefit from, as well as a social media account. The website included information about the key stakeholders in the ecosystem that offer various services and facilities for investors and entrepreneurs. The website also included regulations, a database of startups, a blog and upcoming events for the community. Moreover, the website included complementary resources from private sector organizations such as cloud service provides and marketing firms that offer free credit, mentoring and other resources. The platform also includes a social media account that posts announcements about events and opportunities, enables engagement with the community and hosts live interviews with founders and other key players.

6   Analysis

Bahrain's initiative to set up digital entrepreneurship involved actors from both the public and private sector to collaborate in planning and managing the Startup Bahrain community and digital platform. In this section, we present the public value perspectives of different groups in the stakeholder environment and the negotiated public value from the community perspective. We then present the role of the digital platform itself in supporting the community and the emergent public value.

6.1   Perspectives on the Community and Platform from the Stakeholder Environment

Public Value from a Policy Perspective
One prominent public value associated with digital entrepreneurship and the community is digital entrepreneurship as a means for economic growth and this links to the Economic Vision policy. Setting up a community involves offering them with an opportunity to network, build capacity and improve their business performance. The idea is also to encourage more individuals to set up businesses in a more convenient way with a supportive environment to contribute to economic growth. This public value is associated with the policy aim of economic diversification away from oil. The concept of digital entrepreneurship links to the aim of developing Bahrain as an ICT hub in the region. The country has one of the largest skilled ICT workforce in the region which can be leveraged by attracting businesses in the ICT sector as well as developing local

digital entrepreneurial ventures to hire graduates. Another factor is the legacy of Bahrain as being a pioneer in the banking sector in the region for the past decades. There is a potential for Bahrain's digital entrepreneurial community to set up fintech applications, tools and services that can contribute to the existing banking sector or be the basis for new fintech ventures. In line with this, there have been significant steps taken to set up a fintech sandbox, mentoring activities, hackathons to support the area. There have also been regulatory changes that enables crowdfunding for internet-based platforms (Table 1). As noted by one the managers in the public sector:

Mainly activities in this area are through Startup Bahrain, which is a multi-stakeholder initiative... also working on regulatory reforms and regulatory initia-tives in various areas so this helped push through some of these changes through corporate registration, eliminating minimum capital requirements... they had been working on the new bankruptcy law etc. So, there are broader efforts to try to create a more conducive ecosystem.

Table 1. Policy sector's public value perspective

Policy sector	Factors	Public value perspective
Policymakers The economic vision 2030	Economic diversification policy	Supporting new economic activities that contribute to socioeconomic development
	ICT for development discourse Highly Skilled ICT workforce in the region	Innovation hub in the region to attract FDI and support local developments on ICT
	Historical role of banking	Financial Center in the Region

Public Sector Actors' Conception of Public Value

The public sector actors were driven by a conception of partnerships, private sector growth and empowerment as a public value associated with the Startup Bahrain. First, the community was initially set up and formalized by the EDB which partnered with private sector entities in the process. Setting up this community and platform was an enactment of public-private sector partnerships that is articulated in the Economic Vision 2030. This also links to the Team Bahrain structure which focuses on an agile government model for intersectoral collaboration. As such, the initiative entailed communicating and teaming up with various private sector companies to formulate the aims of the community and platform and plan events and share resources with the community of entrepreneurs. Second, the EDB aimed to play a transitionary role in the management of the community and would hand over the management process once the community gains momentum. The community was set up with the intention of offering the digital entrepreneurs a network of similar businesses that include high-potential start-ups that could leverage

ICTs to scale into the region and beyond. They were aware that there were existing business communities for established businesses that often were large and based on conventional modes of operation and needed a similar one for digital entrepreneurs. This gap in the environment drove the formalization of the community and platform of Startup Bahrain. As such, they were involved in forming a leadership team that consisted of representatives from the public and private sector, such as founders of ICT-based businesses and accelerators who were prominent in the field. The public value of partnerships and private sector empowerment were reflected in actions of developing a formal community, digital platform and leadership team (Table 2). As noted by a senior executive from the private sector:

From the early days they always had conversations with us, but then their conversations became... we need the community to own this, they created it and let it go and said you companies shape it, [...] so finally last year, I said we will take it... the community will take it. Then another company jumped in and said we will take it too, so we said we will figure it out. So, what we did was we created the startup leadership team, some will come for the affiliates some will come to do the work.

Table 2. Public sector public value perspective

Public sector	Factors	Public value perspective
Public sector managers associated with the entrepreneurial ecosystem	Economic vision 2030 Team Bahrain's agile government model Mediated by the startup Bahrain Platform	Public-private partnerships
	Existing business community networks and a gap for tech startups EDB support of the startup field with a transitionary approach Mediated by the startup Bahrain Platform	Private sector empowerment

Private Sector Actors' Conception of Public Value

There were many private sector companies involved in the setup of Startup Bahrain and the platform from financial institutions to accelerators. One prominent public value associated with this initiative from their perspective was to create links with international entrepreneurship experts and enrolling the community into a global network. This was deemed as important in order for the digital entrepreneurs to learn from these experts through mentoring, success stories and this creates the potential to form partnerships. For example, the private sector accelerators were involved in introducing international experts as mentors in various programs they offered. Also, they were involved in taking part and organizing community events such as conferences, hackathons and workshops. In some cases, these experts that were invited came from other international branches of their businesses. The private sector actors involved in the leadership team explained that they found themselves in a situation where they needed to collaborate more than compete to form an environment where businesses could flourish and economic activities between digital entrepreneurs could be enhanced. As noted by one executive from an accelerator during an interview, there was no time to compete and they needed to collaborate with other founders to set up the aims for the digital community and platform and organize events to build capacities (Table 3). As noted by a manager in one of the accelerators (former employee in the public sector):

> And that's when we started to identify 'what are the key pillars of what a startup ecosystem should look like.' So, there were at least 16 pillars that were identified: including government policy, the workforce, costing and, also things like what the ecosystem looked like in community events and all of that. So, each one of those, were different focuses that needed to be put in place. If you want to have a vibrant, startup ecosystem you need to have for instance, community events… we need to put a schedule of community events.

Table 3. Private sector public value perspective

Private sector	Factors	Public value perspective
Private sector managers in organizations such as accelerators, funding agencies, etc	International experts International branches for businesses Best practices	Global networks for Entrepreneurship
	Existing gaps in the marketplace with a need to identify needs from all parties involved	Collaborative Ecosystem Development by members

6.2 Negotiated Public Value by the Community

The digital entrepreneurs' ongoing involvement in Startup Bahrain was shaped by the public values of digital entrepreneurship as a means for scaling to other contexts and contributing to socioeconomic development. This public value is different from traditional businesses in that they saw the potential of using ICTs to scale their businesses into other contexts through the set-up of applications in area such as education-tech and healthcare. As noted by the participants during the focus groups, many founders were driven by a motivation to support the creation of jobs and addressing the employment gap and contributing to socioeconomic growth. These two strands of public value by the community were negotiated and emergent and were shaped through the interaction with other founders and public and private sector organizations involved in the initiative. These community members were interacting with the public and private sector and some of their concepts have been influential such as development aims and scalability. There was often a consultative model approach adopted in townhall like meetings to include entrepreneurs, where the leadership team could collect feedback about needs of the community and this would be communicated to the public sector. As noted by one of the managers in the public sector commented:

> *Town hall meetings at quite a few locations, we also have the leadership team we try to gather feedback as well. We will formalise the feedback, we need to have surveys to everyone to capture opinions, sometimes. The way we capture opinion has been a little bit one to one, a little bit people in the community that haven't had their views shared.*

Other forms of engagement were through the social media account and the organizing of live interviews of founders and other ecosystem members to discuss success stories, advice and emergent opportunities. There was also an influential role for a new narrative of entrepreneurs as successful agents in economic development in the media that came to frame the community's public value as associated with growth, scale and socioeconomic growth.

6.3   Operational Capacity Through the Startup Bahrain Platform

The digital platform, Startup Bahrain, played an important role in supporting the operational capacity of the public sector and partnering firms in supporting public value associated with the initiative. First, the platform formalized the community by identifying the main actors involved. The platform included a database of digital start-ups as well as information about ecosystem members involved that includes background information about them and contact details. Second, the platform supported links to global experts and networks by posting information about upcoming conferences, workshops and events that support the entrepreneurs. Third the platform supported public and private sector partnerships further by offering complementary resources by companies on the platform. For example, Amazon Web Services offered free credits and other services on the platform that start-ups could register for. Finally, the platform's blog and social media engagement such as live interviews presented success stories that linked the community's operations to socioeconomic growth and development (Table 4). As noted by one of the managers from the accelerator:

> *I think we are still in the early stages where we are kind of still drawing how this ecosystem will look in the future. Currently if you look at the different industries that we have, they can all benefit from vibrant entrepreneurial ecosystems. So, whether it is for the financial sector with FinTech, or the manufacturing sector with industry 4.0 or everything that's being done from the industrial side and even tourism also gets effected by technology. So…it has an effect on to the economy, so this is a really important part.*

Table 4. Digital entrepreneurs' negotiated public value

Digital entrepreneurs	Factors	Negotiated public value
Startups that are affiliated with the startup Bahrain initiative and platform	Economic vision 2030 discourse on role of ICT and entrepreneurship	Entrepreneurs as actors that support socioeconomic development
	Role of the Platform as mediating networking between startups and promoting ideas through events	Scalability with ICT based business

7 Discussion and Conclusion

First, the study shows the role of the stakeholder environment as each stakeholder had a perspective on public value (Fig. 1). The national initiative in Bahrain to set up the Start-up Bahrain community and platform involved several public and private sector actors as well as digital entrepreneurs. Even though the idea was to create a community that offers support and resources to digital entrepreneurs there were broader goals of socio-economic development for citizens at large. The link of national ICT initiatives with a broader goal or public value has been discussed extensively in research [8, 25]. The study also shows that the project was embedded in a multi-stakeholder context and each group associated the initiative with a different public value. For example, policy associated it economic goals of diversification, the public sector with partnership and private sector empowerment, the private sector linked it to enrolling into global networks. This contributes to existing studies on multiple public value perspectives in the authoritative environment [15].

Second, the study also showed how the digital platform was an artefact that enacted and reproduced these public values (operational capacity) (Fig. 1). The Startup Bahrain's digital platform offered complementary resources to reinforce partnerships and the blog and social media live interviews to support a narrative for socioeconomic development. This links with work that discusses the potential role of ICTs and digitalization to support operational capacity of the public sector to improve public sector performance and attain better levels of public value [15].

Finally, the study also presented how the stakeholder environment and operational capacity of the digital platform came to shape the community's public value (Fig. 1). The emergent and negotiated public value emphasized digital entrepreneurship as a means for socioeconomic development and scalability of high potential start-ups. This comes in contrast with more common views that businesses focus on economic gains. Our study highlighted that there were efforts to focus on collaboration more than competition between businesses to support the community for an improved environment for economic activity for digital businesses. The case also illustrates a consultative approach to inform the development of the community and platform. There was an adoption of a consultative model where feedback was collected from the digital entrepreneurs and communicated to the public sector to identify needs and aims of the community and inform

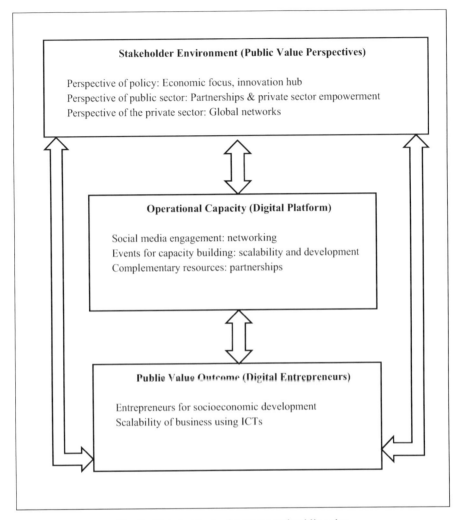

Fig. 1. Stakeholder environment and public value

future decisions. There was also a better understanding gained through engagement as businesses communicated through the social media account.

Many national ICT initiatives carry with them aspirations for change and support in reaching broader socioeconomic aims. The public value of digital entrepreneurship initiatives that often entail support and facilitation of an entrepreneurial ecosystem is conceptualized in different ways by various stakeholders. The case study of Bahrain highlights the collaboration process between the public and private sector which was unique in that it was inclusive of the digital entrepreneurs as well and included a consultative model. We argue that the involvement of the digital entrepreneurs in the shaping of the national ICT project of setting up a community and platform led to an emergent and negotiated public value through interactions. Our study shows that the community of digital start-ups engagement with various sectors came to shape their emergent public value concepts that emphasizes concepts of digital entrepreneurship community and platform for networking, scalability and socioeconomic growth.

This study makes contributions to research in the fields of information systems and digital entrepreneurship. The study emphasizes the social embeddedness of digital entrepreneurship and how the collaborators in such national ICT initiatives have different perspectives on the value of the initiative for society. Our study shows that the community of entrepreneurs enacted a particular set of public values from the environment as they engaged in activities and used the platform. This reinforces existing studies of digital entrepreneurship that focus on the social context and social networks that affect the activities of participants such as the study of digital entrepreneurs that are shaped by social networks in a case study of China [5]. This also links to [26]'s work on digital entrepreneurs in Latin America who are shaped by hybrid networks they are embedded in.

Another contribution to research is that the paper reinforces existing studies that focus on the role of ICTs in reinforcing public values. In this study, we presented the digital platform of Startup Bahrain as supporting public values of partnerships, scaling and development and being part of a global network. Such operational capacity of technology to support public value is explored in [15]'s work.

This paper also has wider implications for practice. The study illustrates the complexity of working on setting up a national ICT project such as digital entrepreneurship initiatives and platforms. The study highlights the importance of identifying various perspectives of stakeholders on the value of these initiatives. Aligning the perspectives of different groups can help in small collaborative ICT projects between them. The study also reframes ICTs, in this case the digital platform, as a tool that can enact certain public values that exist in the environment amongst stakeholders. Thus, practitioners can identify these values when introducing such platforms that support entrepreneurship to get buy in of various parties to use the platform and that ensures its sustainability in such national ICT initiatives.

References

1. Alford, J., Hughes, O.: Public value pragmatism as the next phase of public management. Am. Rev. Public Administr. **38**(2), 130–148 (2008)
2. Alford, J., O'Flynn, J.: Making sense of public value: concepts, critics and emergent meanings. Int. J. Public Adm. **32**, 171–191 (2009)
3. Al Sahaf, M., Al Tahoo, L.: Examining the key success factors for startups in the kingdom of Bahrain. Int. J. Bus. Ethics Gov. **4**(2), 9–49 (2021)
4. Alsamman, A., Ragab, E.: supporting the growth and development of SMEs in Bahrain. In: International Conference on Innovation, Technology, Enterprise and En-trepreneurship Manama, Bahrain, pp.195–207 (2019)
5. Avgerou, C., Li, B.: Relational and institutional embeddedness of web-enabled entrepreneurial networks: case studies of netpreneurs in China. Inf. Syst. J. **23**(4), 329–350 (2013)
6. Benington, J.: From private choice to public value? In: Benington, J., Moore, M.H., (eds.), Public value: Theory and practice. Palgrave Macmillan, Basing-stoke, pp. 31–51 (2011)
7. Benington, J., Moore, M.: Public Value: Theory and Practice. Palgrave Macmillan, London (2010)

8. Bonina, C., Cordella, A.: Public sector reforms and the notion of 'public value': implications for egovernment deployment. In: 15th Americas Conference on Information Systems, San Francisco, California (2009)
9. Bonina, C., Eaton, B.: Cultivating open government data platform ecosystems through governance: lessons from Buenos Aires, Mexico City and Montevideo. Gov. Inf. Q. **37**(3) (2020)
10. Boateng, R., Heeks, R., Molla, A., Hinson, R.: E-commerce and socio-economic development: conceptualizing the link. Internet Res. **18**(5), 562–594 (2020)
11. Chipidza, W., Leidner, D.: A review of the ICT-enabled development literature: towards a power parity theory of ICT4D. J. Strateg. Inf. Syst. **28**(2), 145–174 (2019)
12. Cordella, A., Bonina, C.: A public value perspective for ICT enabled public sector reforms: a theoretical reflection. Gov. Inf. Q. **29**(4), 512–520 (2012)
13. Cordella, A., Iannacci, F.: Information systems in the public sector: the e-Government enactment framework. J. Strateg. Inf. Syst. **19**(1), 52–66 (2012)
14. Cordella, A., Paletti, A., Shaikh, M.: Renegotiating public value with co-production. In: Tucci, C., Afuah, A., Vescusi, G. (eds.), Creating and Capturing Value Through Crowdsourcing, vol. 1, Oxford University Press, Oxford (2012)
15. Cordella, A., Willcocks, L.: Government policy, public value and IT outsourcing: the strategic case of ASPIRE. J. Strat. Inf. Syst. **21**(4), 295–307 (2012)
16. Du, W., Pan, S.L., Zhou, N., Ouyang, T.: From a marketplace of electronics to a digital entrepreneurial ecosystem (DEE): the emergence of a meta-organization in Zhongguancun China. Inf. Syst. J. **28**(6), 1158–1175 (2018)
17. Dunleavy, P., Margetts, H., Bastou, S., Tinkler, J.: Digital Era Governance. Oxford University Press, Oxford (2006)
18. Friederici, N.: Innovation hubs in Africa: what do they really do for digital entrepreneurs? In: Taura, N., Dolat, E., Madichie, O. (eds.) Digital entrepreneurship in sub-Saharan Africa, pp. 9–28. Palgrave Macmillan, Switzerland (2019)
19. Gascó, M.: Living labs: Implementing open innovation in the public sector. Govern. Inf. Q. **34**(1), 90–98 (2017)
20. Goswami, K., Mitchell, J.R., Bhagavatula, S.: Accelerator expertise: understanding the intermediary role of accelerators in the development of the Bangalore entrepreneurial ecosystem. Strateg. Entrep. J. **12**(1), 117–150 (2018)
21. Hui, G., Hayllar, M.R.: Creating public value in e-government: a public-private-citizen collaboration framework in web 2.0. Aust. J. Publ. Administr. **69**, 120–131 (2017)
22. Janssen, M., Estevez, E.: Lean government and platform-based governance: doing more with less. Gov. Inf. Q. **30**, 1–8 (2013)
23. Klievink, B., Bharosa, N., Tan, Y.-H.: The collaborative realization of public values and business goals: governance and infra- structure of public–private information platforms. Gov. Inf. Q. **33**(1), 67–79 (2016)
24. Klievink, B., Janssen, M.: Realizing joined-up government - dynamic capabilities and stage models for transformation. Gov. Inf. Q. **26**(2), 275–284 (2009)
25. O'Flynn, J.: From new public management to public value: paradigmatic change and managerial implications. Aust. J. Publ. Administr. **66**(3), 353–366 (2007)
26. Quinones, G., Heeks, R., Nicholson, G.: Embeddedness of digital start-ups in development contexts: field experience from Latin America. Inf. Technol. Dev. **27**(2), 171–190 (2020)
27. Quinones, G., Nicholson, B., Heeks, R.: A literature review of e-entrepreneurship in emerging economies: positioning research on latin american digital startups. In: Ozório, L., de Jesus Melo, L (eds.), Entrepreneurship in BRICS Policy and Research to Support Entrepreneurs. Springer Nature, Switzerland, pp. 179–209 (2015)
28. Lombardi, P., Giordano, S., Farouh, H., Yousef, W.: Modelling the smart city performance. Innov. Euro. J. Soc. Sci. Res. **25**(2), 137–149 (2012)

29. Lopez, C., Bendix, J, Servin, C.: Bahrain and the Fourth Industrial Revolution (Millken Institute Report) (2020). https://milkeninstitute.org/sites/de-fault/files/reports-pdf/Bahrain-Fourth-Industrial-Revolution-FINAL.pdf
30. Margetts, H., Dunleavy, P.: The second wave of digital-era governance: a quasi-paradigm for government on the web. Philos. Trans. R. Soc. **371**(1987), 20120382 (2013)
31. Meero, A., Rahman, H., Abdul Rahman, A.: The prospects of Bahrain's entrepreneurial ecosystem: an exploratory approach. Prob. Perspect. Manag. **18**, 402–413 (2020)
32. Miles, M.B., Huberman, A.M.: Qualitative Data Analysis: An Expanded Sourcebook. Sage Publications, Thousand Oaks (1994)
33. Modara, M.: The influence of government-private sector collaboration on innovation in a developing knowledge economy: The case of Bahrain (Doctoral dissertation, Bangkok University) (2007). http://dspace.bu.ac.th/bit-stream/123456789/4122/1/marjan_moda.pdf
34. Moore, M.: Creating Public Value. Harvard University Press, Cambridge, Mass (1995)
35. Ramdani, B., Raja, S., Kayumova, M.: Digital innovation in SMEs: a systematic review, synthesis and research agenda. Inf. Technol. Dev. **28**(1), 56–80 (2020)
36. Rangaswamy, N., Nair, S.: The PC in an Indian urban slum: enterprise an entrepreneurship in ICT4D 2.0. Inf. Technol. Dev. **18**, 163–180 (2012)
37. Schmidt, C.: The analysis of semi-structured interviews. In: Flick, U., von Kardorff, E., Steinke, I., (eds.) A Companion to Qualitative Research. Sage, Thousand Oaks (2004)
38. Yin, R.K.: Case Study Research: Design and Methods, Applied Social Research Methods Series. Sage, Thousand Oaks (1994)

Contextual Use of IoT Based Water Quality Control System

Olumide C. Ayeni[1], Taiwo O. Olaleye[2] , Oluwasefunmi T. Arogundade[1,2(✉)] ,
Favour Ifeanacho[1], and A. Kayode Adesemowo[3(✉)]

[1] Department of Mathematical Sciences, Anchor University, Lagos, Nigeria
{oayeni,oarogundade}@aul.edu.ng
[2] Department of Computer Science, Federal University of Agriculture, Abeokuta, Nigeria
[3] SOAMS Consulting, Gqeberha, South Africa
kadesemowo@soams.co.za

Abstract. 'Solutions' are often deployed as interventions without lasting benefit to communities and stakeholders. In the case of water, a basic need and necessity for living and a part of goal 6 of the sustainable development goal, poor water monitoring systems have been one of the reasons for water wastage around communities. The inadequate control of water in and out of the storage has been a part of the cause of water wastage. In Anchor University Lagos, there has been a constant wastage of water. The extents of water in the tanks are likewise not ascertained for proactive measures for enough provision. This is besides the fact that the quality status of the water cannot be asserted before consumption by students. The above-identified issues have therefore become the motivation for this research project. In this paper, considering the ineffectiveness of the current quality control system in Anchor University Lagos, an IoT-based water quantity control- and quality assurance system was implemented following a build, process, and experimental methodology. The system alerts on the possibility of water shortage and the safety of water for consumption. Different sensory modules were connected to raspberry pi 3 devices, a micro-controller, to enable the IoT-based system to function properly. Informed by UTAUT, data was retrieved and analyzed from the sensors through the micro-controller and displayed onto an android based application for end-users. A users' acceptance survey was carried out, influenced by UTAUT, to ascertain the performance and effort expectancy analysis of the system alongside the contextual social influence and the facilitating conditions. We observed a favourable disposition of end-users in welcoming and engaging. More significantly, the belief the users have to expectancy regarding leveraging the system for water quantity and the degree of impact that influencer will have. Further contextual studies shall incorporate the daily consumption rate of water volume to capacity management.

Keywords: Water · Quality · Internet-of-Things · Raspberry pi-3 · Sensor · Android · SDG · Acceptance · UTAUT

© IFIP International Federation for Information Processing 2022
Published by Springer Nature Switzerland AG 2022
A. Elbanna et al. (Eds.): TDIT 2022, IFIP AICT 660, pp. 204–217, 2022.
https://doi.org/10.1007/978-3-031-17968-6_16

1   Introduction

Water is not only a basic, essential need of humankind, it is a necessity for living. Water must be available to meet the 20 to 50L consumption by human daily and must be kept clean. With COVID-19, the importance of water came to fore even more for many. The United Nations recognized the criticality of water and noting majority are without access, stressed the importance of improved water quality in places where water is provided. See Goal 6 of the Sustainable Development Goals – SDG – (www.un.org/sustainabledeve lopment/water-and-sanitation/). There is a need for water to be measured and regulated to avoid wastage and inadequacy. More so, Pasika and Gandla [1] advocate real-time monitoring. This calls for developing solutions that can regulate the flow and monitoring of a water system; a gap that the Internet of Things (IoT) is capable of filling.

The IoT refers to a whole lot of global physical devices that are connected to the internet with data collection and sharing capabilities [2]. This is aided by the prolif-eration of affordable computer chips and the universality of wireless networks which is leveraged in small objects as medicinal pill to something as big as an airplane. The connectivity of the different devices or objects with sensors adds a level of digital intel-ligence to hitherto dumb devices, enabling them to communicate real-time data without the intervention of human beings. The IoT is making the fabric of the world around us smarter and more responsive, merging the digital and physical universes [3], just as Cloud computing likewise advances the possibility of remote functionality in a digi-talized everyday capability [4]. The IoT is a relatively new pattern in information and communication technology (ICT) as it is widely described as the network of objects [5] (things) which is embedded with sensor modules and other technologies for the purpose of connecting and exchanging data with other devices and systems abroad [6]. Hence, IoT has wide deployment and utilitarian value across use cases [7] including everyday tasks and way of life [8]. While the deployment of IoT is widespread for industrial inno-vative disruptions [9], domestic activities that daily touches the life of ordinary citizens could likewise be enhanced by the instrumentality of the Internet of Things [10]. For instance, supposed inconsequential monitoring of water systems in domestic domains could mar water provision intentions if proactive measures are not put in place for effec-tive management [11] as well as the need to ensure quality water for consumption and other domestic use [12]. Hence, monitoring water provisional systems would help crop the incessant wastage of water in communities of developing countries like Nigeria and as well ensure mitigating factors against low quality water for public consumption. In the university community of Anchor University for instance, issues associated with wastages and inadequate water provision is what the water management team struggle with on a daily basis. Consequent upon the foregoing, automation of water monitor-ing and management systems, away from the traditional physical inspection, in no small ways enhances water provisioning efficiency. In this study, the build, process, and exper-imental research methodology is adopted towards automating the water monitoring and management system at the Anchor University Lagos. This research project investigates an IoT-based water control system that keep track of the water level in real-time. The water quality system compares values received from the sensors with some preset water level parameters to accurately ascertain, in real time, the current level of water in various reservoirs through an Android-based technology. The Unified Theory of Acceptance and

Use of Technology – UTAUT [13] approach was used for the evaluation of the automated system in this study.

The rest of the study is structured thus: Sect. 2 discusses related studies and Sect. 3 unveils the proposed methodology. Section 4 discusses the result and Sect. 5 concludes this study with recommendations.

2 Related Studies

The concept of connecting sensors and some level of intelligence to basic objects is a continuous germane discussion [14] apart from some early projects, including an internet-connected vending machine, there is still a growing demand for smart objects. Some of the militating factors were the size of chips with their bulky nature hence no way for objects to communicate effectively until now. The adoption of Radio Frequency Identification (RFID) tags, low-power chips that can communicate wirelessly, solved some of this issue [15], along with the increasing availability of broadband internet and cellular and wireless networking.

The adoption of IPv6, which, among other things, should provide enough IP addresses for every device in the world (or indeed this galaxy) is ever likely to be needed, was also a necessary step for the IoT to scale [16]. IoT has been widely adopted for health services [17] where wearables or sensors are connected to patients in enabling the monitoring of patient's condition remotely in real time. The agriculture use case of IoT is likewise widespread [18] in the area of smart farms in both developing and developed societies. Specifically, the quality of soil etc. is sometimes ascertained through the instrumentality of IoT. Smart homes and smart grid are other areas of applications for real estate [19] and energy industry [20] use cases. More so, water quality monitoring is facilitated by IoT acting as sensors for smart systems [1]. In water quantity control, IoT could be deployed through the instrumentality of an ultrasonic sensor to determine the level of water which can be monitored from the comfort of a mobile phone connected to the internet and the automation system. Indeed, IoTs are burgeoning with their use for secure, smart environment looking promising [21].

Water quality monitoring systems detect water level, amount of water released from the tank, and object detection. The values from the sensors can be obtained from micro devices like Arduino UNO Raspberry Pi and engaged using a Wi-Fi system. Saravanan et al. [22], implemented an Intelligent IoT-based Water Quality Monitoring system, where a PH sensor and TDS meter were deployed for collecting water parameters periodically from different types of water. Collected water parameters are sent to the microcontroller and are sent through serial communication to Raspberry Pi3. The Pi3 processor got the K-Means clustering algorithm in grouping the water parameters into different clusters based on PH and TDS and accordingly trained the data set for predicting the quality of water as good or bad. This information is updated on a cloud-based webpage to aid informed decision of water authorities.

Users can surf web page of a system using a local web browser and can control the industrial devices (micro board), as well as their status from a remote place. The work of [23] proposes an IoT-based cost-effective system that monitors the quality of water in real-time. The design and implementation of the system is done with WeMos D1 mini and sensors (pH, turbidity, temperature, and ultrasonic). The experiment setup was developed and tested for water quality data acquisition, online data transfer, monitoring, recording, and analysis. It is experimentally observed that the system takes less than a minute to update its values, which is an optimal timeframe for residents. Sensor-based water quality monitoring system utilizing microcontrollers leverages Wireless Sensor Network (WSN), a communication system for inter and intra-node communication across several sensors [24]. Access to real-time data is achievable by remote monitoring of IoTs in-situ data collection, aggregation, processing and displaying within an information system. Yasin et al. [25, p. 56] in their review note that such smart water management systems are designed to collect meaningful and actionable data on water supply, pressure, and delivery. Most of the related works present the 'technical' working of their solutions. Pasika and Gandla [1] included the algorithms, while Overmars and Venkatraman [21] presented their process flow diagram for their case study. This paper takes these approaches further by highlighting part of the software engineering use-case and users' 'view' of our implemented IoT-based water quality system for Anchor University's case study.

3   Research Methodology

The question then is how we leverage IoT and micro-boards in deploying water monitoring system based on sound software engineering principles, such as the context of a university environment in a fast-growing mega city (in a third world).

3.1   Research Approach

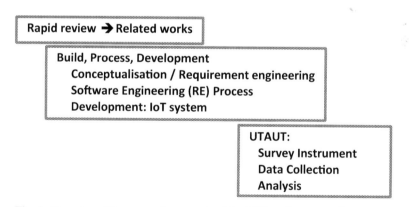

Fig. 1. Overview of the research approach of the IoT-based water quality system.

The approach as depicted in Fig. 1 started off with the rapid literature review of related work as presented in the last section. In this section, we shall look at the build, process, and development which is informed by software engineering principles. The UTAUT informed experimental trial is discussed in the next section (results and discussion).

The Build, Process and Experimental research approach is adopted in this study. The building methodology of the study consist of an IoT system involving the main controller, sensor module, GPIO pins, memory card (storage device). The process methodology of this study is in the areas of Software Engineering and Man-Machine Interface which deals with the way humans build and use computer systems. The experimental methodology used in this study is a 5 scale, UTAUT framework.

3.2   Research Design

The IoT-based system uses a raspberry pi as the main controller with different sensors connected to it and an android based application for end users. Data comes from sensors connected to the raspberry pi controller, which was retrieved by a Python script. The collected data were compared with the World Health Organization (WHO) standards for drinking water. An analysis of the data ensues and is displayed on the mobile application with certain predictions based on the earlier mentioned comparison. The layered architectural framework for the study is as captured in Fig. 2a with the application framework captured in Fig. 2b.

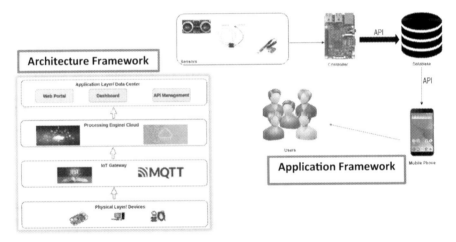

Fig. 2.   Architectural (1a) and application framework (1b) of the water quality system.

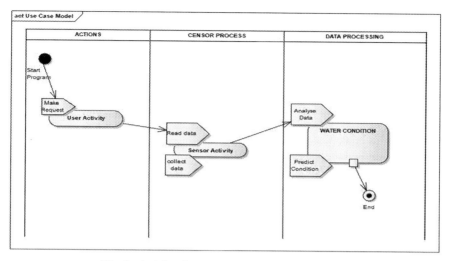

Fig. 3. Activity diagram of the water quality system.

The flow of sequential activities and actions for the functionality of the framework is as captured in the activity diagram depicted in Fig. 3, while the series of messages and interactions between actors and objects are as described in the sequence diagram of Fig. 4 where communications are represented in an orderly manner. The classes of the proposed framework alongside their attributes and consequential behaviors are as described in Fig. 5a while the analysis of the system's functional and non-functional requirements, as expressed by different end users is as captured on the UML use case diagram in Fig. 5b, indicating the actors and their relationships within the design framework.

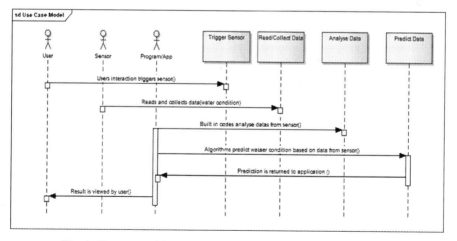

Fig. 4. Use case activity sequence diagram of the water quality system.

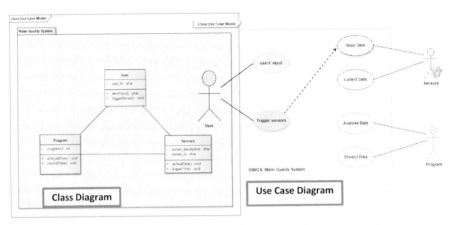

Fig. 5. The class diagram (5a) and use case diagram (5b) of the water quality system.

Requirement gathering (the requirement engineering) based on the architectural and application framework, and the use case activity sequence was done as summarized in Table 1.

Table 1. Listing of the hardware and software requirement.

S/N	Hardware	Function	Remarks
1	GPIO pins	GPIO pins are cables deployed for data and power transmissions, and the overall communication between the raspberry pi microcontroller and the sensors	
2	Resistors	Resistors interfaces the ultrasonic sensor which needed only 3.3 V	The raspberry pi delivers 5 V or 3 V, therefore the resistors used were to step down the 5V to 3.3 V
3	GPIO Extender	Used to extend the communication pins of the micro-controller	
4	Bread board		
5	Memory card	Main storage for the microcontroller	System database
6	Raspberry pi 3b+	A microcontroller	
7	Ph Sensor Module		

(continued)

Table 1. (*continued*)

S/N	Hardware	Function	Remarks
8	TDS sensor module		
9	Ultrasonic Level sensor		
10	Raspbian software		
11	Python coding	Used to build the scripts that communicates with the raspberry pi 3. These files include, firebase.py, distance.py	A scheduler called crontab was used to run the firebase.py script every minute
12	Java coding	Used in android studio to develop the application that will intelligently determine the quantity of water in a tank. Java is also used in to develop the User Interface of the application for the users of the system	Certain water levels were stored in different array list. Then, the distance retrieved from the database is then check in the list to see if it is present, if present, the condition is true else it checks for the next condition

4 Result and Discussion

We shall now discuss the interesting findings from our field experience.

4.1 Water Monitoring App

The interface to the water monitoring system for Anchor University Lagos is an Android-based app, shown in Fig. 6.

Two segments of water quantity and quality status were captured on the device which is easily updated to reflect current status of the water reticulation system. The water quantity is measured in *cm* on the device while the quality segment shows the TDS and pH value of the water. Status label of the water quality segment shows the usability status of the water as *unfit* or *fit* for use. The device was deployed for experimentation by end users to evaluate its performance, questionnaires were administered on end users to evaluate their perception of the new water management control system.

4.2 UTAUT Evaluation

As with other researchers trying to gain insight into the adoption of new innovation, we leverage the UTAUT framework. The UTAUT construct for the water monitoring system was designed to gauge performance (users usage perspective), institutional (social) influence, and the facilitating conditions. We acknowledge and take note of Dwivedi et al. [13, p. 719] call for researchers to go beyond behavioural intention and usage behaviour, to give thought to the contextual relationships that may be potentially important. The

Fig. 6. (Android-based) user interface of the monitor quality state.

test bed is a relatively new university with its own dynamics and reality, yet it exists within another interfacing reality – a fast growing mega city.

The UTAUT construct for the water monitoring system was designed to gauge performance and effort (users usage perspective), institutional (social) influence, and the facilitating conditions. The construct design is as depicted in Fig. 7, which currently shows the Likert scoring in this phase of the research project.

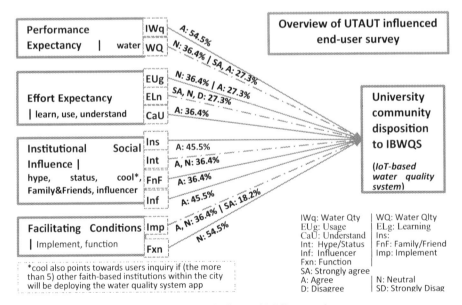

Fig. 7. Summary findings with Likert scoring.

In the current iteration, trust and cost (phase two project deployment and billing) are not a 'factors' and are accordingly excluded. They will be considered in the next iteration along with other contextual factors. Also in the next iteration, the comprehensive UTAUT analysis along with hedonic factors will be finalized and presented (covariance-based structural equation modelling).

Performance and Effort Evaluation

In the current iteration, the performance and effort expectancy analysis of the end user respondents is as presented in Table 2.

Table 2. Performance/effort: water quantity, quality, use, learning and understanding

	Water quantity	Water quality	Use	Learning	Clear & understand
Strongly agree	18.2	27.3	18.2	27.27	18.18
Agree	54.5	27.3	27.2	9.1	36.36
Neutral	9.1	36.4	36.4	27.27	27.27
Disagree	9.1	–	18.2	27.27	9.1
Strongly disagree	9.1	9.0	–	9.1	9.1
Total (n = 11)	100	100	100	100	100

In Table 2, it is seen that "Agree" has 54.5% of the water and work staff choice; we can then conclude that the users see IBWQS as a system that can easily detect the quantity of water in a tank. Regarding quality, IBWQS is having 36.4% as "Neutral" which means the respondents couldn't decide if IBWQS has the capacity to maintain water quality or not. Nonetheless, from the "Agree" and "Strongly Agree" of 27.3% we can conclude that the users see IBWQS as a system that is capable and easy to maintain water quantity. In the same Table 2, "Neutral" has the highest percentage with 36.4% while "Agree" has 27.3%", implying that IBWQS may likely not be easy for them to use or maybe easy. We checked whether IBWQS would be easy for them to learn or not. There was a tie in the decision made by the respondents as "Strongly Agree", "Neutral" and "Disagree" with 27.3% respectively. This implies, slightly so, that IBWQS is easy to learn; some were undecided while some believed that it is not that easy to learn. Many respondents agreed that IBWQS is a system that would be clear and understandable; indicated by 'Agree' having the highest rating of 36.4%.

Contextual Social Influence

The social influence of the new device as perceived by end users was analyzed and presented in Table 3.

Gaining understanding of respondents' opinion to know if the software would be introduced to (higher) institution that needs it, 45.5% agreed with 27.3% further strongly agreeing and a 18.2% neutral. Also, in Table 3, "Agree" and "Neutral" have the same percentage rating of 36.4 for 'water and work' staff choice which indicates that IBWQS may either be introduced to employers or not. Respondents agreed to the fact that IBWQS

Table 3. Respondent feedback to contextual social influence:

	Institutions	Introduce	Family & friends	Influencer
Valid strongly agree	27.3	27.3	27.27	36.3
Agree	45.5	36.4	36.36	45.5
Neutral	18.2	36.4	18.18	9.1
Disagree	9.1	–	9.1	9.1
Strongly disagree	–		9.1	–
Total (n = 11)	100	100	100	100

would definitely be introduced to their family and friends having the highest rating of 36.4%. Respondents overwhelmingly agreed to the fact that if an important or influential person introduces the IBWQS system to them, they would adhere and implement the system; indicated by 'Agree' having the highest rating of 45.5% and another 36.4% strongly agreeing.

Facilitative Conditions in the Context of the University Reality

Respondents' responses to the UTAUT constructs are presented in the charts in Fig. 8. For the two facilitating conditions as analyzed the degree of implementation indicate "Agree" and "Neutral" are tied with 36.4% respectively which means that some agreed to the fact that IBWQS system has an easily implementable system while some are indifferent about the system been an implementable system or not. Finally, the respondents are "Neutral" with 54.5% rating and 18.2% disagreement that IBWQS functions properly.

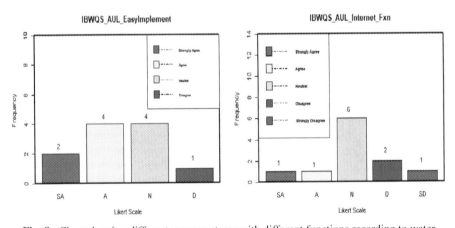

Fig. 8. Chart showing different usage systems with different functions regarding to water

The charts indicate each of the ratings clearly with respect to the IBWQS system usage. In summary, a critical analysis of the UTAUT constructs clearly shows the auspicious utilitarian value of the system with respect to the perception of end users who participated in the acceptance and use of technology analysis.

The response from the small pool of end-users shows a favourable disposition to the IoT-based water quality system. The performance expectancy, an indication of the belief that the end-users hold, and the effort expectancy, a degree of usefulness, are relatively encouraging.

Further compensating evaluation would be considered in future: such as system usability scale (SUS), heuristic evaluation, contextual interview, or hybrid.

4.3 Implication for Research and Practice

Reticulation of water for domestic use could be a source of concern when there are no efficient measures to ensure a proactive system of management and distribution. Lack of portable water for daily use, and the sudden realization of shortage could disrupt daily productive activities of people who cannot do without portable water for food, cleanliness etc. The indispensable nature of water therefore calls for proactive measures towards water distribution and quality assurance policies, per SDG No 6.

In the academic environment of the Anchor University, Lagos, this study conceptualizes an IoT-based water quantity control and quality assurance system that alerts on the possibility of water shortage and the safety status of water for consumption. The system was implemented using the build, process and experimental methodology to design and implement the proposed framework. The UTAUT framework, with its recent update, encouraging contextualization, remains versatile in ascertaining the performance and effort expectancy analysis of the system alongside the social influence and the facilitating conditions. Researchers should, while contextualizing projects such as our IBWQS pay attention to underlying mechanisms. In the next iteration, greater attention will be given to the contextual setting of IBWQS within the university settings and the larger community, as well as unearthing generative mechanisms in the socio-technical setting [26].

5 Conclusion and Recommendation

The water quality monitoring system was deployed in a single institution. The implementation and evaluation were based on the contextual intricacies of the specific institution. Nonetheless, this limitation, the findings provide a rich bed for investigating how water monitoring system can be deployed within an institution in a mega city of a third-world country. Lessons learnt from this adoption are infallible factors towards the United Nations SDG goal 6 and ICT4D researchers/practitioners.

We reported the design, deployment, and evaluation of an IoT based water quality-monitoring system (IBWQS) in a university environment. The UTAUT-based analysis shows a favourable disposition of end users to the solution. We nonetheless note some lapses. Consequently, future study, of larger pool of users, is expected to incorporate the daily consumption rate of water volume as a proactive measure towards making enough provision to last specific timelines. We hope to undertake future research work from socio-technical, systems and complexity theory stand view. Our goal is to explicate underlying contextual causal mechanism towards deepening IT/IS adoption and penetration. In so doing, we frame and factor transformative and emancipatory ethos as espoused in axiology of critical realism [26].

References

1. Pasika, S., Gandla, S.T.: Smart water quality monitoring system with cost-effective using IoT. Heliyon **6**(7), e04096 (2020)
2. Bari, N., Mani, G., Berkovich, S.: Internet of things as a methodological concept. In: Fourth International Conference on Computing for Geospatial Research and Application, San Jose, California, USA (2013)
3. O'Neill, M.: The Internet of Things: do more devices mean more risks? Comput. Fraud Secur. **2014**(1), 16–17 (2014)
4. Arogundade, O., et al.: Cloud computing offered capabilities: threats to software vendors. In: Singh, P.K., Wierzchoń, S.T., Tanwar, S., Ganzha, M., Rodrigues, J.J.P.C. (eds.) Proceedings of Second International Conference on Computing, Communications, and Cyber-Security. LNNS. Springer, Singapore (2021). https://doi.org/10.1007/978-981-16-0733-2_16
5. Zhang, G., Lu, S., Zhang, W.: CAD-Net: a context-aware detection network for objects in remote sensing imagery. IEEE Trans. Geosci. Remote Sens. **57**(12), 10015–10024 (2019)
6. Salam, A.: Internet of Things for Sustainable Community Development, p. 334. Springer, Cham (2020). https://doi.org/10.1007/978-3-030-35291-2
7. Deshpande, A., Pitale, P., Sanap, S.: Industrial automation using Internet of Things (IOT). Int. J. Adv. Res. Comput. Eng. Technol. (IJARCET) **5**(2), 266–269 (2016)
8. Wang, M., Zhang, G., Zhang, C., Zhang, J., Li, C.: An IoT-based appliance control system for smart homes. In: 2013 Fourth International Conference on Intelligent Control and Information Processing (ICICIP), Beijing, China (2013)
9. Kumar, S., Iyer, E.: An industrial IoT in engineering and manufacturing industries–benefits and challenges. Int. J. Mech. Prod. Eng. Res. Dev. **9**(2), 151–160 (2019)
10. Bazhenov, N., Korzun, D.: Use of everyday mobile video cameras in IoT applications. In: FRUCT 2022: Proceedings of the 22st Conference of Open Innovations Association FRUCT, Helsinki, Finland (2018)
11. Kasim, A., Gursoy, D., Okumus, F., Wong, A.: The importance of water management in hotels: a framework for sustainability through innovation. J. Sustain. Tour. **22**(7), 1090–1107 (2014)
12. Vasistha, P., Ganguly, R.: Water quality assessment of natural lakes and its importance: an overview. Mater. Today Proc. **32**(4), 544–552 (2020)
13. Dwivedi, Y.K., Rana, N.P., Jeyaraj, A., Clement, M., Williams, M.D.: Re-examining the unified theory of acceptance and use of technology (UTAUT): towards a revised theoretical model. Inf. Syst. Front. **21**(3), 719–734 (2017). https://doi.org/10.1007/s10796-017-9774-y
14. Bonnaud, O.: New approach for sensors and connecting objects involving microelectronic multidisciplinarity for a wide spectrum of applications. Int. J. Plasma Environ. Sci. Technol. **10**(2), 115–120 (2016)
15. Jia, X., Feng, Q., Fan, T., Lei, Q.: RFID technology and its applications in Internet of Things (IoT). In: 2012 2nd International Conference on Consumer Electronics, Communications and Networks (CECNet), Yichang, China (2012)
16. Savolainen, T., Soininen, J., Silverajan, B.: IPv6 addressing strategies for IoT. IEEE Sens. J. **13**(10), 3511–3519 (2013)
17. Kodali, R.K., Swamy, G., Lakshmi, B.: An implementation of IoT for healthcare. In: 2015 IEEE Recent Advances in Intelligent Computational Systems (RAICS), Trivandrum, India (2015)
18. Shenoy, J., Pingle, Y.: IOT in agriculture. In: 2016 3rd International Conference on Computing for Sustainable Global Development (INDIACom), New Delhi, India (2016)
19. Lin, Y., et al.: Real estate evaluation on thermal diffusivity with IoT sensors. In: 2019 IEEE 8th Global Conference on Consumer Electronics (GCCE), Osaka, Japan (2019)

20. Bedi, G., Venayagamoorthy, G.K., Singh, R.: Navigating the challenges of Internet of Things (IoT) for power and energy systems. In: 2016 Clemson University Power Systems Conference (PSC), Clemson, SC, USA (2016)
21. Overmars, A., Venkatraman, S.: Towards a secure and scalable IoT infrastructure: a pilot deployment for a smart water monitoring system. Technologies **8**(4), 50 (2020)
22. Saravanan, K., Anusuya, E., Kumar, R., Son, L.H.: Real-time water quality monitoring using the Internet of Things in SCADA. Environ. Monit. Assess. **190**, 556 (2018)
23. Ramadhan, J.: Smart water-quality monitoring system based on enabled real-time internet of things. J. Eng. Sci. Technol. **15**(6), 3514–3527 (2020)
24. Chowdury, M.S.U., et al.: IoT based real-time river water quality monitoring system. Procedia Comput. Sci. **155**, 161–168 (2019)
25. Yasin, H.M., et al.: IoT and ICT based smart water management, monitoring and controlling system: a review. Asian J. Res. Comput. Sci. **8**(2), 42–56 (2021)
26. Adesemowo, A.K.: CIPPUA: towards coherence and impact in ICT4D/IS. In: Sharma, S.K., Dwivedi, Y.K., Metri, B., Rana, N.P. (eds.) TDIT 2020. IAICT, vol. 617, pp. 329–340. Springer, Cham (2020). https://doi.org/10.1007/978-3-030-64849-7_30

Working from Home Beyond Covid-19: Technology – Friend or Foe?

Banita Lal[1]([⊠]), Markus Haag[2], and Yogesh K. Dwivedi[3,4]

[1] University of Bradford, Richmond Road, Bradford BD7 1DP, UK
b.lal1@bradford.ac.uk
[2] University of Bedfordshire, University Square, Luton LU1 3JU, UK
markus.haag@beds.ac.uk
[3] School of Management, Swansea University, Bay Campus, Skewen, Swansea SA1 8EN, UK
y.k.dwivedi@swansea.ac.uk
[4] Symbiosis Institute of Business Management, Pune & Symbiosis International (Deemed University), Pune, India

Abstract. As the world aims to start 'getting back to normal' following the hopeful decline of the pandemic, many organisations and employees are questioning whether they will ever return to the old normal, where work for many was conducted within a designated office space. Drawing upon data from a wider study utilizing diary data of 29 participants that was conducted in the early stages of the lockdown, this short paper aims to highlight findings that not only suggest that individuals struggled with managing technology and work, but also that individuals were beginning to develop more control over their use of technology. This short paper ends by highlighting future research that the authors aim to develop.

Keywords: Working from home · Technostress · Qualitative research

1 Introduction

Covid-19 needs no introduction, and the impact of the pandemic and subsequent lockdowns is all too well-known and experienced by many people globally. The way life and work were traditionally conducted underwent a transformation where organisations and employees around the world had no alternative but to adapt to new working conditions: technology has been pivotal in normalising the work and life routines of individuals during this very unique situation [1, 2].

The 'battle' that homeworkers have when it comes to technology is well-documented in the pre-Covid homeworking literature. The 'dark side' of IT use has received significant research attention with two key themes remaining consistent over time with regards to IT-enabled patterns of work and collaboration – "that of quick and easy information access and flexible work patterns vs. addiction, misuse, overuse, overload and stress brought on by IT usage" [3, p. 270]. The benefits and drawbacks cited in earlier literature and that cited in more recent homeworking literature that has transpired since Covid-19

A. Elbanna et al. (Eds.): TDIT 2022, IFIP AICT 660, pp. 218–225, 2022.
https://doi.org/10.1007/978-3-031-17968-6_17

have similarities: the benefits could often be turned on their heads. For instance, increased productivity was deemed a key benefit of working from home, and from a different perspective can be perceived as a negative as individuals become 'over-productive' due to their inability to switch off from Information and Communication Technologies (ICTs).

Whilst a notable amount is now known about individuals' experiences whilst working from home (WFH) during the pandemic, there is potential to explore what their experiences are now that the pandemic's grip seems to be easing. Currently, there is uncertainty of what the future of work will look like: there is some speculation that some organisations and employees will not return to the 'old normal' working styles where work was influenced by time and space [4]. Thus, questions persist, including what are the challenges and impediments faced by individuals and what is the role of technology? As Herath and Herath [2] state: is technology a boon or a bust?

The aim of this short paper is to explore homeworkers' relationship with technology whilst WFH due to Covid-19 and how this has changed in terms of individuals' perceptions and usage of technology for work purposes. This study is currently in its very initial stages: the authors had conducted a wider study examining how homeworkers managed technology-enabled social interaction with colleagues whilst at a distance [5]. It was during this study that a key theme began to emerge which – although not fully integrated into the main, wider study – appeared to be significant in that homeworkers were demonstrating changes in how they perceived and used technology. Thus, the aim of this paper is to demonstrate such changes using findings from the main, wider study and, subsequently, consider how the authors can explore this theme in a future study. The data was collected during the height of the pandemic.

2 Literature Review

When WFH during the pandemic, individuals were overwhelmed with the technology dominance of all things work-related. The role of technology has come to the forefront during the pandemic as online applications have enabled the continuity of personal and business activities [6]. Presently, in the Information Systems/Management area, there is much speculation, expert opinion and suggestions for research and theory in relation to the longer-term implications of Covid-19. The initial stage of immediate panic and high levels of change required to adapt working practices has now passed: organisations and employees have managed to adapt working practices to function remotely using collaborative tools such as Microsoft Teams and Zoom [7].

The relationship that employees have with technology has been studied for some years, particularly given that ICTs have become so embedded in day-to-day life. ICTs have become increasingly "complex, real-time, ubiquitous, and functionally pervasive, often requiring users to process information simultaneously and continually from different applications and devices" [8, p. 304]. This results in multiple challenges for individuals, such as having to deal with a surplus of information, frequent interruptions from – and multitasking on - different devices and applications [8].

Whilst the use of technology facilitates completing tasks, it puts much pressure on employees [9]. This has the potential to result in individuals feeling stressed by ICTs, a phenomenon known as 'technostress' which is the "stress experienced by end users in organizations as a result of their use of ICTs. It is caused by an individual's attempts to deal with constantly evolving ICTs and the changing physical, social, and cognitive responses demanded by their use" [10, pp. 417–418]. In addition to the factors mentioned by Tarafdar et al. [8], other factors that can create technostress include: constant connectivity which can extend the working day, employees being contactable anytime and anywhere, and communication overload due to several mobile communication tools and software resulting in individuals feeling overwhelmed [10]. This can result in increased expectations for individuals to work faster and harder and can have an adverse effect on individuals' ability to make timely decisions [9]. Remaining available anytime and anywhere not only extends individuals' working day and responsiveness to work tasks, but this 'techno-invasion' can lead to personal tensions as a result of work creeping into personal time [9].

As research increases on the impact of homeworking and technology-induced stress during the Covid-19 pandemic, there are clearly different views emerging in light of complex social and organisational factors at play. For example, the likelihood of individuals suffering from workaholism – working excessively hard, being obsessed with work and not respecting the boundaries between home and work [11]; the use of social media to communicate with colleagues for formal and non-formal purposes and the impact on technostress and work exhaustion [12], and understanding the relationship between level of satisfaction when WFH and levels of technostress [4]. The contrasting perspectives in the literature, the range of ICTs available and the fact that that some individuals have now been WFH for over two years makes exploring the relationship between homeworkers and technology a fruitful avenue for further study.

3   Methodology

This study was part of a wider exploratory study utilising the diary-keeping technique [see 5]. Participants completed daily diary entries over a period of ten working days with respect to their homeworking experiences; this included questions about their working hours, their feelings about working remotely each day and their technology use. Not only did this offer an insight into participants' everyday lives as it naturally unfolded [13], but respondents were able to record responses on the day. Diaries were kept between May and June 2020 during the height of the lockdown. Participants were asked to complete an additional information sheet which provided details such as demographic data. Having a record of daily experiences helped the researchers to develop more of a context to each participant's responses. Participants were recruited using a snowballing sampling technique. Diaries were completed by a total of 29 participants. Data was analysed following guidelines by Miles and Huberman [14]: a contact summary sheet, summary sheet, coding, causal diagrams and a matrix of the demographic information.

4   Findings

15 males and 14 females participated in this study. 17 participants were located in the UK, four in India, three in the USA, two in Germany and one each in Nepal, Canada and Luxembourg. Occupations of participants were varied and included: Web Administrator

and Digital Marketer, Software Developers and Academics. Nine participants had never worked from home before the pandemic, whereas 20 participants had. All participants said they had a heavy workload which seemed to have escalated during the shift to working from home. Technology usage also rose hugely given the nature of the pandemic. The key findings relating to technology use are highlighted below with some indicative quotations from the participants' diaries.

4.1 The Changing Nature of Work

A key finding from our study was that work had become a lot more functional: the absence of travel, face-to-face interactions and office-based work meant that several daily routines were omitted – e.g. travel and workplace interactions – which can traditionally be said to constitute an important part of the working day. Now, individuals fit in informal chit-chat with colleagues before/at the end of meetings and, in some cases, were able to keep informal chats going throughout the day via applications such as MS Teams:

Participant 14 (male, 25–34 years, Software Developer): *"I feel like the proportion of casual/personal conversations I am having with colleagues is a lot smaller when working from home (i.e. nearly all conversations are about work matters). For example, today all messages I exchanged with colleagues were about work. Without the casual conversations to break the day up, it can give the work day a more serious feel"*.

4.2 Developing a Balance Between Home and Work-Related Technology Use

In general, participants tried to develop a balance between work and home which helped with managing technology use. For example, Participant 29 (25–34 year old female, Policy and Projects Co-ordinator in local Government) stated the difficulty in trying to strike a balance during each of the ten days' diary entries:

Day 2: *"I'm sat at the computer for so long that I've been feeling it over the last few weeks"* which was leading to physical health problems and affecting sleep."

Day 3: *"I am trying to be very mindful of the stress that work is creating for me at the moment, especially as things are moving to a manageable pace…I am now booking in some days off and trying to create more manageable hours for myself compared to the 10–12 h shifts I had been doing at my computer in the first month or so of the lockdown."*

Participant 27 (male, 25–34 years, Data Analytics Manager, Financial Services) stated the difficulties associated with being connected across time zones and via multiple collaborative platforms throughout the diary entries as well as the opportunity to attend to home commitments. On day 10, he added: *"I may come across as someone who is negatively biased towards remote working concept, but to be honest my experience has been evolving with every single day of the lockdown or rather since 13th March [2020] - 1st day when my company enabled "remote working" across the organisation. The time and experiences encountered since Day 1 compared to Day 50 to Day 100 (and still counting) has allowed and enabled me to become an individual who is not only more flexible than what I used to be 3 months back but has also helped me to be more prepared for such situations in future"*.

4.3 Managing Communication via Social Media Technology

Some participants who had taken up social media communication to retain informal communication with colleagues began to reconsider whether they wanted to continue partaking in such communication. This could prove difficult given that some participants had shared their personal mobile number with more colleagues since the lockdowns. For example, Participant 20 (female, 35–44 years, Researcher):

Day 1: *"someone from another dept has created a whatsapp group. It has people I have never really interacted with before, except for the casual 'hi' in the corridor when we were on-site. It's okay, some funny things shared"*.

Day 7: *"I decided to leave [the Whatsapp group] and I am so happy. I've started managing [other informal colleague communication] better because I ignore their messages after about 9pm"*.

4.4 Balancing Technology and Work: An Ongoing Challenge

How individuals manage technology that is ubiquitous is an ongoing challenge for many. In addition to the issue of sharing personal mobile numbers with more colleagues and engaging in social media interaction with more colleagues, there were other issues that participants had to contend with when working remotely via technology instead of in a designated office space. For example, Participant 19, male, 45–54 years, Head of Service, ICT) highlighted the volume of communication via multiple applications which had to be managed. He stated how his working days have adjusted to enable more video conferences throughout the day which leads to less time for emails and thus a backlog of emails. He also added: *"Made family members understand that noise is amplified during conference calls. They now take out kettle etc. and use it in lounge"*.

Participant 7 (male, 25–34 years, Key Account Manager) was one of the participants who highlighted the problem with being too contactable: *"my team leader called me and asked me to help him with an analysis that needs to be done today by the end of the day and in a short amount of time, he expected me to finish it, however, his requirement was not really clear and that's why I needed more time. After 2 h he kept sending me messages via teams on updates. At some point I felt like I was going crazy"*.

4.5 Technology-Enabled Work as a 'BArrier' from Workplace

There has been a shift in how people relate to technology-enabled work and that shift may be regarded as positive in some cases. For instance, although some participants may have missed the face-to-face interaction with colleagues and the office facilities, others stated the benefit of being able to focus on work when returning to the office on an ad hoc basis:

Participant 7 (male, 35–44 years), IT/Software Professional): *"Today I went to office on need basis, though limited folks critical for project only could come to office, but felt good being in office premise and working at comfort of office desk. And it was productive also than regular days. Being in office without wasting time on office chit chat 😊(as no one to chit chat on politics or social issues)"*.

The issue regarding distancing oneself from organisational politics when working from home was mentioned by other participants, including Participant 4 (female, 25–34 years, Research and Evaluation Officer): *"...having space away from colleagues in a complex political issue means I could respond rather than react, and not be pressured by the immediacy of an in-person interaction"* although she also added at times she felt *"very tired from overwork...and internal politics adding to projects"*.

5 Discussion and Conclusion

There seems to be a wide range of aspects that the diary entries have thrown up, many aspects of which merit further study. In the main study, where the focus was on how homeworkers managed social interaction with colleagues using technology, a somewhat unanticipated finding was how homeworkers' perceptions and usage of technology (beyond that for social interaction purposes) changed. Thus, this short paper only touches upon this theme by presenting some findings related to it. In so doing, the authors wish to use this as a starting point on which to investigate this topic further and would welcome the comments of the conference delegates with regards to advice on relevant theoretical frameworks/theories that may be used to contextualise a future study specifically dedicated to this theme. The brief literature review suggests that technology has often played a stressful role in homeworkers' lives. Indeed, some of the findings in this short paper can concur with this perspective. However, the findings also suggest that individuals are able to form new behaviours and habits, which can ultimately affect how they perceive and use technology.

Even given the term 'technostress' suggests negativity throughout, the reality of a change of working mode is not black and white: e.g. what is regarded in some contexts as positive by some people is regarded rather negatively by other people as negative. This is reflected by the findings, identifying barriers but also balances. Investigating these dynamics more thoroughly is essential for devising recommendations – both in professional as well as private contexts – on how to allow technology into our lives (or not).

For instance, if work is now being perceived as more functional as suggested in the findings, especially given the lack of in-person interactions, then this can affect not only the way in which work is perceived, but also how the tools provided in order to fulfil work tasks are perceived and used – i.e. as a means to an end. The findings also suggest that individuals are trying to develop more of a balance between work and home which is also affecting the time spent on computers which had previously affected them adversely. Also, the longer someone spends working from home, it appears the more 'in control' they can become not just of their work and home lives, but also how they perceive the whole notion of 'work' and what it means to them. This feeling of developing a balance/control can explain why some individuals perceive technology as a barrier/shield to internal politics and distractions from colleagues which enabled them to focus on their work and, thus, reinforces the notion of work becoming more functional.

It goes without saying that it is never the same story with everyone in that the degree to which individuals are able to develop this notion of 'control' depends on many factors. Therefore, in future research, it is planned to investigate the impact of WFH on an individual more holistically, i.e. at the professional, emotional, cultural and individual level. It is expected that these different strands/levels are interdependent and can only be understood properly holistically rather than in isolation.

Cultural situatedness, which has been investigated in some contexts, for example in e-learning [15], should ideally be investigated in a wider range of technology-related scenarios. To this end, thick description [16] and in-depth qualitative study seems most appropriate, as well as maximising the breadth of contexts covered. Insights into this are likely to lead to a more satisfying – and even humane – use of technology in our lives.

References

1. Dwivedi, Y.K., et al.: Impact of COVID-19 pandemic on information management research and practice: Transforming education, work and life. Int. J. Inf. Manag. **55**, 102211 (2020)
2. Herath, T., Herath, H.S.B.: Coping with the new normal imposed by the COVID-19 pandemic: lessons for technology management and governance. Inf. Syst. Manag. **37**(4), 277–283 (2020)
3. Tarafdar, M., Gupta, A., Ture, O.: The dark side of information technology use. Inf. Syst. J. **23**, 269–275 (2013)
4. Taser, D., Aydin, E., Torgaloz, A.O., Rofcanin, Y.: An examination of remote e-working and flow experience: The role of technostress and loneliness. Comput. Hum. Behav. **127**, 107020 (2022)
5. Lal, B., Dwivedi, Y.K., Haag, M.: Working from home during Covid-19: doing and managing technology-enabled social interaction with colleagues at a distance. Inf. Syst. Front. (2021). https://doi.org/10.1007/s10796-021-10182-0
6. Papagiannidis, S., Harris, J., Morton, D.: WHO led the digital transformation of your company? A reflection of IT related challenges during the pandemic. Int. J. Inf. Manag. (2020). https://doi.org/10.1016/j.ijinfomgt.2020.102166
7. Barnes, S.: Information management research and practice in the post-COVID-19 world. Int. J. Inf. Manag. (2020) https://doi.org/10.1016/j.ijinfomgt.2020.102175
8. Tarafdar, M., Tu, Q., Ragu-Nathan, T.S.: Impact of technostress on end-user satisfaction and performance. J. Manag. Inf. Syst. **27**(3), 303–334 (2010)
9. Sarabadani, J., Compeau, D., Carter, M.: An investigation of IT users' emotional responses to technostress creators. In: Proceedings of the 53rd Hawaii International Conference on System Sciences, pp. 6113–6122 (2020)
10. Ragu-Nathan, T.S., Tarafdar, M., Ragu-Nathan, B.S.R., Tu, Q.: The consequences of technostress for end use in organizations: conceptual development and empirical validation. Inf. Syst. Res. **19**(4), 417–433 (2008)
11. Spagnoli, P., Molino, M., Molinaro, D., Giancaspro, M.L., Manuti, A., Ghislieri, C.: Workaholism and technostress during the COVID-19 emergency: the crucial role of the leaders on remote working. Front. Psychol. **11**, 620310 (2020)
12. Oksanen, A., Oksa, R., Savela, N., Mantere, E., Savolainen, I., Kaakinen, M.: COVID-19 crisis and digital stressors at work: a longitudinal study on the Finnish working population. Comput. Hum. Behav. **122**, 106853 (2021)
13. Neupert, S.D., Bellingtier, J.A.: The Ups and Downs of Daily Diary Research. SAGE Research Methods Cases in Psychology (2018). http://methods.sagepub.com/case/the-ups-and-downs-of-daily-diary-research
14. Miles, M.B., Huberman, A.M.: Qualitative Data Analysis: An Expanded Sourcebook, 2nd edn. SAGE Publications Inc., Thousand Oaks (1994)

15. Haag, M.: Personal knowledge development in online learning environments: a personal value perspective. Ph.D. thesis, University of Bedfordshire, Luton, UK (2011)
16. Denzin, N.K., Lincoln, Y.S.: The SAGE Handbook of Qualitative Research, 5th edn. Sage Publications Inc., Thousand Oaks (2017)

Work-From-Home Performance During the Pandemic: How Technology Availability Moderates Job Role, Stress and Family-Work Conflict

Jane Fedorowicz[1] , Safa'a AbuJarour[2(✉)], Haya Ajjan[3], and Dawn Owens[4]

[1] Bentley University, Waltham, MA, USA
[2] An-Najah National University, Nablus, Palestine
safaa.abujarour@najah.edu
[3] Elon University, Elon, NC, USA
[4] University of Texas at Dallas, Richardson, TX, USA

Abstract. Employees working from home (WFH) during the COVID-19 pandemic turned to an array of information and communications technologies (ICT) to support at-home job performance. This study documents the role of ICT in enabling these workers and managers to abruptly transition to WFH and explores the barriers and challenges they faced in working remotely. The goal of the study is to address the research question: How did ICT availability affect the relationship between personal work environment factors (i.e., job role, stress, and family-work conflict) and job performance while WFH due to the onset of the COVID-19 pandemic? We also report on how workers adjusted their ICT usage (hardware, software and Internet access) when moving to remote work. We then compare workers' ICT usage, job performance, and personal stressors across manager and non-manager roles. Our findings from survey responses from 545 workers in 36 countries record a range of personal and professional challenges employees faced when forced to WFH, including whether employer ICT support has successfully met their needs. Our findings will inform employer efforts to establish new WFH policies.

Keywords: ICT · Working from home · WFH · COVID-19 · Pandemic · Survey · Technology availability · Job performance

1 Introduction

As the COVID-19 pandemic spread around the world in early 2020, a large percentage of the global workforce was forced to work from home (WFH) on short notice. For those working in data-centric fields where information is the central commodity, a key enabler of the move to WFH was information and communication technology (ICT). However, many workers were not equipped with the technology they needed to maintain their in-office job performance (Galanti et al. 2021; Morikawa 2022). Only 22% of

A. Elbanna et al. (Eds.): TDIT 2022, IFIP AICT 660, pp. 226–248, 2022.
https://doi.org/10.1007/978-3-031-17968-6_18

respondents to a study by Deloitte said that their organizations supplied the technologies they needed to facilitate remote working before the pandemic, and 42% of organizations planned to invest in new technologies and systems that support remote working in the future (Deloitte 2021). And while ICT is key to moving people to a remote location, there are many other environmental and personal hurdles facing remote workers that also must be overcome (Morikawa 2022). As the physical location of jobs and family life intersect, companies will be well served to identify and support best practices on supporting home-based employees in many possible crisis situations (Choudhury et al. 2020).

The purpose of this study is to document the role of ICT in enabling workers and managers to abruptly transition to WFH due to the global COVID-19 pandemic, and to explore the barriers and challenges these employees faced in working remotely. To do so, we report on the results of an online survey administered soon after the COVID-19 WFH phenomenon began. The study examines the relationship between the technologies available to support remote work and the personal work environment employees contend with when moving to home-based work, and how both affect worker performance. We describe the types and characteristics of technologies used by WFH employees to demonstrate the gulf between office ICT support and employees' home technology setup. We identify those areas where managers and non-managers differed in their ICT-supported WFH performance. We document the effects of stress and family-work conflict on worker performance and suggest that ICT availability can help to ameliorate the impact of these personal environmental factors. To do so, the study first looks at how workers' ICT usage (hardware, software, and Internet access) changed due to WFH during the COVID-19 pandemic. With knowledge of these changes, we then address the following research question:

- *How did ICT availability affect the relationship between personal work environment factors (i.e., job role, stress, and family-work conflict) and job performance while WFH due to the onset of the COVID-19 pandemic?*

2 Related Work

2.1 Working from Home During COVID-19

Office work has evolved to be conducted anywhere and anytime due to its reliance on ICT (Rahim et al. 2018). Environmental and economic factors, such as high operating costs, globalization, and changing workforce demographics, also encouraged the transition to the virtual office (Calvasina et al. 2012; Meinert 2011).

Although not a new notion, WFH was never adopted to the extent forced by the COVID-19 crisis. In addition to causing acute economic and life disruption at an unprecedented scale and rate worldwide (Gopinath 2020), COVID-19 revolutionized the WFH concept by accelerating the move towards remote working (The Economist 2020). About a third of the workforce in the U.S. changed to WFH (Brynjolfsson et al. 2020) and half of Europeans were thought to be WFH at the outset of the pandemic (Ahrendt et al. 2020). As organizations look to the future, many are planning to stay virtual or adopt a hybrid virtual model that combines remote work with time in the office (Paul 2020;

Alexander et al. 2021). Given the widespread and abrupt move to WFH, and companies' continued commitment to supporting this workplace alternative, it is crucial to study how WFH during COVID-19 affects employees in their job-related tasks as well as their personal lives.

The transition to WFH during the COVID-19 pandemic was not easy. Over 70% of employees reported struggling to shift to remote work (Hutzler 2020). Of those, 80% cited the transition to a digital work environment as a challenge (Hutzler 2020). Early in the pandemic, productivity was a concern, however, new research has found that IT innovations related to WFH have facilitated an increase in productivity (Criscuolo et al. 2021). But much depends on the tasks being performed and the WFH environment (Criscuolo et al., 2021). In summary, while there is progress, there are still circumstances and challenges that affect employee performance.

Job Role: Managers vs. Non-managers
Both managers and non-managers moved to remote working under the same circumstances. However, there may be differences in how each group reacts to their work settings. Research has shown that managers experience more ICT-induced stress than non-managers (Boyer-Davis 2019; Stadin et al. 2021) but work-related stress may be lower (Peter et al. 2020; Skaken et al. Skakon et al. 2011). In addition, managers experience greater work-life conflict but higher job satisfaction (Peter et al. 2020). Managers' personality traits might also indicate a differential impact on their job performance. Managers have been shown to score higher on measures of emotional stability than non-managers, and emotional stability is known to be related to job performance (Tett et al. 2000; Salgado 1997; Lounsbury et al. 2016). Managers are held to be more accountable than non-managers for organizational performance (Factor et al. 2013) and therefore may find that their own performance diminishes as their own and their reports' work is affected by WFH challenges. Evidence does confirm a negative relationship between supervisory status and WFH job performance in the public sector during the current pandemic (Fischer et al. 2022).

As many of these findings were based on traditional working environments, it would be useful to assess if these differences persist when employees (including managers) are forced to WFH. This motivates our first hypothesis:

- *H1: Job performance will differ for managers and non-managers while forced to WFH.*

2.2 Stress

A significant concern during the pandemic is that WFH can increase symptoms of stress in those working from home, causing negative impacts on their emotional well-being (Golden 2009; Fornara et al. 2022; Galanti et al. 2021; Moss 2021). Even prior to the pandemic, research documented the challenges around balancing work and family responsibilities, resulting in increased stress levels (Dockery and Bawa 2014; Pfeffer 2018). Although WFH is positively related to overall job satisfaction because of the increased flexibility of achieving work-related tasks, it leads to more job-induced stress and negative personal well-being due to work overload and work-life conflicts (Anderson et al. 2015; Hayman 2010). Moreover, having more job flexibility and autonomy requires greater effort from workers to manage their time at home and this is channeled into their work, causing adverse effects and work-related stress (Curzi et al. 2020; Moss 2021).

WFH also can generate health concerns, some resulting from workers tending to work too much while at home rather than too little (Nickson and Siddons 2004; Pfeffer 2018; Moss 2021). This tendency towards long hours for some can also result in family-work conflicts (Callister 2003).

In addition to job-related adaptation, COVID-19 created a new set of challenges because the entire household unit was in self-isolation together (Vyas 2022). Workers had to develop personal and professional strategies to mitigate the stressful psychological costs from an unanticipated switch to WFH, especially given insufficient time or capacity to effectively manage the trade-off among their work, social and home roles (Choudhury et al. 2020; Moss 2021; Fornara et al. 2022).

In summary, stress is known to be linked to lowered job performance (e.g., Jamal 1985). It is likely that stress levels will increase when WFH, which may further affect an employee's work performance. Hypothesis 2 reflects this prospect.

- H2: An increased stress level will have a negative impact on job performance as employees are forced to WFH.

2.3 Family-Work Conflict

Family-work conflict is the degree to which responsibilities from the family and work domains are incompatible (Greenhaus and Beutell 1985). Conflicts happen when wide-ranging family and work demands cut across each other, resulting in negative performance consequences (Voydanoff 2005). Family-work integration increases both family-to-work conflict and work-to-family conflict, and an inability to disengage from work increases work-to-family conflict (Eddleston and Mulki 2017). Family-work conflict has been shown to be negatively correlated to WFH productivity during the pandemic (Galanti et al. 2021).

Family-work-role conflict comprises time-based, strain-based, and behavior-based reflecting an individual's scarce time and energy resources (Netemeyer et al. 1996; Greenhaus and Beutell 1985). Time-based conflict is the time demanded by one's family roles and responsibilities such as children, spouse, or parent as distinct from time demanded by work-related tasks (Netemeyer et al. 1996; Greenhaus and Beutell 1985). A strain-based conflict results from the anxiety and stress stemming from performing family and work duties (Netemeyer et al. 1996; Greenhaus and Beutell 1985). A behavior-based conflict exists when role demands, such as self-reliance and emotional stability, make it harder to fulfill other roles, such as emotional vulnerability and warmth (Greenhaus and Beutell 1985).

We base the family-work conflict construct used in our study on time-based, strain-based, and behavior-based family-work items. We examine this in Hypothesis 3:

- H3: Family-work conflict will have a negative impact on job performance as employees are forced to WFH.

Employing ICT while WFH

During the COVID-19 lockdown, billions of people were forced to instantly adopt the digital technologies that facilitate communication, data acquisition, research and development, and management to remain productive and efficient (Kamal 2020). Remote teams rely on ICT to communicate, which requires a stable Internet connection to support email, teleconferencing, and document sharing services (McKeown 2016). ICT supports business continuity by maintaining information exchange and enabling business processes, making it a critical tool for WFH particularly in emergency situations. ICT plays a significant role in enabling WFH and coping with negligible work-home boundaries (Cousins and Robey 2005; Gerlach 2018; Golden and Geisler 2007; Kreiner 2006). However, while ICT creates many advantages to enhance worker performance, it can also trigger workplace stress, role overload, and technostress (Ashforth et al. 2000; Boyer-Davis 2019; Sarker et al. 2012; Tarafdar et al. 2007). The "always-on" functionality of technology-based tools makes it difficult to switch off work while WFH (McKeown 2016). While ICT accessibility distinctions can enable work-life boundaries in normal times, they are less feasible during the COVID-19 pandemic. Studies (e.g., Pan et al. 2020) observed that the rapid lockdown produced great challenges for individuals due to the pressure to adapt to a new online- and home-centered life.

Thus, technology availability may be both an enabler of and a source of conflict for employees who WFH. In our study, we differentiate among three categories of ICT artifacts – Internet access, hardware availability and software availability. The closure of offices created a physical challenge to employee access to hardware during the pandemic, even as software could be distributed online (Galanti et al. 2021). In addition, Internet accessibility is constrained by what is available geographically and financially to employees. Hypotheses 1, 2 and 3 will be examined in light of each of these three ICT categories to ascertain whether ICT availability augments or diminishes the relationship between personal environmental WFH characteristics and job performance. Table 1 contains both the direct and moderated hypotheses that address the study's research question.

Demographic Factors Relating to WFH

Trends noted during the pandemic suggest that personal work environment factors may account for some of the job performance differences we expect in our analysis. After testing these hypotheses, we report on relationships in the results that may be linked to age, gender, or family caretaking status of the respondents.

Older workers are more experienced in their jobs and are less likely to have conflicting obligations for dependent care. They may also be less comfortable or practiced with having to switch from in-person to online communications. They have been found to have lower job performance in previous studies (Rhodes 1983; Rodríguez-Cifuentes et al. 2018). However, age was found to correlate both with higher WFH performance (Fischer et al. 2022) and lower WFH productivity (Galanti et al. 2021) during the pandemic. Thus, it is unclear what relationship we might expect of age as a control variable in this study.

There is no doubt that both working men and women have been adversely impacted by the stay-at-home order during the pandemic. Studies have repeatedly shown that working women may have a harder time balancing work and home because women are typically responsible for more of family or home caretaking, even when they earn more than their partner (Craig and Sawrikar 2009). In addition, the link between ICT usage and negative home-to-work spillover has been noted for women, but not for men (Chesley 2005).

Table 1. ICT moderation hypotheses

Hypothesis 1	**Job performance will differ for managers and non-managers while forced to WFH.**
Hypothesis 1a	The relationship between job role and job performance differs based upon available internet speed.
Hypothesis 1b	The relationship between job role and job performance differs based upon the provision of needed hardware.
Hypothesis 1c	The relationship between job role and performance differs based upon the provision of needed software.
Hypothesis 2	**An increased stress level will have a negative impact on job performance as employees are forced to WFH.**
Hypothesis 2a	The negative effect of stress level on job performance is worsened for employees with slower internet speed.
Hypothesis 2b	The negative effect of stress level on job performance is worsened for employees who were not provided with needed hardware.
Hypothesis 2c	The negative effect of stress level on job performance is worsened for employees who were not provided with needed software.
Hypothesis 3	**Family-work conflict will have a negative impact on job performance as employees are forced to WFH.**
Hypothesis 3a	The negative effect of family-work conflict level on job performance is worsened for employees with slower internet speed.
Hypothesis 3b	The negative effect of family-work conflict level on job performance is worsened for employees who were not provided with needed hardware.
Hypothesis 3c	The negative effect of family-work conflict level on job performance is worsened for employees who were not provided with needed software.

During the pandemic, many women took on added responsibility for caring for children, elderly parents, and the home. When given flexible work arrangements, men are expected to improve work performance, while women are expected to increase their caretaking responsibilities, which increase their family-work conflict (Chung and van der Lippe 2018). Prior research has shown that when WFH, total hours worked for women increases dramatically (Dockery and Bawa 2014), and this leads to more family-work conflict (van der Lippe and Lippényi 2018). Early in the pandemic, mothers with children under 13 reduced their work hours four to five times more than fathers (Collins et al. 2020). However, gender alone may not predict performance decrease, as at least one study found women in government roles experienced an increase in performance during the pandemic shutdown (Fischer et al. 2022). We expect that women, especially those who are responsible for caretaking of family members, will experience higher levels of stress and family-work conflict than men or those without family caretaking obligations, and this will affect their performance.

These demographic factors will be evaluated after the hypotheses in Table 1 to suggest personal characteristics that may drive differences noted by job role, stress, and family-work conflict.

3   Research Design

Our conceptual model (shown in Fig. 1) reflects the hypotheses listed in Table 1. The model depicts the expected moderating relationship of ICT between job role, stress level, and family-work conflict and job performance. The model will test whether ICT can ameliorate the effects of these personal environmental factors, to specifically identify the benefits (or costs) that ICT provision (or lack) adds when employees' work environment becomes dispersed.

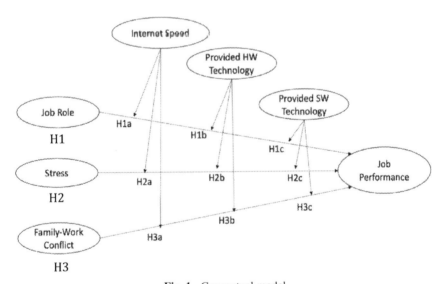

Fig. 1. Conceptual model

4   Methodology and Sampling

We developed an online survey instrument using Qualtrics to collect data from employees who have had to move their jobs home during the COVID-19 pandemic. The survey instrument, which was approved by a university institutional review board, combined demographic questions with items characterizing the WFH environment and covering employees' current use of technology. In line with previous literature assessing technology availability (Bélanger et al. 2001; Prezza et al. 2004), we asked respondents whether they had access to needed ICT including high-speed Internet, and whether the company has provided access to adequate WFH-enabling hardware and software.

We measured family-work conflict experienced by the employees using a five-item scale measuring the demands of family (Netemeyer et al. 1996). We asked employees to assess their stress levels before and during the pandemic. We measured job performance using a three-item scale from Becker et al. (1996) that is commonly used to analyze people's work outcomes. Demographic variables included the person's gender, age, and caregiver status. Each respondent also indicated their job role (as manager or non-manager).

A pilot test of the survey was conducted using a convenience sample. Due to the desire to reach a large and disparate global audience for the full survey, we employed a combination of social media channels and email distribution lists to reach a wide online audience. Personal connections also shared the survey with their professional contacts, creating a snowball distribution network. The final version of the questionnaire was distributed over these channels during the 12-day period of April 27 to May 8, 2020.

We obtained a total of 545 usable responses from 36 countries. 456 of the respondents were living with others. Of these, 21.4% reported they are mainly responsible for family/home caretaking, 41% are not the main family/home caretakers, and 34% had

Table 2. Demographic information

Description	Frequency	Percent	Description	Frequency	Percent
Gender			**Job role**		
Male	210	38.5	Management	134	24.6
Female	326	59.8	Non-Management	405	74.3
Other/ Missing	9	1.7	Missing	6	1.1
Age			**Country (Top 6 of 36 are shown here)**		
18-24	57	10.5	United States	240	44.0
25-34	128	23.5	Germany	192	35.2
35-44	125	22.9	Greece	22	4.0
45-54	104	19.1	Mexico	13	2.4
55-64	105	19.3	Canada	7	1.3
65 or older	19	3.5	Egypt	6	1.1
Missing	7	1.3	Other	58	10.6
			Missing	7	1.3
Marital status			**Living Alone**		
Single	169	31.0	Yes	89	16.3
Married/In Partnership	369	67.7	No	456	83.7
Missing	7	1.3			

equally distributed responsibilities (3% had missing responses). Table 2 reports on the demographic characteristics of the respondents. For privacy reasons, demographic questions included an option for those choosing not to respond, resulting in a small number of missing values for those items.

5   Results

We first present descriptive statistics capturing WFH trends in technology use. Then, we perform a hierarchical regression analysis to examine the main study variables in three models to control for the selected variables. All analysis was conducted using SPSS.

5.1   Descriptive Statistics

Technology Usage
We asked participants to compare their current use of ICT to before the stay-at-home order, by enquiring about their use of teleconferencing tools, VPN, productivity tools, company applications, and shared storage. As expected, reliance on ICT increased for many of the respondents, with few reporting a decrease in ICT use (See Fig. 2). The largest increase was in use of teleconferencing technologies such as Zoom, Skype, GotoMeeting, Webex, and Microsoft Teams. This was unsurprising given the forced isolation of this population.

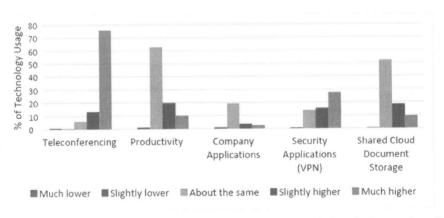

Fig. 2. A % of respondents technology usage compared to the time before the "stay-at-home" order

We also noted an increase in productivity tool usage (e.g., Word, PowerPoint, Google Docs, Project Management, Calendar, Email), with over half of the respondents saying they used them about the same and another third using them somewhat more or much more than before WFH. Of the relatively few working with company applications at home (e.g., SAP, Quickbooks, CRM), usage stayed the same for most, with some noting they used these more or much more. Over half of respondents reported the use of security applications like Virtual Private Networks (VPN) once they began to WFH, and of these, most reported an increase in use, again not surprising given their reliance on remote access. Finally, most respondents reported using shared cloud document storage while at home, with most acknowledging accessing the cloud as much or more than before WFH. Some respondents also mentioned "Other" tools they used while WFH such as project management, software development and screen recording tools.

5.2 Regression Analysis

Table 1 lists the three sets of hypotheses that address our research question: *How did ICT availability affect the relationship between personal work environment factors (i.e., job role, stress, and family-work conflict) and job performance while WFH due to the onset of the COVID-19 pandemic?*

A hierarchical regression analysis that incorporates the personal environment, ICT and job performance variables tests the model in Fig. 1. To do so, several categorical variables were dummy coded: job role (manager (reference group) and non-manager), hardware available (adequate (reference group) and inadequate), and software provided (adequate (reference group), and inadequate). To control for respondent characteristics, we included three additional variables used in previous work-related perception studies (e.g., Agle and Caldwell 1999; Keyes 2002; Brammer et al. 2007; Factor et al. 2013; Scandura and Lankau 1997): age, gender (female (reference group) and family responsibility/main caregiver (yes (reference group), no, and equally divided).

Measurement Model

The reliability of all multi-item constructs was assessed using Cronbach's alpha. Cronbach's alpha coefficient ranged from 0.83 to 0.94, all greater than 0.7 (Nunnally 1978). The correlations among the variables ranged from 0.26 to 0.02, indicating no evidence of multicollinearity (r's > 0.8). Convergent and discriminant validity of all scales were evaluated. Factor loading of all items in the family-work conflict and performance constructs exceeded 0.7, providing evidence for convergent validity. The AVE scores exceeded 0.5, with family-work conflict (AVE $= 0.81$) and for job performance (AVE $= 0.745$).

Regression Results

Three hierarchical regression analyses were used to assess the ability of the independent variables together in predicting performance. For each regression model, we ran three regression levels (control, main effect, and interactions) including a new set of variables at each level.

The first regression analysis included demographics control variables (age, gender and family responsibility status). In the second model, we included the main effect variables, job role, stress, family-work conflict and the relevant ICT variable (for example, access to high-speed Internet). In the third model we included three interaction terms calculated using a product term with each of the main effect variables with the specific

ICT variable. To minimize the effect of multicollinearity, we centered all main effect variables to calculate the product term (Edwards and Lambert 2007).

ICT Moderation Model for Internet Speed

In step 1, analysis of the controls (gender, age, family responsibility status = yes, main caregiver = equal), age (B = 0.15, P < 0.01), main caregiver = No (B = 0.64, P < 0.01), and main caregiver = Equal (B = 0.34, P < 0.01) all predicted performance, as shown in Table 3.

Table 3. Hierarchical regression analysis for internet speed predicting job performance

	Model 1		Model 2		Model 3	
	B	Std. Error	B	Std. Error	B	Std. Error
Gender = Female	-0.03	0.09	0.02	0.07	0.02	0.07
Age	0.15**	0.03	0.06*	0.03	0.07**	0.03
Family Responsibility = No	0.64**	0.11	0.22*	0.09	0.22*	0.09
Family Responsibility = Equal	0.34**	0.11	0.18*	0.09	0.18*	0.09
Role = Not Management			-0.27**	0.08	-0.27**	0.08
Stress			-0.09**	0.03	-0.09**	0.03
Family-work conflict			-0.42**	0.03	-0.42**	0.03
Internet Speed			0.13*	0.06	0.11	0.06
Internet Speed X Role					0.10	0.14
Internet Speed X Stress					-0.09	0.05
Internet Speed X Conflict					0.12*	0.05
R^2	0.11		0.45		0.46	
Change in R^2	0.11		0.34		0.01	
F Change	13.09**		64.44**		2.43	

*p < .05. **p < 01, n= 422

In step 2, the main effects for job role = Not Management (B = −0.27, P < 0.01), family-work conflict (B = −0.42, P < 0.01), and stress (B = −0.09, P < 0.01) all predicted job performance. Thus, the main hypotheses H1, H2, and H3 were supported.

Internet speed (B = 0.13, P < 0.05) was also significant in Step 2. Hypotheses 1a, 2a, and 3a proposed a moderator role for Internet speed between job role, stress, and family-work conflict and performance.

In the final step, the entry of three interaction terms contributed to a small added explained variance that is not significant (change in R2 = 0.01, P = 0.06). Job role's interaction with Internet speed (B = 0.09, P = 0.49) and stress interaction with Internet speed (B = 0.10, P = 0.08) were not significant in predicting job performance (H1a, H2a). However, family-work conflict interaction with Internet speed (B = 0.12, P < 0.05) was significant in predicting job performance (H3a).

To further analyze differences in the interaction term, we examined the performance means across the interaction term in Fig. 3. We reviewed the job performance scores at a combination of the mean ± 1 SD (high and low levels) for family-work conflict at three levels of Internet speed (slow, acceptable, and fast). The figure shows that the negative relationship between family-work conflict and job performance is worsened by slow Internet speed, thus supporting hypothesis H3a. Hypotheses 1a and 2a were rejected due to the insignificant interaction effect; a non-management job role and increased stress are associated with negative job performance regardless of Internet speed.

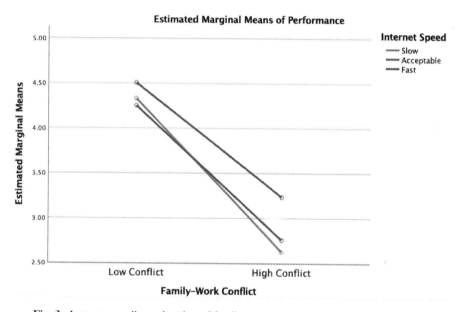

Fig. 3. Internet speed's moderation of family-work conflict's impact on performance

ICT Moderation Model for Hardware

We next evaluate the moderating role of adequate hardware support between job role (hypothesis 1b), stress (hypothesis 2b), family-work conflict (hypothesis 3b) and job performance. As shown in Table 4, job role (B = −0.26, P < 0.01), stress (B = −0.10, P < 0.01), and family-work conflict (B = −0.42, P < 0.01) all predict job performance, supporting the main effects noted in H1, H2 and H3. Hardware availability (B = −0.19, P < 0.05) was also significant.

The entry of three interaction terms contributed to added explained variance (change in $R^2 = 0.01$, $P < 0.05$). We find the interaction of available hardware and role (H2a, B $= -.43$, $P < 0.05$) and the interaction of available hardware and family-work conflict (H2c, B $= -.16$, $P < 0.05$) were significant in predicting job performance. Hypotheses 2b was rejected due to the insignificant interaction effect between available hardware and stress (B $= -0.01$, $P = 0.80$).

To further analyze differences in the interaction term, we examined the mean differences in Fig. 4 and Fig. 5. We reviewed the job performance scores at a combination of the mean ± 1 SD (high and low levels) for family-work conflict. Figure 4 shows that the negative relationship between non-managers and job performance is worsened with inadequate access to hardware, thus supporting hypothesis H1b. Figure 5 shows that the negative relationship between family-work conflict and job performance is worsened with inadequate hardware, in support of hypothesis H3b. Despite the lack of moderating effect of inadequate hardware (H2b is not supported), it is important to note that stress has a significant negative main effect on job performance (B $= -0.10$, $P < 0.01$). This shows that higher stress leads to negative job performance regardless of hardware availability.

Table 4. Hierarchical regression analysis for hardware availability predicting job performance

	Model 1		Model 2		Model 3	
	B	Std. Error	B	Std. Error	B	Std. Error
Gender = Female	-0.03	0.09	0.02	0.07	0.03	0.07
Age	0.15**	0.03	0.06*	0.03	0.06*	0.03
Family Responsibility = No	0.64**	0.11	0.23*	0.09	0.22*	0.09
Family Responsibility = Equal	0.34**	0.11	0.17*	0.09	0.18*	0.09
Role= Not Management			-0.26**	0.08	-0.31**	0.08
Stress			-0.10**	0.03	-0.10**	0.03
Family-work conflict			-0.42**	0.03	-0.43**	0.03
Hardware Availability			-0.19*	0.08	-0.10	0.08
Hardware Availability X Role					-0.43*	0.20
Hardware Availability X Stress					-0.02	0.06
Hardware Availability X Conflict					-0.16*	0.07
R^2	0.11		0.45		0.47	
Change in R^2	0.11		0.34		0.01	
F Change	13.09**		64.44**		3.71*	

*$p < .05$. **$p < 01$, n= 423

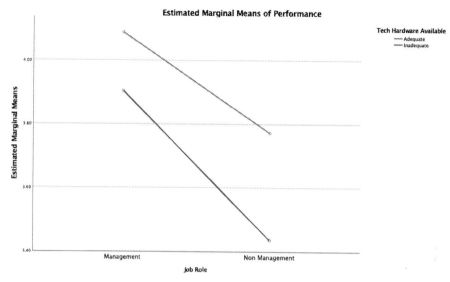

Fig. 4. Hardware's moderation of job role's impact on performance

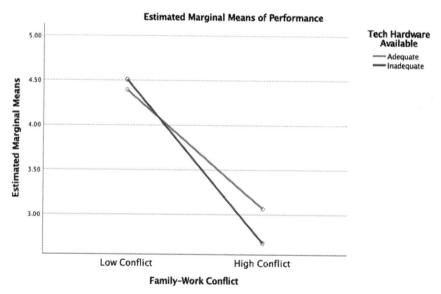

Fig. 5. Hardware's moderation of family-work conflict's impact on performance

ICT Moderation Model for Software

Hypotheses 1c, 2c, and 3c examine available software as a moderator between job role, family-work conflict, and performance. As shown in Table 5, the main effects in model 2 for job role (B = −0.26, P < 0.01), stress level (B = −0.11, P < 0.01), and family-work conflict (B = −0.41, P < 0.01) all predicted job performance, as did inadequate software availability (B = −0.24, P < 0.01). The change in R2 was significant (change in R2 = 0.34, P < 0.01) relative to the variance explained. In the final step, job role interaction with inadequate software (B = −0.36, P = 0.07), stress and inadequate software (B = 0.02, P = 0.67), and family-work conflict and inadequate software (B = −0.06, P = 0.43) were not significant in predicting job performance. Thus, hypotheses 1c, 2c and 3c were rejected due to the insignificant interaction effect. Also, the change in R2 for model 3 was insignificant (change in R2 = 0.01, P > 0.05). Despite the lack of moderating effect, it is important to note that job role, family-work conflict and stress all have a negative main effect on job performance. This shows that a non-management job role is associated with negative job performance regardless of the software availability. It also shows that higher stress and higher family-work conflict led to lower job performance regardless of software availability.

Table 5. Hierarchical regression analysis for software availability predicting job

	Model 1		Model 2		Model 3	
	B	Std. Error	B	Std. Error	B	Std. Error
Gender = Female	-0.03	0.09	0.02*	0.07	0.02	0.07
Age	0.14**	0.03	0.06*	0.03	0.06*	0.03
Family Responsibility = No	0.64**	0.11	0.23*	0.09	0.24**	0.09
Family Responsibility = Equal	0.33**	0.11	0.18**	0.09	0.19*	0.09
Role = Not Management			-0.26**	0.08	-0.29**	0.08
Stress			-0.11**	0.03	-0.11**	0.03
Family-work conflict			-0.41**	0.03	-0.41**	0.03
Software Availability			-0.24**	0.08	-0.18*	0.09
Software Availability X Role					-0.36	0.20
Software Availability X Stress					0.03	0.07
Software Availability X Conflict					-0.06	0.08
R2	0.11		0.46		0.46	
Change in R2	0.11		0.34		0.01	
F Change	13.04**		66.06**		1.39	

*p < .05. ** p < 01, n= 423

Figure 6 provides a summary of these results.

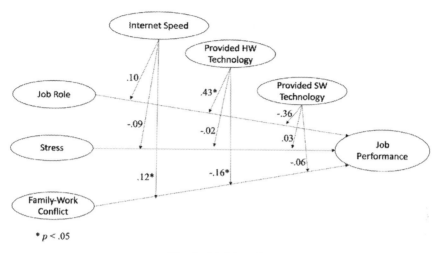

Fig. 6. Model results

6   Discussion

As organizations look to the future, many realize the future of work may look different than what we experienced during pre-pandemic times, with many planning to stay virtual or adopt a hybrid virtual model (Paul 2020; Alexander et al. 2021; Vyas 2022). With several unknown factors on the horizon, we help address this future scenario by exploring how ICT influences the effect of remote workers' personal work environments on their job performance.

We first documented how technology usage changed when workers had to WFH during the pandemic. Respondents reported an increase in ICT use, notably teleconferencing technologies and cloud storage. Less common were increases in productivity tools, company applications such as ERP, and security applications such as a VPN. Our results corroborate prior research that shows ICT enhances the feasibility of WFH (Curzi et al. 2020), and ICT availability with a stable Internet connection is necessary for a team to be able to work well remotely (McKeown 2016). This justifies investigation as to their efficacy in improving worker performance when employees encounter unique challenges or roadblocks due to the colocation of work and home. ICT adoption accelerated during the pandemic and is considered to be the primary enabler of the future of work (Vyas 2022).

Testing of our research question explored whether ICT could influence the relationship among several personal work environmental factors (i.e., job role, stress, and family-work conflict) and job performance, as these factors are likely to be affected by having to WFH. Three core themes emerged in our analysis. First, all three personal work environment factors - job role, stress, and family-work conflict - have a direct effect on job performance. Second, low Internet speed and hardware availability increase the negative impact of family-work conflict. Finally, two demographic factors, family caregiver responsibility and age, also significantly explain performance differences.

6.1 Job Role

Job role has a direct effect on job performance with provided hardware technology having a moderating effect, while Internet speed and provided software technology did not. Non-managers self-reported lower job performance than managers and this difference increased when they did not have adequate access to hardware. This may mean that managers are more likely to be provided with hardware for home use by the employer, or that they are more inclined to purchase their own hardware and do not need any provided by their employer. In either situation, non-managers are less able to perform given the hardware with which they must accomplish their work.

Although Internet speed and provided software technology did not have a significant effect on job performance differences between the two job roles, they were still important factors. When asked about Internet speed and reliability, managers were more likely to have good, reliable Internet access than non-management respondents.

This raises the question "who is responsible for ensuring that employees, when forced to WFH, have a suitable work environment?" Complications ensue if there are multiple people WFH, a situation rarely encountered widely in the past. Few organizations have pre-planned ways to support an office environment for every employee who is WFH.

Looking ahead, workers should gain experience using ICT tools on a regular basis, to ensure that they are prepared during future WFH scenarios. In addition to hardware and software, employers should consider the WFH workspace so employees have the proper office equipment (e.g., ergonomics, screen size, monitors) to remain productive Fornara et al. 2022).

6.2 Stress

Employees often struggled with the shift to remote work, with the transition to a digital work environment a particular challenge (Hutzler 2020; Galanti et al 2021). These struggles bear out as stress, whether caused by different tasks, changed work processes, the home setting, or learning to use new ICT. Our findings confirm that stress has a direct effect on job performance while WFH. Participants reported higher stress levels than pre-pandemic times, and respondents with higher stress levels during the pandemic reported lower performance. We found no moderating effect from provided hardware technology, provided software technology, or Internet speed, which implies that sources other than technostress (Hung et al. 2011; Tarafdar et al. 2007) are the drivers of WFH stress.

However, it is important to note that Internet speed's impact on job performance was close to significant with a P value of .08. Respondents with fast Internet speed experienced somewhat lower stress than those with acceptable Internet speed or with slow Internet. This is corroborated in a survey reported by Computerworld (Oct. 2020), as unreliable home broadband connectivity was noted as the primary technical challenge businesses faced with remote work during the COVID-19 pandemic.

There was no significant difference in stress levels between those that regularly performed work-related tasks from home prior to the pandemic than those that did not. This suggests that stress levels are not related solely to WFH. In addition, stress levels did not differ markedly between management and non-management levels. While prior research has shown that managers experience more ICT-induced stress than non-managers (Boyer-Davis 2019; Stadin et al. 2021), this does not consider WFH.

Work-related stressors were magnified by respondents' living arrangements - respondents living alone experienced lower stress than those living with others. This is supported by Dockery and Bawa (2014) who found that remote workers found it challenging to balance work and family responsibilities simultaneously which resulted in higher stress. Studies show that although WFH is positively related to overall job satisfaction because of the increased flexibility of achieving work-related tasks, it leads to more job-induced stress and negative personal well-being due to work overload and work-life conflicts (Anderson et al. 2015; Hayman 2010; Fornara et al. 2022). Thus, it is not surprising that both stress and family-work conflict were associated with lowered job performance.

6.3   Family-Work Conflict

Perhaps the biggest visible change to the pandemic-time work environment is its colocation. Not only were workers suddenly making do with whatever home office equipment they may own, they also must contend with the many distractions of working alongside family members or roommates, who contend for space, attention, and silence (Fornara et al. 2022). The removal of a boundary between work and home life is a significant source of individual work-related conflict (Eddleston and Mulki 2017; Greenhaus and Beutell 1985; van der Lippe and Lippényi 2018; Voydanoff 2005). We found a negative relationship between family-work conflict and job performance, meaning job performance decreased with heightened family-work conflict. Further, the effect of family-work conflict is worsened by slow Internet access and deficient employer provision of hardware technology.

WFH during COVID-19 creates a new set of technology challenges that did not exist before. Household members may compete for access to the Internet or the family's hardware (Galanti et al. 2021). This can lead to conflict due to reduced Internet speed if they all need to be on Zoom at the same time or are forced to vie for a single-family computer or printer. Therefore, it is not surprising that insufficient ICT lowered job performance for those experiencing family-work conflict.

Family-work conflict is especially significant for those who might have insufficient time or capacity to effectively manage the trade-off among their work, social and home roles (Choudhury et al. 2020; Galanti et al. 2021). This corroborates the results of our demographic analysis, in which gender had no direct effect on job performance, a relationship that appears to counter intuition and the popular press about how women are under more pressure than men during these times (Alon et al. 2020; Giurge et al. 2021; Lyttelton et al. 2020; Peters 2021). While the gender of remote workers was not a meaningful predictor of performance, we do note that family or caregiving responsibility is a strong determinant of performance, even when the respondent reports equal responsibility. These responsibilities are likely to be carried by women, and these are also the demographic that the popular press documents as withdrawing from the workforce due to conflicting work-family demands (Alon et al. 2020; Petts et al. 2020).

Even without the distraction of family responsibility, the lack of a boundary between work and home was a notable challenge for many. Employers need to enable boundaries in their WFH strategies and put into place mechanisms for remote workers to control the number and timing of work hours considering personal commitments (Galanti et al. 2021; Pfeffer 2018).

One other interesting demographic finding was the significance of age as having a positive direct relationship with job performance. Some of this may be attributable to the likelihood that older workers are less likely to have small or school-age children at home. They are also more likely to be managers, and that job role was demonstrated to lead to higher performance. Or it may be that older workers have had more time to garner experience with remote work prior to COVID19, and therefore find the transition less dramatic. There is more to learn here, and we suggest that further research be conducted on how these demographic variables relate to characteristics of the personal work environment to provide guidance for companies' ability to support all of their employees who WFH.

The results of this study will be valuable to employers concerned with the welfare of their workers who may prefer to WFH post-pandemic. Companies will need to establish workable WFH policies that fit with the expectations of both employers and employees as we enter the "new normal" world where ICT will be a key enabler (Vyas 2022).

7 Limitations and Directions for Future Research

Like any study, this one suffers from limitations. We chose to distribute a survey to capture a global snapshot of a dynamic situation that is changing quickly. Due to the need for timely and widespread dissemination of our instrument, we employed a convenience sample and snowball survey distribution. This led to uneven representation globally as the countries where the authors reside are overly represented in the sample. Only an English version was distributed. We are unable to estimate how well the sample represents the actual population of WFH workers, as there is little hard evidence of the true distribution of WFH employees around the world. We also acknowledge that pandemic closures occurred in countries at different times and with different limitations, which might affect how long participants had been working at home before responding and what their personal situation might be. This could also affect their expectations about the future of their WFH experience and the nature of the tasks they are responsible for during this period. In addition, data reflect respondent perceptions of the constructs in the study and were not corroborated by other independent sources or measures.

This study reported on the results of the first of three surveys planned to assess WFH job-related, personal and ICT characteristics of remote workers. Added constructs in the follow-up surveys will ascertain the longer-term effects of forced WFH to contrast with the initial reactions of this sample. To illustrate, we will explore the nature and sources of stress attributable to WFH during the pandemic. Our broader project aims to build upon the Job Demands and Resources model (Demerouti et al. 2001) by adapting it to the WFH setting. The multi-time-period study will allow us to distinguish the short-term and longer-term relationships among a larger number of WFH factors and demographic characteristics. Once the third survey is conducted in summer 2022, we will have a better window into the benefits and challenges of WFH that should help to inform businesses about the assistance needed to ensure performance enhancement in the home environment (Vyas 2022).

References

Agle, B.R., Caldwell, C.B.: Understanding research on values in business: a level of analysis framework. Bus. Soc. **38**(3), 326–387 (1999)

Ahrendt, D., Cabrita, J., Clerici, E., et al.: Living, Working and Covid-19, pp. 1–80. Publications Office of the European Union, Luxembourg (2020)

Alexander, A., De Smet, A., Langstaff, M., Ravid, D.: Employees want more certainty about postpandemic working arrangements – even if you don't yet know what to tell them, McKinsey & Company (2021). https://www.mckinsey.com/business-functions/people-and-organi zational-performance/our-insights/what-employees-are-saying-about-the-future-of-remote-work. Accessed 03 Mar 2022

Alon, T., Doepke, M., Olmstead-Rumsey, J., Tertilt, M.: The impact of COVID-19 on gender equality. National Bureau of Economic Research (2020)

Anderson, A.J., Kaplan, S.A., Vega, R.P.: The impact of telework on emotional experience: when, and for whom, does telework improve daily affective well-being? Eur. J. Work Organ. Psy. **24**(6), 882–897 (2015)

Ashforth, B.E., Kreiner, G.E., Fugate, M.: All in a day's work: boundaries and micro role transitions. Acad. Manag. Rev. **25**(3), 472–491 (2000)

Becker, T.E., Billings, R.S., Eveleth, D.M., Gilbert, N.L.: Foci and bases of employee commitment: implications for job performance. Acad. Manag. J. **39**(2), 464–482 (1996)

Bélanger, F., Collins, R.W., Cheney, P.H.: Technology requirements and work group communication for telecommuters. Inf. Syst. Res. **12**(2), 155–176 (2001)

Boyer-Davis, S.: The empirical relationship between leadership style and technostress. ASBBS Proc. **26**, 99–112 (2019)

Brammer, S., Millington, A., Rayton, B.: The contribution of corporate social responsibility to organizational commitment. Int. J. Hum. Resour. Manag. **18**(10), 1701–1719 (2007)

Brynjolfsson, E., Horton, J., Ozimek, A., Rock, D., Sharma, G., Ye, H.Y.T.: Covid-19 and remote work: an early look at us data. Unpublished work (2020). https://john-joseph-horton.com/papers/remote_work.pdf?utm_source=npr_newsletter&utm_medium=email&utm_content=20200427&utm_term=4544910&utm_campaign=money&utm_id=33857746&orgid=310. Accessed 01 June 2020

Callister, P.: Overwork, work schedules, working at home and time spent with family members: how time use data can inform work/life policy. In: Working Paper (2003). http://citeseerx.ist.psu.edu/viewdoc/download?doi=10.1.1.517.324&rep=rep1&type=pdf

Calvasina, G.E., Calvasina, R.V., Calvasina, E.J.: The virtual office: HRM legal, policy, and practice issues. Bus. Stud. J. **4**(2), 37–46 (2012)

Chesley, N.: Blurring boundaries? Linking technology use, spillover, individual distress, and family satisfaction. J. Marriage Fam. **67**(5), 1237–1248 (2005)

Choudhury, P., Koo, W.W., Li, X.: Working (from home) during a crisis: online social contributions by workers during the coronavirus shock. In: Harvard Business School Working Paper, no. 20–096, March 2020 (2020)

Chung, H., van der Lippe, T.: Flexible working, work–life balance, and gender equality: introduction. Soc. Indicat. Res. 1–17 (2018)

Collins, C., Landivar, L.C., Ruppanner, L., Scarborough, W.J.: COVID-19 and the gender gap in work hours. Gender Work Organ. (2020)

Cousins, K.C., Robey, D.: Human agency in a wireless world: patterns of technology use in nomadic computing environments. Inf. Organ. **15**(2), 151–180 (2005)

Craig, L., Sawrikar, P.: Work and family: how does the (gender) balance change as children grow? Gend. Work. Organ. **16**(6), 684–709 (2009)

Criscuolo, C., Gal, P., Leidecker, L., Losma, F., Nicoletti, G.: The role of telework for productivity during and postCOVID-19: results from an OECD survey among managers and workers. In: OECD Productivity Working Papers, 2021-31. OECD Publishing, Paris (2021)

Curzi, Y., Pistoresi, B., Fabbri, T.: Understanding the stressful implications of remote e-working: evidence from Europe (No. 0165). University of Modena and Reggio Emilia, Department of Economics (2020)

Deloitte: Building the Resilient Organization - 2021 Deloitte Global Resilience Report. Deloitte Insights (2021). https://www2.deloitte.com/content/dam/insights/articles/US114083_Global-resilience-and-disruption/2021-Resilience-Report.pdf?icid=learn_more_content_click

Demerouti, E., Bakker, A.B., Nachreiner, F., Schaufeli, W.B.: The job demandsresources model of burnout. J. Appl. Psychol. **86**(3), 499 (2001)

Dockery, A.M., Bawa, S.: Is working from home good work or bad work? Evidence from Australian employees [online]. Aust. J. Labour Econ. **17**(2, Aug 2014), 163–190 (2014)

Eddleston, K.A., Mulki, J.: Toward understanding remote workers' management of work–family boundaries: the complexity of workplace embeddedness. Group Org. Manag. **42**(3), 346–387 (2017)

Edwards, J.R., Lambert, L.S.: Methods for integrating moderation and mediation: a general analytical framework using moderated path analysis. Psychol. Methods **12**(1), 1–22 (2007)

Factor, R., Oliver, A.L., Montgomery, K.: Beliefs about social responsibility at work: comparisons between managers and non-managers over time and cross-nationally. Bus. Ethics Eur. Rev. **22**(2), 143–158 (2013)

Fischer, C., Siegel, J., Proeller, I., Drathschmidt, N.: Resilience through digitalisation: how individual and organisational resources affect public employees working from home during the COVID-19 pandemic. Public Manag. Rev., 1–28 (2022)

Fornara, F., et al.: Space at home and psychological distress during the Covid-19 lockdown in Italy. J. Environ. Psychol. **79**(101747), 1–10 (2022)

Galanti, T., Guidetti, G., Mazzei, E., Zappala, S., Toscano, F.: Work from home during the COVID-19 outbreak: the impact on employees' remote work productivity, engagement, and stress. J. Occup. Environ. Med. **63**(7), e426–e432 (2021)

Gerlach, J.P.: Work, home, and technology: towards a framework of IT-based boundary management. In: 26th European Conference on Information Systems (ECIS 2018) (2018)

Giurge, L.M., Whillans, A.V., Yemiscigil, A.: A multicountry perspective on gender differences in time use during COVID-19. PNAS Proc. Natl. Acad. Sci. U.S.A. **118**(12), e2018494118 (2021)

Golden, A.G., Geisler, C.: Work–life boundary management and the personal digital assistant. Hum. Relat. **60**(3), 519–551 (2007)

Golden, T.D.: Applying technology to work: toward a better understanding of telework. Organ. Manag. J. **6**(4), 241–250 (2009)

Gopinath, G.: The great lockdown: worst economic downturn since the great depression. IMF Blog, April, 14 (2020). https://blogs.imf.org/2020/04/14/the-great-lockdown-worst-economic-downturn-since-the-great-depression/. Accessed 01 June 2020

Greenhaus, J.H., Beutell, N.J.: Sources of conflict between work and family roles. Acad. Manag. Rev. **10**(1), 76–88 (1985)

Hayman, J.: Flexible work schedules and employee well-being. N. Z. J. Employ. Relat. **35**(2), 76 (2010)

Hung, W.H., Chang, L.M., Lin, C.H.: Managing the risk of overusing mobile phones in the working environment: a study of ubiquitous technostress. In: PACIS, p. 81 (2011)

Hutzler, A.: More than 7 in 10 employers are struggling to adapt to remote work, survey shows. News Week (2020). https://www.newsweek.com/more-7-10-employers-are-struggling-adapt-remote-work-survey-shows-1499236?utm_source=npr_newsletter&utm_medium=email&utm_content=20200427&utm_term=4544910&utm_campaign=money&utm_id=33857746&orgid=310. Accessed 06 Jan 2020

Jamal, M.: Type A behavior and job performance: some suggestive findings. J. Hum. Stress. 11(2), 60–68 (1985)

Kamal, M.M.: The triple-edged sword of COVID-19: understanding the use of digital technologies and the impact of productive, disruptive, and destructive nature of the pandemic. Inf. Syst. Manag. 37(4), 310–317 (2020)

Keyes, C.L.: The mental health continuum: from languishing to flourishing in life. J. Health Soc. Behav, 207–222 (2002)

Kreiner, G.E.: Consequences of work-home segmentation or integration: a person-environment fit perspective. J. Organ. Behav. 27(4), 485–507 (2006)

Lounsbury, J.W., Sundstrom, E.D., Gibson, L.W., Loveland, J.M., Drost, A.W.: Core personality traits of managers. J. Manag. Psychol. 31(2) (2016)

Lyttelton, T., Zang, E., Musick, K.: Gender differences in telecommuting and implications for inequality at home and work (2020). SSRN 3645561

McKeown, S.: Dealing with the causes of stress in remote teams. Human Made (2016). https://humanmade.com/uploads/sites/3/2016/11/dealing_with_the_causes_of_stress_in_remote_teams.pdf

Meinert, D.: Make telecommuting pay off. HRMagazine 56(6), 33–37 (2011)

Moss, J.: The Burnout Epidemic: The Rise of Chronic Stress and How We Can Fix It, pp. 1–269. Harvard Business Review Press, Boston (2021)

Morikawa, M.: Work-from-home productivity during the COVID-19 pandemic: evidence from Japan. Econ. Inq. 60, 508–527 (2022)

Netemeyer, R.G., Boles, J.S., McMurrian, R.: Development and validation of work–family conflict and family–work conflict scales. J. Appl. Psychol. 81(4), 400 (1996)

Nickson, D., Siddons, S.: Remote working: linking people and organizations. Ind. Commercial Train. 36(2) (2004)

Nilles, J.M., Carlson, F.R., Gray, P., Hanneman, G.: Telecommunications-transportation tradeoffs. Final report. 1 July 1973–31 December 1974 University of Southern California, Los Angeles (1974)

Nunnally, J.C.: An overview of psychological measurement. Clin. Diagn. Mental Disord, 97–146 (1978)

Pan, S.L., Cui, M., Qian, J.: Information resource orchestration during the COVID-19 pandemic: a study of community lockdowns in China. Int. J. Inf. Manag. 54, 102143 (2020). ISSN 0268-4012

Paul, K.: Twitter announces employees will be allowed to work from home 'forever'. The Guardian (2020). https://www.theguardian.com/technology/2020/may/12/twitter-coronavirus-covid19-work-from-home

Peter, K.A., Schols, J.M., Halfens, R.J., Hahn, S.: Investigating work-related stress among health professionals at different hierarchical levels: a cross-sectional study. Nurs. Open 7(4), 969–979 (2020)

Peters, E.: What you want is not always what you get: gender differences in employer-employee exchange relationships during the COVID-19 pandemic. Soc. Sci. 10(8), 281 (2021)

Petts, R.J., Carlson, D.L., Pepin, J.R.: A gendered pandemic: childcare, homeschooling, and parents' employment during COVID-19. Gender Work Organ. (2020)

Pfeffer, J.: Dying for a Paycheck, pp. 1–258. Harper Business, New York (2018)

Prezza, M., Pacilli, M.G., Dinelli, S.: Loneliness and new technologies in a group of Roman adolescents. Comput. Hum. Behav. **20**(5), 691–709 (2004)

Rahim, N.I.M., Rahman, A.A., Iahad, N.A.: The overview for implementing work from home (WFH) in Malaysia higher education institution (HEI) context. Int. J. Innov. Comput. **8**(3) (2018)

Rhodes, S.R.: Age-related differences in work attitudes and behavior: a review and conceptual analysis. Psychol. Bull. **93**, 328–367 (1983)

Rodríguez-Cifuentes, F., Farfán, J., Topa, G.: Older worker identity and job performance: the moderator role of subjective age and self-efficacy. Int. J. Environ. Res. Public Health **15**(12), 2731 (2018)

Salgado, J.F.: The five factor model of personality and job performance in the European Community. J. Appl. Psychol. **82**(1), 30 (1997)

Sarker, S., Sarker, S., Xiao, X., Ahuja, M.: Managing employees' use of mobile technologies to minimize work-life balance impacts (2012)

Scandura, T.A., Lankau, M.J.: Relationships of gender, family responsibility and flexible work hours to organizational commitment and job satisfaction. J. Organ. Behav. Int. J. Ind. Occup. Organ. Psychol. Behav. **18**(4), 377–391 (1997)

Skakon, J., Kristensen, T.S., Christensen, K.B., Lund, T., Labriola, M.: Do managers experience more stress than employees? Results from the Intervention Project on Absence and Well-being (IPAW) study among Danish managers and their employees. Work **38**(2), 103–109 (2011)

Stadin, M., Nordin, M., Broström, A., Hanson, L.L.M., Westerlund, H., Fransson, E.I.: Technostress operationalised as information and communication technology (ICT) demands among managers and other occupational groups–results from the Swedish longitudinal occupational survey of health (SLOSH). Comput. Hum. Behav. **114**, 106486 (2021)

Tarafdar, M., Tu, Q., Ragu-Nathan, B.S., Ragu-Nathan, T.S.: The impact of technostress on role stress and productivity. J. Manag. Inf. Syst. **24**(1), 301–328 (2007)

Tett, R.P., Guterman, H.A., Bleier, A., Murphy, P.J.: Development and content validation of a "hyperdimensional" taxonomy of managerial competence. Hum. Perform. **13**(3), 205–251 (2000)

The Economist: Covid-19: is working from home really the new normal? The Economist (2020). https://www.youtube.com/watch?v=MxDVucUZCnc&feature=youtu.be

van der Lippe, T., Lippényi, Z.: Beyond formal access: organizational context, working from home, and work–family conflict of men and women in European workplaces. Soc. Indicat. Res. 1–20 (2018)

van der Lippe, T., Lippényi, Z.: Co-workers working from home and individual and team performance. N. Technol. Work. Employ. **35**(1), 60–79 (2020)

Voydanoff, P.: Toward a conceptualization of perceived work-family fit and balance: a demands and resources approach. J. Marriage Fam. **67**(4), 822–836 (2005)

Vyas, L.: "New normal" at work in a post-COVID world: work-life balance and labor markets. Policy Soc. **41**(1), 155–167 (2022)

The State of Health Information Systems Research in Africa: A Scoping Review

Josue Kuika Watat[1](✉) ⓘ and Ebenezer Agbozo[2] ⓘ

[1] HISP Centre, Department of Informatics, University of Oslo,
Ole-Johan Dahls Hus Gaustadalleèn 23B, 0373 Oslo, Norway
josuekw@ifi.uio.no
[2] Ural Federal University, Mira 32, 620078 Yekaterinburg, Russia
eagbozo@urfu.ru

Abstract. Research on health information systems is gaining momentum, given the importance of the topic in curbing various healthcare issues which are challenging the African health system. The relevance of the topic is reflected in the exponential growth of technological innovations for health and scientific research that assesses their impact. This plethora of research avenues poses a situation of missing evidence on the state of the art of the topic in its diversity. In this research, we report on an overview of research on health information systems across Africa, outlining key insights such as current trends and institutions addressing the topic. We examined 353 articles collected in the Scopus database, and screened them using the biblioshiny. Based on the findings, we ascertained the intricacy of the topic and pinpointed key areas for future research. The outcomes of our research provide information for practitioners engaged in understanding the advancement and state of the art of technology for healthcare in Africa, and research analysis for scholars and researchers on health technologies in Africa.

Keywords: Health information systems · Healthcare · Africa · Bibliometrics

1 Introduction

Since the onset of recent healthcare crises and pandemics such as Ebola and Covid19, it has become more challenging to envision a safe and effective health environment without the use of Information and Communication Technologies. The health fabric of many states is now based on critical data and information for health needs analysis and quality service delivery [1]. The African context represents a significant window of opportunity regarding the sheer volume of information produced but not aggregated due to their states, which makes its use difficult and unstructured [2]. The advent of technological tools has significantly reshaped the health landscape, its data and information, and working practices. For clinicians, the ever-growing demand for health services ought to be at the core of innovations that pertain to the health care system, and they should be key performers in monitoring the evolution of needs by disease, and any resulting technological changes [3].

A. Elbanna et al. (Eds.): TDIT 2022, IFIP AICT 660, pp. 249–258, 2022.
https://doi.org/10.1007/978-3-031-17968-6_19

The use of health information systems in Africa has been presented as a solution to address shortcomings related to cost-effectiveness, quality of health care delivery, data security and process efficiency [4]. Thus, policymakers and government decision-makers emphasized the necessity for the health sector to emulate the examples set by other industries, where the use of technology has been instrumental in expanding access to critical data for decision making, automating formerly resource-intensive processes and tasks, and minimizing human error [5–7].

A number of previous investigations have employed bibliometric analysis to construe the research evidence on health information systems, the role of technology in health within Africa, and the relevance of cutting-edge technologies in the fight against epidemics. To our knowledge, no research has documented the emerging literature on mapping health information systems research in Africa, explicitly through the use of bibliometric analysis. Pertaining to our topic, a systematic review is a relevant source of the progress and state of the art which will provide statistics, information on affiliations, origin of studies, as well as the thematic overview of the topic. Thus, a major contribution of this research for practitioners and scholars lies in the documentation of the state of the art of the current literature on health information systems in Africa. In addition, one of the contributing components of our research is the prioritization of themes that drive research on this topic in Africa, along with the compilation of lacunae and promiscuous avenues of research that serve as a foundation for future research and a forum for practitioners to engage in dialogue.

This research underscores the complex nature of discussions around health information systems in Africa, especially the technological, social and economic endeavors that need to be made. Also, it demonstrates the relevance of such an innovation in transforming the African health landscape, which has a significant impact on the One Health vision [8, 9]. The research enables a variety of institutions to engage in prioritized, results-oriented thinking with efficient resource allocation. The remainder of this paper focuses on the methodology identified and applied to this research, the associated findings, and the implications.

2   Methodology

The study is based on a systematic literature review methodology, which is built upon the PRISMA (Preferred Reporting Items for Systematic Reviews and Meta-Analyses) paradigm. Systematic reviews have been applied by researchers in providing insights on how empirical studies employed co-design strategies in mobile health (mHealth) systems development [10]. The PRISMA statement guidelines undergirds this study by adopting the four (4) steps - identification, screening, eligibility and inclusion criteria [11–13]. A systematic literature review acts as an instrumental source of summarize evidence relating to efficacy of any domain of discourse accurately and reliably [14]. The PRISMA guidelines have been adopted by studies focused on information systems in Africa, as such it was deemed as an efficient backing for this study [15, 16].

2.1 Setting the Academic Scope and Study Background

The academic field engaged in this study is health information systems, and the background to the study is Africa. Recognizing that health information systems contribute to improving the health system throughout all levels of performance (strategic, social), health information systems research in Africa has the substantial promise of providing transformational proof to issues surrounding the use of technology in health, in a weakened environment, and amidst uncertainty.

2.2 Identification and Curation of Relevant Publications on the Subject

We compiled bibliometric records from the Scopus database due to its completeness, inclusivity, ease of use, comprehensiveness, and credibility with regards to research sources [17, 18]. Studies have recommended Scopus as enough for systematic reviews because it is an effective search engine and contains majority of the credible research publications [19, 20]. Figure 1 illustrates the research methodology by visually depicting keyword combinations. The results of our keyword combination yielded a sample size of N = 572 articles published and indexed until March 2022. By applying the PRISMA guidelines, we furthermore derived a subset of the final list of articles to N = 353, by excluding non-English articles, undefined authors, articles in press (due to the fact that

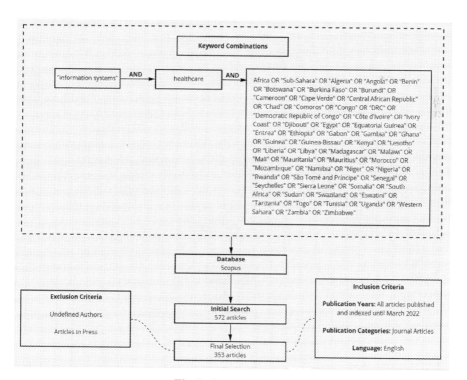

Fig. 1. Research design

articles in press are likely to be withdrawn since they are not yet officially published), and limiting sources to scientific journals only.

2.3 Bibliometric Assessment

In order to obtain the relevant results for the study, we adopted the bibliometrix package - an open-source scientometrics and bibliometrics research tool - in R and used the biblioshiny tool as our knowledge extraction tool [21]. The tool has a proven track record of performing elaborate analysis of a large set of compiled data, generating reliable outputs with an easily readable and understandable layout [21, 22]. In the next section, we present the results of our knowledge extraction and data analysis.

3   Findings

In this section, we uncover our research findings. The bibliometric analysis generated essential insights that highlighted the scientific production and cited sources, most relevant affiliations of authors, topic trends based on keywords, and a co-occurrence map network with respect to healthcare information systems research in Africa. From our data source, Scopus, the earliest research papers on information systems and healthcare with respect to Africa were published as early as 1995. Out of 353 articles, the average citations per document was 10.73, with 1973 authors and 5.59 authors per document.

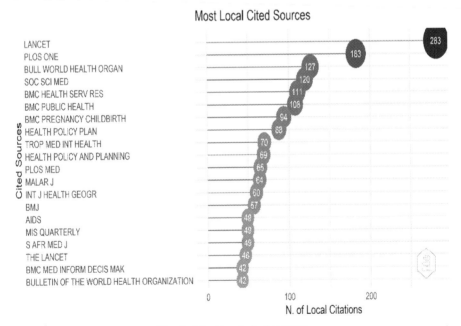

Fig. 2. Most local cited sources.

Figure 2 highlights the most cited sources with the number of local clusters on the x-axis and the cited sources on the y-axis. Lancet topped the number of cited sources for research on healthcare and information systems research in Africa.

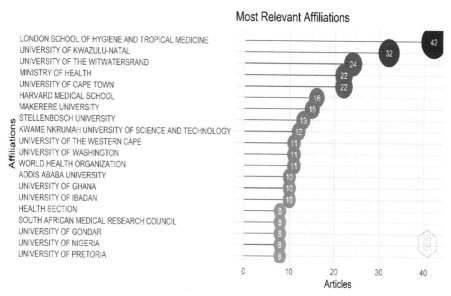

Fig. 3. Most relevant affiliations

Another relevant statistic is the affiliation of authors (as highlighted in Fig. 3) with the London School of Hygiene and Tropical Medicine (UK), University of Kwazulu Natal (South Africa), Ministry of Health (which is as a result of affiliation name disambiguation), and the University of Cape Town (South Africa) being the topmost institutions. The presence of Ministry of Health research, indicates the immense contribution by scientists and academics associated with government institutions as a means of improving healthcare delivery within the various countries in Africa. Also, corresponding authors and their countries of affiliation by publication count are South Africa (53), USA (48), United Kingdom (34), Ghana (15), Nigeria (14), Ethiopia (13), Kenya (10), Canada (7), Netherlands (6), and Australia (5) respectively. This is indicative of the fact that researchers within the sub-Saharan region are putting in the effort to tell the story of the state of healthcare and information systems within their region and contribute towards its development.

Figure 4 illustrates topical trends with respect to research on information systems and healthcare in Africa. By observation, one can infer that topics such as public health, data quality, and primary healthcare will be the focus of future studies with regards to information systems in African healthcare studies. Themes such as malaria and health systems continue to be studied. One can also observe the sudden decline in certain topics right after 2019, and this could most probably be linked to the covid-19 pandemic and a shift of research focus. Studies confirm this observation (publication boom) by indicating

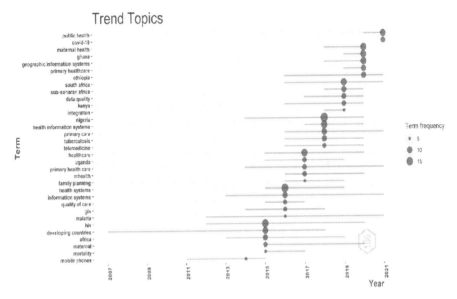

Fig. 4. Trend topics (Author keywords)

the fact that there was an urgency to disseminate new research findings, with Nigeria ranking second (2nd) in research productivity with respect to covid-19 studies [23–25].

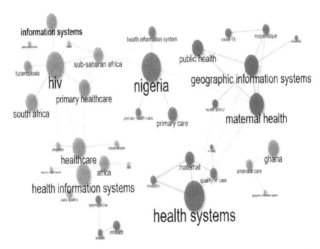

Fig. 5. Co-occurrence network map (based on Authors' keywords) (Color figure online)

Figure 5 illustrates the co-occurrence network map of health care and information systems research in Africa, drawn from the authors' keywords. A co-occurrence network is graph $G(V, E, W)$, where V is the vertex set (representative of entities - keywords in this case), E is indicative of the set of edges that connect vertices, and W is a set of weights associated with the edges (it is indicative of the strength of the relationship) [26]. The network parameters include: (a) the Louvain clustering algorithm which is used to cluster words, after which each word is scored based on the sum of several scoring approaches such as word score based on dependency relations, and term frequency score of each word [27] (b) graph normalization by association, the number of nodes (50) and the minimum number of edges (2). The graph is composed of seven (7) clusters. The red cluster shines a light on geographic information systems (GIS) linked to public health, maternal health, accessibility, healthcare policy, covid-19 and the country of Mozambique. From these nodes, one can conclude that one of the key components of IS and healthcare research in Africa is targeted at providing accessible services to maternal healthcare as well as the utilization of GIS for healthcare provision especially with respect to contact tracing during the COVID-19 pandemic in 2020.

The blue cluster links maternal health (from the red cluster) to Nigeria (the central node) which is linked to health information systems and primary healthcare. It can be deduced that healthcare and information systems research focused on Nigeria has been narrowed down to the need for quality primary healthcare delivery via IS within the rural and public health scope.

The green cluster is an isolated cluster with three (3) nodes: Ghana, antenatal care and GIS. This cluster buttresses the points made in studies that highlight the use of GIS in evaluating the impact of community-based health initiatives in rural Ghana [28]. Studies have also focused on the application of GIS (road network analysis) to analyze the distance from the homes of women living in Bo, Sierra Leone to the nearest healthcare providers and to their preferred acute care providers [29].

The orange cluster has the keywords HIV, information systems, primary healthcare, tuberculosis, South Africa, Sub-Saharan Africa, Malawi, and healthcare workers. Studies have revealed the positive strides South Africa has taken in curbing the HIV crisis and tuberculosis related issues via formidable policies and health information systems [30]. Such initiatives have eased the burden on health workers and optimized the process of delivering quality healthcare.

The pink cluster which is healthcare information systems, healthcare, Africa, data quality, mobile phones, integration, and health. In recent years, studies on data quality interventions (i.e. effective management) have been a priority of healthcare research in Africa [31]. One study highlighted the improvement in data quality with respect to reports submitted to health authorities in South Africa [32]. Studies continue to focus on assessing and improving data quality in electronic healthcare records for optimal service delivery [33].

The brown cluster comprises the following keywords: health system, maternal, new-born, quality of care, and mortality. Previous studies have revealed the huge rate of infant and maternal mortality within African countries [34, 35]. Conversely, research has also focused on countering child and maternal mortality [36].

Finally, the purple cluster which constitutes the tokens mhealth, ehealth, and telemedicine reveal the adoption of technology within Africa's healthcare sector. Digital healthcare initiatives have been integrated in the African healthcare experience for health-care education, disease prevention initiatives, medical appointments and drug adherence programs [37]. They were adopted as a form of sustainable technology capable of protecting patients, medical practitioners during the covid-19 pandemic to reduce patients' social mobility (so as to decrease viral spread) [38]. It is evident that technological integration within healthcare in Africa has come a long way and will continue to make progressive strides.

4   Conclusion and Research Avenues

In this research, we report on a systematic overview of the nascent literature on health information systems in Africa. The methodology applied revealed how complex the topic is, considering the major interests at stake, and the importance of Africa's health system in the global health agenda as spurred on by the World Health Organization (WHO). Various research priorities such as health data quality, primary health care and telemedicine emerged as key factors that warrant further investigation by researchers. The fight against diseases such as tuberculosis and HIV/AIDS is still a major issue for the African continent [30, 39, 40]. In our research, we note some limitations. One practical implication of our study includes validating the efficacy of data-driven methodologies as tools for furthering knowledge discovery research in order to provide factual insights to researchers and knowledge workers. Another implication is in the adoption, utilization and management of digital transformation tools as decision support systems for quality healthcare delivery. Theoretical implications of the study include the necessity of developing and integrating data-driven mobile-based frameworks in healthcare delivery for the sub-region owing to the fact that mobile usage in Africa is at an all-time high.

Our research derives its entire analytical focus and implication from articles indexed in Scopus only. This restriction would indicate a level of bias at a scale, as well as an underestimation of the state of the art. We therefore advocate for further research to extend our reflections to other databases and publication sources.

References

1. Smith, M., et al.: Integrated health information systems in Tanzania: experience and challenges. Electron. J. Inf. Syst. Dev. Ctries. **33**(1), 1–21 (2008)
2. Katuu, S.: Transforming South Africa's health sector: the eHealth Strategy, the implementation of electronic document and records management systems (EDRMS) and the utility of maturity models. J. Sci. Technol. Policy Manag. **7**(3), 330–345 (2016)
3. Rodrigues, J.J.P.C.: Health Information Systems: Concepts, Methodologies, Tools, and Applications, vol. 1. IGI Global, Hershey (2009)
4. Kuika Watat, J., Jonathan, G.M.: Transforming Marginalized communities through virtual healthcare during a pandemic. In: ACIS 2021 Proceedings, p. 44 (2021). https://aisel.aisnet.org/acis2021/44
5. Agbozo, E., Watat, J.K., Olaleye, S.A.: 5 - COVID-19 outlook in the United States of America: a data-driven thematic approach. In: Kose, U., et al. (eds.) Data Science for COVID-19, pp. 77–93. Academic Press, London (2022)
6. Kuika Watat, J., et al.: Health is wealth: a conceptual overview of virtual healthcare & future research directions [1995–2021]. In: Themistocleous, M., Papadaki, M. (eds.) EMCIS 2021. LNBIP, vol. 437, pp. 463–473. Springer, Cham (2022). https://doi.org/10.1007/978-3-030-95947-0_33

7. Kuika Watat, J., Moukoko Mbonjo, M.: Social media and public health emergency of international concern: the COVID-19 outbreak. In: Sharma, S.K., Dwivedi, Y.K., Metri, B., Rana, N.P. (eds.) TDIT 2020. IFIP AICT, vol. 617, pp. 623–634. Springer, Cham (2020). https://doi.org/10.1007/978-3-030-64849-7_55

8. Ledikwe, J.H., et al.: Improving the quality of health information: a qualitative assessment of data management and reporting systems in Botswana. Health Res. Policy Syst. **12**(1), 1–10 (2014)

9. Guetibi, S., Hammoumi, M.E., Brito, A.C.: Process approach for information systems in health care: a systematic review and PRISMA method. In: Proceedings of the 2018 International Conference on Software Engineering and Information Management, Casablanca, Morocco, pp. 108–112. Association for Computing Machinery (2018)

10. Noorbergen, T.J., et al.: Co-design in mHealth systems development: insights from a systematic literature review. AIS Trans. Hum. Comput. Interact. **13**(2), 175–205 (2021)

11. Gough, D., Oliver, S., Thomas, J.: An Introduction to Systematic Reviews. Sage, Thousand Oaks (2017)

12. Rojon, C., Okupe, A., McDowall, A.: Utilization and development of systematic reviews in management research: what do we know and where do we go from here? Int. J. Manag. Rev. **23**(2), 191–223 (2021)

13. Selçuk, A.A.: A guide for systematic reviews: PRISMA. Turk. Arch. Otorhinolaryngol. **57**(1), 57 (2019)

14. Liberati, A., et al.: The PRISMA statement for reporting systematic reviews and meta-analyses of studies that evaluate health care interventions: explanation and elaboration. J. Clin. Epidemiol. **62**(10), e1–e34 (2009)

15. Ayanore, M.A., et al.: Towards resilient health systems in Sub-Saharan Africa: a systematic review of the English language literature on health workforce, surveillance, and health governance issues for health systems strengthening. Ann. Glob. Health **85**(1), 113 (2019)

16. Otieno, P., et al.: Chronic care models and opportunities for improving health care practice and outcomes in Sub-Saharan Africa: protocol for systematic review. Research Square (2020)

17. Pech, G., Delgado, C.: Assessing the publication impact using citation data from both Scopus and WoS databases: an approach validated in 15 research fields. Scientometrics **125**(2), 909–924 (2020). https://doi.org/10.1007/s11192-020-03660-w

18. Jalali, M.S., et al.: Health care and cybersecurity: bibliometric analysis of the literature. J. Med. Internet Res. **21**(2), e12644 (2019)

19. Almeida-Filho, N., et al.: Research on health inequalities in Latin America and the Caribbean: bibliometric analysis (1971–2000) and descriptive content analysis (1971–1995). Am. J. Public Health **93**(12), 2037–2043 (2003)

20. Wahle, F., et al.: Toward the design of evidence-based mental health information systems for people with depression: a systematic literature review and meta-analysis. J. Med. Internet Res. **19**(5), e191 (2017)

21. Aria, M., Cuccurullo, C.: bibliometrix: an R-tool for comprehensive science mapping analysis. J. Informetr. **11**(4), 959–975 (2017)

22. Ahmi, A., Bibliometric Analysis using R for Non-Coders: a practical handbook in conducting bibliometric analysis studies using Biblioshiny for Bibliometrix R package (2022)

23. Aggarwal, A., et al.: Scientometric analysis of medical publications during COVID-19 pandemic: the twenty-twenty research boom. Minerva Med. **112**(5), 631–640 (2021)

24. Gai, N., et al.: General medical publications during COVID-19 show increased dissemination despite lower validation. PLoS ONE **16**(2), e0246427 (2021)

25. Anwar, M., Zhewei, T.: Research productivity of library philosophy and practice during the period of COVID 19. Libr. Philos. Pract. (e-journal), 1–11 (2020)

26. Carvalho, D., et al.: A process to support analysts in exploring and selecting content from online forums. Soc. Netw. **03**, 86–93 (2014)

27. Babu, M.H.A., Mani, G.: Customized news filtering and summarization system based on personal interest. Procedia Eng. **38**, 2214–2221 (2012)
28. Ebener, S., et al.: The geography of maternal and newborn health: the state of the art. Int. J. Health Geogr. **14**(1), 19 (2015)
29. Fleming, L.C., et al.: Health-care availability, preference, and distance for women in urban Bo, Sierra Leone. Int. J. Public Health **61**(9), 1079–1088 (2016). https://doi.org/10.1007/s00 038-016-0815-y
30. Koivu, A., et al.: Vertical interventions and parallel structures: a case study of the HIV and tuberculosis health information systems in South Africa. J. Health Inform. Dev. Ctries. **11**(2) (2017)
31. Mphatswe, W., et al.: Improving public health information: a data quality intervention in KwaZulu-Natal, South Africa. Bull. World Health Organ. **90**, 176–182 (2012)
32. English, R., et al.: Health information systems in South Africa. S. Afr. Health Rev. **2011**(1), 81–89 (2011)
33. Darko-Yawson, S., Ellingsen, G.: Assessing and improving EHRs data quality through a socio-technical approach. Procedia Comput. Sci. **98**, 243–250 (2016)
34. Adjiwanou, V., LeGrand, T.: Gender inequality and the use of maternal healthcare services in rural sub-Saharan Africa. Health Place **29**, 67–78 (2014)
35. Akinyemi, J.O., et al.: Independent and combined effects of maternal smoking and solid fuel on infant and child mortality in sub-Saharan Africa. Trop. Med. Int. Health **21**(12), 1572–1582 (2016)
36. Budu, E., et al.: Maternal healthcare utilsation and complete childhood vaccination in sub-Saharan Africa: a cross-sectional study of 29 nationally representative surveys. BMJ Open **11**(5), e045992 (2021)
37. Tapera, R., Singh, Y.: A bibliometric analysis of medical informatics and telemedicine in sub-Saharan Africa and BRICS nations. J. Public Health Res. **10**(3), 1903 (2021)
38. Adetunji, C.O., et al.: eHealth, mHealth, and telemedicine for COVID-19 pandemic. In: Pani, S.K., Dash, S., dos Santos, W.P., Chan Bukhari, S.A., Flammini, F. (eds.) Assessing COVID-19 and Other Pandemics and Epidemics using Computational Modelling and Data Analysis, pp. 157–168. Springer, Cham (2022). https://doi.org/10.1007/978-3-030-79753-9_10
39. Hochgesang, M., et al.: Scaling-up health information systems to improve HIV treatment: an assessment of initial patient monitoring systems in Mozambique. Int. J. Med. Inform. **97**, 322–330 (2017)
40. Nicol, E., Dudley, L., Bradshaw, D.: Assessing the quality of routine data for the prevention of mother-to-child transmission of HIV: an analytical observational study in two health districts with high HIV prevalence in South Africa. Int. J. Med. Inform. **95**, 60–70 (2016)

Metaverse and Social Media

As Time Goes By: Temporal Characteristics of Social Media and Information Objective-Subjective Tensions in Crisis Communication

Deborah Bunker[✉], Maryam Shahbazi, Christian Ehnis, and Tania C Sorrell

University of Sydney, Camperdown, Australia
deborah.bunker@sydney.edu.au

Abstract. Social media communication is integral to framing an effective crisis response but is generally impacted by high volumes and an overload of information and misinformation, i.e., infodemic conditions. The social media connection content (i.e., information) and connection type (i.e., communications strategies) that are shared between actors (e.g., emergency response organisations and the public) underpins the development of trusted shared situational awareness for effective crisis management. This study investigates how local public health organisations use Facebook to mitigate COVID-19 misinformation and create effective trusted shared situational awareness. We show how the nature of the event and social media temporal characteristics can create information objective-subjective tensions and create misinformation on public health social media channels. This undermines an agreed and accurate representation of reality that is expected of trusted, shared situational awareness. We conclude that developing communications strategies to manage information objective-subjective tensions becomes especially important during an evolving crisis scenario where situational awareness and knowledge are developed over time and information and advice may change in response to a changing crisis conditions.

Keywords: Social media · Crisis communication · Infodemic · Trust · Misinformation · Health communication

1 Introduction

Widespread social media use has exacerbated infodemics, defined as a rapid spread of all kinds of information, including misleading or false information (misinformation) in digital and physical environments during an epidemic [1]. Even though the word "infodemiology" was coined in 2002 [2], concerns about the digital spread of misinformation have been present since the World Wide Web was first launched [3]. Misinformation spread globally alongside the COVID-19 pandemic on social networks, e.g., Twitter, Facebook, TikTok, and other social media platforms, which became a major concern for societies [4, 5]. The infodemic phenomenon influenced and fragmented social response,

© IFIP International Federation for Information Processing 2022
Published by Springer Nature Switzerland AG 2022
A. Elbanna et al. (Eds.): TDIT 2022, IFIP AICT 660, pp. 261–276, 2022.
https://doi.org/10.1007/978-3-031-17968-6_20

impacted the efficiency of government countermeasures, and resulted in the pandemic's acceleration [6].

Information technologies such as social media platforms became a critical means of social interaction during the COVID-19 pandemic [7]. Social media use in the initial stages and during the COVID-19 outbreak resulted in the generation of a vast amount of information (both accurate and inaccurate), creating an infodemic not seen in previous viral epidemics like SARS and MERS. The COVID-19 infodemic disseminated information, misinformation, and rumours with a range, reach, velocity, and volume, which complicated the pandemic response, creating confusion and distrust among the public as well as risks to public health, hampering effective crisis management [8].

Official and trusted social media channels, including those located on Facebook, Weibo, Instagram, Twitter, LinkedIn, Pinterest, and official public health agency websites, were also actively used to provide timely and accurate information to mitigate infodemic and misinformation impacts. However, the flood of misinformation countered by a flood of corrective information caused public confusion about which sources of information were reliable [9]. This problem contributed to the destruction of mental model alignment, i.e., public trust in shared situational awareness [10], and resulted in worldwide panic and fear [11].

Boell [54] discusses the *Four Stances on Information* which encompass the physical, objective, subject-centred and sociocultural perspectives of information depiction. Each stance is underpinned by assumptions regarding information existence in the world, the condition for that existence, data (definition), knowledge (definition), signs, human beings (as creators, interpreters, and appropriators), social context, technology use and relevance to IS research.

As mental model alignment [10] is essential for the creation of trusted shared situational awareness, the development of an objective stance of information and its underlying assumptions for use in crisis communications, is a critical factor. Information and the communication solutions in this space must "be researched as an objectively existing artifact, with a particular interest in the accuracy of representations enabled or captured by IT artifacts" [54 - p. 11]. Given that it can be argued that social media as an IT artifact, is subject-centred in its underlying information systems assumptions [10] this presents us with a *stance tension* in the IT artifact where an information objective-subjective divide must be bridged for effective infodemic solutions.

It is here that we turn to Seppänen et al., [12] which highlights the importance of shared understanding of situational awareness for emergency response and which identifies the critical factors that affect the formation of shared situation awareness 1) information, 2) communication, and 3) trust.

As shown in Fig. 1, the connection between actors via content (information), type (communication), and quality (trustworthiness) are all key elements in creating shared situational awareness during a crisis. However, processing high volumes of information communicated through social media platforms is problematic for emergency response agencies because it is difficult to authenticate the trustworthiness of actors to establish the accuracy and relevance of the information itself [13]. This presents us with an information objective-subjective tension in the *condition of existence*, where information needs to be both 'a representation of reality' but also 'meaningful and relevant to a human being'.

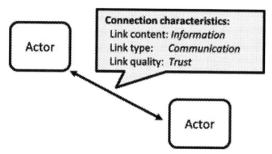

Fig. 1. Information, communication, and trust affect the formation of shared situational awareness for emergency response (source; [12])

As we have seen in the pandemic infodemic, social media is effective at providing subject-centred meaningful and relevant information but is not well suited to providing an objective representation of reality due to its underlying algorithmic design which reinforces individual subjective perspectives [10].

This study intends to bridge the information objective-subjective divide by utilising Seppänen et al., and their approach [12] to determine how the spread of misinformation on social media i.e., Facebook affects the formation of trusted shared situation awareness. Within our study, we investigate *how local health organisations in Australia, at state levels, use social media i.e., Facebook content (information) and type (communication strategies) to mitigate COVID-19 misinformation propagation and how this knowledge might be used to enhance the development of the quality of shared situational awareness (trust)*.

Our study reveals the factors that should be considered in creating the *content (information) and type (strategies)* of official social media crisis communication to bridge the information objective-subjective divide that fuels infodemics.

The COVID-19 pandemic and the disruption it has produced in the age of social media is remarkable. The COVID-19 infodemic is a current and urgent information systems problem, which requires an effective solution, so our research is timely. Furthermore, our analysis has revealed how the nature of the event leads to the creation and spread of misinformation in a previously unidentified manner. Emergency management agencies such as public health agencies can use our results as a first step in the development of effective crisis communication strategies to fight an infodemic in a digital context.

2 Background - Social Media Crisis Communication

Our social connections, individual and collective activities, and dominant attitudes are all influenced by social media [14]. During crises, the public's interest in using social media increases [15]. People seek timely and unfiltered information during a crisis or an emergency to raise their concerns and express sentiments [16, 17]. They also use these platforms to determine disaster magnitude, check-in with family and friends, maintain a sense of community, seek and express physical and emotional support, and to make sense of an event [18, 19].

Although social media platforms are well-known as crisis communication tools, information is also created, catalysed, and distributed by these channels due to their nature and characteristics [20]. These platforms provide an enormous opportunity for "fake news" and "misinformation" to reach a mass audience [10, 21].

For instance, the propagation of vast amounts of accurate or inaccurate COVID-19 related messages during the pandemic was remarkably confusing and misleading for an uninformed public [22]. Social media amplified misinformation, disinformation, and unverifiable content at an alarming rate that hampered effective crisis communication about the pandemic [23]. To counteract this situation and mitigate the risks associated with misinformation propagation, the WHO Information Network for Epidemics (EPI-WIN) was launched by the WHO risk communication team as a new information platform to share timely, tailored, accurate and relevant information with target audiences [24]. Furthermore, government and health officials provided daily updates on the virus's growth and information on how to guard against it [25].

The urgent need to conduct information systems research on social media infodemics has been highlighted by the research community [26], who highlighted that the term "*misinformation*" is unclear and imprecise. Baines and Elliott [26] introduced a taxonomy of false information examining the communicator's intention to deceive, the message and its embodied proposition.

Research on a COVID-19 information typology [27] highlighted that our understanding of risks associated with the crisis and knowledge of the situation influence the type of information created and disseminated via social media. While technology allows information to be coded, transformed, stored, and transmitted at high speeds [28], the uncertainty and temporality of crisis-related information can cause crucial problems. Crisis decision-making follows the rhythm of knowledge production in which phases of '*known,*' '*partly-known,*' '*not-yet-known,*' '*will-be-known,*' '*unable-to-know*' and '*unable-ever-to-know*' differ; this is because assessments of uncertainties and risks change constantly. From time to time, decisions must precede what is not yet known, but the decisions must be able to be reversed or corrected if the assumptions prove to be wrong.

Due to the legislative constraints and responsibilities of crisis management agencies such as health agencies, it is difficult to coordinate their decisions with the daily updated crisis information, so the 'epistemic constellation' forms a complex system that needs constant reassessment of previous situational perceptions and decisions [29]. Correspondingly, we argue that the temporal and uncertain nature of advice and crisis communications in the COVID-19 outbreak are also significant drivers of misinformation production and the resulting infodemic.

At the same time, we understand that if government agencies fail to establish an early and regular flow of factual and trusted information in their crisis communications that this could *result in the proliferation of rumours, misinformation, and information overload to 'fill the gap' and drastically accelerate the effects of a crisis as it impacts social behaviour* [15]. Hence, further understanding of governmental crisis communication strategies is required to treat the resulting infodemic effectively. To date, researchers and government health authorities are still seeking 'treatments' for the infodemic of misinformation and the general information overload caused by social media communications.

Our study focuses on developing an understanding of social media use for combating misinformation and increasing shared situational awareness during a crisis by studying the COVID-19 pandemic as an example; examining information posted by a trusted public health authority on their Facebook channel during the early days of the pandemic; and analysing communications strategies involved in those posts.

To align with prior studies [30, 31], we focus on *falsehood* and *ambiguity* to identify misinformation in our data cleaning process. We define falsehood as the degree to which a piece of news/information concerning a real-world event is perceived to be false and ambiguity as the level of uncertainty about a piece of information truthfulness. We also identify, define, and classify the information typologies used to combat misinformation and explore how the organisational response to deal with misinformation and the nature of the event influenced pandemic response. Our study is the first phase of a larger study that investigates how health agencies use of Facebook during the pandemic affected public trust in health officials, their communications channels, and trusted shared situational awareness.

This paper is structured as follows. We firstly summarise the crisis communications literature which deals with the COVID-19 pandemic to outline the problem. Next, we explain the research approach and dataset and outline our findings and discussion. Our paper concludes by providing insights and an immediate recommendation to assist public crisis managers and decision-makers to improve their social media communication policies and practices to enhance shared situational awareness.

3 Crisis Communications and the COVID-19 Pandemic

3.1 The Role of Misinformation

The term *infodemic* has been defined by the World Health Organisation [32] as an overabundance of information about a (public health-related) crisis, some accurate and some not, in digital and physical environments that complicates the problem-solving process. The lack of a readily available solution to the COVID-19 pandemic and a lack of relevant clinical data to support successful public health communications stifled information-sharing efforts. As a result, information systems worldwide were failing to provide timely and accurate information allowing the COVID-19 infodemic to flourish and disseminate false information [28]. Researchers intended to identify a COVID-19 crisis-related information topology and define different types of false information [27, 28].

Misinformation has been defined as false, inaccurate, or misleading information intentionally disseminated to, or not to deceive (regardless of intent to mislead). Misinformation denotes falsehoods or distorted information, which means any information that does not directly reflect the generally accepted 'true' state of the world can be considered misinformation [33].

Disinformation, instead, is a subset of misinformation and refers to false information *deliberately disseminated* to confuse or manipulate people. An infodemic may be fuelled by deliberate attempts to spread misinformation to undermine the public confidence in disaster response which can be used to advance alternative agendas of individuals or groups. Therefore, in an emergency, people struggle to find trustworthy information and reliable guidance when they need it.

The infodemic of COVID-19 misinformation can be classified into four major thematic areas, including (1) the cause and source of the disease and virus; (2) the symptoms and patterns of transmission; (3) existing treatments, cures, and prophylactics; (4) the outcome of interventions by health authorities and organisations [32].

Some examples of this misinformation from RMIT ABC Fact Check[1] include:

- "Bill Gates would use COVID-19 vaccines to track people" (FactCheck.org – 14 April, 2020) CoronaCheck #66;
- "COVID-19 vaccines are 'in violation of all 10 of the Nuremberg Codes'" CoronaCheck #66;
- "people vaccinated against COVID-19 can "shed" the virus and infect those around them" CoronaCheck #64;
- "masks are "useless" and "actively damaging to individual health and social wellbeing"" CoronaCheck #62;
- "Xi Jinping invented the lockdown" CoronaCheck #61;
- "PCR tests are unable to distinguish between the flu and COVID-19" CoronaCheck #76; and
- "50% of animals in Australian COVID-19 vaccine trials died" CoronaCheck #73.

Mian and Khan [34] reported that unverified sources of COVID-19 related information on social media were prevalent and even more popular compared to reliable sources like official online health channels among internet users. For instance, some false claims like *"the virus cannot survive in the hot weather"*, or *"taking a high dose of chloroquine medication can protect you"*, and *"consuming large quantities of ginger and garlic can prevent the virus from going viral"* were spreading faster than the virus itself. Therefore, it is essential and timely to understand how the spread of misinformation impacts effective crisis communication and the creation of shared situational awareness.

3.2 Infodemics and Crisis Response

"We're not just fighting an epidemic; we're fighting an infodemic[2]"
Tedros Adhanom Ghebreyesus, Director-General of the WHO.

The spread of misinformation during crisis like an infectious disease epidemic can inhibit crisis response and hamper risk communication efforts by undermining the trust and credibility of the information source [35]. For example, the effect of misinformation about the preventative impact of white vinegar on the spread of disease caused a dramatic increase in the price of vinegar and panic buying during the 2003 pneumonia scare in China [36].

---

[1] https://www.abc.net.au/news/factcheck/.

[2] WHO Director-General Tedros Adhanom Ghebreyesus at Munich Security Conference, 15 February 2020.

Misinformation spread has also impacted the management of the COVID-19 pandemic. For instance, even though scientists condemned and attempted to dispel the rumour that 5G lowers the immune system and helps COVID-19 to be more readily transmitted, mobile phone masts were still set on fire by an enraged public in Birmingham and Merseyside in early April 2020 [37]. Likewise, scientists emphasised that the Malaria drug, hydroxychloroquine, should not be used to treat coronavirus, but the infodemic of misinformation around the effectiveness of this drug as a COVID-19 treatment triggered its overuse and a shortage of the medicine in pharmacies.

"The spread of misinformation during an outbreak event and the fear and uncertainty of the situation can weaken the national and global response, encourage nativist narratives, and provide opportunities for those who may seek to take advantage of this moment to deepen social divisions,"; said Melissa Fleming[3]. Correspondingly, public health decision-makers need to find a way to mitigate this issue. Pennycooke et al. [38] stated that people share misinformation about COVID-19 because they fail to think about the trustworthiness of the information source, and they suggest that pushing people to think about the source and accuracy of information may improve their choices about what to share on social media. As a result, social media providers like Twitter, Facebook, and Weibo can decide to censor actors who spread misinformation; however, they cannot stop conspiracy theorists, liars, and trolls [39]. Furthermore, public health organisations employ information and communication technology (ICT)-enabled channels like Facebook to combat the infodemic of COVID-19 misinformation.

Adhanom Ghebreyesus, *Director-General of the WHO*, believed that in the COVID-19 crisis, fake news spread faster and easier than the virus itself. Zarocostas [40] investigated how health officials responded to the infodemic during the pandemic outbreak to ensure people were informed to act appropriately to control the disease or mitigate its impact. WHO was at the forefront of the battle against the pandemic and was also fighting against the spread of misinformation. WHO communications teams in six regional offices included social media personnel, risk communications consultants, and communications officers. WHO's Information Network for Epidemics (EPI-WIN) provides access to regular updates on accurate and easy-to-understand information on public health events and outbreaks such as the COVID-19 pandemic. A technical risk communications team and their colleagues working at WHO's Information Network for Epidemics (EPI-WIN) closely interact with Facebook, Twitter, Pinterest, Tencent, Tik-Tok, and Chinese social media platforms to provide them with evidence-based answers to public concerns, address rumours and misinformation about COVID-19, as well as to supply timely information.

WHO has launched various messaging services in several languages and interactive chatbots by partnering with WhatsApp, Facebook, and Rakuten Viber to communicate with billions of people worldwide in their local language. WHO and the International Telecommunication Union (ITU), supported by UNICEF, requested that all worldwide telecommunication companies send text messages to billions of people who do not have access to online information to help save lives from COVID-19.

---

[3] Melissa Fleming is Under-Secretary-General for Global Communications, taking up her functions as of 1 September 2019.

Alongside these services, the UN uses all available channels, including social media and radio, to counter misinformation and rumours; for instance, the organization's 59 UN Information Centres fight disinformation in local languages.

The UN formed a rapid response team to overcome a surge of misinformation by sharing facts and science-based evidence and is tackling the spread of misinformation by (1) producing and propagating facts and reliable information through various communication channels, (2) partnering with businesses, (3) working with media and journalists, (4) mobilising civil society to respond to the COVID-19 crisis, and (5) speaking out for rights of global citizens [41].

Priority COVID-19 communications actions for many governments around the world included (a) advising social media companies on removing contentious pandemic content (e.g., India); (b) creating special units to combat misinformation (e.g., UK, EU); and (c) criminalising malicious coronavirus deception concerning public health measures (e.g., South Africa, Hungary) [42]. It is noted that governments worldwide take various actions to counter misinformation, many of which have yet to be proven effective.

3.3 Misinformation and Public Trust

During a public health crisis, public health officials are responsible for providing trustworthy information; however, there has been little research on how the public reacts when their expectations for such information are not met. Jang and Baek [43] showed less credible information from public health organisations resulted in increased use of interpersonal networks, online news, and social media to obtain health crisis-related information. COVID-19 is spreading throughout an increasingly interconnected globe in which people are maintaining connectivity using global digital social networks, such as Facebook, to enable their interaction and information sharing about the virus [44].

During the COVID-19 pandemic, the public trust in information sources and confidence in institutions determined public response to the health measures and defined public health decisions, e.g., willingness to take up vaccines [45]. In contrast, misinformation and mistrust contributed to hesitancy and rejection of vaccinations [46]. In the circumstances where trust in the government is critical to crisis response, communication content, type and quality are critical factors in managing a crisis. Fletcher et al. [47] showed public trust in information about coronavirus provided by the UK government decreased during the pandemic. The erosion of trust in public institutions and health crisis information drove the government in Italy (i.e., the Ministry of Health) to use Facebook to fight misinformation [48]. Our study investigates Australian public health (communication) strategies against misinformation, develops a better understanding of the factors that impact (information) content of governmental communication, to enhance social media communication capabilities in creating quality shared situational awareness (trust) during a public health crisis.

4   Research Approach

Our study seeks to better understand:

- How do local health organisations in Australia, at state levels, use social media (i.e., Facebook) content (information) and type (communication strategies) to mitigate COVID-19 misinformation propagation? (RQ1)
- How can this knowledge help to improve the development of shared situational awareness during crisis events? (RQ2)

We develop our understanding through an analysis of Australian public health agency Facebook pages by exploring post content and related public comments that were published during the early stage of the pandemic. Our analysis looked at NSW Health and the Victorian Department of Health official Facebook communications. New South Wales (NSW) and Victoria (VIC) are two of Australia's most populous states that also reported the highest number of COVID-19 cases during the first four months of the outbreak (3,045 and 1,366 patients, respectively). The NSW Public Health system is also the largest public health system in Australia. Facebook pages are one of the official channels that agencies use for public health communication. Our qualitative exploratory study allowed us to focus on the nature and content of public health agency Facebook communications during the early stages of the COVID-19 pandemic. Our approach is appropriate for exploratory research [49], allowing us to uncover operational processes [50] that are tight to the context under study aiming at development of findings to the 'how' question [51].

We randomly sampled 765 posts and their linked public comments published from 1 January to the end of April 2020 on the NSW and VIC of Health agency Facebook pages[4]. This four-month sampling window allowed us to study communications around two major events; 1) the start of the pandemic in Australia in late January 2020 and 2) the first COVID-19 peak in March/April 2020, affecting all states and territories [52]. We utilised a general inductive research approach [53] that provided an efficient way of analysing qualitative data. After a close reading of the post content, we removed posts that provided facts, news, or information that had been scientifically accepted at the time of the post. To achieve this, we conducted a thematic analysis, and unlocked insights in the data to code posts. This assisted us to *"condense extensive and varied raw text data into a brief, summary format"* and *"establish clear links between the research objectives and the findings derived from the raw data"* [53 p. 2].

Finally, we further analysed the post content and manually selected 29 posts that addressed the uncertainty or unreliability of COVID-19 related information available on social media or other sources/channels of communication. We selected these posts because they address the four major thematic areas[5] of the COVID-19 misinformation outlined in *"Coronavirus disease 2019 (COVID-19) Situation Report–85"* [32]. By doing

---

[4] https://www.facebook.com/NewSouthWalesHealth & https://www.facebook.com/VicGovDH.

[5] 1) the cause and origin of the virus and disease; 2) the symptoms and patterns of transmission; 3) the treatments, prophylactics, and cures that are available; and 4) the effectiveness and impact of interventions by health authorities or other institutions.

this, we investigated how local public health organisations, employed social media to combat misinformation. Our study methodology could be further employed for similar or more complex examples of crisis communication.

Subsequently, the content of the posts was read several times to identify themes and categories, i.e., open coding. The posts were read by researchers individually, and the coding frame was developed after group discussion sessions. The posts were reread again and recategorized according to the agreed coding structure, then abstracted into a higher logical level, which, after further discussion, were conceptualised into final themes. Major themes emerged through rigorous and systematic reading and coding of post content. The themes were developed to address the research questions.

We also observed a new phenomenon during the process; the old posts containing obsolete information contradicted subsequent new 'current' knowledge, which could be considered misinformation. Consequently, a new code, i.e., *Contradictory Information*, emerged, and the coding frame was slightly changed. All posts were then reread according to the new structure. The new theme, i.e., *contradictory information*, was a significant insight and finding as: 1) this directly undermines the connection between content and type undermining the trustworthiness of the source and consequently trust in the shared situational awareness, and 2) the phenomenon has not been reported in the literature. This finding revealed a new factor shaped by the temporary nature of the crisis-related information that directly impacts social media content and thus situational awareness quality and therefore, public trust in the official channel Crisis response agencies should carefully consider this knowledge to improve the development of shared situational awareness during crisis events.

5   Findings and Discussion

Our coding revealed three official *information typologies,* i.e., misinformation, counter-information, and myth-busting information. These information typologies are described as (1) *contradictory information*, (2) *countering fabricated information*, and (3) *myth-busting cynical information*.

Our analysis also revealed how social media *communication strategies* could spread and combat misinformation on COVID-19. The public health agencies used different strategies to fight the infodemic of misinformation using Facebook. Our analysis indicates that official posts to the health agency Facebook channels: (1) *contained the propagation of misinformation by posting counter-information, or 'corrections'* of these imprecise posts, as well as (2) *mitigated the infodemic by posting 'myth-busting' information* related to general rumours and inaccuracies about COVID-19. However, public health agency posts also *accelerated the infodemic of misinformation* through posting imprecise information, which, as it 'aged' then became misinformation.

We now explain our findings in detail.

5.1 Connections - Information Topologies and Communication Strategies

How do local health organisations in Australia, at state levels, use social media (i.e., Facebook) content (information) and type (communication strategies) to mitigate COVID-19 misinformation propagation? **(RQ1)**

Contradictory Information – Infodemic Acceleration. The public health agencies used Facebook extensively to inform the public about the outbreak; however, the uncertain nature of COVID-19 impacted the consistency and sometimes the accuracy of the information that was broadcast on the channel. The organisations posted accurate information (to the best of their knowledge at the time), and then as the outbreak changed and new scientific evidence emerged, new information was published that conflicted with previous posts. Earlier posts of information and advice, therefore, became outmoded and inaccurate as the pandemic evolved. This resulted in the information and advice in later posts contradicting that which was contained in the earlier posts. Contradictory information can be recognised as misleading/fabricated information if it is still accessible on the Facebook channel. For instance, a short video with the caption: *"Should I wear a facemask to protect myself from novel coronavirus? No. Unless you are a health professional*[6]*"* was published (in February 2020) to inform the audience that <u>at that time,</u> they did not need to wear facemasks in public. The video was watched 244K times and received 304 likes and 115 comments by July 2021 after our data collection frame. However, another post (in July 2020) contradicted the previous February post *"We strongly recommend wearing a face mask in situations where social distancing is not possible"*[7] this post received 486 comments and was shared 502 times by other users. As at the time we were writing this paper (i.e., July 2021), the initial post was still available to the public on the channel.

Countering Fabricated Information – Infodemic Containment. From the early stages of the outbreak in Australia (i.e., January 2020), the agencies used their Facebook channel to contain the infodemic of misinformation about COVID-19. In this sense, publishing relevant information based on scientific evidence was a strategy. In doing so, the agencies published accurate, relevant, and timely information on COVID-19 to increase public situational awareness. For instance, the agencies published posts to address the rumours, and misleading information about the cures and treatment for COVID-19, e.g., *"NSW Health is aware of people self-medicating to treat COVID-19 or using medications in an attempt to prevent COVID-19 disease.*[8]*"* The spread of fabricated information created a substantial life-threatening risk to public health as well as made managing the crisis more complex. This information typology and communication strategy also included posts to increase public awareness about the existence and spread of misinformation, including disinformation (i.e., information intentionally disseminated to mislead audiences). This containment strategy aims to improve both individual health literacy

---

[6] https://www.facebook.com/watch/?v=620993142046514.

[7] https://www.facebook.com/NewSouthWalesHealth/photos/a.232420926957256/134936006 5263331.

[8] https://www.facebook.com/NewSouthWalesHealth/photos/a.232420926957256/125433442 8099229/.

and community risk awareness regarding misinformation threats e.g., "*NSW Health has been made aware of a social media post that is being widely circulated warning people to … there is no such entity as the "Department of Diseasology Parramatta.*[9]

Mythbusting Cynical Information - Infodemic Mitigation. When disputed or imprecise information was circulated between people on social media or other sources, the health agency posted information with a tag that there was insufficient evidence on the accuracy of the information. This was done to provide some *yet-to-be-confirmed* information to the public to address the uncertain nature of the COVID-19 outbreak. It must be remembered that COVID-19 at this stage was a newly emerging disease and that there was a great deal of uncertainty regarding the evolution and spread of the pandemic. The health agencies admitted to the uncertain nature of some information in their posts, e.g., "*According to World Health Organization (WHO) it's not certain how long the virus that causes COVID19 survives on surfaces,…,*[10]" or "*… people gain immunity to the virus, but because it is a new virus, we don't know how long….*[11]".

5.2   Managing Objective-Subjective Information Tensions

How can this knowledge help to improve the development of shared situational awareness during crisis events? (**RQ2**)
The spread of misinformation has been an increasing challenge in managing crises since the development of social media facilitated mass communication. The infodemic of COVID-19 information and related misinformation has created a significant threat to public health and significant challenges for health systems. We investigated how misinformation impacted official health agencies' Facebook communication with the public on the NSW and VIC Health Facebook page during the COVID-19 outbreak from January to April 2020.

   This study revealed that use of social media, i.e., Facebook for emergency and crisis communication, assisted public health agencies to mitigate the infodemic by 1) posting counter information or corrections of these imprecise posts and 2) posting myth-busting information related to general rumours and inaccuracies about COVID-19 by providing scientific information to increase community health literacy. However, on the downside, it accelerated the infodemic through posting of imprecise information due to the uncertain and changing nature of the event, which, as it 'aged' became misinformation. Identifying that the very communications strategies in use to counter the infodemic were in fact, contributing to it, highlights the necessity of developing alternative, or at least, other supplementary strategies.

   It is recommended that government agencies should develop communications strategies which focus on information *objective-subjective tensions* to better accommodate

---

[9] https://www.facebook.com/NewSouthWalesHealth/photos/a.232420926957256/121115870
5750135/.

[10] https://www.facebook.com/225158094350206/posts/1234523503413655/.

[11] https://www.facebook.com/NewSouthWalesHealth/photos/a.232420926957256/128009261
8856743/.

and deal with variations in advice to the public over time. Changing crisis conditions and impacts e.g., knowledge of the virus and its effects, access to services, government funding, vaccines and RATS, community support and leadership, social dislocation, and mental health outcomes etc. as well as public digital health and safety literacy are all risk factors in infodemic generation. It is in the interest of both government and platform providers to carefully develop and utilise platforms in a way that manages objective-subjective tensions to retain and enhance trusted shared situational awareness effectively.

As a starting point, we would suggest that the content of old posts on social media crisis communications pages need to be regularly reviewed and backward audited to detect and eliminate misinformation before it has a chance to impact public response to health advice and confidence in trusted sources of information. There is also scope to be more proactive by closely monitoring changing crisis conditions and probable impacts to better anticipate possible niche communications strategies to specific audiences. These strategies may also be useful for shaping convergence behaviours in some crisis event conditions [16].

6   Conclusions and Recommendations

The inconsistency that is created over time between the information contained within posts can undermine shared and trusted situational awareness, the channel users' understanding and expectations of trusted sources, i.e., the health agency.

While trust, credibility, consistency, timeliness, and reliability are essential character- istics for effective, persuasive health communication, we observed that the unpredictable and changing nature of the COVID-19 outbreak, as well as social media temporal char- acteristics, facilitated information aging resulting in the spread of inconsistent and inac- curate information. This had the potential to undermine public confidence in agencies and trusted COVID-19 situational awareness.

In the context of our study, the connection type, i.e., Facebook, facilitated the dissem- ination of information, but the unpredictable nature of the event as it unfolded, increased the possibility and damage caused by the infodemic of misinformation.

From our study, we conclude that social media has significant advantages when it comes to infodemic containment and mitigation by health agencies, but it can also accel- erate the size and velocity of an infodemic as information ages and becomes inconsistent. Disseminating timely information during a crisis is necessary to producing accurate sit- uational awareness at any given point in time. The COVID-19 pandemic, however, was a very uncertain and changing situation in its early stages. This fuelled informational objective-subjective tensions as the temporal characteristics of a crisis, i.e., uncertainty and change over time, presented challenges for using social media channels for crisis communications.

While these channels are effective broadcast mechanisms for current situational awareness and advice, they also retain and enable the interrogation of changing com- munications over time without an accompanying reflection of the changing situation at each point in time when the information is posted.

As we have seen in our study, aging social media information has the potential to become inconsistent and inaccurate, which can then accelerate an infodemic and consume valuable resources required to contain and mitigate it. It can also directly undermine communication quality i.e., trusted sources. More research is required to better understand this problem and to develop more effective social media policies and applications for crisis communications.

Our research also calls into question the definition of trusted situational awareness and how information is defined and communicated during crisis and emergency circumstances.

7   Future Research

We know that the public places trust in official information sources like health agencies when it comes to assessing crisis situational awareness [4]; however, in this study we observed that social media information and communications strategies had been involved in disseminating contradictory information. As a next stage we call for information systems studies investigating situational awareness development on other social media platforms, e.g., Twitter and Instagram as these platforms target different audiences and may require different treatments of objective-subjective tensions of information, its impact on communication strategy and quality in developing trusted shared situational awareness.

References

1. WHO: Infodemic (2021). https://www.who.int/health-topics/infodemic#tab=tab_1. Accessed 21 Feb 2022
2. Eysenbach, G.: Infodemiology: the epidemiology of (mis)information. Am. J. Med. **113**(9), 2 (2002)
3. Eysenbach, G.: How to fight an infodemic: the four pillars of infodemic management. J. Med. Internet Res. **22**(6), e21820 (2020)
4. Bermes, A.: Information overload and fake news sharing: a transactional stress perspective exploring the mitigating role of consumers' resilience during Covid-19. J. Retail. Consum. Serv. **61**, 102555 (2021)
5. Buchanan, M.: Managing the Infodemic. Nature Publishing Group (2020)
6. Kim, L., Fast, S.M., Markuzon, N.: incorporating media data into a model of infectious disease transmission. PLoS ONE **14**(2), e0197646 (2019)
7. PAHO: The potential of frequently used information technologies during the pandemic. WHO (2020). https://iris.paho.org/handle/10665.2/52021. Accessed 21 Feb 2022
8. DGC, The United Nations Department of Global Communications: COVID-19 Response (2020). https://www.un.org/en/un-coronavirus-communications-team/un-tackling-%E2%80%98infodemic%E2%80%99-misinformation-and-cybercrime-covid-19. Accessed 21 Feb 2022 (2020)
9. Agley, J., Xiao, Y.: Misinformation about COVID-19: evidence for differential latent profiles and a strong association with trust in science. BMC Public Health **21**(1), 1–12 (2021)
10. Bunker, D.: Who do you trust? The digital destruction of shared situational awareness and the COVID-19 infodemic. Int. J. Inf. Manag. **55**, 102201 (2020)
11. Vaezi, A., Javanmard, S.H.: I'nfodemic and risk communication in the era of COVID-19. Adv. Biomed. Res. **9**, 10 (2020)

12. Seppänen, H., Mäkelä, J., Luokkala, P., Virrantaus, K.: Developing shared situational awareness for emergency management. Saf. Sci. **55**, 1–9 (2013)
13. Ehnis, C., Bunker, D.: Repertoires of collaboration: Incorporation of social media help requests into the common operating picture. Behav. Inf. Technol. **39**(3), 343–359 (2020)
14. Bunker, D., Ehnis, C., Shahbazi, M.: Managing influenza outbreaks through social interaction on social media: research transformation through an engaged scholarship approach. In: Healthcare of the Future, pp. 39–44. IOS Press (2019)
15. Mirbabaie, M., Bunker, D., Stieglitz, S., Marx, J., Ehnis, C.: Social media in times of crisis: learning from Hurricane Harvey for the coronavirus disease 2019 pandemic response. J. Inf. Technol. **35**(3), 195–213 (2020)
16. Bunker, D., Mirbabaie, M., Stieglitz, S.: Convergence behaviour of bystanders: an analysis of 2016 munich shooting twitter crisis communication. Paper presented at the 28th Australasian Conference on Information Systems, Hobart, University of Tasmania (2017)
17. Shahbazi, M., Ehnis, C., Shahbazi, M., Bunker, D.: Tweeting from the shadows: social media convergence behaviour during the 2017 Iran-Iraq earthquake. In: ISCRAM Asia Pacific 2018, Wellington, NZ (2018)
18. Fraustino, J.D., Liu, B., Jin, Y.: Social Media Use During Disasters A Research Synthesis and Road Map. Routledge, New York (2017)
19. Mirbabaie, M., Bunker, D., Deubel, A., Stieglitz, S.: Examining convergence behaviour during crisis situations in social media - a case study on the Manchester bombing 2017. In: Elbanna, A., Dwivedi, Y.K., Bunker, D., Wastell, D. (eds.) TDIT 2018. IAICT, vol. 533, pp. 60–75. Springer, Cham (2019). https://doi.org/10.1007/978-3-030-04315-5_5
20. Apuke, O.D., Tunca, E.A.: Social media and crisis management: a review and analysis of existing studies. LAÜ Sosyal Bilimler Dergisi **9**(2), 199–215 (2018)
21. Tandoc, E.C., Jr., Lim, Z.W., Ling, R.: Defining "fake news" a typology of scholarly definitions. Digit. J. **6**(2), 137–153 (2018)
22. Ashrafi-rizi, H., Kazempour, Z.: Information diet in covid-19 crisis; a commentary. Arch. Acad. Emerg. Med. **8**(1), e30 (2020)
23. Ramez, K., et al.: Coronavirus goes viral: quantifying the COVID-19 misinformation epidemic on Twitter. Cureus **12**(3), e7255 (2020)
24. WHO: About EPI-WIN (2021). https://www.who.int/teams/risk-communication/about-epi-win. Accessed 21 Feb 2022
25. Rao, H.R., Vemprala, N., Akello, P., Valecha, R.: Retweets of officials' alarming vs reassuring messages during the COVID-19 pandemic: Implications for crisis management. Int. J. Inf. Manag. **55**, 102187 (2020)
26. Baines, D., Elliott, R.J: Defining misinformation, disinformation and malinformation: An urgent need for clarity during the COVID-19 infodemic. Discussion Papers, 20 (2020)
27. Ashrafi-Rizi, H., Kazempour, Z.: Information typology in coronavirus (Covid-19) crisis; a commentary. Arch. Acad. Emerg. Med. **8**(1), e19 (2020)
28. Flender, C.: Information and temporality. Front. Phys. **4**, 40 (2016)
29. Parviainen, J.: 'We're flying the plane while we're building it': epistemic humility and non-knowledge in political decision-making on COVID-19. Soc. Epistemol. Rev. Reply Collect. **9**(7), 6–10 (2020)
30. Pennycook, G., Bear, A., Collins, E.T., Rand, D.G.: The implied truth effect: Attaching warnings to a subset of fake news headlines increases perceived accuracy of headlines without warnings. Manag. Sci. **66**(11), 4944–4957 (2020)
31. Velichety, S., Shrivastava, U.: Quantifying the impacts of online fake news on the equity value of social media platforms–evidence from Twitter. Int. J. Inf. Manag. **64**, 102474 (2022)
32. WHO: Coronavirus disease 2019 (COVID-19) Situation Report–85 (2020). https://www.who.int/docs/default-source/coronaviruse/situation-reports/20200415-sitrep-86-covid-19.pdf?sfvrsn=c615ea20_4. Accessed 21 Feb 2022

33. Zhou, L., Zhang, D.: An ontology-supported misinformation model: toward a digital misinformation library. IEEE Trans. Syst. Man Cybern. Part A Syst. Hum. **37**(5), 804–813 (2007)
34. Mian, A., Khan, S.: Coronavirus: the spread of misinformation. BMC Med. **18**(1), 1–2 (2020)
35. Glik, D.C.: Risk communication for public health emergencies. Annu. Rev. Public Health **28**, 33–54 (2007)
36. Rosling, L., Rosling, M.: Pneumonia causes panic in Guangdong province. In: British Medical Journal Publishing Group (2003)
37. Schraer, R., Lawrie, E.: Coronavirus: Scientists brand 5G claims 'complete rubbish'. BBC News (2020)
38. Pennycook, G., McPhetres, J., Zhang, Y., Rand, D. Fighting COVID-19 misinformation on social media: Experimental evidence for a scalable accuracy nudge intervention. PsyArXiv Preprints, 10 (2020)
39. Garrett, L.: COVID-19: the medium is the message. Lancet **395**(10228), 942–943 (2020)
40. Zarocostas, J.J.: How to fight an infodemic. Lancet **395**(10225), 676 (2020)
41. U N, T. D. O. G. C.: 5 Ways the Un Is Fighting 'Infodemic' of Misinformation. COVID-19 Response (2020). https://www.un.org/en/un-coronavirus-communications-team/five-ways-united-nations-fighting-%E2%80%98infodemic%E2%80%99-misinformation
42. Radu, R.: Fighting the 'Infodemic': legal responses to Covid-19 disinformation. Soc Media Soc. **6**(3), 2056305120948190 (2020). https://doi.org/10.1177/2056305120948190, PMID: 34192029, PMCID: PMC7399562
43. Jang, K., Baek, Y.M.: When information from public health officials is untrustworthy: the use of online news, interpersonal networks, and social media during the MERS outbreak in South Korea. Health Commun. **34**(9), 991–998 (2019)
44. Limaye, R.J., et al.: Building trust while influencing online COVID-19 content in the social media world. Lancet Digit. Health **2**(6), e277–e278 (2020)
45. De Freitas, L., Basdeo, D., Wang, H.I.: Public trust, information sources and vaccine willingness related to the COVID-19 pandemic in Trinidad and Tobago: an online cross-sectional survey. Lancet Reg. Health Am. **3**, 100051 (2021)
46. Rodriguez-Morales, A.J., Franco, O.H.: Public trust, misinformation and COVID-19 vaccination willingness in Latin America and the Caribbean: today's key challenges. Lancet Reg. Health Am. **3**, 100073 (2021)
47. Fletcher, R., Kalogeropoulos, A. Nielsen, R.K.: Trust in UK government and news media COVID-19 information down, concerns over misinformation from government and politicians up. Reuters Institute for the Study of Journalism (2020)
48. Lovari, A.: Spreading (dis) trust: Covid-19 misinformation and government intervention in Italy. Media Commun. **8**(2), 458–461 (2020)
49. Siggelkow, N.: Persuasion with case studies. Acad. Manag. J. **50**(1), 20–24 (2007)
50. Gephart, R.P., Jr.: Qualitative Research and the Academy of Management Journal. Academy of Management, Briarcliff Manor, NY 10510 (2004)
51. Pan, S.L., Tan, B.: Demystifying case research: a structured–pragmatic–situational (SPS) approach to conducting case studies. Inf. Organ. **21**(3), 161–176 (2011)
52. AIHW: The first year of COVID-19 in Australia: direct and indirect health effects. Cat. no. PHE 287. AIHW, Canberra (2021)
53. Thomas, D.R.: A general inductive approach for qualitative data analysis. School of Population Health, University of Auckland, August 2003
54. Boell, S.K.: Information: Fundamental positions and their implications for information systems research, education and practice. Inf. Organ. **27**, 1–16 (2017)

Examining the Role of Social Media in Emergency Healthcare Communication: A Bibliometric Approach

Keshav Dhir[1,2] ⓘ, Prabhsimran Singh[2(✉)] ⓘ, Yogesh K. Dwivedi[4,5] ⓘ,
Sargun Sawhney[2], and Ravinder Singh Sawhney[3] ⓘ

[1] Department of Computer Science and Engineering, Chandigarh University, Gharuan, Mohali,
India
kesdhir@gmail.com, keshavcet.rsh@gndu.ac.in
[2] Department of Computer Engineering and Technology, Guru Nanak Dev University, Amritsar,
India
prabhsimran.dcet@gndu.ac.in, prabh_singh32@yahoo.com
[3] Department of Electronics Technology, Guru Nanak Dev University, Amritsar, India
sawhney.ece@gndu.ac.in
[4] School of Management, Emerging Market Research Center (EMaRC), Swansea University,
Swansea, UK
y.k.dwivedi@swansea.ac.uk
[5] Department of Management, Symbiosis Institute of Business Management, Pune & Symbiosis
International (Deemed University), Pune, Maharashtra, India

Abstract. Social media has been extensively used for the communication of health-related information and consecutively for the potential spread of medical misinformation. The aim of this study was to perform a bibliometric analysis of the current literature from Scopus database to discover the prevalent trends and topics related to communication regarding healthcare emergencies via social media. To accomplish this task, the research work has been carried in form of defending three research questions related to most impactful sources, most impactful publications and most impactful authors. The adopted methodology has been successful towards answering the research questions in the light of our collected dataset of Scopus articles.

Keywords: Bibliometric analysis · Crisis communication · Emergency communication · Healthcare communication · Social media · Scopus · Twitter

1 Introduction

COVID-19 pandemic has turned out to be the greatest enemy of the humankind in recent years (Singh et al. 2020c). This pandemic has exposed vulnerability of our medical system. With the advancement in information technology, people were able to combat this deadly pandemic through better communication for information diffusion (Dwivedi et al. 2020). Social media platforms, especially Twitter played an important role in passing the critical information to people around the world in real time breaking the

A. Elbanna et al. (Eds.): TDIT 2022, IFIP AICT 660, pp. 277–290, 2022.
https://doi.org/10.1007/978-3-031-17968-6_21

traditional geographical barriers (Haman 2020; Singh et al. 2018; Xue et al. 2020). The proliferation of Internet has led to exponential rise in social media users worldwide (Singh et al. 2019). Social media has now become more of an information-sharer platform rather than just a media related fun service or a tool. It has been observed that people now share all sorts of information, whether related to politics, sports, disaster etc. (Dwivedi et al. 2018; Kapoor et al. 2018; Singh et al. 2020b).

Medical emergencies at global levels can be threatening to the human race. Extensive use of social media, in the recent years has helped many people across the globe to make use of the shared information related to medical healthcare whether disease specific or the precautionary measures related to an outbreak. People are becoming comparatively more knowledgeable about the crisis management through the information being shared by other people through their own experiences via social media channels or groups. Social media is a competitive differential towards the provision of health services and it has revolutionized the methods how any kind of information can be transferred to the masses (Margus et al. 2021; Riaz et al. 2020).

Hence, this paper explores the use of social media in emergency healthcare communications. To accomplish our research objectives towards completion of this task, we made use of bibliometric analysis. Pritchard and Wittig (1981) first coined the term "bibliometrics". This approach has evolved quite well reaching the crescendo towards growth of new age technologies. In order to effectively assess and analyze the overall outcome of the research undertaken by researchers in managing the cooperation among the universities, authors, countries etc., bibliometrics has become an extremely predominant tool (Gutiérrez-Salcedo et al. 2017).

This research work reviews the literature concerning utilization of social media in emergency healthcare communications over a decade between 2014 and 2021. In doing so, we try to investigate and defend the following research questions (RQs):

RQ1: What are the most impactful sources (journals)?
RQ2: What are the most impactful documents (publications)?
RQ3: Who are the most impactful authors?

The rest of the paper is structured as follows: Sect. 2 describes the methodology and selection criteria. Section 3, deals with various results and findings, followed by discussions in Sect. 4. Finally, we make concluding remarks in Sect. 5.

2   Methodology

The task of accomplishing the bibliographic analysis is performed in numerous stages. To explore the favorable bibliographic database (e.g. PubMed, EMbase, SpringerLink, Scopus, Web of Science etc.) and to heap up the essential articles as well as journals, is considered as the most crucial stage, and this happens to be our initial stage. Here, it is to be noted that not all the databases provide us with the information or data in order to directly perform the bibliometric analysis. In this study, Scopus database is considered for bibliometrics on the retrieved sources (articles, journals, etc.) as it gives access to the citation data and huge databases related to social sciences, health sciences, physical as well as life sciences. Scopus database can be accessed through Elsevier website and it covers three types of sources: book series, journals and trade journals.

To gather the data the following search query was used: (*'Social Media' OR 'Twitter' OR 'Tweet' OR 'Social Media Analytic') AND ('Medical' OR 'M-Health' OR 'Health' OR 'Healthcare') AND ('Emergency' OR 'Crisis' OR 'Epidemic' OR 'Pandemic') AND ('Management' OR 'Awareness' OR 'Info-Management').* In addition to this, the period of publication was selected as 2014–2021, as we wanted to concentrate on the latest literature articles related to the utilization of social media in emergency healthcare communications. Further, only highly rated journal publications were considered for our analysis.

In bibliometric analysis, the data preprocessing and cleaning is an important as well as daunting task that should be performed as the first step. Scopus data collected using the query string resulted in a total of 1273 published articles, which was then refined manually on the basis of relatable titles from the total list, bringing the bibliographic data down to 756 articles. Then to narrow it down further, the remaining articles were filtered one by one on the basis of useful abstracts by reading them individually, bringing the whole count to a solid 251 but after thoroughly analyzing each paper and data munging, which required removal of unwanted keyword data, filtering and manual inspection of every article based on the their abstract, methodology and conclusion, the outcome reduced to a favorable 67 unique articles, on which this whole analysis was conducted. An overview of collected articles is given in Table 1.

Table 1. Overview of collected articles

Main information		Authors		Authors collaboration	
Sources	56	Authors	300	Single-authored documents	8
Documents	67	Author Appearances	311	Documents per author	0.233
Average years from publication	2.14	Authors of single-authored documents	7	Authors per document	4.29
Average citations per documents	13.44	Authors of multi-authored documents	293	Co-authors per documents	4.44
Average citations per year per document	3.498			Collaboration index	4.73
References	3272				

For this research study, an open-source R Package, "bibliometrix" was used which incorporates several analysis options. It is a powerful library that can perform complete bibliometric and scientometric analysis (Aria and Cuccurullo 2017). Furthermore, it allows us to obtain multiple types of graphs and features not common in other libraries and any non-coder can also use this tool as well.

3   Results and Findings

In this section, we share the results and findings of bibliometric analysis. This section has been divided in four sub-sections. The first sub-section deals with most impactful sources (journals), while, second sub-section deals with most impactful documents. Third sub-section deals with most impactful authors, while prominent publication themes are discussed in fourth sub-section.

3.1   Impactful Sources

In order to identify the most impactful sources, we first check the relevance of the sources i.e. number of articles published from a particular source in our shortlisted 67 articles (shortlisted local database). The result of this analysis is shown in Table 2. With five articles Journal of Medical Internet Research (Himelein-Wachowiak et al. 2021; Iyu et al. 2021; Margus et al. 2021; Nagar et al. 2014; Park et al. 2021) made the maximum contribution, followed by Plos One (Allen et al. 2016; Buchanan et al. 2021; Hartley et al. 2017; Rivieccio et al. 2021) with four articles.

Table 2. Journals with maximum publications

Rank	Journals	Number of articles published
1	Journal of Medical Internet Research	5
2	Plos One	4
=3	International Journal of Environmental Research and Public Health	3
=3	Online Social Networks and Media	3
=5	IEEE Access	2
=5	Indonesian Journal of Geography	2
=5	Journal of Information and Knowledge Management	2

Next, we attempt to identify most locally cited sources. The term locally cited refers to the citations that an article receives from other articles in the review corpus only citations (Donthu et al. 2021). With 45 citations Plos One was the most locally cited source, followed by Journal of Medical Internet Research with 37 citations. The result of top ten locally cited sources is shown in Table 3.

Table 3. Most Local Cited Sources

Rank	Journals	Number of citations
1	Plos One	45
2	Journal of Medical Internet Research	37
3	Government Information Quarterly	30
4	Science	19
5	Nonprofit and Voluntary Sector Quarterly	18
6	Nature	17
=7	Computers in Human Behavior	16
=7	Public Relations Review	16
9	American Journal of Public Health	15
10	Information	14

3.2 Impactful Documents

In order to investigate the most impactful document, we first find the most globally cited documents. Islam et al. (2020), is the most globally cited article with 198 citations, followed by Gaspar et al. (2016) and Nagar et al. (2014) with 94 citations each. The results most globally cited documents is shown in Table 4.

Table 4. Most globally cited documents

Rank	Publication	Total citations	Total citations per year	Normalized total citations
1	Islam et al. (2020)	198	66.000	7.8628
=2	Gaspar et al. (2016)	94	13.429	1.9583
=2	Nagar et al. (2014)	94	10.444	1.4242
4	Allen et al. (2016)	68	9.714	1.4167
5	Sutton et al. (2015)	57	7.125	1.0000
6	Plotnick and Hiltz (2016)	55	7.857	1.1458
7	Househ (2016)	47	6.714	0.9792
8	Shahi et al. (2021)	44	22.000	10.8736
9	Teufel et al. (2020)	32	10.667	1.2708
10	Li et al. (2020)	21	7.000	0.8339

Next, we compute the most locally cited documents. To our surprise only four documents were locally cited. The results of the most locally cited documents are shown in Table 5. Nagar et al. (2014), was the most locally cited document with three local citations.

Table 5. Most locally cited documents

Rank	Publication	Local citations (LC)	Global citations (GC)	LC/GC ratio (%)	Normalized local citation	Normalized global citation
1	Nagar et al. (2014)	3	94	3.19	2.00	1.42
2	Shahi et al. (2021)	2	44	4.55	43.00	10.87
=3	Islam et al. (2020)	1	198	0.51	5.50	7.86
=3	Hassan et al. (2020)	1	11	9.09	5.50	0.44

3.3 Impactful Authors

In order to identify the most impactful authors, we first check the relevance of the authors i.e. number of articles published by an author in shortlisted local database. There were a total of four authors (Benítez De Gracia, E; Herrera-Peco, I; Jiménez-Gómez, B; Ruiz Núñez, C) who published two articles and coincidently they authored the same two articles. The results of same is shown in Table 6.

Table 6. Most relevant authors

Author	Publications	Number of articles	Article fractionalized
Benítez De Gracia, E	Herrera-Peco et al. (2021a, b)	2	0.34
Herrera-Peco, I	Herrera-Peco et al. (2021a, b)	2	0.34
Jiménez-Gómez, B	Herrera-Peco et al. (2021a, b)	2	0.34
Ruiz Núñez, C	Herrera-Peco et al. (2021a, b)	2	0.34

Next, major question emanates that the authors of which country made the maximum impact. So, in order to investigate this question, we check the corresponding authors' country. The maximum impact was observed to be created by USA with 18 articles. The results of the same are shown in Table 7.

Table 7. Corresponding author country

Rank	Country	Number of articles	Frequency	Simple country publication	Multiple country publication	MCP_ratio
1	USA	18	0.3673	17	1	0.0556
=2	Indonesia	4	0.0816	4	0	0.0000
=2	United Kingdom	4	0.0816	3	1	0.2500
=4	Egypt	3	0.0612	3	0	0.0000
=4	Saudi Arabia	3	0.0612	2	1	0.3333
=6	China	2	0.0408	2	0	0.0000
=6	Korea	2	0.0408	1	1	0.5000
=6	Spain	2	0.0408	2	0	0.0000
=6	Tunisia	2	0.0408	2	0	0.0000

3.4 Prominent Publication Themes

When analysisng the multiple articles, it becomes significant to find the most prominent themes in order to cluster them into groups. Further it also helps us to identify the under-explored themes that can be taken by researchers in future work. In order to get themes of these articles, latent dirichlet allocation (LDA) based topic modeling is used (Jeong et al. 2019; Singh et al. 2020a). Three prominent themes were identified namely (a) **Theme-1:** Government use of social media during healthcare emergency (b) **Theme-2:** Public use of social media during healthcare emergency (c) **Theme-3:** Spread of fake news and misinformation during healthcare emergency. Though many can argue that theme-1 and theme-2 overlap each other as both are related to use of social media during healthcare emergency; however, the main difference lies between the context of major stake holders using the social media; in theme-1 it is the government, while in theme-2 it is the general public. The results of topic modeling are shown in Table 8.

Table 8. Results of topic modeling

Themes	Total number of publications	References
Government use of social media during healthcare emergency	21	Adriani et al. (2020), Akbar et al. (2021), Alomari et al. (2021), Al-Sarem et al. (2021), Arpaci et al. (2021), Bélanger and Lavenex (2021), Crook et al. (2016), Ilyas et al. (2021), Islam et al. (2020), Jing and Ahn (2021), Laserna et al. (2021), London Jr and Matthews. (2021), Machmud et al. (2021), Mansoor (2021), O'Leary and Storey (2020), Park et al. (2021), Rivas-De-roca et al. (2021), Santoso et al. (2019), Solnick et al. (2021), Teufel et al. (2020), Thelwall (2021)
Information Diffusion through social media during healthcare emergency	33	Ahmed et al. (2020), Al-Dulaimi et al. (2018), Allen et al. (2016), Andreadis et al. (2021), Botero-Rodríguez et al. (2021), Buchanan et al. (2021), Cherichi and Daiz (2019), Chong and Park (2021), Enoki et al. (2017), Galindo Neto et al. (2021), Gaspar et al. (2016), Hartley et al. (2017), Haupt et al. (2021), Househ (2016), Li et al. (2020), Lyu et al. (2021), Mann et al. (2021), Margus et al. (2021), Nagar et al. (2014), Nikolovska et al. (2020), O'Connor et al. (2021), Plotnick and Hiltz (2016), Priyadarshini et al. (2021), Riaz et al. (2020), Rivieccio et al. (2021), Schweinberger et al. (2021), Shakeri (2020), Sun and Gloor (2021), Tsai and Wang (2021), Tully et al. (2019), Wang et al. (2021), Wu (2021),

(*continued*)

Table 8. (*continued*)

Themes	Total number of publications	References
Spread of fake news and misinformation during healthcare emergency	12	Abdelminaam et al. (2021), Burel et al. (2021), Hassan et al. (2020), Herrera-Peco et al. (2021a, b), Himelein-Wachowiak et al. (2021), Jemielniak and Krempovych (2021), Muric et al. (2021), Qureshi et al. (2021), Safarnejad et al. (2020), Shahi et al. (2021), Sutton et al. (2015)

4 Discussions

Social media is so deeply embedded in our everyday lives, that we have become helplessly reliant on it for every source of information. This is also true for healthcare related information. This research explores the use of social media in emergency healthcare communication. Our research was based upon three research questions, namely, the most impactful resource, the most impactful document and lastly, the most prominent author(s) and additionally, the country too. According to our results, Journal of Medical Internet Research and Plos One were the most impactful sources (journals). Similarly, Islam et al. (2020) and Nagar et al. (2014) were the most impactful documents (publications). Benítez De Gracia, E; Herrera-Peco, I; Jiménez-Gómez, B; Ruiz Núñez, C were the most impactful authors, while USA was the most impactful country.

This study also reveals that the current subject matter in discussion is not limited to a single domain like information systems (IS), healthcare sciences, information technology (IT) and the social media, but has further advanced into multidisciplinary connotation. People from different disciplines like sciences, healthcare and information systems are working together to explore this area of knowledge.

Like any other research work, this research work also has its own limitations: Firstly, all the sources have been retrieved from a single database, 'Scopus'. The articles from most other prominent databases e.g. PubMed, EMbase, SpringerLink, Web of Science etc. are not considered for bibliometric analysis. Within the selected database, only peer-reviewed articles are ruminated and leaving behind all the other forms of publications, such as conference papers, review papers, book chapters, etc. Secondly, we have considered only the literature written in the English language and no other language is included for the analysis which might have impacted the overall outcome of the findings of this study. Thirdly, the search query used for this study also poses a limitation to the whole analysis as any other combination of search query might have given different results. Finally, even if different initials or surnames have been used by the authors, still, this analysis does not capture common names for active researchers.

Regardless of these limitations, this study can play a vital role in contributing towards the methodological review of active journals published in the area of medical emergencies, related to the communication via famous social media platforms by performing bibliometrics on them. Furthermore, these limitations can be addressed in future studies.

5 Conclusions

This research analyzes the evolution of research trends in the use of social media for information sharing and communication during global medical emergency situations. In this research work, we have used the bibliometric analysis to investigate and defend our three research questions. Though the limitations of this research work have been listed, yet the purpose of completing this investigation seems fulfilled. Further, as highlighted from our research results that spread of fake news and misinformation during healthcare emergency was under explored research domain, which the researchers can explore in future studies.

References

Abdelminaam, D.S., Ismail, F.H., Taha, M., Taha, A., Houssein, E.H., Nabil, A.: CoAID-DEEP: an optimized intelligent framework for automated detecting COVID-19 misleading information on Twitter. IEEE Access **9**, 27840–27867 (2021)

Adriani, M., Azzahro, F., Hidayanto, A.N.: Disease surveillance in Indonesia through Twitter posts. J. Appl. Res. Technol. **18**(3), 214–228 (2020)

Ahmed, M.A., Sadri, A.M., Amini, M.H.: Data-driven inferences of agency-level risk and response communication on COVID-19 through social media based interactions. arXiv preprint arXiv: 2008.03866 (2020)

Akbar, G.G., Kurniadi, D., Nurliawati, N.: Content analysis of social media: public and government response to COVID-19 pandemic in Indonesia. Jurnal Ilmu Sosial Dan Ilmu Politik **25**(1), 16–31 (2021)

Al-Dulaimi, O.H.Z.: Image content based topological analysis for friend recommendation on Twitter. Jour of Adv Res. Dyn. Control Sys. **10**(9) (2018)

Allen, C., Tsou, M.H., Aslam, A., Nagel, A., Gawron, J.M.: Applying GIS and machine learning methods to Twitter data for multiscale surveillance of influenza. PLoS ONE **11**(7), e0157734 (2016)

Alomari, E., Katib, I., Albeshri, A., Mehmood, R.: COVID-19: detecting government pandemic measures and public concerns from Twitter Arabic data using distributed machine learning. Int. J. Environ. Res. Public Health **18**(1), 282 (2021)

Al-Sarem, M., Alsaeedi, A., Saeed, F., Boulila, W., AmeerBakhsh, O.: A novel hybrid deep learning model for detecting COVID-19-related rumors on social media based on LSTM and concatenated parallel CNNs. Appl. Sci. **11**(17), 7940 (2021)

Andreadis, S., et al.: A social media analytics platform visualising the spread of COVID-19 in Italy via exploitation of automatically geotagged tweets. Online Soc. Netw. Media **23**, 100134 (2021)

Aria, M., Cuccurullo, C.: bibliometrix: an R-tool for comprehensive science mapping analysis. J. Informetr. **11**(4), 959–975 (2017)

Arpaci, I., Alshehabi, S., Mahariq, I., Topcu, A.E.: An evolutionary clustering analysis of social media content and global infection rates during the COVID-19 pandemic. J. Inf. Knowl. Manag. **20**(03), 2150038 (2021)

Bélanger, M.E., Lavenex, S.: Communicating mobility restrictions during the COVID-19 crisis on Twitter: the legitimacy challenge. Swiss Polit. Sci. Rev. **27**(4), 822–839 (2021)

Botero-Rodríguez, F., et al.: Análisis de percepciones y repercusiones emocionales en usuarios de Twitter en Colombia durante la pandemia de COVID-19. Revista Colombiana de Psiquiatría (2021)

Buchanan, K., Aknin, L.B., Lotun, S., Sandstrom, G.M.: Brief exposure to social media during the COVID-19 pandemic: doom-scrolling has negative emotional consequences, but kindness-scrolling does not. PLoS ONE **16**(10), e0257728 (2021)

Burel, G., Farrell, T., Alani, H.: Demographics and topics impact on the co-spread of COVID-19 misinformation and fact-checks on Twitter. Inf. Process. Manag. **58**(6), 102732 (2021)

Cherichi, S., Faiz, R.: Upgrading event and pattern detection to big data. Int. J. Comput. Sci. Eng. **18**(4), 404–412 (2019)

Chong, M., Park, H.W.: COVID-19 in the Twitterverse, from epidemic to pandemic: information-sharing behavior and Twitter as an information carrier. Scientometrics **126**(8), 6479–6503 (2021). https://doi.org/10.1007/s11192-021-04054-2

Crook, B., Glowacki, E.M., Suran, M., Harris, J.K., Bernhardt, J.M.: Content analysis of a live CDC Twitter chat during the 2014 Ebola outbreak. Commun. Res. Rep. **33**(4), 349–355 (2016)

Donthu, N., Kumar, S., Mukherjee, D., Pandey, N., Lim, W.M.: How to conduct a bibliometric analysis: an overview and guidelines. J. Bus. Res. **133**, 285–296 (2021)

Dwivedi, Y.K., et al.: Impact of COVID-19 pandemic on information management research and practice: transforming education, work and life. Int. J. Inf. Manag. **55**, 102211 (2020)

Dwivedi, Y.K., Kelly, G., Janssen, M., Rana, N.P., Slade, E.L., Clement, M.: Social media: the good, the bad, and the ugly. Inf. Syst. Front. **20**(3), 419–423 (2018)

Enoki, M., Yoshida, I., Oguchi, M.: Capacity control of social media diffusion for real-time analysis system. IEICE Trans. Inf. Syst. **100**(4), 776–784 (2017)

Galindo Neto, N.M., Sá, G.G.D.M., Pereira, J.D.C.N., Barbosa, L.U., Henriques, A.H.B., Barros, L.M.: COVID-19: comments on official social network of the Ministry of Health about action Brazil Count on Me. Rev. Gaucha Enferm. **42**, e20200167 (2021)

Gaspar, R., Pedro, C., Panagiotopoulos, P., Seibt, B.: Beyond positive or negative: qualitative sentiment analysis of social media reactions to unexpected stressful events. Comput. Hum. Behav. **56**, 179–191 (2016)

Gutiérrez-Salcedo, M., Martínez, M.Á., Moral-Munoz, J.A., Herrera-Viedma, E., Cobo, M.J.: Some bibliometric procedures for analyzing and evaluating research fields. Appl. Intell. **48**(5), 1275–1287 (2017). https://doi.org/10.1007/s10489-017-1105-y

Haman, M.: The use of Twitter by state leaders and its impact on the public during the COVID-19 pandemic. Heliyon **6**(11), e05540 (2020)

Hartley, D.M., et al.: Coughing, sneezing, and aching online: Twitter and the volume of influenza-like illness in a pediatric hospital. PLoS ONE **12**(7), e0182008 (2017)

Hassan, N., Gomaa, W., Khoriba, G., Haggag, M.: Credibility detection in Twitter using word n-gram analysis and supervised machine learning techniques. Int. J. Intell. Eng. Syst. **13**(1), 291–300 (2020)

Haupt, M.R., Jinich-Diamant, A., Li, J., Nali, M., Mackey, T.K.: Characterizing Twitter user topics and communication network dynamics of the "Liberate" movement during COVID-19 using unsupervised machine learning and social network analysis. Online Soc. Netw. Media **21**, 100114 (2021)

Herrera-Peco, I., et al.: Antivaccine movement and COVID-19 negationism: a content analysis of Spanish-written messages on Twitter. Vaccines **9**(6), 656 (2021a)

Herrera-Peco, I., Jiménez-Gómez, B., Romero-Magdalena, C.S., Benítez De Gracia, E.: COVID-19 and vaccination: analysis of public institution's role in information spread through Twitter. Revista espanola de salud publica **95**, e202106084 (2021b)

Himelein-Wachowiak, M., et al.: Bots and misinformation spread on social media: implications for COVID-19. J. Med. Internet Res. **23**(5), e26933 (2021)

Househ, M.: Communicating Ebola through social media and electronic news media outlets: a cross-sectional study. Health Inform. J. **22**(3), 470–478 (2016)

Ilyas, H., Anwar, A., Yaqub, U., Alzamil, Z., Appelbaum, D.: Analysis and visualization of COVID-19 discourse on Twitter using data science: a case study of the USA, the UK and India. Glob. Knowl. Mem. Commun. **71**, 140–154 (2021)

Islam, A.N., Laato, S., Talukder, S., Sutinen, E.: Misinformation sharing and social media fatigue during COVID-19: an affordance and cognitive load perspective. Technol. Forecast. Soc. Chang. **159**, 120201 (2020)

Jemielniak, D., Krempovych, Y.: An analysis of AstraZeneca COVID-19 vaccine misinformation and fear mongering on Twitter. Public Health **200**, 4–6 (2021)

Jeong, B., Yoon, J., Lee, J.M.: Social media mining for product planning: a product opportunity mining approach based on topic modeling and sentiment analysis. Int. J. Inf. Manag. **48**, 280–290 (2019)

Jing, E., Ahn, Y.-Y.: Characterizing partisan political narrative frameworks about COVID-19 on Twitter. EPJ Data Sci. **10**(1), 1–18 (2021). https://doi.org/10.1140/epjds/s13688-021-00308-4

Kapoor, K.K., Tamilmani, K., Rana, N.P., Patil, P., Dwivedi, Y.K., Nerur, S.: Advances in social media research: past, present and future. Inf. Syst. Front. **20**(3), 531–558 (2018)

Laserna, M.S.S., Marí-Sáez, V.M., Ceballos-Castro, G.: Analysis of the solidarity discourse of Spanish NGOS on the coronavirus on Twitter. Tonos Digital (2021)

Li, Y., et al.: Constructing and communicating COVID-19 stigma on Twitter: a content analysis of tweets during the early stage of the COVID-19 outbreak. Int. J. Environ. Res. Public Health **17**(18), 6847 (2020)

London, J., Jr., Matthews, K.: Crisis communication on social media-lessons from Covid-19. J. Decis. Syst. **31**, 1–21 (2021)

Lyu, J.C., Le Han, E., Luli, G.K.: COVID-19 vaccine–related discussion on Twitter: topic modeling and sentiment analysis. J. Med. Internet Res. **23**(6), e24435 (2021)

Machmud, M., Irawan, B., Karinda, K., Susilo, J.: Analysis of the intensity of communication and coordination of government officials on Twitter social media during the Covid-19 handling in Indonesia. Acad. J. Interdiscip. Stud. **10**(3), 319 (2021)

Mann, M., Byun, S.E., Ginder, W.: B Corps' social media communications during the COVID-19 pandemic: through the lens of the triple bottom line. Sustainability **13**(17), 9634 (2021)

Mansoor, M.: Citizens' trust in government as a function of good governance and government agency's provision of quality information on social media during COVID-19. Gov. Inf. Q. **38**(4), 101597 (2021)

Margus, C., Brown, N., Hertelendy, A.J., Safferman, M.R., Hart, A., Ciottone, G.R.: Emergency physician Twitter use in the COVID-19 pandemic as a potential predictor of impending surge: retrospective observational study. J. Med. Internet Res. **23**(7), e28615 (2021)

Muric, G., Wu, Y., Ferrara, E.: COVID-19 vaccine hesitancy on social media: building a public Twitter data set of antivaccine content, vaccine misinformation, and conspiracies. JMIR Public Health Surveill. **7**(11), e30642 (2021)

Nagar, R., et al.: A case study of the New York City 2012–2013 influenza season with daily geocoded Twitter data from temporal and spatiotemporal perspectives. J. Med. Internet Res. **16**(10), e3416 (2014)

Nikolovska, M., Johnson, S.D., Ekblom, P.: "Show this thread": policing, disruption and mobilisation through Twitter. An analysis of UK law enforcement tweeting practices during the Covid-19 pandemic. Crime Sci. **9**(1), 1–16 (2020)

O'Connor, C., et al.: Bordering on crisis: a qualitative analysis of focus group, social media, and news media perspectives on the Republic of Ireland-Northern Ireland border during the 'first wave' of the COVID-19 pandemic. Soc. Sci. Med. **282**, 114111 (2021)

O'Leary, D.E., Storey, V.C.: A Google–Wikipedia–Twitter model as a leading indicator of the numbers of coronavirus deaths. Intell. Syst. Account. Financ. Manag. **27**(3), 151–158 (2020)

Park, S., et al.: COVID-19 discourse on Twitter in four Asian countries: case study of risk communication. J. Med. Internet Res. **23**(3), e23272 (2021)

Plotnick, L., Hiltz, S.R.: Barriers to use of social media by emergency managers. J. Homel. Secur. Emerg. Manag. **13**(2), 247–277 (2016)

Pritchard, A., Wittig, G.R.: Bibliometrics. AllM Books, Watford (1981)

Priyadarshini, I., Mohanty, P., Kumar, R., Sharma, R., Puri, V., Singh, P.K.: A study on the sentiments and psychology of Twitter users during COVID-19 lockdown period. Multimedia Tools Appl., 1–23 (2021). https://doi.org/10.1007/s11042-021-11004-w

Qureshi, K.A., Malick, R.A.S., Sabih, M., Cherifi, H.: Complex network and source inspired COVID-19 fake news classification on Twitter. IEEE Access **9**, 139636–139656 (2021)

Riaz, M., Wang, X., Guo, Y.: An empirical investigation of precursors influencing social media health information behaviors and personal healthcare habits during coronavirus (COVID-19) pandemic. Inf. Disc. Deliv. **49**, 225–239 (2020)

Rivas-De-roca, R., García-Gordillo, M., Rojas-Torrijos, J.L.: Communication strategies on Twitter and institutional websites in the Covid-19 second wave: analysis of the governments of Germany, Spain, Portugal, and the United Kingdom. Revista Latina de Comunicacion Social **79**, 49–72 (2021)

Rivieccio, B.A., et al.: CoViD-19, learning from the past: a wavelet and cross-correlation analysis of the epidemic dynamics looking to emergency calls and Twitter trends in Italian Lombardy region. PLoS ONE **16**(2), e0247854 (2021)

Safarnejad, L., Xu, Q., Ge, Y., Krishnan, S., Bagarvathi, A., Chen, S.: Contrasting misinformation and real-information dissemination network structures on social media during a health emergency. Am. J. Public Health **110**(S3), S340–S347 (2020)

Santoso, A.D.: Tweets flooded in Bandung 2016 floods: connecting individuals and organizations to disaster information. Indones. J. Geogr. **51**(3), 242–250 (2019)

Schweinberger, M., Haugh, M., Hames, S.: Analysing discourse around COVID-19 in the Australian Twittersphere: a real-time corpus-based analysis. Big Data Society **8**(1), 20539517211021436 (2021)

Shahi, G.K., Dirkson, A., Majchrzak, T.A.: An exploratory study of covid-19 misinformation on Twitter. Online Soc. Netw. Media **22**, 100104 (2021)

Shakeri, S.: A framework for the interaction of active audiences and influencers on Twitter: the case of Zika virus. J. Inf. Knowl. Manag **19**(04), 2050032 (2020)

Singh, P., Dwivedi, Y.K., Kahlon, K.S., Rana, N.P., Patil, P.P., Sawhney, R.S.: Digital payment adoption in India: insights from Twitter analytics. In: Pappas, I.O., Mikalef, P., Dwivedi, Y.K., Jaccheri, L., Krogstie, J., Mäntymäki, M. (eds.) I3E 2019. LNCS, vol. 11701, pp. 425–436. Springer, Cham (2019). https://doi.org/10.1007/978-3-030-29374-1_35

Singh, P., Dwivedi, Y.K., Kahlon, K.S., Sawhney, R.S., Alalwan, A.A., Rana, N.P.: Smart monitoring and controlling of government policies using social media and cloud computing. Inf. Syst. Front. **22**, 315–337 (2020a)

Singh, P., Dwivedi, Y.K., Kahlon, K.S., Pathania, A., Sawhney, R.S.: Can Twitter analytics predict election outcome? An insight from 2017 Punjab assembly elections. Gov. Inf. Q. **37**(2), 101444 (2020b)

Singh, P., Sawhney, R.S., Kahlon, K.S.: Sentiment analysis of demonetization of 500 1000 rupee banknotes by Indian government. ICT Express **4**(3), 124–129 (2018)

Singh, P., Singh, S., Sohal, M., Dwivedi, Y.K., Kahlon, K.S., Sawhney, R.S.: Psychological fear and anxiety caused by COVID-19: insights from Twitter analytics. Asian J. Psychiatry **54**, 102280 (2020c)

Solnick, R.E., Chao, G., Ross, R.D., Kraft-Todd, G.T., Kocher, K.E.: Emergency physicians and personal narratives improve the perceived effectiveness of COVID-19 public health recommendations on social media: a randomized experiment. Acad. Emerg. Med. **28**(2), 172–183 (2021)

Sun, J., Gloor, P.A.: Assessing the Predictive power of online social media to analyze COVID-19 outbreaks in the 50 US states. Future Internet **13**(7), 184 (2021)

Sutton, J., et al.: A cross-hazard analysis of terse message retransmission on Twitter. Proc. Natl. Acad. Sci. **112**(48), 14793–14798 (2015)

Teufel, M., et al.: Not all world leaders use Twitter in response to the COVID-19 pandemic: impact of the way of Angela Merkel on psychological distress, behaviour and risk perception. J. Public Health **42**(3), 644–646 (2020)

Thelwall, M.: Can Twitter give insights into international differences in Covid-19 vaccination? Eight countries' English tweets to 21 March 2021. arXiv preprint arXiv:2103.14125 (2021)

Tsai, M.H., Wang, Y.: Analyzing Twitter data to evaluate people's attitudes towards public health policies and events in the era of COVID-19. Int. J. Environ. Res. Public Health **18**(12), 6272 (2021)

Tully, M., Dalrymple, K.E., Young, R.: Contextualizing nonprofits' use of links on Twitter during the West African Ebola virus epidemic. Commun. Stud. **70**(3), 313–331 (2019)

Wang, B., Liu, B., Zhang, Q.: An empirical study on Twitter's use and crisis retweeting dynamics amid Covid-19. Nat. Hazards **107**(3), 2319–2336 (2021). https://doi.org/10.1007/s11069-020-04497-5

Wu, V.C.S.: Beyond policy patrons: A 'MADE' framework for examining public engagement efforts of philanthropic foundations on Twitter. Public Manag. Rev., 1–25 (2021)

Xue, J., et al.: Twitter discussions and emotions about the COVID-19 pandemic: Machine learning approach. J. Med. Internet Res. **22**(11), e20550 (2020)

The Effect of Technostress on Cyberbullying in Metaverse Social Platforms

Zainah Qasem[1](✉), Hazar Y. Hmoud[2], Doa'a Hajawi[1], and Jumana Ziad Al Zoubi[3]

[1] The School of Business Department of Marketing, The University of Jordan, Amman, Jordan
{z.qasem,d.hajawi}@ju.edu.jo
[2] The School of Business, Department of Management Information Systems,
The University of Jordan, Amman, Jordan
h.hmoud@ju.edu.jo
[3] The School of Business, Department of Public Administration, University of Jordan, Amman,
Jordan
j.zoubi@ju.edu.jo

Abstract. Facebook and platforms such as Second Life3 and Roblox5 have contributed to the late interest in Metaverse. The metaverse is a three-dimensional virtual world inhabited by avatars of real people. After the prolonged pandemic people have got engaged more with the metaverse and used social metaverse platforms such as VRchat to communicate and interact. However, the lack of regulation that controls content creation on the Metaverse, and the democratized environment have presented a rich environment for people not only to escape stress but also to find an outlet for this stress by cyberbullying other avatars. In this conceptual paper, we are proposing a conceptual model based on the stress-strain model that explains the relationship between technostress elements and cyberbullying. This paper is also a call for policymakers and metaverse social platform owners to put clear policies to prevent cyberbullying on these platforms.

Keywords: Technostress · Metaverse · Antisocial behaviour · Cyberbullying · Escapism

1 Introduction

Since launching its new vision to bring the Metaverse to life by moving into the complete virtual ecosystem, Facebook has paved the road to a new era in online consumer interaction (Facebook, 2022; Han et al. 2022). Along with Facebook, platforms such as Second Life3 and Roblox5 have contributed to the late interest in Metaverse (Fernandez and Hui, 2022).

Metaverse is a term that refers to a "three-dimensional virtual world inhabited by avatars of real people" (Kim, 2021, p141). The global Metaverse market is growing fast; it is expected to be worth 280 billion U.S. dollars by 2025 (Jeon, 2021). Generally, the Metaverse is changing the face of trading from both the consumer and business sides. For example, people are shifting towards owning and trading virtual online assists that serve

A. Elbanna et al. (Eds.): TDIT 2022, IFIP AICT 660, pp. 291–296, 2022.
https://doi.org/10.1007/978-3-031-17968-6_22

their avatars, such as real estate and fashion products for their avatars (Fernandez and Hui, 2022). From the business, side metaverse has created an opportunity for businesses to market their services to potential customers (Collins, 2008).

The Metaverse is also significantly affecting societies and human lives. The Metaverse is a 3D world that mimics the physical world. In this 3D world, users can interact with each other and their digital space surroundings using avatars that represent them and imitate their movements (Hollensen et al. 2022). As a result, many people have started to resort to the Metaverse and engage in social metaverse experiences and activities with other fellow avatars. One of the reasons people use social Metaverse such as VRchat is to escape their everyday stress (Panova and Lleras 2016).

One aspect that people might escape is the stress caused by different technologies such as mobiles and emails, which extend working hours and allow reachability of employees during their off-work hours (Tarafdar et al. 2007). In addition, the nature of the Metaverse allows people to overcome physical world limitations (Davis et al.2009), which is not limited to activities but extends to the availability of regulations that rule how people interact and play. As a result, several antisocial behaviours might occur while in the Metaverse such as cyberbullying (Jamison, 2022).

In this paper, we propose a conceptual model based on the stress-strain model as a theoretical background to explain how technostress results in antisocial behaviour in the Metaverse, such as cyberbullying.

The following parts of this paper are organized as the following. First, it will present a literature review that covers the main concepts of this paper. The second section will present the stress-strain model as a theoretical background, followed by some prepositions.

2 Literature Review

2.1 The Metaverse

The Metaverse has received significant attention since 2020. The term refers to a "three-dimensional virtual world inhabited by avatars of real people" (Kim, 2021, p141). The Metaverse is a computer-generated world that goes beyond the physical world (Lee et al. 2011). The Metaverse has also been described as a "3D virtual world with collapsed reality and virtual boundaries, along with technological developments such as virtual reality and augmented reality" (Jeon, 2021, p81). Communicating using social metaverse platforms is one of the various uses of the Metaverse. Since the pandemic has forced people to adopt a non-face-to-face culture using social metaverse (Lee et al. 2021). People have resorted to social metaverse platforms such as VRchat to connect and communicate. One of the significant characteristics of the Metaverse is being a democratized platform that permits anybody to produce interactive content (MacCallum and persons, 2019). As such, and with the lack of regulations that controls the produced content (low inhibitors), there is a growing presence of inappropriate behaviour among users of Metaverse. The "Centre for Countering Digital Hate" has reported that Metaverse is a rich environment for antisocial behaviour such as cyberbullying and hate speech (Centre for Countering Digital Hate, 2021).

2.2 Cyberbullying on the Metaverse Social Platforms

There are a number of acts that can be referred to as antisocial behavior on the metaverse platforms. However, in this paper we will focus on cyberbullying as a general form of antisocial behavior that includes in it more than one type of antisocial behavior like cyber harassment and cyber stalking (Lowry et al. 2016).

Cyberbullying is "any behavior performed through electronic or digital media by individuals or groups that repeatedly communicate hostile or aggressive messages intended to inflict harm or discomfort on others (Gonzalez-Cabrera et al. 2017. P153).

Modern Information Communication Technology and electronic media artifacts such as anonymity (Slonje et al. 2013), and lack of regulations that control content creation have significantly influenced cyberbullying (Jamison, 2022).

2.3 Self-indulging Escapism and the Metaverse

The blaring between the physical world and the Metaverse creates a novel consumer experience, presenting a potentially negative consequence. The fast-paced life of modern humans and the existence of Information Communication Technology have led to many mental and physical health issues such as stress. The Metaverse allows people to spend a vast amount of time in a virtual environment where they have the luxury of interacting with other avatars sheltered in the illusion of the alternative reality (Han et al. 2022).

Self-indulgent escapism proposes that a person can use Information Communication Technology to escape from and cope with everyday stressors such as workload (Panova and Lleras 2016). Yee (2006) has proposed that escapism is one of the motives people engage with the virtual environment.

2.4 Technostress and Technostressors

Technostress represents the dark side of technology and focuses on the negative effect of Information Communication Technology on individuals' mental and physical health by studying topics such as techno stressors and outcomes of dealing with Technostressors (Tarafdar et al. 2010). Technostress was defined as the direct or indirect effect of interacting with Information Communication Technology on users' cognition, attitudes, emotions, thoughts and behaviours (Rosen, 1997, Weil and Rosen, 1997; Brooks et al. 2017).

Technostress is generated by a number of causes known as technostressors or stressors (Ayyagari et al. 2011). Since Information Communication Technology has become part of modern human lives, the negative effect of these technologies is becoming more significant. For example, the invasive nature of technologies (e.g., instant messaging) and overloading (e.g., emails on smartphones) nature allow work to overwhelm and interrupt people's lives out of working hours.

This conceptual paper adopts the stressor-strain model (Yan et al. 2013). We will be focusing on two stressors; these are first, techno invasion, which refers to the stress caused by Information Communication Technology's ability to continuously allows reaching people. Second, techno-overload which refers to the stress caused by being forced to increase the amount and speed of work because of Information Communication Technology (Tarafdar et al. 2007).

In this paper we assume that one expected outcome to the existence of techno-overload and techno-invasion as stressors is anger and aggression (Barlett et al. 2021). People are expected to search for a way to eliminate anger. As people are already escaping their reality to an uncontrolled environment it is expected that people will ease their anger by attaching and cyberbullying fellow avatars in social metaverse platforms.

3 Theoretical Background and Propositions

In this conceptual paper, we propose using the stress-strain model as the theoretical background that will explain the relationship between variables of our proposed model. Stress-strain relationship refers to stressors -the stimuli that cause technostress (Ayyagari et al. 2011, Qasem, 2019), and strains which are the outcomes of being exposed to a specific stressor (Ayyagari et al. 2011). This paper proposes two main stressors: technology overload and technology invasion. Being faced with these stressor people are expected to show anger as a strain. In the existence social metaverse platforms which allows people to escape reality, and in the lack of regulations that inhibit creating negative content people are expected ease their anger by cyberbullying other avatars. Hence, we propose the following prepositions.

Preposition one: there is a positive relationship between technology-overload and anger.

Preposition two: there is a positive relationship between technology-invasion and anger.

Preposition three: there is a positive relationship between anger and self-indulgent escapism.

Preposition four: there is a positive relationship between self-indulgent escapism and cyberbullying.

Preposition Five: the relationship between self-indulgent escapism and cyber bullying in social metaverse platforms is moderated by low inhibitors.

4 Proposed Research Methodology

This research aims to study the effect of workload related technostressors on cyberbullying on social metaverse platforms. Therefore, the sample of this study will be employees who use social metaverse platforms. Quantitative survey-based research is recommended to test the proposed model.

5 Conclusion

The importance of the Metaverse is increasing daily specially after being adopted by big companies like Facebook. This increased importance makes it very cruccial for researchers and businesses alike to understand how people interact on this virtual world. Hence, this paper comes as a call for social metaverse platforms owners to start putting policies and regulations to protect the Metaverse users from different misbehavior that might harm users such as cyberbullying. In this paper we are focusing on one aspect that might lead to cyberbullying which is stress caused by workload. The prepositions of this paper suggest that people might ease their stress on metaverse social platforms by cyberbullying their fellow users.

References

Ayyagari, R., Grover, V., Purvis, R.: Technostress: technological antecedents and implications. MIS Q. **35**(4), 831–858 (2011)

Bradshaw, R., Zelano, J.A.: Exploring themes of technostress for end users working with hardware and software technology. Retrieved on July (2013)

Barlett, C.P., Rinker, A., Roth, B.: Cyberbullying perpetration in the COVID-19 era: an application of general strain theory. J. Soc. Psychol. **161**(4), 466–476 (2021)

Brooks, S., Longstreet, P., Califf, C.: Social media-induced technostress and its impact on Internet addiction: a distraction-conflict theory perspective. AIS Trans. Human-Computer Interaction **9**(2), 99–122 (2017)

Centre for Countering Digital Hate. New research shows Metaverse is not safe for kids. [online][15.04.2022] (2021). available on the world wide web at: https://www.counterhate.com/post/new-research-shows-metaverse-is-not-safe-for-kids

Collins, C.: Looking to the future: higher education in the metaverse. Educause Review **43**(5), 51–63 (2008)

Davis, A., Murphy, J.D., Owens, D., Khazanchi, D., Zigurs, I.: Avatars, people, and virtual worlds: foundations for research in metaverses. J. Assoc. Inf. Syst. **10**(2), 90 (2009)

Fernandez, C.B., Hui, P.: Life, the Metaverse and Everything: An Overview of Privacy, Ethics, and Governance in Metaverse. arXiv preprint arXiv:2204.01480 (2022)

González-Cabrera, J., Calvete, E., León-Mejía, A., Pérez-Sancho, C., Peinado, J.M.: Relationship between cyberbullying roles, cortisol secretion and psychological stress. Comput. Hum. Behav. **70**, 153–160 (2017)

Kim, J.: Advertising in the metaverse: research agenda. J. Interact. Advert. **21**(3), 141–144 (2021)

Han, D.I.D., Bergs, Y., Moorhouse, N.: Virtual reality consumer experience escapes: preparing for the Metaverse. Virtual Reality, pp.1–16 (2022)

Hollensen, S., Kotler, P., Opresnik, M.O.: Metaverse–the new marketing universe. Journal of Business Strategy (2022)

Jamison, M.: The dark side of the Metaverse, part I. American enterprise institute (AEI). [online][15.04.2022] (2022). available on the world wide web at: https://www.aei.org/technology-and-innovation/the-dark-side-of-the-metaverse-part-i/#:~:text=As%20such%2C%20in%20some%20areas,data%20exploitation%20becoming%20well%20established.&text=Antisocial%20behavior%20includes%20assault%2C%20bullying%2C%20harassment%2C%20and%20hate%20speech.]

Jeon, J.E.: The effects of user experience-based design innovativeness on user-metaverse platform channel relationships in south Korea. Journal of Distribution Science, **19**(11), 81-90 (2021).

Lee, S.G., Trimi, S., Byun, W.K., Kang, M.: Innovation and imitation effects in Metaverse service adoption. Serv. Bus. **5**(2), 155–172 (2011)

Lee, L.H., et al.: All one needs to know about metaverse: a complete survey on technological singularity, virtual ecosystem, and research agenda. *arXiv preprint* arXiv:2110.05352 (2021)

Lowry, P.B., Zhang, J., Wang, C., Siponen, M.: Why do adults engage in cyberbullying on social media? an integration of online disinhibition and deindividuation effects with the social structure and social learning model. Inf. Syst. Res. **27**(4), 962–986 (2016)

MacCallum, K., Parsons, D.: Teacher perspectives on mobile augmented reality: the potential of metaverse for learning. In: World Conference on Mobile and Contextual Learning , pp. 21–28 (2019)

Tarafdar, M., Tu, Q., Ragu-Nathan, T.S.: Impact of technostress on end-user satisfaction and performance. J. Manag. Inf. Syst. **27**(3), 303–334 (2010)

Weil, M.M., Rosen, L.D.: Technostress: Coping with technology @ work @ home @ play , Vol. 13, p. 240. J. Wiley, New York (1997)

Yan, Z., Guo, X., Lee, M.K., Vogel, D.R.: A conceptual model of technology features and technostress in telemedicine communication. Inf. Technol. People **26**(3), 283–297 (2013)

Religiously Polarised Message Diffusion on Social Media

Seema Naula[✉], Sujeet K. Sharma, and Jang Bahadur Singh

Indian Institute of Management Tiruchirappalli, Tiruchirappalli, India
`seema.f170204@iimtrichy.ac.in`

Abstract. The study intends to examine the relationship between religious polarisation and message diffusion on social media. Communal and religious messages are shared heavily on social media such as Facebook, WhatsApp, and Twitter (Purnell & Horwitz, 2021). The diffusion of such messages translates into real-life crises many times. The study aims to collect and use the tweets collected using a Twitter API to examine the relationship. We plan to encode the religious polarity of messages manually as religious polarisation is a complex subject. The study uses the diffusion of innovation theory (Rogers, 1962) to understand the diffusion of religiously polarised messages on Twitter. In the study, we propose to test if religious polarisation diffuses more than non-polarised tweets and whether negatively polarised tweets disseminate more than positively polarised tweets. The proposed hypotheses will be tested using Twitter data which will collected usingTwitter API about a religious congregation. The paper aims to contribute to understanding the diffusion of religiously polarised messages on social media and hence to policymakers and governing bodies to mediate the spread of hatred and communal messages on social media.

Keywords: Polarisation · Message diffusion · Religious polarisation · Social media · Diffusion of innovation · Negativity bias

1 Introduction

Social media gives users a stage to discuss and share information. However, at the same time, it poses a threat of spreading hatred, false news, and misinformation which even leads to real-life crimes sometimes (Chan et al. 2016). One of the vital issues is religious hatred in religiously polarised messages (Soundararajan et al. 2020). The extant literature on social media information diffusion focuses highly on the sentiment and content of messages in viral/online marketing (Ullah et al. 2016), diffusion of false information or rumour (Oh et al. 2013; Volety et al. 2018), information travel during and after a disaster (natural or human-made) (Pang and Ng, 2016). On many social media platforms, such as products of Facebook, Facebook, and WhatsApp content diffusion is heavily communal. The communal messages diffused over such platforms even translated into communal riots in February 2020 in the capital city of India (Purnell and Horwitz, 2021). The diffusion of religiously polarised messages on social media is a grave concern but the

© IFIP International Federation for Information Processing 2022
Published by Springer Nature Switzerland AG 2022
A. Elbanna et al. (Eds.): TDIT 2022, IFIP AICT 660, pp. 297–303, 2022.
https://doi.org/10.1007/978-3-031-17968-6_23

research paucity on the topic. In this essay, we test the relationship between tweets' religious polarity and diffusion using diffusion of innovation theory as a lens. The study will help us better understand the dissemination of religious polarisation on social media.

Social media research is heavily focused on content features such as hashtags, URL inclusion, sentiment (emotions) of the message, and network features such as the number of followers associated with information diffusion (Stieglitz and Dang-Xuan, 2013). It has been shown that the presence of negative emotions/sentiments, the subject of the tweet, and the number of followers of the publisher of the tweet affect the message diffusion (Stieglitz and Dang-Xuan, 2013). We focus on the religious polarity of tweets and their impact on message diffusion. We propose that religiously polarised tweets will diffuse more than not polarised tweets due to the presence of extremity displayed in the tweets. Social media such as Twitter facilitate speedy information dissemination, leading to public opinion formation (Vosoughi et al. 2018). Although most information and news consumption are guided by social media (Vosoughi et al. 2018), we lack understanding their contribution in disseminating religious polarity online.

Existing literature discusses the role of different emotions present in the tweet's content, the sentiment of the tweet, and whether the tweet is accurate or not on its diffusion on social media. However, inquiries are lacking on how religious polarisation spreads on such platforms or if religious polarity plays a role in the fast diffusion of messages on social media. Understanding such diffusion on social media is required as social media is creating public opinion, setting trends, and is capable of causing panic or stress situations (Henry et al. 2017). This study proposes two hypotheses: religiously polarised tweets spread more than non-polarised, and negatively polarised tweets spread more than positively polarised ones.

2   Literature Review

Information diffusion studies have a long history in communication, social, and computational sciences. Other than that, researchers in marketing and business have always been curious about factors that influence message diffusion in the context of viral and online marketing (e.g., Ullah et al., 2016). With time message diffusion research started focussing on different social media platforms such as SNS, weblogs, picture-sharing platforms, and others. However, a large set of research was inclined towards Twitter (e.g., Lee et al. 2015; Oh et al. 2015; Oh et al. 2013; Volety et al. 2018) as it was becoming a most popular medium to put opinions and platform for accessing news, especially during a crisis. As of 2022, Twitter has 436 million active users per month (Statista, 2022), making it one of the most used social networking sites. Now, Twitter has evolved to be a platform for the public to share and discuss any topic ranging from public policies, crises and calling out different entities (organizations, politicians, ministers, policies, practices, actions). Tweets reach several users by word-of-mouth, impacting trends and contributing to public opinions about the subject of the tweet in society (Pang and Ng, 2016). Extant literature has shown the impact of the user's influence (J. Lee et al., 2015), the sentiment of the tweet (Stieglitz and Dang-Xuan, 2013), the distance between the place of crisis and the user who is tweeting (Volety et al. 2018), mood displayed in the tweet, use of URLs, use of hashtags on the extent to which a tweet is diffused.

2.1   Message Diffusion on Twitter

The researchers have inquired about the content of messages that impact their diffu-sion on social media. Studies such as Stieglitz and Dang-Xuan (2013) dwell on how the sentiment of tweets impacts the extent of diffusion by retweeting and the rate of retweeting. Gruzd (2013) claims that users post more positive tweets than negative ones, and positive tweets spread more than negative, suggesting the Twitter user interface is partially responsible. However, Stieglitz & Dang-Xuan (2013) stated that though sen-timents spread more on Twitter, negative sentiments diffuse more than positive ones. Researchers also investigated the role of different sentiments, such as visual and textual, on information dissemination and found out that visual and textual sentiment dissonance enhances the shareability of information (Yim et al. (2020). The sentiment analysis lacks the understanding of the emotions of tweets and their impact on diffusion by retweeting. Researchers then focused on the impact of emotions on message dissemination. Kwon and Gruzd (2017) studied the emotions present in the comments of a YouTube video and found out negative emotion like anger is mimicked and displayed more in subsequent comments if earlier comments display similar emotion. Berger (2011) claimed the con-tent with emotions creating more psychological arousal, such as disgust, is shareable than emotions that evoke low psychological arousals, such as sadness or contentment. Chang et al. (2015) used the elaboration likelihood model to explain the impact of the persuasiveness of messages, measured by argument quality, post popularity, and post attractiveness on the intent of users to like and share the messages in the context of media marketing.

One significant stream of literature on Twitter information diffusion is rumour/non-rumour diffusion amid crises and fake news dissemination (Vosoughi et al. 2018). Researchers have studied the impact of emotion, i.e., anxiety, ambiguity of information provided in the tweet, the tweeter's involvement, and its impact on rumourmongering (Oh et al. 2013). Additionally, studies have found the significant impact of the num-ber of followers, reaction time, and hashtags in the diffusion of information on Twitter measured by the number of retweets (J. Lee et al. 2015). The literature on social media diffusion is skewed by the diffusion of sentiments, emotions, and fake/false information on social media.

In addition, social media research vastly covers research on communicative responses during/immediately after crises and disasters (Spence et al. 2016). J. Lee et al. (2015) studied the message diffusion during the extreme event of a man-made disaster and claim that number of followers and hashtags positively impact message diffusion on Twitter. Heo et al. (2016) discloses that social media allows users to consume information about some events and enables them to form its discourse. Pang and Ng (2016) studied an ongoing riot and found that emotive cues were dominant in the beginning, predominantly negative sentiment, but tweets with positive sentiments were more likely to be shared. The dissemination of messages on Twitter is vastly measured using retweet counts, and it is positively influenced by the number of followers and the use of hashtags in every context of information dissemination research.

In social media research, scholars have explored the polarisation of content on social media. Polarisation means extreme opinion towards an issue, group, or agenda (Buder et al. 2021); therefore, extremity (extreme positive or negative position towards a religion) to any religion is considered religious polarisation. The study found out that tweets become affectively polarised, whereas on social media platforms WhatsApp and Facebook, depolarisation happens over time. Hong and Kim (2016) also proves that politically polarised messages by politicians get more readership on Twitter, suggesting that they may be motivated to deliver a polarizing discourse to increase the reach of their opinions. The extant literature is concentrated on political polarisation diffusion on social media, whereas religion-based nationalism highly impacts politics and political control (Poruthiyil, 2020). We propose to study the diffusion of religiously polarised messages on social media by measuring the religious polarity of tweets and exploring its impact on tweet diffusion.

3 Theoretical Background and Hypothesis Development

3.1 Diffusion of Innovation Theory

Diffusion of innovation theory (DOI) was introduced by Rogers (1962), where he defined diffusion by four main elements as the process by which an **innovation** is communicated through specific **channels** over **time** among the members of a **social system**. Innovation is an idea, practice, or object perceived as new by an individual where perceived newness is not drawn from just new knowledge but persuasion or a decision to adopt the innovation. DOI is vastly used in a myriad of domains of Information systems research, such as the adoption of technological innovation, message diffusion on Twitter (J. Lee et al. 2015), and the influence of virtual community interactions on innovations (Stanko, 2016). The practice of sharing or forwarding messages (posts, links) via social media or email can be understood as information diffusion or innovation adoption (Weber et al. 2013). Also, the diffusion of messages associated with social issues is akin to the diffusion of innovation (J. Lee et al. 2015). Religiously polarised messages are high in emotion and connected with social issues. Therefore, this essay examines the diffusion of religiously polarised messages by applying DOI by considering retweets, Twitter, and the public affected by message diffusion, communication channel, and social system, respectively. The context of our study is a congregation event in Delhi, India. The controversial congregation amid the pandemic was a unique type of extreme event as the world was facing a pandemic after more than a decade. We used diffusion innovation theory as a lens to study diffusion by retweets and replies.

This essay explores the difference between religiously polarised and religiously non-polarised information diffusion. According to Stieglitz and Dang-Xuan (2013), emotionally charged messages get faster retweets than neutral messages, and negative sentiment travels faster than positive sentiment. Polarisation means extreme opinion towards an issue, group, or agenda (Buder et al. 2021); therefore, extremity to any religion is considered religious polarisation. The extremity in attitude implies polarisation (Weber et al. 2013); therefore, in our context, aggressive support for religion and blatant unkind remarks toward religion are considered polarised tweets and rest as non-polarised tweets. This extremity is measured by emotions in the tweets, implying that the religiously polarised tweets have a higher emotion charge than non-religiously polarised tweets.

Therefore, we developed hypothesis 1 as follows:

Hypothesis 1: Religiously polarised messages diffuse more than non-religiously polarised messages.

3.2 Negativity Bias

Human beings give weight to negative entities compared to positive entities because of their innate disposition and experience (Rozin & Royzman, 2001). This human behaviour is called negativity bias. People feel more impact of an equivalent negative entity than the positive entity (negative potency). Stieglitz and Dang-Xuan (2013) state and prove that negative sentiment travels faster and more than positive sentiment on social media. People's bias to negativity contributes to more diffusion of negatively religiously polarised tweets than positively religiously polarised ones. Therefore, we propose:

Hypothesis 2: Negatively religiously polarised tweets diffuse more than positively religiously polarised tweets.

4 Proposed Methodology

The data for the study will be collected by using Twitter API for a hashtag that was regarding a religious congregation occurred in Delhi, India in March 2020. After collecting and cleaning the data we plan to extract dependent variable, religious polarisation from every tweet. Each tweet will be encoded using modified guidelines provided by Yardi and Boyd (2010) and Kelly, Fisher, and Smith (2005) to annotate polarity. The independent variable, message diffusion will be measured by number of retweets of a tweet (Oh et al. 2013). The diffusion of messages on twitter is positively influenced by number of followers, presence of hashtags, and presence of URL(s) in the tweet (Stieglitz and Dang-Xuan, 2013). In our research model (Fig. 1) we plan to control for all three variables to test our hypotheses.

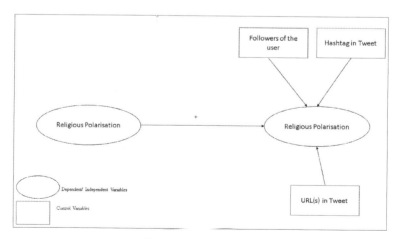

Fig. 1. Research Model

5 Concluding Remarks

In this paper, we intend to address the problem of diffusion of religiously polarised messages on social media. We plan to use Twitter data (tweets and other features of tweets) to examine the hypotheses mentioned earlier. This work aims to understand the role of religious polarisation on message diffusion on social media, which can be helpful for policymakers and governing bodies to mediate the spread of hatred and communal messages on social media. This study provides a model to test the role of religious polarisation on social media message diffusion and can be a stepping stone for future researchers to test the relationship in different contexts. We plan to extend the study to one more context of religious polarisation to increase the generalizability of the model used in the study.

References

Berger, J.: Arousal Increases Social Transmission of Information. Psychological Science, Vol. 22 (2011)

Chan, J., Ghose, A., Seamans, R.: The internet and racial hate crime: offline spillovers from online access. MIS Q. **40**(2), 381–403 (2016)

Chang, Y.T., Yu, H., Lu, H.P.: Persuasive messages, popularity cohesion, and message diffusion in social media marketing. J. Bus. Res. **68**(4), 777–782 (2015)

Gruzd, A.: Emotions in the twitterverse and implications for user interface design. AIS Trans. Human-Computer Interaction **5**(1), 42–56 (2013)

Henry, D., Stattner, E., Collard, M.: Social media, diffusion under influence of parameters: survey and perspectives. In: Procedia Computer Science, Vol. 109, pp. 376–383. Elsevier B.V (2017)

Heo, Y.C., Park, J.Y., Kim, J.Y., Park, H.W.: The emerging viewertariat in South Korea: the seoul mayoral tv debate on twitter, facebook, and blogs. Telematics Inform. **33**(2), 570–583 (2016)

Hong, S., Kim, S.H.: Political polarization on Twitter: implications for the use of social media in digital governments. Gov. Inf. Q. **33**(4), 777–782 (2016)

Kapoor, K.K., Tamilmani, K., Rana, N.P., Patil, P., Dwivedi, Y.K., Nerur, S.: Advances in social media research: past, present and future. Inf. Syst. Front. **20**(3), 531–558 (2017)

Kelly, J., Fisher, D., Smith, M.: Debate, division, and diversity: political discourse networks in USENET newsgroups. In: Online Deliberation Conference 2005, pp. 1–35 (2005)

Kwon, K.H., Gruzd, A.: Is aggression contagious online? a case of swearing on donald trump's campaign videos on youtube. Proceedings of the 50th Hawaii International Conference on System Sciences, pp, 2165–2174 (2017)

Lee, J., Agrawal, M., Rao, H.R.: Message diffusion through social network service: the case of rumor and non-rumor related tweets during Boston bombing 2013. Inf. Syst. Front. **17**(5), 997–1005 (2015)

Oh, O., Eom, C., Rao, H.R.: Role of social media in social change: an analysis of collective sense-making during the 2011 Egypt Revolution. Inf. Syst. Res. **26**(1), 210–223 (2015)

Oh, O., Manish, A., Rao, H.R.: Community intelligence and social media services: a rumor theoretical analysis of tweets during social crises. MIS Q. **37**(2), 407–426 (2013)

Pang, N., Ng, J.: Twittering the little India riot: audience responses, information behavior and the use of emotive cues. Comput. Hum. Behav. **54**, 607–619 (2016)

Poruthiyil, P.V.: Religious ethics: an antidote for religious nationalism. Bus. Soc. **59**(5), 1035–1061 (2020)

Purnell, B.N., Horwitz, J.: Facebook services are used to spread religious hatred in India, Internal Documents Show. Wall Street Journal, pp. 1–9 (2021)

Rogers, E.M.:. Diffusion of Innovations. A Division of Macmillan Publishing Co (1962)

Rozin, P., Royzman, E.B.: Negativity bias, negativity dominance, and contagion. Pers. Soc. Psychol. Rev. **5**(4), 296–320 (2001)

Soundararajan, T., Kumar, A., Nair, P., Greely, J.: CORONAJIHAD: An Analysis of Islamophobic Covid19 Haterspeech and Disinformation: The Implications on Content Moderation and Social Media Policy. Equality Labs (2020)

Spence, P.R., Lachlan, K.A., Rainear, A.M.: Social media and crisis research: data collection and directions. Comput. Hum. Behav. **54**, 667–672 (2016)

Stanko, M.A.: Toward a theory of remixing in online innovation communities. Inf. Syst. Res. **27**(4), 773–791 (2016)

Stieglitz, S., Dang-Xuan, L.: Emotions and information diffusion in social media - sentiment of microblogs and sharing behavior. J. Manag. Inf. Syst. **29**(4), 217–248 (2013)

Ullah, R., Amblee, N., Kim, W., Lee, H.: From valence to emotions: exploring the distribution of emotions in online product reviews. Decis. Support Syst. **81**, 41–53 (2016)

Volety, T., Valecha, R., Vemprala, N., Kwon, H., & Rao, R. (2018). Cyber-rumor Sharing: The Case of Zika Virus. AMCIS 2018 Proceedings, 2017–2018

Vosoughi, S., Roy, D., Aral, S.: The spread of true and false news online. Science **359**(6380), 1146–1151 (2018)

Weber, I., Garimella, V.R.K., Batayneh, A.: Secular vs. Islamist Polarization in Egypt on Twitter. In: 2013 IEEE/ACM International Conference on Advances in Social Networks Analysis and Mining, pp. 290–297 (2013)

Yarchi, M., Baden, C., Kligler-Vilenchik, N.: Political polarization on the digital sphere: a cross-platform, over-time analysis of interactional, positional, and affective polarization on social media. Polit. Commun. **38**(1–2), 98–139 (2021)

Yardi, S., Boyd, D.: Dynamic debates: an analysis of group polarization over time on Twitter. Bull. Sci. Technol. Soc. **30**(5), 316–327 (2010)

Yim, D., Gao, Q., Khuntia, J.: Semantic and sentiment dissonant framing effects on online news sharing. Commun. Assoc. Inf. Syst. **46**, 638–655 (2020)

Climate Policy and e-Participation Resilience: Insights from Social Media

Sreejith Alathur[1]([⊠]) [iD] and Naganna Chetty[2] [iD]

[1] Indian Institute of Management Kozhikode, Kozhikode, India
asreejith@iimk.ac.in
[2] A. J. Institute of Engineering and Technology, Mangaluru, India

Abstract. Social media content on climate change and geological hazards show an exponential increment in recent years. The citizens' narratives about threats to ecosystems are largely mobilized by protests against resource exploitations or disaster rescue operations. This database is less captured or reported for gaining insights about participants' competency in influencing the climate policies. The proposed study aims to address the knowledge gap on how to improve the climate policies by enabling e-participation from the citizens. Required data for the study is collected from Twitter social media content pertinent to climate and metaphorical analysis of resilience issues with an automated system. Sentiment analysis and community detection of Twitter content are carried out using a program developed in R. The people have expressed trust in the rehabilitation and other efforts by the government during the flood. Though the people show trust, anger and disgust are also part of the opinions. Despite the diverse attitudes and beliefs, the people exhibited an interest in inclusiveness. In its entirety, the study captured factors influencing the competency of e-participants in influencing the climate change issues effectively. Policy recommendations for improving the citizens' competency for meaningful e-participation on climate issues are provided.

Keywords: Climate change · e-Participation · Social media · Policy · Inclusion · Twitter

1 Introduction

Disaster management (DM) agencies largely adopt social media (SM) in their rescue and awareness initiatives to reach out to the citizens (Velev and Zlateva 2012; Xiao et al. 2015). Social media as a channel for the government to citizens' communications will be effective if the content has significant value addition to the receivers. The DM agencies overly depend on automated tools and analysis for gaining insights from Citizens-to-Citizens interactions, and efforts for public input on policies have less success rate (Koswatte et al. 2015; Poblet et al. 2013).

Social Media content on climate issues limits its usefulness for impactful policy decisions as the citizens' interactions on digital platforms are less focused and fail to identify their target audience. New technologies, including Artificial Intelligence and

© IFIP International Federation for Information Processing 2022
Published by Springer Nature Switzerland AG 2022
A. Elbanna et al. (Eds.): TDIT 2022, IFIP AICT 660, pp. 304–313, 2022.
https://doi.org/10.1007/978-3-031-17968-6_24

Machine learning tools, are in their nascent state to capture the citizens' metaphors of regional communications in their local language. DM agencies often require quick information processing for their rescue and relief activities (Egelhoff and Sen 1992; Lee and Bui 2000). Thus, formulating the climate policies is based on a backward-looking process. Further, real-time policies have input mainly from the satellite or Internet of Things (IoT) enabled cyber-physical systems.

And the ever-changing dynamicity of the climate hazards is capable of catastrophic impact leaves the existing climate policies void. Trust in government and the safeguarding capacity of the disaster management agencies are affected as the investment in policies decisions is less likely to bring its best outcome. Fewer studies identified why e-participants are limited in their capacity to influence policy matters directly (Lee and Kim 2018; Wang et al. 2020). Climate policies can be analyzed through the lenses of citizens' e-participation with their discussion on climate change through social media. This is to deliver policies that support critical consciousness and climate change education in India.

Therefore, the study aims to understand e-participation dynamics and design citizen-government co-production of climate policies. In 2020, the flood in southern India was very disastrous and impacted the lives of human beings. For this study, the data is collected from Twitter social media on the ongoing discussion on flood and remedy work by the governmental authorities in 2020. The study tried to attain the objectives from the analysis of Twitter data concerning floods.

The rest of the paper is organized as follows. Section 2 reviews the concerned literature for the current study. In Sect. 3, the methodology applied to collect and analyze the data is presented. The results of the analysis are depicted in Sect. 4. In Sect. 5, the discussion on the results is made. In the end, Sect. 6 concludes the work.

2   Literature Review

Cartoons and visual representations like trolls are the most frequent form of awareness campaigns and citizens' responses to public policy (Saji et al. 2021). However, research on policy cartoons focusing on climate change is reported largely from a global perspective or from organized news media at the national level (Manzo 2012). Regional representation of climate policies is mainly under-reported in comparison with health policies or terror incidents. Scholars consider that climate policies have a significant regional impact on tourism, travel restrictions, investment decisions, and thus the overall economy (Belle and Bramwell 2005; Adano et al. 2012). The social media content on climate responses influences decision-making and mobilizes the public to influence policymaking (Leong and Ho 2020; Hestres 2014). Cross-national relations and global resource business activities are susceptible to climate policies (Adam et al. 2019; Koch and Perreault 2019). The climate policy content is censored by the Internet search policing agencies that are operationalized by the resource exploitation geo-political groups (Szulecki et al. 2016). From these studies, content on climate policies is politically flavored, economically rewarding, and technologically regulated.

The regional problems of pollution, water scarcity, landslides, floods etc. are often #taged in social media as a short-term entity (Alathur et al. 2021; Chen and Wang

2020). This is because the interrelations ship between climate policy and regional economy is less conceptualized as novel issues but coined as political gains (Berglund and Helander 2015; Aiyer 2007; Zhang 2013). Scholars consider the trade strategies not necessarily sensitive to climate change. This is due to the initial investment cost, and the current design won't be sufficient to meet the climate requirements of the future (Kumar, and Chakrabarty 2020; Lydgate and Anthony 2020). Thus, the policymakers and the leadership always have less adequate information regarding technology requirements to mitigate the impact of climate change in the future. This has forced agencies and investors to limit strategies with short-term goals, resulting in uncertainties in global and regional climate models (Foley 2010). Policies relaying simple climate models with anomalies (Williams et al. 2010) further weaken the climate change education (CCE) programs (Schrot et al. 2021) and ultimately influence citizens' perceptions of risk, critically evaluate and contribute to climate policies (Bojovic et al. 2021). Limited critical consciousness about multi-climate changes and inconsistent policies also influences the e-participants resilience in ensuring sustainable policies.

In social media, fake news is more than real, and misinformation (Seo et al. 2021) receives more engagement than real. Many studies reported that the participants tend to follow the 'desirable category and perceptual judgments' behavior (Leong et al. 2021). Thus the mobilization effort is highly influenced by how effective the governance is to tackle the extreme or exploitation incidents. In disasters, trafficking of the vulnerable population is, and most frequently, Internet technologies facilitate exploitations of climate incidents or meet the political expectations. Inaccessible and lack of trust in social media among the vulnerable communities (Alathur et al. 2021) also hinders inclusive real-time policy inputs.

Grassroots mobilization for climate policy implementation and support for climate change educational challenges, particularly with regional climate models (Banwell et al. 2020). Internet resources become the primary form of knowledge acquisition and sensitizing multi climate change incidents. The e-participation literature less reported on citizens' climate learning and analyzed the social assistance with a focus on climate risk. Existing climate models fail to capture regional representation largely because fewer efforts are reported in assessing citizens' consciousness perceptions expressed through social media. The dynamics of e-participation in climate policies, local resistance, and community needs during seasonal hazards are rarely analyzed or utilized in policy reforms. Impact assessment of climate change education in citizens' e-participation is not significantly reported in the Indian context. Thus, curriculum restructuration for local climate hazard representations to cater to the regional requirements is missing in the literature. Multi-level, multi-criteria maturity assessment of climate knowledge in regional languages will be helpful for climate capacity building, however, in the Indian context, uneven access to knowledge resources and indigenous climate governance structures are hardly digitized by voluntary community engagement. Disaster agencies adopt social media in their rescue operations. Still, sustainable models are never reported as an integrative climate service approach is yet to develop, even in climate search behavior.

3 Methodology

The use of social media platforms to capture the views of online users is prevalent in this digital era (Chetty and Alathur 2020; Ramachandran and Parvathi 2019). Hence, the data is collected from Twitter social media during the flood in the southern part of India in 2020. The data consists of the discussions on flood and remedy work by the governmental authorities as tweets. In its entirety, 12265 tweets are collected using different keywords such as flood, diversity, and inclusiveness. The collected tweets are analyzed for insights using the R programming tool.

Pre-processing of Twitter social media content is essential before its analysis (Abdullah et al. 2020; Rustam et al. 2019). Therefore, first, the data is pre-processed to remove unwanted information such as stop words, URLs, digits, and punctuations. The stemming is performed to retain the root of the words. Secondly, the emotion analysis is applied to pre-processed tweets to identify and understand the emotions of social media participants during the flood disaster. Third, the community detection algorithm is used to identify the possible communities centered around different themes in the Twitter content. In the end, the results are interpreted and inference is made.

4 Results

Capturing emotions during the discussions of natural disasters like flood is essential to take corrective actions and facilitate the victims of the flood. Figure 1 shows score values for different emotions. The emotion anger is used to express dissatisfaction and is occurred around 2000 times in the tweets. The expectation about future events is expressed through anticipation emotion in 4000+tweets. Disgust expresses the dislike about the incidents and is appeared in a few tweets around 1000. Next panic is expressed through fear emotion in around 6000 tweets.

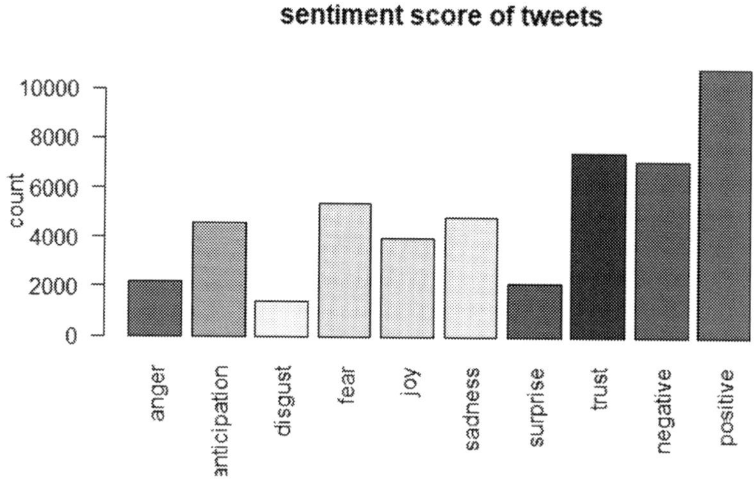

Fig. 1. Emotions during flood and rehabilitation work

The happiness about the rehabilitation work during the flood is expressed from joy emotion and is around 4000 tweets. The sadness emotion is used to express sorrow during floods and related incidents in around 5000 tweets. Surprise represents a sudden or unexpected incident occurrence. The expression of trust by the people during floods is more than the other emotions and indicates the beliefs in governmental authorities concerning the restoration of the damages. Overall, the positive sentiments are more than the negative during the flood and related acts. The occurrence of common words with other associated words is shown in Table 1.

Table 1. Frequency and occurrence of words together

	People	Diversity	Inclusion	Just	Need	Equity	Time	Work	Get	Great
People	767	17	43	22	24	4	19	19	38	15
Diversity	17	1126	850	32	19	192	17	34	14	28
Inclusion	43	850	1856	55	32	193	26	68	27	67
Just	22	32	55	360	10	4	4	15	5	7
Need	24	19	32	10	235	3	3	4	6	4
Equity	4	192	193	4	3	262	2	11	5	1
Time	19	17	26	4	3	2	334	5	11	8
Work	19	34	68	15	4	11	5	262	2	28
Get	38	14	27	5	6	5	11	2	275	4
Great	15	28	67	7	4	1	8	28	4	270

The principal diagonal elements in Table 1 indicate the occurrence of words in the tweets. The words inclusion and diversity are more frequent words during discussion. For particular words along the x and y axes, the corresponding cell value indicates their occurrence together. For example, inclusion and diversity appeared 850 times together. Different communities identified are shown in Fig. 2.

The set of tweets in one community discusses inclusion and diversity. The community discussing inclusion is shown with light green background in Fig. 2. Other associated words with inclusion are great, equity, need, and work. The community with light orange color background discusses the Kerala floods and related places, and incidents. Similarly, the third community with blue background discusses the Karnataka flood and related incidents.

5 Discussion

Sentiment analysis of social media content plays a significant role in policymaking (Georgiadou et al. 2020; Hubert et al. 2018). The emotions expressed by the citizens on a particular topic could act as the preferences for policymaking (Georgiadou et al. 2020). Though there is a presence of negative emotions such as anger, disgust, and sadness in the discussions during the flood (Garske et al. 2021; Karmegam and Mappillairaju 2020), the score values for positive associated emotions such as trust and anticipation are more. This indicates that despite the issues, people are happy with the governmental rehabilitation activities. The frequent and together occurrence of the words diversity and inclusion indicate that despite the different beliefs and faith, the people want to be associated with a common group or community. This inclusiveness of people depicts and presents as input to policymaking concerning climate change such as floods.

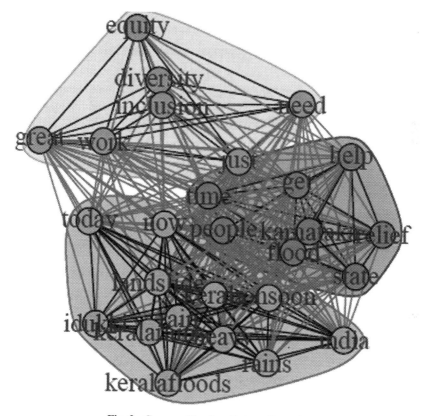

Fig. 2. Communities in a Twitter discussion

Few studies reported on regional climate models with a focus on the influence of social media e-participation. Barriers to e-participation in availing climate services, the perception, and knowledge of e-participant in climate policy are less captured in the Indian context. The proposed study is nascent in this direction as the Internet Governance Framework on climate policies is yet to be in place. Such a framework is as helpful to integrate the Internet content on climate policies designed by the risk-mitigating agencies and under-reported mobilization of climate change education efforts at regional levels. Empowering the e-participants with climate knowledge and co-production of climate policies with social media integration is a promising approach to Internet governance and climate change policy adoption.

5.1 Implications to Practice and Theory

Existing regional climate models do not adequately accommodate the potential input from the citizens to government (C2G) and citizens to citizens (C2C) content from the social networks. The current study emphasizes the compound policy-making strategies by utilizing the new technologies and knowledge resources. The importance of climate change education and voluntary community engagement using social media-enabled platforms is important for improving the policy dimensions and becoming more inclusive. Understanding the level of citizen engagement in climate policies will help to identify the limitations and knowledge gaps. The study gives an Internet governance framework for the climate policy, hence pointing to the multi-dimensional aspects of such policies, including the multi-seasonal, global, and local climate change strategies.

Table 1 shows that the words diversity and inclusion are expressed more times in isolation as well as together. According to Fig. 2, these words are expressed by a particular set of Twitter users. These findings indicate that though India has people with different cultures, traditions, religions, gender, and languages, they demand equal treatment irrespective of their belonging to a particular protected characteristic. During the flood and climate change, women and the marginalized communities face problems (Azad et al. 2013; Bukhari and Rizvi 2015; Grineski et al., 2015; Mitchell et al. 2007). Therefore, the adoption of inclusion, diversity, and emotions in policy-making could help to provide equal; treatment to the people facing problems during climate change.

The dynamics of e-participation resilience in climate policies will help the mobilizers to frame better strategies for engaging the citizens in their movements. Citizens will get better opportunities for the inclusive policy making process as the study give recommendations for capturing local language sentiment in risk and rescue awareness initiatives. A framework that integrates the social movements in the policy formulations will help to design effective platforms in which the citizens with varying knowledge levels can contribute and empower themselves for meaningful e-participation.

5.2 Limitations and Future Research Recommendations

The current study uses only Twitter social media content. As there is a limitation on obtaining tweets beyond a week freely, the tweets collected may not be more (12265 tweets). Sometimes with fewer tweets, it is difficult to generalize the outcome. Though the collected tweets are fewer, considering the topic of discussion the tweets' quantity is encouraging and supportive. The current study could not consider any personal interviews with the experts on climate change incidents.

In the future, the study can be enhanced by incorporating other social media platforms and by extracting more tweets from Twitter media. The study can also be strengthened by conducting interviews with experts in handling similar incidents.

6 Conclusion

The use of social media is significant in disaster management and coping with climate change. People interact and share information during climate change such as floods and other disasters. E-participation and the opinions of flood-affected victims are important for policy-making and restoration works.

The people have shown more trust in the rehabilitation and other related works by the concerned government during floods. Anger and disgust are also part of the opinions. Despite the diverse attitudes and beliefs, the people exhibited an interest in inclusiveness. This inclusive nature of e-participants or social media users during climate change indicates the importance of inclusion for policymaking. The deliberation of e-participants is centered on the topics of inclusion, and two parts of southern India.

The design of policy frameworks for handling climate change situations could be driven by social media users. Inclusion and diversity are important factors in policy design for climate change. The study can be strengthened by incorporating expert views by conducting interviews on climate change incidents.

References

Abdullah, M., AlMasawa, M., Makki, I., Alsolmi, M., Mahrous, S.: Emotions extraction from Arabic tweets. Int. J. Comput. Appl. **42**(7), 661–675 (2020)

Adam, S., Häussler, T., Schmid-Petri, H., Reber, U.: Coalitions and counter-coalitions in online contestation: an analysis of the German and British climate change debate. New Media Soc. **21**(11–12), 2671–2690 (2019)

Adano, W.R., Dietz, T., Witsenburg, K., Zaal, F.: Climate change, violent conflict and local institutions in Kenya's drylands. J. Peace Res. **49**(1), 65–80 (2012)

Aiyer, A.: The allure of the transnational: notes on some aspects of the political economy of water in India. Cult. Anthropol. **22**(4), 640–658 (2007)

Alathur, S., Kottakkunnummal, M., Chetty, N.: Social media and disaster management: influencing e-participation content on disabilities. Transforming Government: People, Process and Policy **15**(4), 566–579 (2021)

Azad, A.K., Hossain, K.M., Nasreen, M.: Flood-induced vulnerabilities and problems encountered by women in northern Bangladesh. International Journal of Disaster Risk Science **4**(4), 190–199 (2013)

Belle, N., Bramwell, B.: Climate change and small island tourism: policy maker and industry perspectives in Barbados. J. Travel Res. **44**(1), 32–41 (2005)

Berglund, H., Helander, S.: The popular struggle against coca-cola in Plachimada. Kerala. J. Developing Societies **31**(2), 281–303 (2015)

Bukhari, S.I.A., Rizvi, S.H.: Impact of floods on women: with special reference to flooding experience of 2010 flood in Pakistan. J. Geography Natural Disasters **5**(2), 1–5 (2015)

Bojovic, D., et al.: Engagement, involvement and empowerment: three realms of a coproduction framework for climate services. Glob. Environ. Chang. **68**, 102271 (2021)

Chen, C.C., Wang, H.-C.: Using community information for natural disaster alerts. J. Inf. Sci. (2020). https://doi.org/10.1177/0165551520979870

Chetty, N., Alathur, S.: Developing Indian smart cities: insights from social media. In: International Working Conference on Transfer and Diffusion of IT. pp. 209–218 (2020). Springer, Cham https://doi.org/10.1007/978-3-030-64861-9_19

Egelhoff, W.G., Sen, F.: An information-processing model of crisis management. Manag. Commun. Q. **5**(4), 443–484 (1992)

Foley, A.M.: Uncertainty in regional climate modelling: a review. Progress in Physical Geography: Earth and Environ. **34**(5), 647–670 (2010)

Garske, S.I., et al.: Space-time dependence of emotions on Twitter after a natural disaster. Int. J. Environmental Res. Public Health **18**(10), 5292 (2021)

Georgiadou, E., Angelopoulos, S., Drake, H.: Big data analytics and international negotiations: sentiment analysis of Brexit negotiating outcomes. Int. J. Inf. Manage. **51**, 102048 (2020)

Grineski, S., Collins, T.W., Chakraborty, J., Montgomery, M.: Hazardous air pollutants and flooding: a comparative interurban study of environmental injustice. GeoJournal **80**(1), 145–158 (2015)

Hestres, L.E.: Preaching to the choir: internet-mediated advocacy, issue public mobilization, and climate change. New Media Soc. **16**(2), 323–339 (2014)

Hubert, R.B., Estevez, E., Maguitman, A., Janowski, T.: Examining government-citizen interactions on Twitter using visual and sentiment analysis. In: Proceedings of the 19th annual international conference on digital government research: governance in the data age. pp. 1–10 (2018)

Karmegam, D., Mappillairaju, B.: Spatio-temporal distribution of negative emotions on Twitter during floods in Chennai, India, in 2015: a post hoc analysis. Int. J. Health Geogr. **19**(1), 1–13 (2020)

Koch, N., Perreault, T.: Resource nationalism. Prog. Hum. Geogr. **43**(4), 611–631 (2019)

Koswatte, S., McDougall, K., Liu, X.: SDI and crowdsourced spatial information management automation for disaster management. Surv. Rev. **47**(344), 307–315 (2015)

Kumar, P., Chakrabarty, S.: Total cost of ownership analysis of the impact of vehicle usage on the economic viability of electric vehicles in India. Transp. Res. Rec. **2674**(11), 563–572 (2020)

Lee, J., Kim, S.: Citizens'e-participation on agenda setting in local governance: do individual social capital and e-participation management matter? Public Manag. Rev. **20**(6), 873–895 (2018)

Lee, J., Bui, T.: A template-based methodology for disaster management information systems. In: Proceedings of the 33rd annual Hawaii international conference on system sciences, pp. 1–7 (2000). IEEE, Maui, HI, USA

Leong, A.D., Ho, S.S.: Perceiving online public opinion: the impact of Facebook opinion cues, opinion climate congruency, and source credibility on speaking out. New Media Soc. **23**(9), 2495–2515 (2020)

Leong, Y.C., Dziembaj, R., D'Esposito, M.: Pupil-linked arousal biases evidence accumulation toward desirable percepts during perceptual decision-making. Psychol. Sci. **32**(9), 1494–1509 (2021)

Lydgate, E., Anthony, C.: Coordinating UK trade and climate policy ambitions: a legislative nd policy analysis. Environ. Law Rev. **22**(4), 280–295 (2020)

Manzo, K.: Earthworks: the geopolitical visions of climate change cartoons. Polit. Geogr. **31**(8), 481–494 (2012)

Mitchell, T., Tanner, T., Lussier, K. 'We know what we need': South Asian women speak out on climate change adaptation. Institute of Development Studies (IDS) at the University of Sussex, UK (2007)

Poblet, M., García-Cuesta, E., Casanovas, P.: Crowdsourcing tools for disaster management: a review of platforms and methods. In: International Workshop on AI Approaches to the Complexity of Legal Systems. pp. 261–274 (2013). Springer, Berlin, Heidelberg https://doi.org/10.1007/978-3-662-45960-7_19

Ramachandran, D., Parvathi, R.: Analysis of twitter specific preprocessing technique for tweets. Procedia Computer Science **165**, 245–251 (2019)

Rustam, F., Ashraf, I., Mehmood, A., Ullah, S., Choi, G.S.: Tweets classification on the base of sentiments for US airline companies. Entropy **21**(11), 1078 (2019)

Saji, S., Venkatesan, S., Callender, B.: Comics in the time of a pan (dem) ic: COVID-19, graphic medicine, and metaphors. Perspect. Biol. Med. **64**(1), 136–154 (2021)

Schrot, O.G., Peduzzi, D., Ludwig, D., Riede, M., Keller, L.: Is it possible to build adolescents' cognitive adaptive capacity through climate change education? insights into a two-year long educational programme in North Tyrol (Austria) and South Tyrol (Italy). Clim. Risk Manag. **33**, 100327 (2021)

Seo, H., Blomberg, M., Altschwager, D., Vu, H.T.: Vulnerable populations and misinformation: a mixed-methods approach to underserved older adults' online information assessment. New Media Soc. **23**(7), 2012–2033 (2021)

Szulecki, K., Fischer, S., Gullberg, A.T., Sartor, O.: Shaping the 'Energy Union': between national positions and governance innovation in EU energy and climate policy. Climate Policy **16**(5), 548–567 (2016)

Velev, D., Zlateva, P.: Use of social media in natural disaster management. Int. Proceedings Economic Dev. Res. **39**, 41–45 (2012)

Wang, G., Chen, Q., Xu, Z., Leng, X.: Can the use of government Apps shape citizen compliance? the mediating role of different perceptions of government. Comput. Hum. Behav. **108**, 106335 (2020)

Williams, C.J.R., Kniveton, D.R., Layberry, R.: Idealized SST anomaly regional climate model experiments: a note of caution. Progress in Physical Geography: Earth Environ. **34**(1), 59–74 (2010)

Xiao, Y., Huang, Q., Wu, K.: Understanding social media data for disaster management. Nat. Hazards **79**(3), 1663–1679 (2015)

Zhang, Z.: Energy, climate and environmental policy in China: introduction to the special double issue. Energy Environ. **24**(7–8), 1201–1207 (2013)

Metaverses and Business Transformation

Ariana Polyviou[1]([⊠]) [iD] and Ilias O. Pappas[2,3] [iD]

[1] Department of Management, School of Business, University of Nicosia, 2417 Nicosia, Cyprus
`polyviou.a@unic.ac.cy`
[2] Department of Information Systems, University of Agder, 4639 Kristiansand, Norway
`ilias.pappas@uia.no`
[3] Department of Computer Science, Norwegian University of Science and Technology (NTNU), 7491 Trondheim, Norway
`ilpappas@ntnu.no`

Abstract. Metaverses refer to virtual worlds which enable the interaction between users and simulate people, places and things of the physical world. The wider use of metaverses can disrupt how we interact and bring a plethora of implications for businesses and society. While the term metaverse received increased attention recently due to the interest of tech giants, researchers have been exploring virtual world interactions for over a decade. In light of new exciting metaverse implementations, it is necessary to consolidate information via existing research on how the use of metaverses can transform businesses. As a first step, this paper outlines the methodology to be followed by future researchers aiming to shed light on metaverse and business transformation. It proposes a framework to assist authors in organizing existing literature on metaverses and guide them in identifying future research avenues.

Keywords: Virtual reality · Augmented reality · Avatars · Digital twins · Virtual worlds

1 Introduction

The term 'metaverse' has been initially coined by the science fiction writer Neal Stephenson in his Snow Crash book in 1992, to refer to a computer-generated universe [1] –a massive collective virtual environment that simulates the physical world, where users can get together to play games, socialize and work. Here, we define metaverse as an immersive virtual world where people, places and things of the physical world are represented by their digital representations (e.g., avatars) and can meet, communicate, interact and collaborate. The notion of virtual three-dimensional world has existed ever since tools like Open Simulator project, Second Life and VR-head mounting displays (e.g., Oculus Rift) appeared in the market. The virtual world is defined as a reality-inspired digital multimedia 3-dimensional online environment where users can interact by using avatars [2]. A virtual world comprises certain characteristics [3]; it has a three-dimensional format offering an immersive experience, it involves an active user role through the avatar, and

A. Elbanna et al. (Eds.): TDIT 2022, IFIP AICT 660, pp. 314–319, 2022.
https://doi.org/10.1007/978-3-031-17968-6_25

there is a collaborative relationship with other users who exist through their avatars in the specific virtual environment. Avatars in virtual environments have been used in different contexts and situations such as e-commerce, e-therapy, virtual worlds, videogames, collaborative online design etc. [4]. Research on these topics provides valuable knowledge on metaverse's predecessors.

Metaverse is currently receiving increased attention. The maturity of technologies including extended reality, human-computer interaction, artificial intelligence, blockchain, computer vision, edge and cloud computing and mobile networks, is currently driving the wider use of metaverses [5]. Enhanced accessibility, wider use of mobile technologies, social distancing due to the pandemic and the need for alternative ways of investing are some of the drivers of recent interest of the wider population. For example, Decentraland[1] is a 3D virtual platform that goes beyond interaction with users, as they can create, explore, and purchase virtual property through it. Such property ownership is supported by non-fungible token (NFT) which is based on Ethereum blockchain, serving as public certificate of authenticity or proof of ownership.

Tech giants (e.g., Facebook, Microsoft) recently made announcements on their intention to transform their platforms towards metaverse. In October 2021, Facebook announced its rebranding into Meta[2], bringing together all applications and technologies offered by the company under a new company brand. The company aims to elevate its online social experiences into three dimensions or even sometimes project them in the physical world, so that users can share their experiences and connect with others, even when they are not able to be in the same physical location. Meta also aims to enable users to complete activities that they cannot do in the physical world. Along the same lines, in November 2nd, 2021, Microsoft announced the mesh features for its Mesh for Teams application in an effort to offer mixed reality capabilities and enable users in different physical locations to make their meetings more collaborative and share holographic experiences [6]. Mesh for Teams release is expected in the first half of 2022.

3D avatar-based virtual and augmented reality tools have been available for more than a decade. However, recent announcements of tech giants on enhancing online social media and communication tools using immersive virtual environments are expected to advance advancements in the area, thus most likely leading to a significant increase on our use of metaverse soon. As metaverse brings new capabilities and challenges to businesses, it is expected to inspire changes in their strategies, operations, policies and organizational structure, similar to the ones that social media brought two decades ago. Our goal here is to facilitate a discussion on how the information system field can help uncover the potential of metaverses for business transformation and how should a systematic literature review be designed to address this goal.

2 Background and Motivation

Existing literature has focused on reviewing the technical aspects of the technologies related to metaverse. Lee et al. [5], examine the latest metaverse developments on the

---

[1] https://decentraland.org/.

[2] https://about.fb.com/news/2021/10/facebook-company-is-now-meta/.

state-of-the-art technologies which are serving as metaverse enablers and reflect on the user-centric factors that enable metaverse ecosystems. Information Systems (IS) scholars have also focused on reviewing existing literature on tools and technologies related to metaverse and their impact to specific application domains (e.g., Second Life, Open Simulator, use of head-mounted displays etc.). Most of this work has focused on reviewing such technologies with respect to its impact for the e-learning field. For example, in [7] the authors provide a review of virtual reality technologies in e-learning. In [8], they review empirical studies on e-learning and organizational learning and exhibit how existing research in these areas has made use of metaverse related technologies. In [9] the authors conduct a systematic review of how researchers have applied immersive VR (head-mounted displays) in higher education. Other scholars have also focused on reviewing existing literature on 3D virtual worlds on collaboration and their impact for businesses [10].

Despite the potential of the metaverse to bring the next 'digital big bang' [5], IS literature currently lacks a systematic review which reflects on our so far knowledge on its business transformation potential. This gap signals scarcity of sufficient information sources and leaves researchers as well as practitioners in unchartered territories when in need to decide upon new research experiments in virtual worlds or sketch new strategies and policies to respond to the rapid changes in the tech arena. To extract useful theoretical and practical implications and identify research avenues related to the metaverse, it is necessary for future researchers to map existing IS research on the intersection of metaverse (and related technologies) and business transformation).

To address this gap, researchers may review existing research on metaverse related technologies (e.g., Open Simulator project, Second Life, VR-head mounted displays etc.) of the past decade. Below we include a couple of research questions which could shape this body of research:

RQ1: What is the status of the research on metaverses and its predecessors from a business transformation perspective?

RQ2: Which are the potential future research avenues at the intersection of metaverse and business transformation?

As a first step towards this direction, in this paper we outline a methodological approach and framework which could guide future researchers in organizing existing research. Section 3 describes the methodological approach to be followed for conducting a systematic literature review framed by the research questions of this paper and Sect. 4 outlines a proposed research framework that can be employed for analyzing the extant literature.

3   Methodology

Reflecting on the research questions proposed earlier in this paper, this Section suggests a structured process for identifying papers which could be included in a structured literature review analysis. Inspired by [11], scoping review approach for this purpose could include a comprehensive overview of relevant papers while remaining open on excluding papers on metaverse related topics which go beyond the proposed research questions. More specifically, such a process will encapsulate sources of research scan, the means to retrieve the papers identified and the criteria for inclusion and exclusion of papers depending on their relevance to the research questions [11]. In particular, this process may include a search approach for identifying relevant conference and journal papers in databases that cover the major venues of IS publications. In particular, the databases to be addressed may include the AIS Senior Scholar's Basket of Journals (basket of 8), AIS Electronic Library, ScienceDirect, IEEE Xplore and other major databases related to IS. We suggest that the process will only accounts for scientific knowledge as arising by scientific papers on the topic and exclude publications such as press releases, media, white papers, book chapters, communications, encyclopedias and reviews.

The approach of [12] may be followed to cover the three main issues which need to be examined when evaluating the quality of shortlisted papers; rigor, credibility and relevance. Such criteria have also been used in the past for reviewing adjunct IS research areas, e.g., e-Learning [8]. Relevance could also be associated with application area, use, design, impact, benefits, challenges associated with the use of metaverse related technologies for individuals, society, organizations and industries. During the review process, the samples of the approach followed may also be discussed among authors to ensure a consistent process will be followed across all databases and papers identified minizine in this way the risk of subjectivity in the shortlisting process. Paper duplicates should be excluded from the paper count process.

After finalizing the list of papers to be reviewed, a qualitative content analysis can be followed. The qualitative content analysis may encapsulate three steps as illustrated in Fig. 1 leading to the final number of papers to emerge from this process.

Researchers may adopt the predefined set of categories and descriptions of [13] to organize advancements relevant to metaverse. They may follow Morris' five-step process for directed content analysis [14]. For each paper researchers may begin with determining the unit of analysis, then categorize the papers with respect to the academic discipline and research method employed. Then, researchers may use the selected framework to further organize papers and related knowledge.

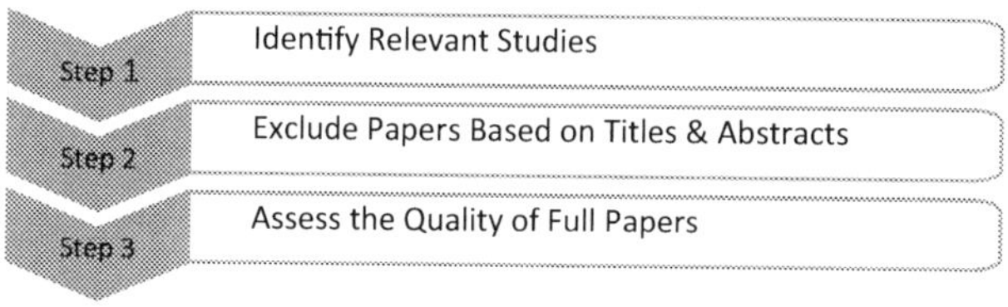

Step 1 Identify Relevant Studies

Step 2 Exclude Papers Based on Titles & Abstracts

Step 3 Assess the Quality of Full Papers

Fig. 1. Stages of paper selection process

4   An Organizing Framework for Metaverse Research

In [13] the authors, propose a framework for reviewing the social medical literature. In their proposed framework, acknowledge the framework's intention to guide research in the areas of social media and digital transformation. As the social media research area holds a plethora of similarities with metaverse (e.g., virtual profiles, communication, user interaction etc.), we consider this framework as a viable starting point for reviewing existing research on the metaverse topic. Other IS scholars have already employed this framework to review research in other IS domains e.g., blockchain research [15]. In their framework, the authors identify four thematic research areas which span across three (overlapping) units of analysis: Users and society; Intermediaries and platforms; Firms and industries. Researchers may employ these 4 thematic areas, to describe how users and business create and use metaverse related technologies. Adding to the existing discussion [16], we present examples that can guide researchers further towards realizing the role of IS to uncover the potential of metaverses for business transformation.

1. **Design and features.** How users and organizations interact with metaverse features; whether metaverse features serve the objectives of the users; how platforms, organizations and governments design, implement, standardize and regulate these features to foster or control the use of metaverse related technologies; how can metaverse platform providers transfer sensed information from real world to virtual world objects; what features should firms consider when developing metaverses.

2. **Strategy and tactics:** How users, organizations and governments can make the most out of their use of metaverse; how they may use metaverse tools and create strategies (e.g., product development, pricing etc.) which meet their requirements or goals; what new market opportunities arise for metaverse platforms and intermediaries; how can metaverse platforms serve organizations in order to achieve their business goal.

3. **Management and organization:** How should users adjust their routines in order to better facilitate the use of metaverses; what skills do users need to develop in order to benefit by the use of metaverses; how should platform providers create and maintain metaverse platforms; what is the role of intermediaries in re-training the population on the use of metaverses.

4. **Measurement and value:** What is the emotional and behavioral impact of metaverses on users; what are the factors shaping positive user experiences; what is the impact of using metaverses for the environment; what is the impact of ownership ambiguity in virtual worlds for platform providers; how do metaverses add value to firms in different industries

In this paper we propose an approach for mapping existing research on metaverse for business transformation as well as a framework for analyzing existing research. We note that the mapping of existing research may vary on depth and the breadth and researchers may choose to select keywords to be included in their search accordingly (e.g., may only include "metaverse" or may also include "virtual worlds", "avatars" etc.) Reflecting on the proposed framework, we highlight the adequacy of this framework for analyzing metaverses literature with regards to business transformation. In particular, the framework distinguishes across three levels of analysis which can be employed to reflect on existing research from a specific viewpoint. Consumers and society such as individuals who make use of metaverse. Platforms and intermediaries such as for example, organizations or Governmental actors that build, operate, or innovate using metaverse. Firms and industries, such as for example firms or industries that use and interact with metaverse. We hope that the approach and framework will inspire future researchers to map and analyze existing knowledge on this topic.

References

1. Stephenson, N.: Snow Crash. Bantam Books, New York (1992)
2. Chandra, Y., Leenders, M.A.A.M.: User innovation and entrepreneurship in the virtual world: a study of second life residents. Technovation **32**(7–8), 464–476 (2012)
3. Badilla Quintana, M.C., Fernández, S.M.: A pedagogical model to develop teaching skills. The collaborative learning experience in the Immersive Virtual World TYMMI. Computers in Human Behavior, 51B, pp. 594–603 (2015)
4. Diego-Mas, J.A., Alcaide-Marzal, J.: A computer based system to design expressive avatars. Computers in Human Behavior **44**, 1–11 (2015)
5. Lee, L.-H., et al.: All one needs to know about metaverse: a complete survey on technological singularity. Virtual Ecosystem, and Research Agenda (2021)
6. Roach, J.: Mesh for Microsoft Teams aims to make collaboration in the 'metaverse' personal and fun. Microsoft Inc. https://news.microsoft.com/innovation-stories/mesh-for-microsoft-teams/. Access 12 Nov 2021
7. Muller Queiroz, A.C., et al.: Immersive virtual environments in corporate education and training. In: Americas Conference in Information Systems (2018)
8. Giannakos, M.N., Mikalef, P., Pappas, I.O.: Systematic literature review of e-learning capabilities to enhance organizational learning. Information Systems Frontiers (2021)
9. Radianti, J., Majchrzak, T., A., Fromm, J., Wohlgenannt, I.: A systematic review of immersive virtual reality applications for higher education: Design elements, lessons learned, and research agenda. Computers & Education **147**, 103778 (2020)
10. Bououd, I., Rouis, S., Boughzala, I.: Social loafing impact on collaboration in 3D virtual worlds: an empirical study. In: Proceedings of 19th Americas Conference on Information Systems, AMCIS, pp. 3014–3022 (2013)
11. Pare, G., Trudel, M.C., Kitsiou, J.M.: Synthesizing information systems knowledge: a typology of literature reviews. Inf. Manage. **52**(2), 183–199 (2015)
12. Dybå, T., Dingsøyr, T.: Empirical studies of agile software development: a systematic review. Inf. Softw. Technol. **50**(9–10), 833–859 (2008)
13. Aral, S., Dellarocas, C., Godes, D. Introduction to the special issue—social media and business transformation: a framework for research. Information Systems Res. **24**(1), 3–13 (2013)
14. Morris, R.: Computerized content analysis in management research: a demonstration of advantages & limitations. J. Manag. **20**(4), 903–931 (1994)
15. Risius, M., Spohrer, K.: A blockchain research framework. Business Information Systems Eng. **59**, 385–409 (2017)
16. Dwivedi, Y.K., et al.: Metaverse beyond the hype: multidisciplinary perspectives on emerging challenges, opportunities, and agenda for research, practice and policy. Int. J. Inf. Manage. **66**, 102542 (2022)

Blockchain and Cryptocurrency

Theoretical Framework for Blockchain Technology Adoption in Public Sector Organizations: A Transaction Cost Theory Perspective

Sujeet Kumar Sharma[✉]

IS and A Area, Indian Institute of Management Tiruchirappalli, Sooriyur, India
sujeet@iimtrichy.ac.in

Abstract. The Indian economy, driven by multiple digital initiatives in the past couple of years, is considered as a fast-growing economy among developing countries. In digital initiatives, Blockchain is one of the promising technologies with potential to transform organizations in particular public sector organizations. There are concerns related to the nature of Blockchain technology and benefits offered by the same in organizational settings. This study attempts to identify critical factors influencing Blockchain technology adoption in public sector organizations. This research attempts to develop a theoretical framework for value based Blockchain technology adoption by integrating task-technology-fit theory, transaction cost theory, and the unified theory of acceptance and use of technology (UTAUT) in Indian public sector organizations. The proposed research framework may provide insights to public sector organizations, technology service providers, academicians and researchers. Researchers may collect data from public sector organizations to test the proposed research framework using structural equation modeling or other statistical models. This is a working paper and intends to further test the proposed theoretical model as the ongoing work.

Keywords: Blockchain technology · Task-technology-fit theory · UTAUT · Transactions cost theory · India

1 Introduction

Blockchain technology, which supported the bitcoin revolution, has the potential to change the way organizations store, retrieve and share information. In 2021, the blockchain market worldwide was valued at $4.67 billion and is expected to grow from $ 7.18 to $163.83 billion, showing a CAGR of 56.3% during 2022 to 2029 (https://www.fortunebusinessinsights.com/). Blockchain is a secure and append only ledger for peer to peer transactions without any third party. The main advantage blockchain technology offers are transparency and traceability of the transactions. It reduces dependency on third parties and also mitigates risk of manipulation or even risk of system failure as

A. Elbanna et al. (Eds.): TDIT 2022, IFIP AICT 660, pp. 323–330, 2022.
https://doi.org/10.1007/978-3-031-17968-6_26

all nodes of the network keep the same information (Olnes et al. 2017) . In general, blockchain technology (BCT) stores transactional data such as educational certificates, land records, birth and marriage certificates, social benefits, votes among others. BCT may offer several benefits to public sector organizations such as reduction in the transaction cost and complexities in the procedures involved in public service deliveries and also may help in ensuring trust in government records. It is reported in the literature that BCT offers several benefits, however, there is uncertainty in the business value offered by this promising technology which has slowed down the adoption of blockchain technology (Liang et al. 2021). It is also reported in the extant literature that the public sector are laggards in adopting new technologies and hence adoption of blockchain technology among executives in public sector organizations is an important concern that requires comprehensive investigation.

The extant literature in the information systems domain has significant research in terms of theoretical models and empirical evidence to understand the phenomenon of intention to adopt an emerging technology. The prominent theoretical frameworks in the literature includes technology adoption model (TAM: Davis 1989), task-technology-fit (TTF), unified theory of acceptance and use of technology (UTAUT: Venkatesh et al. 2003), among others. These theoretical frameworks help in understanding factors that influence adoption of a new technology. It is important for middle level executives to understand the interaction of technology, process and people in the context of a new technology and also how new technology will provide business value. Therefore, it is important to identify the critical factors that executives in public sector organizations keep in mind while adopting blockchain technology.

This study attempts to make three contributions to extend the extant literature of information systems in the Indian public sector context. First, this study develops a research model for understanding blockchain adoption by middle level executives in public sector organizations. Second, this study integrates task-technology-fit theory, transaction cost theory, value-based model, and the unified theory of acceptance and use of technology (UTAUT) to develop the research model. Finally, this study proposed the blockchain adoption framework in the Indian context, which is the one of fastest growing economies in the world.

2   Literature Review and Theoretical Background

2.1   Blockchain in Government

Blockchain technology has huge potential to change the way the working of public sector organizations to deliver better and faster services. For example, Blockchain technology adoption in Government is needed for tamper proofing of digital assets, and protecting them against an 'insider-job'. It is quite common in government services, almost all the documents and certificates issued by governments and government run institutions and universities are in digital format and there is always a lurking danger of tampering with these documents in the 'back end' at the database level. Across India, there have been hundreds of cases of fake degrees and fake mark sheets from colleges and universities. Many of them were issued with connivance of staff with access to university's database and the staff had added an unauthorized entry into the database and as a result when verification is done the fake degree gets verified as genuine ("Pan-India links in fake degree scam" 2015). There have been cases of manipulating marks by university employees. Many of the aforementioned and similar case in public sector organizations can be addressed using blockchain technology capabilities such as traceability and transparency. In addition, the tamper proof quality of blockchain can significantly help cyber security digital resource protection for Governments as well. It is virtually impossible to monitor thousands of Government websites and their contents, especially if there are dormant script injections attacks. The dormant scripts remain undetected till they maliciously manifest themselves. These challenges can also be addressed with the effective use of Blockchain hashing would help detect any unauthorized change in any digital resource, in near real time.

As per Gartner (2019), by 2025, the business value added by Blockchain is expected to grow to slightly more than $176 billion – then move past $3.1 trillion by 2030. However, surprisingly, Gartner (2019) further predicts that in 90% of the overall enterprises, blockchain projects will become obsolete by 2021. Realizing such massive growth of the Blockchain technology in the next one decade and the expected decline for a high percentage of the Blockchain projects in enterprises in the near future, it would be very much timely and imperative to understand and analyze the challenges of Blockchain implementation for the massive projects, which are being rolled out in the Government settings such as the Government of Tamil Nadu in India.

2.2   Task-Technology Fit (TTF)

The TTF is an important model in the extant literature of information systems that plays a critical role in new technology adoption within an organizational setting. This model helps in understanding the impact of technology in organizations with the help of performing tasks faster and with greater efficiency. There are two components in the TTF model namely task and technology characteristics. Task characteristics means some challenging activities an individual may face while using an IT artifact. Next, technology characteristics related to the IT artifact designed to complete a set of tasks (Aljukhadar et al. 2014).

2.3   Value-Based Model

The value-based model helps in the evaluation of importance, usefulness and worth of a new technology (Kim et al. 2007). The overall value of a new technology can be categorized in two components namely perceived benefits and perceived sacrifices (Zeithaml et al. 1988). Perceived benefits mean how much an individual save in terms of cost and time. Furthermore, perceived benefits play an important role in the adoption of a new technology.

2.4   Functional Benefits

Business value of IT of an artifact means the benefits received from the use of a new IT with existing resources to gain and sustain competitive advantage for a firm (Chau et al.

2007). In general, business value obtained from the effective use of IT can be categorized into functional value and symbolic value. In the context of blockchain adoption in public sector organizations, functional value is of greater importance than symbolic value so functional value is included in the proposed research model in this study. Functional value in the context of public sector organizations means alignment between new technology and tasks in the organizations and also how blockchain technology capabilities are aligned with the objectives of the public sector organizations.

2.5 Transaction Cost Theory

TCT, Transaction Cost Theory, primarily developed by Williamson aimed to understand the organization and governance structures of its economic activities (Devaraj et al. 2002). Consumers while proceeding with transactions must conduct activities such as searching for information, negotiating terms, and monitoring the on-going process to ensure a favorable deal (Liang and Huang 1998). The costs involved with such transaction-related activities are called transaction costs. TCT, in the past two decades, has undergone a tremendous amount of change, especially with the advent of technological improvements and digital initiatives. With the rapid growth of the ICT and Internet-enabled service delivery platforms, citizens are participating in various types of online transactions like never before. The extant technological advancements and innovation in the IT sector of the Government of India have persuaded it to proactively apply its features to the rural areas with an aim to bridge the urban and rural divide. The emergence of the ICT enabled governance system as a force in developing India has helped it in discovering numerous innovative ways to deliver public services to citizens and businesses with the prime focus on the rural sector (Dwivedi et al. 2016).

2.6 Unified Theory of Acceptance and Use of Technology (UTAUT)

Technology Acceptance Model (Davis 1989) is the leading theory of IS acceptance and use in the extant literature. Scholars (Irani et al. 2009; Chong 2013; Sharma et al. 2019) have adopted TAM and explained the IS use phenomenon in the extant literature. Next, UTAUT (Venkatesh et al. 2003) is the extension of the TAM to further explain and understand IS acceptance and use in organizational context. The UTAUT includes four main independent variables namely performance expectancy, effort expectancy, social influence and facilitating conditions and four moderating variables namely gender, age, experience and voluntariness of use to explain intention and usage relationship in the context of an adoption of a new technology. The UTAUT model has been used to understand the user behavior in various information technology domains such as mobile banking (Alalwan et al. 2017), mobile health (Dwivedi et al. 2016), mobile government Apps (Sharma et al. 2018), mobile payments (Slade et al. 2015; Sharma and Sharma 2019), online information services (Oh and Yoon 2014). Dwivedi et al. (2017) re-examined the UTAUT model and provided some useful insights to researchers and practitioners. In case of the applications of the UTAUT model, the aforementioned researchers have adapted hypotheses from the original UTAUT model developed by Venkatesh et al. (2003).

3   Hypothesis Development

The task technology fit is a conceptual framework that helps in matching the requirements of a task with the capabilities of a new technology so that it can be completed in a faster and efficient way and also can reduce the cost also (McGill and Klobas 2009). The extant literature reports that TTF helps in improving performance of a task in an organizational context and relates with the benefits offered by the technology (Liang et al. 2021). In this study, it is hypothesized that blockchain technology and organizational capabilities will positively influence the perceived benefits offered by the blockchain technology.

H1: Task-technology-fit (TTF) positively influences the perceived benefits offered by blockchain technology.

Keller (1993) defined benefits offered by a product or services that meet the need after consuming the same. Blockchain as a new technology brings a set of benefits including transparency and traceability that will motivate organizations to adopt the technology. In the public sector organization context, blockchain may help in building trust between government and citizens. Therefore, it is hypothesized that perceived benefits offered by blockchain technology will have a positive influence on the intention to adopt the technology.

H2: Perceived benefits positively influence the intention to adopt blockchain technology in public sector organizations.

Facilitating conditions is one the critical factors motivating users to adopt a new technology is reported in the extant literature and defined by Venkatesh et al. (2003) in the seminal work as "the degree to which the individual perceives the existence of resources and support to use certain technology whenever necessary". For example, Zuiderwijk et al. (2015) observed that facilitating conditions plays a critical role in determining an intention to use a new information technology. Many scholars in the extant literature (Crabbe et al. 2009; Venkatesh et al. 2012; Chong 2013; Hew et al. 2015) have proved that facilitating conditions are a very strong predictor to determine the intention to adopt (m-commerce and mobile apps). It is expected that blockchain technology adoption will also get influenced by the facilitating conditions available in the public sector organizations. In this study, the following hypothesis is proposed on the basis of aforementioned arguments.

H3: Facilitating conditions in public sector organizations positively influences intention to adopt blockchain technology.

Devaraj et al. (2002) contextualized Transaction Cost Theory (TCT) to understand economic activities in the organizational context. The costs involved in transaction-related activities searching for information, passing information from one organization to another, negotiating terms, and monitoring are known as transaction costs. In the context of public sector organizations, transaction costs are huge. Blockchain technology has the potential to reduce the transaction cost significantly in public sector organizations. Therefore, it is hypothesized that.

H4: Transactions costs in public sector organizations positively influences intention to adopt blockchain technology (Fig. 1).

4 Proposed Research Model

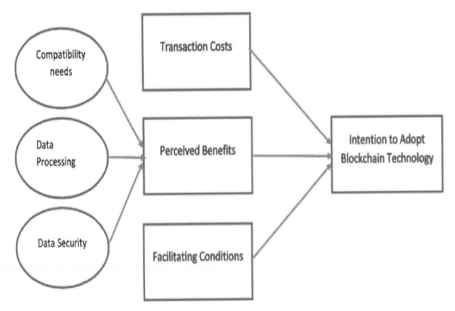

Fig. 1. Research model (adapted from Liang et al. 2021)

5 Concluding Remarks

Public sector organizations are also attempting to use emerging technologies to connect citizens better and deliver more value in public services. Blockchain being an innovative and general- purpose technology, is one of the prominent emerging technologies provides opportunities to organizations to deliver services to citizens in efficient and transparent manner. In particular, blockchain provides new ways to public sector organizations to record transactions, certificates, and ownership in multiple domains. To achieve this, it is essential to middle level executives in public sector organizations to adopt blockchain technologies to deliver public services. Consequently, this study attempts to develop a research framework to understand critical factors influencing adoption of blockchain technology in public sector organizations. The research framework to understand adoption of value based blockchain technology is developed by integrating task-technology-fit theory, transaction cost theory, and the unified theory of acceptance and use of technology (UTAUT) in Indian public sector organizations. The objective of this study is to develop a theoretical framework that can help decision makers to promote blockchain technology adoption in public sector organizations. The proposed research framework may provide some initial insights to senior executives working in public sector organizations and also for senior executive who develops blockchain based solutions. In addition, researchers are encouraged to collect data from public sector organizations to empirically test the proposed research framework. Furthermore, it is also recommended to conduct a rigorous qualitative research study (interviews of middle level and senior level executive working in public sector organizations) using proposed research framework. This approach may provide deeper insights about blockchain adoption in public sector organizations. Researchers may also explore longitudinal quantitative study using the proposed research framework to provide consistent and generalizable insights for decision makers to take strategic and informed decisions. Finally, researchers from two or more cultural settings may test the proposed research framework and recommend more generalizable and deeper insights about blockchain technology adoption in public sector organizations. This is a working paper and author is planning to collect primary data in a structured survey questionnaire from middle-level executives who are involved in the decision to adopt blockchain technology in Indian public sector organizations to test the proposed research model to provide deeper and generalizable insights for multiple stakeholders.

References

Alalwan, A.A., Dwivedi, Y.K., Rana, N.P.: Factors influencing adoption of mobile banking by Jordanian bank customers: extending UTAUT2 with trust. Int. J. Inf. Manage. **37**(3), 99–110 (2017)

Aljukhadar, M., Senecal, S., Nantel, J.: Is more always better? Investigating the task-technology fit theory in an online user context. Information Manage. **51**(4), 391–397 (2014)

Chau, P.Y., Kuan, K.K., Liang, T.P.: Research on IT value: what we have done in Asia and Europe. Eur. J. Inf. Syst. **16**(3), 196–201 (2007)

Chong, A.Y.L.: Predicting m-commerce adoption determinants: a neural network approach. Expert Syst. Appl. **40**(2), 523–530 (2013)

Crabbe, M., Standing, C., Standing, S., Karjaluoto, H.: An adoption model for mobile banking in Ghana. Int. J. Mobile Commun. **7**(5), 515–543 (2009)

Davis, F.: Perceived usefulness, perceived ease of use, and user acceptance of information technology. MIS Q. **13**(3), 319–340 (1989)

Devaraj, S., Fan, M., Kohli, R.: Antecedents of B2C channel satisfaction and preference: validating e-commerce metrics. Inf. Syst. Res. **13**(3), 316–333 (2002)

Dwivedi, Y.K., Sahu, G.P., Rana, N.P., Singh, M., Chandwani, R.K.: Common Services Centers (CSCs) as an approach to bridge the digital divide. Transforming Government: People, Process and Policy **10**(4), 511–525 (2016)

Dwivedi, Y.K., Rana, N.P., Jeyaraj, A., Clement, M., Williams, M.D.: Re-examining the unified theory of acceptance and use of technology (UTAUT): Towards a revised theoretical model. Information Systems Frontiers, pp. 1–16 (2017)

Dwivedi, Y.K., Shareef, M.A., Simintiras, A.C., Lal, B., Weerakkody, V.: A generalised adoption model for services: a cross-country comparison of mobile health (m-health). Gov. Inf. Q. **33**(1), 174–187 (2016)

Hew, J.J., Lee, V.-H., Ooi, K.-B., Wei, J.: What catalyses mobile apps usage intention: an empirical analysis. Ind. Manag. Data Syst. **115**(7), 1269–1291 (2015)

Irani, Z., Dwivedi, Y.K., Williams, M.D.: Understanding consumer adoption of broadband: an extension of the technology acceptance model. J. Operational Res. Soc. **60**(10), 1322–1334 (2009)

Kim, H.W., Chan, H.C., Gupta, S.: Value-based adoption of mobile internet: an empirical investigation. Decis. Support Syst. **43**(1), 111–126 (2007)

Keller, K.L.: Conceptualizing, measuring, and managing customer-based brand equity. J. Mark. **57**(1), 1–22 (1993)

Kuo, Y.-F., Wu, C.-M., Deng, W.-J.: The relationships among service quality, perceived value, customer satisfaction and post-purchase intention in mobile value-added services. Comput. Hum. Behav. **25**, 887–896 (2009)

Liang, T.P., Huang, J.S.: An empirical study on consumer acceptance of products in electronic markets: a transaction cost model. Decis. Support Syst. **24**(1), 29–43 (1998)

Liang, T.P., Kohli, R., Huang, H.C., Li, Z.L.: What drives the adoption of the blockchain technology? a fit-viability perspective. J. Manag. Inf. Syst. **38**(2), 314–337 (2021)

McGill, T.J., Klobas, J.E.: A task–technology fit view of learning management system impact. Comput. Educ. **52**(2), 496–508 (2009)

Oh, J.-C., Yoon, S.-J.: Predicting the use of online information services based on a modified UTAUT model. Behaviour Inf. Technol. **33**(7), 716–729 (2014)

Ølnes, S., Ubacht, J., Janssen, M.: Blockchain in government: Benefits and implications of distributed ledger technology for information sharing. Gov. Inf. Q. **34**(3), 355–364 (2017)

Pikkarainen, T., Pikkarainen, K., Karjaluoto, H., Pahnila, S.: Consumer acceptance of online banking: an extension of the technology acceptance model. Internet Res. **14**(3), 224–235 (2004)

Sharma, S.K., Sharma, H., Dwivedi, Y.K.: A hybrid SEM-neural network model for predicting determinants of mobile payment services. Inf. Syst. Manag. **36**(3), 243–261 (2019)

Sharma, S.K.: Integrating cognitive antecedents into TAM to explain mobile banking behavioral intention: a SEM-neural network modeling. Inf. Syst. Front. **21**(4), 815–827 (2017)

Sharma, S.K., Al-Badi, A., Rana, N.P., Al-Azizi, L.: Mobile applications in government services (mG-App) from user's perspectives: a predictive modelling approach. Gov. Inf. Q. **35**(4), 557–568 (2018)

Sharma, S.K., Sharma, M.: Examining the role of trust and quality dimensions in the actual usage of mobile banking services: an empirical investigation. Int. J. Inf. Manage. **44**, 65–75 (2019)

Slade, E.L., Dwivedi, Y.K., Piercy, N.C., Williams, M.D.: Modeling consumers' adoption intentions of remote mobile payments in the United Kingdom: extending UTAUT with innovativeness, risk, and trust. Psychol. Mark. **32**(8), 860–873 (2015)

Venkatesh, V., Morris, M.G., Davis, G.B., Davis, F.D.: User acceptance of information technology: toward a unified view. MIS Q. **27**(3), 425–478 (2003)

Venkatesh, V., Thong, J.Y., Chan, F.K., Hu, P.J.: Managing citizens' uncertainty in e- government services: the mediating and moderating roles of transparency and trust. Inf. Syst. Res. **27**(1), 87–111 (2016)

Venkatesh, V., Thong, J.Y.L., Xu, X.: Consumer acceptance and use of information technology: extending the unified theory of acceptance and use of technology. MIS Q. **36**(1), 157–178 (2012)

Zeithaml, V.A.: Consumer perceptions of price, quality, and value: a means-end model and synthesis of evidence. J. Mark. **52**(3), 2–22 (1988)

Zuiderwijk, A., Janssen, M., Dwivedi, Y.K.: Acceptance and use predictors of open data technologies: drawing upon the unified theory of acceptance and use of technology. Gov. Inf. Q. **32**(4), 429–440 (2015)

Users' Awareness Towards Digital Financial Transactions: A Study Conducted in India

K. Kajol(✉) ⑩ and Ranjit Singh ⑩

Department of Management Studies, Indian Institute of Information Technology Allahabad,
Allahabad, India
Kajol.1096@gmail.com, ranjitsingh@iiita.ac.in

Abstract. The growing use of smartphones is boosting the demand for such digital services in the financial space. The digital financial transaction is gaining popularity all over the globe; however, there are numerous challenges as well at the global level, especially for a person not familiar with changing technology. Therefore, the purpose of the study is to access the level of awareness of digital financial transactions among digital payment users in India. Authors have used the recall method to access the level of awareness. The structured questionnaire was used to collect primary data from 208 individuals having a sufficient level of literacy to operate a digital transaction. The data was analyzed using SPSS software. The finding shows that Indian users have a moderate level of awareness of digital financial transactions. The level of awareness was high among the male respondents. There are some significant differences between researchers' demographic and personal characteristics and their levels and actions with regard to digital payment. The implications provided in the study will not only help scholars in further research in the concerned area but also for policymakers and managers in formulating policies and strategies to promote the adoption of digital financial transactions. The study also sets the future research agenda.

Keywords: Digital financial transactions · Awareness · Mis-information · Digital innovation

1 Introduction

In the era of digitization, a transaction using technology is the best way of being agile and giving better service to customers [1]. The use of non-cash transactions caught attention during the 1990s, with the growing popularity of electronic banking among developed nations. The technological breakthroughs and regulatory reforms of the past decades have brought payment media to the forefront of business, social and political interests [2]. Today, the digitalization of transactions has become essential for banking and financial institutions for their survival and growth. India is not untouched by this digital revolution and the ever-increasing number of digital transactions in the financial sector is moving it up the ladder among other nations. India has rapidly digitized its payment systems and promises huge potential in the area. The Digital India initiative started by the Indian

© IFIP International Federation for Information Processing 2022
Published by Springer Nature Switzerland AG 2022
A. Elbanna et al. (Eds.): TDIT 2022, IFIP AICT 660, pp. 331–345, 2022.
https://doi.org/10.1007/978-3-031-17968-6_27

government has given a tremendous boost to the usage of digital payment systems throughout the country. The progress in digital payments has been driven by a healthy mix of technological innovation, policy interventions, and expansion and strengthening of existing infrastructure on the supply side, coupled with an increasing proportion of the population adopting financial and digital instruments on the demand side.

Digital payments offer not only convenience by saving time and labor, but also help the government in its fight against black money and counterfeiting currency [3]. Usage of digital financial transactions (DFTs) provides speed, security, and transparency of data [4]. However, there are huge implicit costs to digitizing the existing systems and nudging people to change. The use of cash still seems to be on the uptick in India [5]. While cash may appear to be convenient, as it's ingrained in habits and is still readily accepted in more places, and free of any direct transactional cost; it is still costly for both governments and end-users [6]. As per a survey conducted in 2014, the Reserve Bank of India (RBI) and commercial banks collectively spent nearly 210 billion rupees on currency-related operating expenses in the year 2014, while the people of Delhi spent approximately 91 million rupees to access cash in the same year [7].

There are two main characteristics of the Indian economy. First, it is a developing economy characterized by a middle-class population with huge opportunities for employment and entrepreneurship. And second, the population is mostly made up of people who live in rural areas that don't have as much knowledge about innovations as people who live in urban areas [8]. There is strong evidence that awareness can alter the perception or response of people towards a given product to a large extent, and thus, consequently change their final decisions [9]. Therefore, the existence of awareness among individuals about financial transactions acts as a motivator and enhances their engagement in the banking system [10–12]. An extensive review of past studies showed that research on awareness towards DFTs or related financial innovation is extremely sparse [13–19]. Thus, accessing awareness is critical to explain the DFTs adoption pattern. The study's novelty stems from the authors' attempt to shed light on one of the most critical factors, 'awareness'. The key objectives of the present study are to (1) examine the overall level of awareness among the individuals towards DFTs; (2) find out if there is any miss-awareness about the same; and (3) finally to identify the factors affecting awareness towards DFTs. The study attempts to answer the following key research questions:

RQ1. What is the overall level of awareness towards DFTs among people?
RQ2. Is there any mis-awareness towards the DFTs among people?
RQ3. Are there some people who are pretending to be aware about DFTs?
RQ4. What are the demographic factors that affect the awareness towards DFTs?

2   Theoretical Background and Literature Review

Ajwani-Ramchandani [20] found that a very large segment of the population around the world is not conversant with the use of digital payment alternatives. Many people are not using digital payment due to a lack of knowledge and interest [21]. Lack of awareness is a serious problem for a developing country like India [22]. It would take a lot of effort to steer the country on the path to a cashless economy because millions of people are yet to cultivate the banking habit [23]. Antitrust concerns in the market for payment media stem from the lack of information, improving consumer awareness could be a remedy [24]. The goal of awareness measurement is to determine what people know as well as what they do not know [25]. The concept of awareness attempts to explore how the customers establish their knowledge of the products or services and to what extent they are lacking information about it [26]. Past researchers have provided various models and theories of awareness [13, 22, 24, 25, 27–30]. One of the classic explanations for the level of awareness was given by Smith in the year 1999 [31]. He propounded that there are three levels of awareness [31] consciousness, precociousness, and unconsciousness. Consciousness encompasses an individual's instantaneous thinking and reasoning. According to Nilsson [32], conscious individuals are more likely to use provided services. Conscious users have a better understanding of the benefits of the given innovation and thus they adopt the given innovation quickly. The preconscious is a repository of information that exists just beneath the level of awareness. It is easily retrievable and is frequently referred to as memory or recollection. Albert [33] discovered that the preconscious mind has a greater role in trust acquisition than previously believed. According to Singh and Malik [8], those who are aware of DFTs do not use them and do not trust the virtual channel supporting the banking transactions. Individuals at a preconscious level need to be informed about the privacy and security risks associated with digital payment systems. This consequently may help in the acceptance of digital payments [34, 35]. The unconscious mind contains buried thoughts, memories, and desires. Even though individuals are unaware of the stages involved in financial decision-making (planning, decision-making, execution, and feedback), they have a significant influence on their behaviour [36]. Training and development programs are used to bring unconscious people to the level of conscious. Thus, the level of awareness of individuals toward DFTs must be assessed at the mastery level, where it is assumed that users possess all information.

Awareness could be measured through the recall and recognition method [37]. The recall is the mental reproduction of some target item experienced or learned earlier, whereas recognition is the awareness of having previously experienced those stimuli. Operationally, in the recall, some contextual cue is provided and the respondent must retrieve the target item from memory. In recognition, the target item is provided and the contextual circumstances of the earlier event or experience must be retrieved. The present study uses the recall method of testing awareness about DFTs because of their relative merit over the recognition method [37]. The study is expected to fill this research gap one from the perspective of its geographical coverage, i.e., India, and secondly from the perspective of its timeline, i.e., post COVID-19, by shedding some light on the impact of the Indian government's initiatives to promote DFTs adoption during the nationwide lockdown. The authors design the following hypothesis:

H_{01}: *There is no significant association between demographic variables and awareness of DFTs.*

3 Methodology

The study is based on the analysis of primary as well as secondary data. The primary data was collected using a structured questionnaire while the secondary data was obtained from relevant sources such as journals, official reports, newspapers, etc. for providing necessary background information on the study area. Individuals having a sufficient level of literacy to operate a DFTs were considered as a sample unit in the study. Using simple random sampling methods, a sample of 208 respondents was collected through an online survey.[38–42] are some of the scholars who attempted to measure the awareness level of different subjects. Even though their works were not related to measuring the awareness level of DFTs, their approach needs special mention. These studies have provided a base to the authors for accessing awareness levels. There were certain limitations in the methodology adopted in these papers. It was observed that the respondents were unaware of their level of awareness, and sometimes they were confused about the product. Moreover, some respondents pretended to be more knowledgeable. There are two types of awareness measures: recall and recognition [37]. A recall is the mental recreation of a previously experienced or learned target item, whereas recognition is the awareness of having previously experienced those stimuli. In the recall, a contextual cue is given, and the respondent must retrieve the target item from memory. The target item is provided in recognition, and the contextual circumstances of the previous event or experience must be retrieved. The recall method of testing awareness about DFTs was used in this research due to its superiority over the recognition method [37]. A questionnaire was designed to evaluate the awareness of individuals about DFTs. The questionnaire was so designed to examine the conscious, preconscious, and unconscious levels of mind for DFTs. The questionnaire is framed using the variables identified by [42–45], and several other documents issued by the government. Thirty-one multiple-choice questions were designed based on DFTs. For measuring awareness levels using the recall method, there were five options. Only one of the five options was correct, three were incorrect, and the fifth was "not aware of." Thus, a respondent who gave the correct answer was thought to be aware and knowledgeable, whereas a respondent who gave the incorrect answer was thought to be pretending to be aware. In addition, information such as their age, gender, income, qualification, and occupation was requested.

We apply multiple regression models to find the impact of select variables on the awareness of DFT. The SPSS software is used to execute the analysis process. SPSS and Microsoft Excel have been used to analyze and interpret the data and Cronbach's alpha method has been used to verify the reliability and validity of the questionnaire. The profile of the respondents is given in Table 1.

Table 1. Profile of the respondents

Variable	Frequency	Percentage (%)
Gender		
Male	112	53.8
Female	96	46.2
Age		
15–30 years	198	95.2
30–40 years	7	3.4
40–60 years	1	0.5
60 years and above	2	1
Education		
Uneducated	1	0.5
Primary	0	0
Secondary	7	3.4
Higher secondary	38	18.3
Graduate	0	0
Post graduate	123	59.1
Others	39	18.8
Occupation		
Business	18	8.7
Service	20	9.6
Agriculturist	4	1.9
Student	154	74
Home maker	11	5.3
Retired	1	5
Annual family income (Rs)		
Below 1 lakhs	176	84.6
1–2 lakhs	22	10.6
2–4 lakhs	8	3.8
4–6 lakhs	1	0.5
6 lakhs and above	1	0.5
Physically challenged		
Yes	44	21.2
No	164	78.8
Locality		
Rural	101	48.6
Urban	107	51.4
Email		
Yes	155	74.5
No	53	25.5

Source: Compiled by authors

4 Results

There were total 31 numbers of multiple-choice questions in the questionnaire. By applying item-total correlation in the above items it was found that the item-total correlation value of question no. 31 was less than 0.2, which means that there does not correlate very well with the overall score and thus it can be dropped. So, a total of 30 questions were used to analyze the awareness level.

The reliability of the scale constructed to measure awareness about DFTs is tested using Cronbach's alpha. A Cronbach's alpha of more than 0.70 is considered to be a good measure of the reliability of the scale [46]. Thus, in the present study, it can be inferred that the scale is a reliable one, since the value of Cronbach's Alpha is 0.821, and it is measuring the latent variable namely awareness of DFTs.

Each question carries a score of one. Then a total score has been found by adding the scores of all the questions. The maximum possible score of awareness level was 30 (30 × 1) and the minimum possible score was zero (30 × 0). The difference between the maximum and minimum possible score was 30. To ascertain the awareness level at five levels, this range was divided by 5. It is found to be 6. Adding 6 with 0 (lowest possible score), it was obtained the very low awareness level (0–6). Similarly, adding 6 with subsequent values, the next higher range was obtained. The interpreted score of awareness level for DFTs is given in Table 2.

Table 2. Interpretation of score on awareness about DFTs

Score value	Interpretation of score value
0–6	Very low level of awareness
6–12	Low level of awareness
12–18	Moderate level of awareness
18–24	High level of awareness
24–30	Very high level of awareness

The overall awareness level of the entire respondent is, calculated by adding their score from the questionnaire and it is given in Table 3.

Table 3. Overall awareness level

Level of awareness level	Frequency	Percent
Very low level of awareness	20	9.62
Low level of awareness	76	36.54
Moderate level of awareness	85	40.87

(*continued*)

Table 3. (*continued*)

Level of awareness level	Frequency	Percent
High level of awareness	25	12.02
Very high level of awareness	2	0.95
Total	208	100
Mean	12.95	
Std. deviation	5.15	
Minimum	0	
Maximum	26	

Similarly, those who have given the wrong answer are considered they are not informed but pretending to be informed or to be aware of DFTs. Similar to Table 3, another table is prepared to interpret the pretending to be informed score or misinformed score and it is given in Table 4.

Table 4. Interpretation of pretending to be informed score

Score value	Interpretation of score value
0–6	Very low level of mis-information
6–12	Low level of mis-information
12–18	Moderate level of mis-information
18–24	High level of mis-information
24–30	Very high level of mis-information

Overall, the level of mis-information of the respondent is calculated by adding their score from the questionnaire. Then its value is interpreted using Table 4. The overall frequencies of mis-awareness are presented in Table 5.

Table 5. Overall level of mis-information

Level of awareness level	Frequency	Percent
Very low level of mis-information	82	39.42
Low level of mis-information	88	42.31
Moderate level of mis-information	25	12.02

(*continued*)

Table 5. (*continued*)

Level of awareness level	Frequency	Percent
High level of mis-information	10	4.81
Very high level of mis-information	3	1.44
Total	208	100
Mean	8.72	
Std. deviation	5.01	
Minimum	1	
Maximum	26	

To study the impact of select demographic and socio-economic variables on awareness towards digital transactions, all the statements in the questionnaire used to measure awareness are added to get the total awareness score (Table 6).

Table 6. Item analysis for information among DFTs users

Particulars	Mean	Std. deviation
About Unstructured Supplementary Service Data (USSD)	0.0673	0.25116
Maximum limit of making transactions through Bharat Interface for Money (BHIM)	0.1587	0.36623
About National Electronic Funds Transfer (NEFT)	0.1635	0.37068
About the number of accounts to be linked with a single digital wallet	0.1635	0.37068
About only transfer mechanism that transfer money between different accounts and does not hold money	0.1635	0.37068
The idea about mobile applications that do not have a digital wallet	0.1875	0.39125
Awareness about payment gateway	0.1971	0.39878
Awareness about Unified Payment Interface (UPI)	0.2115	0.40938
Transaction limit in UPI for a single transaction	0.2115	0.40938
Devices require for making payment through a banking card at a shop	0.25	0.43406
Awareness about Immediate Payment Service (IMPS)	0.2692	0.44463
Idea about QR code	0.3173	0.46655
Devices required for making a payment with Aadhaar Enabled Payment System (AEPS)	0.351	0.47842

(*continued*)

Table 6. (*continued*)

Particulars	Mean	Std. deviation
Services offered by Aadhaar Enabled Payment System (AEPS)	0.3558	0.4799
Different forms of UPI	0.3558	0.4799
Details UPI app collects for user bank account verification	0.3894	0.4888
Regarding regulators of the functioning of UPI in India	0.3942	0.48986
Awareness about internet banking	0.4423	0.49786
Details that are necessary while requesting for Real-Time Gross Settlement (RTGS) transfer	0.4663	0.50007
About means of making digital payment	0.5673	0.49664
About adding money to a digital wallet	0.5721	0.49597
Devicesneeded to make DFTs	0.5769	0.49524
About transferring money through the Unified Payment Interface (UPI)	0.6298	0.48402
The document is mandatory to avail of any kind of digital payment services	0.6827	0.46655
About debit cards	0.6827	0.46655
Types UPIs mechanism	0.6971	0.46061
About debit card	0.7452	0.4368
Awareness about debit cards regulator	0.851	0.35699
Awareness about the usage of digital wallets	0.8654	0.34214
Payment Security	0.9038	0.29551

Source: Compiled by authors

A multiple regression model was used by considering awareness score as the dependent variable. The corresponding independent variables are gender, locality, age, education, occupation, and income. The findings of the multiple regressions are presented in Tables 7, 8, and 9.

Table 7. Model summary

Model	R	R square	Adjusted R Square	Std. Error of the estimate
1	.388	.151	.125	4.81565

Thus, Table 7 shows the value of R square to be 0.151 which implies that the independent variables are 15.1% responsible for explaining variations in the dependent variable, i.e., awareness score. Table 8, ANOVA test provides that the regression is significant with p-value 0.000 and Table 9 shows locality (p = 0.000), age (p = 0.037) and education (p = 0.000) are significant in determining dependent variable awareness score.

Table 8. ANOVA

Model		Sum of squares	df	Mean square	F	Sig.
1	Regression	826.238	6	137.706	5.938	.000
	Residual	4661.281	201	23.190		
	Total	5487.519	207			

Table 9. Coefficients

Model		Unstandardized coefficients		Standardized coefficients	t	Sig.
		B	Std. error	Beta		
1	(Constant)	2.199	2.567		.857	.393
	Gender	.016	.696	.002	.023	.982
	Locality	2.513	.680	.244	3.696	.000
	Age	1.540	.732	.142	2.105	.037
	Education	1.230	.304	.268	4.044	.000
	Occupation	.258	.331	.052	.780	.436
	Income	−.129	.599	−.014	−.215	.830

5 Discussion

The analysis and results have provided three important insights. First, there is a moderate level of awareness among the people living in Nagaland, India, since the mean value of awareness score is 12.95 which falls in the category of 'moderate level of awareness'. The responses under this category are also highest among all the class intervals, i.e., 85. Table 3 also shows that 'low level of awareness has significant frequency i.e., 76, thus, as per the results; there is a high need to educate people towards the DFTs. Second, the overall level of mis-information about DFT is low as the mean value is 8.72 as per Table 5 which falls in the category of 'low level of misinformation as per Table 4. The third insight is from the demographic and social-economic variables. The results show that education, locality, and age are significantly influencing the level of awareness about DFT. Co-efficient of 1.54 for age signifies that if age is increased by one unit, the level of awareness is increasing by 1.54 units. Here age was taken in the range of 15–30 years, 30–40 years, 40–60 years, and 60 years and above. Increasing one unit means the person is placed from a lower age group to the next higher age group. Similarly, if the locality is changed from rural to urban the net impact on the awareness score is 2.513 times, and if education is increased by one unit, the awareness score increases by 1.23 times. Similar to the age, education was also taken at a particular level, and increasing one unit of education means, placing the person from one level of education to the next higher level of education. From the findings, it could be interpreted that, the younger population, educated and someone living in the urban area possesses a high level of awareness. Table 9 provides us with the estimated Regression equation which is given by,

$$Awarenesslevel = 2.199 + 2.513 \; locality + 1.54 \; age + 1.23 \; education$$

6 Conclusion

The technological breakthroughs and regulatory reforms of the past decades have brought payment media to the forefront of business, social and political interests [2]. In the era of digitization, a transaction using technology is the best way of being agile and giving better service to customers [1]. The research shows the level of awareness toward DFTs in the North-East Indian state of Nagaland. The study presents a comprehensive analysis of the level of information, level of misinformation, and socio-economic and demographic variables for DFT. The analysis was done using primary data. A structured questionnaire was used to collect the responses from an online survey. The results depicted that individuals were not aware of their appropriate level of awareness if they were to rate their awareness level. It indicates that some people still pretend to be more informed but they are not. Results also suggest that demographic variables such as education, age, and locality have a significant influence on the level of awareness while other variables such as income, gender, and occupation have a very weak influence on the level of awareness. The usage of DFT will raise only when the awareness level of the individuals will improve [47] also with the increase in awareness level trust will build up and attitude towards DTF improves [48]. The authors concentrated on the level of awareness, throughout enhancing research understanding towards DFT. The findings of the present study provide numerous managerial, policy, and theoretical implications.

6.1 Practical Implications

India is a developing economy characterized by a middle-class population, an emerging standard of living, a young population with huge opportunities for employment and entrepreneurship, high purchasing power of the people, and growth in voluminous business transactions. Therefore, the service providers need to increase the visibility of their innovation or payment service. The visibility could be increased in advertising the products. Today, a large segment of the population, especially the younger generation follows social media influencers. The Internet is considered a most valuable tool for sharing data and other relevant information [49, 50]. Thus, service providers could appoint famous social media influencers to advertise their products. Awareness about digital instruments for financial transactions results in their actual use for various day-to-day transactions. Mobile service providers need to engender users' innovativeness to facilitate the usage of mobile payments [51]. Banks should take necessary steps to create awareness among semi-urban and rural people about the advantages of e-banking/internet banking services available in the banks.

6.2 Policy Implications

The awareness campaign about the use of digital instruments may prove to be an advantage for the prime objective. The government must focus its awareness programs [27]. The government needs to put more effort to educate people about the benefits of electronic payment systems and improving the security features of the electronic payment system [52]. The Government should organize financial literacy campaigns from time to time to make the population aware of the benefits of electronic payment. Efforts must be taken to increase awareness about digital payments among rural people [22]. The level of education has a major influence on financial product awareness among youths [53]. A necessary awareness program should be given to the students because they are the future of India [54]. Antitrust concerns in the market for payment media stem from the lack of information, improving consumer awareness could be a remedy [55]. There is a need for proper infrastructure facilities first to make them aware of the technology.

6.3 Theoretical Implications

The current study makes a theoretical addition to the field of research researchers who are now working in, or willing to work in the concerned area. As stated above the research on awareness towards DFTs is limited, therefore awareness, as a factor, needs to be explored more carefully in future research. Technology has had a significant impact on the financial sector, and as a result, financial innovations are becoming more commonplace. Emotional intelligence-related approaches could be used to identify the conscious, preconscious, and, unconscious levels of awareness. Another scope of research is the investigation of the rural-urban divide. A comparative study could be done to understand the pattern of awareness in rural as well as urban areas so that suitable actions could be taken.

7 Limitations

Although the authors have made effort to present a comprehensive analysis, the study is not free from limitations. The methodology adopted to measure the awareness suffers from certain limitations. The study has used primary data collected from people living in Nagaland, India, therefore, results might vary in a similar study conducted in other countries. The authors have conducted a cross-sectional study which is another limitation. The study has provided a basic framework for the researchers willing to work in the concerned area. Tracing and revocation of malicious users can be regarded as future work. Future work could explore the causes of the presence of misinformation among digital payment users. Moreover, there is a need for a comprehensive model that could help in increasing the level of awareness. The factors that affect the awareness towards DFTs could be identified for future research.

References

1. Verma, S., Chaurasia, S., Singh, V.: Understanding the corpus of mobile payment services research: an analysis of the literature using co-citation analysis and social network analysis. J. Inf. Syst. Technol. Manag. **17**, 1–36 (2020)

2. Hyytinen, A., Takalo, T.: Investor protection and business creation. Int. Rev. Law Econ. **28**(2), 113–122 (2008)
3. Balsmeier, B., Woerter, M.: Is this time different? How digitalization influences job creation and destruction. Res. Policy **48**(8), 103765 (2019)
4. Nandal, N., Nandal, M.N., Mankotia, K., Jora, M.N.: Investigating digital transactions in the interest of a sustainable economy. Int. J. Mod. Agric. **1**(10), 1150–1162 (2021)
5. Chodorow-Reich, G., Gopinath, G., Mishra, P., Narayanan, A.: Cash and the economy: evidence from India's demonetization*. Q. J. Econ. **135**(1), 57–103 (2020)
6. Sarker, M.N.I., Khatun, M.N., Alam, G.M.: Islamic banking and finance: potential approach for economic sustainability in China. J. Islam. Mark. **11**(6), 1725–1741 (2019)
7. Shree, S., Pratap, B., Saroy, R., Dhal, S.: Digital payments and consumer experience in India: a survey based empirical study. J. Bank. Financ. Technol. **5**(1), 1–20 (2021). https://doi.org/10.1007/s42786-020-00024-z
8. Singh, R., Malik, G.: Impact of digitalization on Indian rural banking customer: with reference to payment systems. Emerg. Econ. Stud. **5**(1), 31–41 (2019)
9. Merikle, P.M.: Toward a definition of awareness. Bull. Psychon. Soc. **22**(5), 449–450 (1984). https://doi.org/10.3758/BF03333874
10. Iradianty, A., Aditya, B.R.: Student awareness of digital payment services (case study in Indonesia). J. Phys. Conf. Ser. **1823**(1), 012036 (2021)
11. Adam, N.D., Adhariani, D.: Sustainable finance for sustainability: a case study analysis. In: E3S Web of Conferences, vol. 74, p. 08007, December 2018
12. Sathye, M.: Adoption of Internet banking by Australian consumers: an empirical investigation. Int. J. Bank Mark. **17**(7), 324–334 (1999)
13. Gichuki, C.N., Mulu-Mutuku, M.: Determinants of awareness and adoption of mobile money technologies: evidence from women micro entrepreneurs in Kenya. Womens. Stud. Int. Forum **67**, 18–22 (2018)
14. See-To, E.W.K., Ngai, E.W.T.: An empirical study of payment technologies, the psychology of consumption, and spending behavior in a retailing context. Inf. Manag. **56**(3), 329–342 (2019)
15. Cao, Q., Niu, X.: Integrating context-awareness and UTAUT to explain Alipay user adoption. Int. J. Ind. Ergon. **69**, 9–13 (2019)
16. Al-Okaily, M., Lutfi, A., Alsaad, A., Taamneh, A., Alsyouf, A.: The determinants of digital payment systems' acceptance under cultural orientation differences: the case of uncertainty avoidance. Technol. Soc. **63**, 101367 (2020)
17. Balakrishnan, V., Shuib, N.L.M.: Drivers and inhibitors for digital payment adoption using the Cashless Society Readiness-Adoption model in Malaysia. Technol. Soc. **65**, 101554 (2021)
18. Schulz, C., Ioris, A.A.R., Martin-Ortega, J., Glenk, K.: Prospects for payments for ecosystem services in the Brazilian Pantanal: a scenario analysis. J. Environ. Dev. **24**(1), 26–53 (2015)
19. Bayero, M.A.: Effects of cashless economy policy on financial inclusion in Nigeria: an exploratory study. Procedia Soc. Behav. Sci. **172**, 49–56 (2015)
20. Ajwani-Ramchandani, R.: Less cash or cashless: what about the common man? In: The Role of Microfinance in Women's Empowerment, pp. 275–281. Emerald Publishing Limited (2017)
21. Kumar, B., Kumar, B.P.: Fattening the long tail items in e-commerce. J. Theor. Appl. Electron. Commer. Res. **12**(3), 27–49 (2017)
22. Thatte, S., Kulkarni, S.M.: A study on awareness of M-banking app in rural areas of Jalgaon district, June 2019
23. Chopdar, P.K., Sivakumar, V.J.: Understanding continuance usage of mobile shopping applications in India: the role of espoused cultural values and perceived risk. Behav. Inf. Technol. **38**(1), 42–64 (2019)
24. Hyytinen, A., Takalo, T.: Consumer awareness and the use of payment media: evidence from young Finnish consumers. Rev. Netw. Econ. **8**(2), 164–188 (2009)

25. Gafoor, K.A.: Considerations in the measurement of awareness. In: Seminar on Emerging Trends in Education, p. 6 (2012)
26. Kotler, P.: Ten Deadly Marketing Sins: Signs and Solutions. Wiley, New York (2004)
27. Saini, S.: Digital financial literacy: awareness and access. Int. J. Manag. IT Eng. 9(4), 201–207 (2019)
28. Mohamad, S.A., Kassim, S.: Examining the relationship between UTAUT construct, technology awareness, financial cost and e-payment adoption among microfinance clients in Malaysia. Adv. Soc. Sci. Educ. Humanit. Res. 292(1), 351–357 (2018)
29. van Benthem, J., Velázquez-Quesada, F.R.: The dynamics of awareness. Synthese 177(Suppl. 1), 5–27 (2010)
30. Kalyani, P.: An empirical study about the awareness of paperless e-currency transaction like e-wallet using ICT in the youth of India. J. Manag. Eng. Inf. Technol. 3(3), 2394–8124 (2016)
31. Smith, P.K., Mahdavi, J., Carvalho, M., Tippett, N.: An investigation into cyberbullying, its forms, awareness and impact, and the relationship between age and gender in cyberbullying. Research Brief, vol. RBX03-06 (2006)
32. Nilsson, U.: The anxiety- and pain-reducing effects of music interventions: a systematic review. AORN J. 87(4), 780–807 (2008)
33. Albert, W., Gribbons, W., Almadas, J.: Pre-conscious assessment of trust: a case study of financial and health care web sites. Proc. Hum. Factors Ergon. Soc. Annu. Meet. 53(6), 449–453 (2009)
34. Singh, S., Sahni, M.M., Kovid, R.K.: What drives FinTech adoption? A multi-method evaluation using an adapted technology acceptance model. Manag. Decis. 58(8), 1675–1697 (2020)
35. Sivathanu, B.: Adoption of digital payment systems in the era of demonetization in India: an empirical study. J. Sci. Technol. Policy Manag. 10(1), 143–171 (2019)
36. Lan, Y., et al.: A pilot study of a group mindfulness-based cognitive-behavioral intervention for smartphone addiction among university students. J. Behav. Addict. 7(4), 1171–1176 (2018)
37. Copland, B.D.: The study of attention value: a review of some available material (1958)
38. Bhushan, P.: Insights into awareness level and investment behaviour of salaried individuals towards financial products. Int. J. Eng. Bus. Enterp. Appl. 8(1), 53–57 (2014)
39. Choudhury, S., Pattnaik, S.: Emerging themes in e-learning: a review from the stakeholders' perspective. Comput. Educ. 144, 103657 (2020)
40. Prathap, G., Rajamohan, A.: A study on status of awareness among mutual fund investors in Tamil Nadu. J. Exclus. Manag. Sci. 2(12), 1–7 (2013)
41. Rajeswari, N., Mary, S.T.: E-filing of income tax returns: awareness and satisfaction level of salaried employees. Int. J. Curr. Res. Acad. Rev. 2(9), 39–45 (2014)
42. Singh, R., Kar, H.: Do the highly educated subscribers aware of it. New Pension Scheme in India. SIBACA Manag. Rev. 1(1), 8–16 (2011)
43. Bhattacharjee, J., Singh, R.: Awareness about equity investment among retail investors: a kaleidoscopic view. Qual. Res. Financ. Mark. 9(4), 310–324 (2017)
44. Deb, S., Singh, R.: Impact of risk perception on investors towards their investment in mutual fund. Iran. J. Manag. Stud. 11(2), 407–424 (2018)
45. Kajol, K., Biswas, P., Singh, R., Moid, S., Das, A.K.: Factors affecting disposition effect in equity investment: a social network analysis approach. Int. J. Account. Financ. Rev. 5(3), 64–86 (2020)
46. Nunnally, J.C.: Psychometric Theory. McGraw-Hill, New York (1978)
47. Das, A., Das, S., Jaiswal, A., Sonthalia, T.: Impact of COVID-19 on payment transactions. Stat. Appl. 18(1), 239–251 (2020)
48. Chen, R., Yu, J., Jin, C., Bao, W.: Internet finance investor sentiment and return comovement. Pac. Basin Financ. J. 56(May), 151–161 (2019)

49. Kaushik, A.K., Rahman, Z.: Perspectives and dimensions of consumer innovativeness: a literature review and future agenda. J. Int. Consum. Mark. **26**(3), 239–263 (2014)
50. Porter, M.E., Millar, V.E.: How information gives you competitive advantage. Harv. Bus. Rev. **63**, 149–160 (1985)
51. Thakur, R., Srivastava, M.: Adoption readiness, personal innovativeness, perceived risk and usage intention across customer groups for mobile payment services in India. Internet Res. **24**(3), 369–392 (2014)
52. Choudrie, J., Pheeraphuttranghkoon, S., Davari, S.: The digital divide and older adult population adoption, use and diffusion of mobile phones: a quantitative study. Inf. Syst. Front. **22**(3), 673–695 (2018). https://doi.org/10.1007/s10796-018-9875-2
53. Gikandi, J.W., Bloor, C.: Adoption and effectiveness of electronic banking in Kenya. Electron. Commer. Res. Appl. **9**(4), 277–282 (2010)
54. Girija, K., Nandhini, M.: Awareness about cash less economy among students. Int. J. Econ. Commer. Res. **8**(5), 5–12 (2018)
55. Takalo, T.: Switching costs in the Finnish retail deposit market (2019)

Creating Endogenous Growth: Introducing Community Inclusion Currencies Within Rural Communities

Josue Kuika Watat[1,2(✉)] 🆔 and William O. Ruddick[2,3] 🆔

[1] HISP Centre, Department of Informatics, University of Oslo, Ole-Johan Dahls Hus Gaustadalleèn 23B, 0373 Oslo, Norway
josuekw@ifi.uio.no
[2] Grassroots Economics Foundation, Kilifi 80108, Kenya
will@grassecon.org
[3] Institute for Leadership and Sustainability, University of Cumbria, London 146JE, UK

Abstract. Although economic cooperation has significantly enhanced countries' development, the countryside remains an economically underprivileged region in Africa. The scarcity of mainstream financial resources is mentioned as a contributing factor to difficulties experienced by rural communities. This research explores mechanisms for introducing blockchain based community currency in African rural areas to mitigate social and economic challenges. To achieve the objective of the study, extant literature was scoured to distil past studies and expand on a theoretical framework. The results reflect on the intricacies of financial systems in the continent's economies, including the necessity to pinpoint key areas that drive willingness to embrace alternative financial instruments. The study's findings will be invaluable for financial institutions and organizations engaged in economic cooperation and lay a crucial theoretical basis for future research.

Keywords: Blockchain · Diffusion of Innovation · Community inclusion currencies · Rural Africa · Digital divide

1 Introduction

The emergence of contemporary technologies has generated novel innovative financial options for many individuals. Among others, microfinance, crowdfunding and peer-to-peer lending have garnered widespread attention from researchers and practitioners. Nevertheless, the access to financial options has been out of reach for many people in sub-Saharan Africa. Based on some predictions, few households and families in many regions of Africa have access to a bank account, as contrasted with other regions of the world [1, 2]. Recently, the spectrum of affordable financial services in Africa has broadened with increasing Internet access and the widespread acceptance of smartphones in communities [3, 4]. This technological boom has afforded new opportunities for the underserved, who are able to use technology to turn once tedious daily tasks into profitable ones. For

A. Elbanna et al. (Eds.): TDIT 2022, IFIP AICT 660, pp. 346–352, 2022.
https://doi.org/10.1007/978-3-031-17968-6_28

instance, mobile money has been one of the technologies enabling peer-to-peer financial transactions. Mobile financial services (MFS) such as mobile money enabled users to deposit or withdraw money without a bank account [5]. Considering the huge number of unbanked families and households (over 1 billion households), there is strong pent-up demand for alternative financial services such as peer-to-peer transactions [3].

The merits of implementing community inclusion currency through blockchain technology for the "unbanked" are manifold. For instance, it eliminates intermediate operations by encoding information about transactions, thus making the process foolproof [6]. Blockchain technology also enables secure peer-to-peer transactions while boosting the acceptance rate of rural populations [7]. Through blockchain technology, individuals who do not have access to traditional bank accounts can benefit from a range of ownership for any decentralized peer-to-peer payment solution [8].

In this study, we outline an economic and social framework for blockchain-based community currencies that addresses the critical drivers of acceptance within developing countries. We commence with a cursory discussion of the state of the art regarding the use of community currencies and their impact on the national economy. Based on these structural premises, we describe our theoretical framework and the associated hypotheses. The subsequent portions of the paper are allocated to elaborating on our research methodology and presenting the expected managerial and organizational implications of our study.

2 Theoretical Underpinning and Hypotheses

2.1 Related Research on Community Currency

By definition, a community currency is a local currency intended to exchange goods and services to complement the national currency [9]. An institution's objective to set up a local currency can vary—stimulate the local economic growth, increase social cohesion of a rural community, or decrease the constraints related to employment. Besides, community currency can be expressed in convertible community bonds, a mutual credit network, or even a Local Exchange and Trading Systems (LETS) [10].

The idea behind the use of several currencies at different scales was thought of by [11]. The incentive was to design a complementary mechanism to the national currency, which was often not widespread in impoverished rural areas. The model was extensively tested in a study on the economic recession in Argentina in 2009 [12]. The study results pointed out a positive effect of using the local community currency to offset the effects of the national currency shortage triggered by the country's economic turmoil [12]. The adoption of such an alternative system in Argentina due to the financial crisis increased the country's national GDP by 0.6 [12]. In Kenya, Grassroots Economic Foundation has launched Community Currency has introduced a community currency known as Sarafu Credit, with the rural communities [13, 14]. The Sarafu is backed by the Kenyan Shillings and is supported by a local community (backers). Backers can be merchants, farmers, street vendors. In a context where having access to national currency remains a challenge, and where the rate of bank penetration is low, Sarafu endorsers are leaning more and more on this alternative as a complement to the national currency [13].

In rural communities, community currencies may offer a unique alternative for accessing financial services. The legitimacy of these currencies derives from trust and mutual agreement within communities and from the establishment of monetary agreements between individuals. Such agreements therefore regulate different social contracts [15]. The sustainability of such a system stems from community members' social behaviour, which in turn has a relatively positive impact on the local economy. The strongest argument for the success of such a system is the stimulation of local consumption of goods and services as a result of the local financial system [10]. [15] has documented evidence of the positive effects of community currency for economically vulnerable countries. The evidence implies an increase in financial inclusion and enhanced inter-household connections within a community due to high levels of trust. We contend that community currencies can also play a vital role in sub-Saharan Africa. The area has experienced political, economic and social crises for several years. Offering alternative financial solutions to families and individuals in a community can be crucial for survival, especially in times of economic insecurity. Community currencies could empower communities by enabling financial independence, reinforcing existing local institutions and augmenting local know-how on a solid social basis.

2.2 Core Constructs

This study draws its theoretical foundations from the emerging literature on blockchain acceptance in developing countries and previous work on community currencies in Africa. The study's theoretical foundation derives from several constructs resulting from models of the Diffusion of Innovation theory and the Technology Acceptance Model. The framework is anchored on institutional considerations (regulatory support) as key determinants of community currency acceptance within the Central African Economic and Monetary Community. Thus, we present various constructs of our research framework as follows:

Relative Advantage refers to "the degree to which an innovation is perceived as providing more benefits than its predecessor" [16, 17].

H1: Relative Advantage has a positive influence on Perceived Ease of Use

H2: Relative Advantage has a positive influence on Perceived Usefulness

Compatibility refers to the extent to which a technological system is perceived as harmonious and fair to citizens' local beliefs, attitudes, and past experiences [16].

H3: Compatibility has a positive influence on Perceived Ease of Use

H4: Compatibility has a positive influence on Perceived Usefulness

Complexity refers to the degree to which technological innovation is deemed difficult to understand and use [16, 18].

H5: Complexity has a negative influence on Perceived Ease of Use

H6: Complexity has a negative influence on Perceived Usefulness

Trialability refers to the degree of technological innovation experimentation on a benchmark limited in time [18].

H7: Trialability has a positive influence on Perceived Ease of Use

H8: Trialability has a positive influence on Perceived Usefulness

Observability refers to the degree of visibility of technological innovation outputs by different actors [18].

H9: Observability has a positive influence on Perceived Ease of Use

H10: Observability has a positive influence on Perceived Usefulness

Perceived Ease of Use refers to the degree of a citizen's belief in increasing his work performance through the use of technological innovation [19].

H11: Perceived Ease of Use has a positive influence on Perceived Usefulness

H12: Perceived Ease of Use has a positive influence on Attitude

Perceived Usefulness refers to the belief of a citizen that the use of technological innovation would be effortless [19].

H13: Perceived Usefulness has a positive influence on Attitude

Perceived Risk refers to the degree of prudence and uncertainty (positive and/or negative) associated with technological innovation's potential use [20].

H14: Perceived Risk has a positive influence on Attitude

Perceived Knowledge refers to the self-assessment provisions of citizens' understanding of local community currency and blockchain technology [21].

H15: Perceived Knowledge has a positive influence on Attitude

Social Influence refers to the degree of acceptance and use of technological innovation based on the influence of leaders' opinion in its community [22].

H16: Social Influence has a positive influence on Attitude

Regulatory Support refers to the implementation of a regulatory and institutional framework as a prelude to the introduction of technological innovation [23].

H17: Regulatory Support moderates the impact of Attitude on Community Currency acceptance

Attitude refers to the attitudinal assessment (positive or negative) of technological innovation [24].

H18: Attitude has a positive influence on Community Currency Acceptance

We present in « Fig. 1 » The Theoretical Framework of the research.

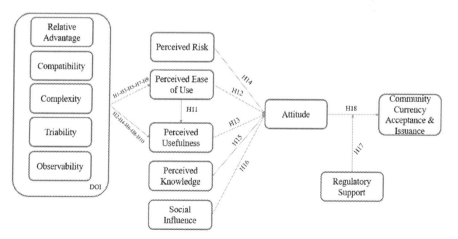

Fig. 1. Research framework

3 Methodology

To test the measurement items of our theoretical framework, we opted for a mixed methodology. [25] recognizes the mixed-method approach's complementary nature overcoming the shortcomings of studies where the qualitative and quantitative methodologies were applied separately. Thus, the present research begins with a qualitative study to justify the results of our quantitative analysis. Interviews and focus group discussions were conducted in the traditional chiefdoms of Batoufam, Bameka, and Fondjomekwet. These are the selected sites for the deployment of the community currency project based on blockchain technology. The purpose of the interviews was to gauge the level of understanding and acceptance of such technology in an environment particularly known to be resistant to new technologies. Subsequently, we developed a survey questionnaire based on our research model. For a better understanding of our measurement elements, the questionnaire developed was translated into local dialect as follows: Ngemba (for the kingdom of Bameka), Ndanda (for the kingdom of Batoufam), Ghomala' (For the kingdom of Fondjomekwet) [26]. To make sure our informants understood our study, we hired three interpreters for the kingdoms where the study took place. The interpreters possessed the expertise to better explain our study's objective as they are familiar with the local pronunciation, expressions, and terms. Besides, caution was taken to ensure that the intonation of the local language is respected. We opted for on-site data collection approaching rural communities and collecting the first-hand information necessary for our study. This proximity to the communities is essential for us as we formulate technological and administrative recommendations. We will use the Partial Least Square Structural Equation Modelling (PLS-SEM) approach for the structural analysis of our theoretical representation, and the SmartPLS software version 3.2.8 will be used.

4 Outlook

This research explores the extent to which the introduction of community currency will impact on rural communities that might not be ready to embrace technological change. One aim is to capture key elements of the acceptance of such a technological innovation for the sake of local economic development, and endogenous and social growth. We opted first for a mixed methodology to overcome the shortcomings observed in previous studies applying qualitative or quantitative methodologies separately. The findings of our study contribute to the existing literature on community currency and its importance in the African social and economic landscape. The study also has practical and managerial contributions. Institutional actors and technology organizations will find the results of our study invaluable in refining their technology implementation strategies based on a human-centered design approach.

References

1. Léon, F., Zins, A.: Regional foreign banks and financial inclusion: evidence from Africa. Econ. Model. **84**, 102–116 (2020)

2. Aga, G.A., Peria, M.S.M.: International remittances and financial inclusion in Sub-Saharan Africa. The World Bank (2014)
3. Pankomera, R., Van Greunen, D.: Challenges, benefits, and adoption dynamics of mobile banking at the base of the pyramid (BOP) in Africa: a systematic review. Afr. J. Inf. Commun. **21**, 21–49 (2018)
4. Kuika Watat, J., Jonathan, G.M.: Breaking the digital divide in rural Africa. In: AMCIS 2020 Proceedings, p. 2 (2020). https://aisel.aisnet.org/amcis2020/global_dev/global_dev/2
5. Watat, J.K., Madina, M.: Towards an integrated theoretical model for assessing mobile banking acceptance among consumers in low income African economies. In: Themistocleous, M., Papadaki, M. (eds.) EMCIS 2019. LNBIP, vol. 381, pp. 165–178. Springer, Cham (2020). https://doi.org/10.1007/978-3-030-44322-1_13
6. Beck, R., Avital, M., Rossi, M., Thatcher, J.B.: Blockchain technology in business and information systems research. Bus. Inf. Syst. Eng. **59**(6), 381–384 (2017). https://doi.org/10.1007/s12599-017-0505-1
7. Chiang, C.-W., et al.: Designing blockchain technology to transform rural communities (2019)
8. Rajnak, V., Puschmann, T.: The impact of blockchain on business models in banking. IseB **19**(3), 809–861 (2020). https://doi.org/10.1007/s10257-020-00468-2
9. Kim, S.M., Lough, B., Wu, C.-F.: The conditions and strategies for success of local currency movements. Local Econ. **31**(3), 344–358 (2016)
10. Zhan, Y.: Local currency networks in rural communities in Africa: a feasibility study of blockchain based community currency, Vrije Universiteit Amsterdam, Amsterdam, p. 36 (2019)
11. Kiyotaki, N., Wright, R.: On money as a medium of exchange. J. Polit. Econ. **97**(4), 927–954 (1989)
12. Colacelli, M., Blackburn, D.J.H.: Secondary currency: an empirical analysis. J. Monet. Econ. **56**(3), 295–308 (2009)
13. Wang, F., De Filippi, P.: Self-sovereign identity in a globalized world: credentials-based identity systems as a driver for economic inclusion. Front. Blockchain **2**, 28 (2020)
14. Zeller, S.: Economic advantages of community currencies. J. Risk Financ. Manag. **13**(11), 271 (2020)
15. Telalbasic, I.: Redesigning the Concept of Money: a service design perspective on complementary currency systems. J. Des. Bus. Soc. **3**(1), 21–44 (2017)
16. Al-Jabri, I.M., Sohail, M.S.: Mobile banking adoption: application of diffusion of innovation theory. J. Electron. Commer. Res. **13**(4), 379–391 (2012)
17. Moore, G.C., Benbasat, I.: Development of an instrument to measure the perceptions of adopting an information technology innovation. Inf. Syst. Res. **2**(3), 192–222 (1991)
18. Friedlmaier, M., Tumasjan, A., Welpe, I.M.: Disrupting industries with blockchain: the industry, venture capital funding, and regional distribution of blockchain ventures. In: Proceedings of the 51st Annual Hawaii International Conference on System Sciences (HICSS) (2018)
19. Folkinshteyn, D., Lennon, M.: Braving Bitcoin: a technology acceptance model (TAM) analysis. J. Inf. Technol. Case Appl. Res. **18**(4), 220–249 (2016)
20. Soon, K.W.K., Lee, C.A., Boursier, P.: A study of the determinants affecting adoption of big data using integrated technology acceptance model (TAM) and diffusion of innovation (DOI) in Malaysia. Int. J. Appl. Bus. Econ. Res. **14**(1), 17–47 (2016)
21. Alqaryouti, O., Siyam, N., Alkashri, Z., Shaalan, K.: Users' knowledge and motivation on using cryptocurrency. In: Themistocleous, M., Papadaki, M. (eds.) EMCIS 2019. LNBIP, vol. 381, pp. 113–122. Springer, Cham (2020). https://doi.org/10.1007/978-3-030-44322-1_9
22. Nuryyev, G., et al.: Blockchain technology adoption behavior and sustainability of the business in tourism and hospitality SMEs: an empirical study. Sustainability **12**(3), 1256 (2020)
23. Wong, L.-W., et al.: Unearthing the determinants of Blockchain adoption in supply chain management. Int. J. Prod. Res. **58**(7), 2100–2123 (2020)

24. Ajzen, I., Fishbein, M.: Understanding Attitudes and Predicting Social Behavior. Prentice-Hall, Englewood Cliffs (1980)
25. Caruth, G.D.: Demystifying mixed methods research design: a review of the literature. Online Submiss. 3(2), 112–122 (2013)
26. Kouega, J.P., Ndzotom, W.: Language use in multi-ethnic Christian congregations: The case of the Evangelical Church of Cameroon. Annales de la Faculté des Arts, Lettres et Sciences Humaines 1(13), 67–86 (2011)

A Call for Research: Cryptocurrencies as a Disruptive Technology for Governments, Organizations, and Society

Michael Lapke[1][✉] and Leevi Jan Folke Lindfors[2]

[1] Christopher Newport University, Newport News, VA, USA
mike.lapke@gmail.com
[2] Aalto University, Helsinki, Finland

Abstract. With the potential for significant effects on financial systems, societal order, and organizational strategy, cryptocurrencies and blockchain technologies stand as a potentially major disruptive force (Rossi et al. 2019). As such, Information Systems Research should focus resources on this still emerging technology. The objective of this research is to identify and analyze what research has found since these technologies have emerged in the last decade. An inductive study was conducted where articles from the AIS Basket of 8 journal list in the domain of cryptocurrencies and blockchain were examined and categorized into emergent themes. These themes were analyzed and supplemented with other research. Resultantly, the ramifications for future trends in research were discussed.

Keywords: Cryptocurrencies · Blockchain · Literature review

1 Introduction

With a total market cap in the trillions of dollars and exponential growth in the last two years (bitcoin.org 2022), the impact of cryptocurrencies on economic markets and governments' fiscal policy cannot be overstated. Indeed, the total market cap of cryptocurrencies has grown by over 1000% in the last 24 months alone (bitcoin.org 2022). Though known for severe volatility in valuation, cryptocurrency growth has recently begun to align with market indexes such as the Dow Jones and S&P 500.

Cryptocurrencies, such as Bitcoin, Ethereum, and Litecoin, are defined as virtual currencies that are based on blockchain technology and secured by cryptography. Blockchain technology itself is a specific type of database in which the information is stored in blocks. Moreover, these blocks are chained together (Convey 2021; Frankenfield 2021). Cryptocurrency is a blockchain-based payment network, which is considered to be an information system (Serapiglia et al. 2015).

The specific type of database that is called blockchain is maintained by the nodes, which are computers. The computers validate the transactions and therefore upkeep the payment network based on the blockchain. While validating the transactions in

© IFIP International Federation for Information Processing 2022
Published by Springer Nature Switzerland AG 2022
A. Elbanna et al. (Eds.): TDIT 2022, IFIP AICT 660, pp. 353–362, 2022.
https://doi.org/10.1007/978-3-031-17968-6_29

a blockchain the computers are rewarded the specific cryptocurrency to compensate their electricity costs. The computers validating the transactions are called miners. The existence of these miners utilizing their computing power is the requirement for the functional payment network, which can validate transactions as they occur. This is one way of validating transactions in a blockchain called proof-of-work, PoW. However, there are already other existing validating methods, such as proof-of-stake. (Tschorsch and Scheuermann 2016; Conti et al. 2018; Pernice and Scott 2021; Convey 2021).

This emerging area has limited exposure in major publications. Across the eight elite journals in the AIS Basket of 8, only a handful of publications focusing on cryptocurrencies have been published. These have all been within the last two to three years. Given the potential for momentous change at the organizational, personal, and governmental sectors, further research is urgently needed (La Paz et al. 2020). This literature review intends to highlight the themes emergent in extant literature and identify fruitful areas for future research. The body of this paper is divided into sections for each of the themes identified. The final discussion section analyzes the potential research streams and discusses future possibilities.

2   Methodology

As stated in the introduction, the intention of this review is to identify emerging themes and potential future research directions. The domain of the data was initially confined to the eight elite journals in the Information Systems field as defined by the Association for Information Systems. Keywords, which included cryptocurrency, bitcoin, and decentralized finance, were used to discover publications in the study domain. No date restriction was utilized but the journal was restricted to the eight journals in the AIS list. Articles that referenced the keywords only in passing were not included as relevant studies. This search revealed 19 total publications across the eight elite journals. The breakdown of the distribution of relevant articles is listed below in Table 1:

Table 1. Breakdown of relevant article count for major journals

Journal name	Code	Count
European Journal of Information Systems	EJIS	2
Information Systems Journal	ISJ	2
Information Systems Research	ISR	2
Journal of the AIS	JAIS	2
Journal of Information Technology	JIT	3
Journal of MIS	JMIS	6
Journal of Strategic Information Systems	JSIS	1
MIS Quarterly	MISQ	1

The marginal number of publications in major journals is in line with a new and emerging domain. Despite this perceived reality, cryptocurrencies have been in circulation since 2009 (bitcoin.org 2022) which means there was a decade long gap between their introduction and the first analysis in major journals. The cause for this delay could have a myriad of reasons that are beyond the scope of this paper however it is apparent that research is lagging behind the real world situation.

Once articles were determined to be relevant, they were divided into respective thematic groupings. There were four major themes and two minor themes. Themes were established as major if more than one paper fell into that thematic group. If only one paper formed a theme, it was established as a minor theme. As seen in Table 2 below, the major themes were fintech innovation, end Users (Fees, motivations, etc.), governance, and business models/strategy/integration. The minor themes were security and entrepreneurship.

Table 2. Listing of journal articles assigned to given themes

Themes	Journal article(s) assigned to theme					
Entrepreneurship	ISJ					
User attitudes and perceptions	MISQ	EJIS	EJIS			
Business integration	JAIS	JMIS	JSIS			
Governance	JAIS	JMIS	JMIS	JMIS		
Fintech innovation	ISJ	ISR	JMIS	ISR	JMIS	JIT
Security	JIT					

Two additional articles were found that spoke to potential research agendas in the cryptocurrency domain area. As this is a meta-theme, it was not included in any of the assigned themes. They were included in the discussion at the conclusion of the paper in a comparative analysis with our findings. The four major themes identified in Table 2 formed the basis for the breakdown of the sections below. Supporting articles outside of the group articles identified in the elite journals were included to facilitate a broader discussion.

3   Major Theme 1: User Attitudes and Perceptions

For end users, there are many barriers to entry into this platform. There is significant literature that examines how trust is an ongoing issue. Comfort with the status quo of traditional banking mechanisms is a significant barrier to the realization of blockchain banking applications benefits, additional awareness of consumer privacy protections can persuade customers to use the blockchain-based applications (Raddatz et al. 2021). The user attitudes towards information systems should be considered influential, especially when it comes to cryptocurrencies where the trusted party is the system itself. More specifically speaking the trust lies in cryptography (Serapiglia et al. 2015).

There are both internal and external factors identified that might affect users' attitudes of which trust is found to be the most influential one for blockchain-based technology adoption (Albayati et al. 2020). Further, the most influential aspects affecting the trust itself are the regulatory support, and user experience of which the first one is lagging substantially behind the development of the technology (Asheer 2018; Cousins et al. 2019; Parveen and Alajmi 2019; Albayati et al. 2020).

Internal factors are behavior intention, attitude, perceived usefulness, perceived ease of use, and trust. Beyond these factors, external ones identified were regulatory support, experience, social influence, and design (Albayati et al. 2020). The identified factors indicate the challenging business environment the developers and founders have to face while developing cryptocurrencies. The development should go far beyond the technology to meet the users' needs as a blockchain-based currency.

The trust of the users is hindered by the lack of available, easy to access knowledge regarding cryptocurrencies. Although there and hundreds and hundreds of news articles and discussion forums discussing cryptocurrencies as an alternative payment method, the information of such sources is mostly superficial and biased ultimately causing puzzlement. The rather complex blockchain technology behind cryptocurrencies is complicating the understanding further. Moreover, it is identified that the fundamental value of cryptocurrencies is still unclear, which should evoke skepticism among the people currently utilizing the cryptocurrencies (Giudici et al. 2020).

Security issues behind cryptocurrencies will also affect the trust of the users. There are multiple security issues identified such as double-spending, mining pool attacks, and client-side security threats regarding specifically the bitcoin (Conti et al. 2018). Conti et al. (2018) suggest that these identified bitcoin security aspects should be researched further. For individual users, the client-side security threats might be viewed as the most critical, even though the security aspects should be evaluated as a whole. The credibility of the payment system security should be based on the overall security evaluation including all the aspects. Currently, the security research is in the initial stage while new cryptocurrencies and related technologies arise. Therefore, the cryptocurrency industry, especially the users' trust viewpoint of it is still in the initial stage of evolving. At the moment it is reasonable to argue that people should have healthy skepticism whilst researching and collaborating with the cryptocurrency industry.

A final barrier to entry for end users are the fees involved with utilizing cryptocurrencies. Ilk et al. (2021) found that market equilibrium forms between users who demand data space for conducting crypto-transactions while trying to avoid transaction delays, and miners who supply data space while trying to maximize fee revenues. Their findings indicated that the inelastic nature of demand signals the utility of Bitcoin as a niche platform for transactions that are otherwise difficult to conduct. Reading between the lines, this seems to support the perception that cryptocurrencies are mostly used for illicit transactions as being mostly true. Why would a user go through the trouble and cost unless there was a motivation to hide the transaction itself?

Beyond illicit transactions, there are two major drivers towards end user adoption of cryptocurrencies. One is as a new investment vehicle (Mattke et al. 2021) and the other is as a crypto-miner (Ilk et al. 2021). It is debatable if either of these groups of people could truly be considered "end-users" as they are not using the currency for transactions.

However, they are not acting as part of an organization or government for the most part so their place as stakeholders in the cryptocurrency scheme is at least ambiguous.

4 Major Theme 2: Business Integration

In Darwin's "On the Origin of Species", a major premise postulated was that the species that is most adaptable to change is the one that survives. The same can be said of organizations in the modern day. Cryptocurrencies and blockchain presents a potential inflection point for businesses where adaptation is critical. The adaptation in this context refers to matching the existing user requirements with the characteristics of blockchain-based cryptocurrencies. For businesses, cryptocurrencies should be cost-effective and fast compared to fiat currencies, such as EUR and USD. For individuals, customer convenience should be a priority on which to focus.

While some early studies have indicated that effectively implementing blockchain into an organization remains unknown (Du et al. 2019), other research has shown there are specific cases for potential implementation (Chong et al. 2019). These include blockchain support for businesses, replacing incumbents in the value chain, resolving inefficiencies in the value chain, revolutionizing contemporary business practices, and co-developing rival blockchain solutions to preexisting business practices (Chong et al. 2019). Furthermore, strategies for the integration of blockchain into existing businesses have been explored (Kohli and Ting-Peng 2021).

Despite these hurdles, the growth and use of blockchain is not something that organizations can ignore. According to the Deutsche Bank (Laboure and Reid 2020), there are currently around 50 million blockchain wallet users, and the estimations argue that there might be 200 million by 2030. Moreover, Bezhovski et al. (2021) argue that the estimated usage of cryptocurrencies as an e-¬commerce payment method is currently less than 1%. However, the estimation that Bezhovski et al. (2021) make is ambiguous and should be as a directive, rather than absolute truth. The number of current wallet users and usage amount indicates that the cryptocurrencies are still in the initial phase of the adaption while fiat currencies remain dominant ones.

Regarding the lack of incentives specifically, the already existing trustworthy payment systems discourage the users from taking a step forward towards cryptocurrency payment systems. In developing countries, these incentives can be seen higher compared to the developed countries, where the financial infrastructure is more stable. For example, the lack of trust towards third parties in developing countries might inhibit growth, and therefore the adaption of cryptocurrencies (Saiedi et al. 2021). Also, hyperinflation could increase the adaption of cryptocurrencies, while citizens prefer to use cryptocurrencies over the existing legal currencies (Tu and Meredith 2015; Denison et al. 2019; Saiedi et al. 2021).

The adaptation of cryptocurrencies by businesses and organizations is still in the early stages although the industry is widely noticed in the media. As more academic literature and research will be published more precise analysis can be done relating to the speed of adaptation, and possible ways of adaptation. At a high level, cryptocurrencies as information systems should be developed substantially further by focusing especially on convenience regarding usability for both individuals and businesses.

5   Major Theme 3: Governance

As noted in the "User Attitudes and Perception" section, there is a high degree of probability that a significant portion of crypto transactions are illicit in nature. This results in an obvious motivation for governments to attempt to legislate and control the currency. Specifically, there are multiple legal issues to be solved regarding the taxation of cryptocurrencies, and the definition of which instrument they are considered to be. Some countries view cryptocurrencies, like bitcoin, as currencies, while some of the countries lack the specific definition of what these instruments are (Asheer 2018; Cousins et al. 2019; Parveen and Alajmi 2019).

Some countries, such as Australia, Canada, Finland, and Germany have legalized its use and have made it clear to apply normal earned income rules on Bitcoin, while many countries have yet not made a clear statement with the legalization and use of bitcoin' (Parveen and Alajmi 2019). Given the novelty of cryptocurrencies, it is not surprising that there is a lack of legislative clarity. This tends to limit the practical adaptation of the cryptocurrencies due to a high threshold of initiating the use of such currencies with ambiguous legislation (Asheer 2018; Cousins et al. 2019; Parveen and Alajmi 2019).

A likely cause to the slow adaptation by governments with regards to legislating cryptocurrencies is the built in anonymous nature of transactions. If it is near impossible to track who is doing what with this system, how could legislation actually be enforced? On a promising note for governments, a recent study has shown the practicality of using Machine Learning to de-anonymize the Bitcoin Blockchain to predict the type of yet-unidentified entities (Sun Yin et al. 2019). This study was successful in their predictions and was able to predict the type of a yet-unidentified entity with an accuracy of 80.42% (Sun Yin et al. 2019). This could provide the basis for legislation for many governments.

Other research has found that blockchain can actually assist in combating corruption in international commerce (Sarker et al. 2021). It was found that blockchain, with its capacity to provide full transactional disclosure and thereby reduce uncertainty, insecurity, and ambiguity in transactions, has been lauded in its potential to fight against corruption. This was a surprising finding given the previously discussed issues with the very anonymous nature of cryptocurrencies.

Governance appears to be a ripe area for research given competing motivations and seemingly contradictory research. While it might seem impossible to expect governance given the nature of blockchain, there is not only the possibility for sound and effective legislation but even the potential for a positive use by way of combating corruption. At the end of the day however, the question of governance in the traditional sense may be moot given that governance in the blockchain economy might radically depart from established notions of governance (Beck et al. 2018).

6   Major Theme 4: Innovation

The primary research profile in the most prolific thematic area is the place that blockchain and cryptocurrencies have in the context of financial technologies (FinTech). At a high level, FinTech is the application of technological innovations to financial services and processes (Lagna and Ravishankar 2022). It is often discussed alongside other innovative

FinTech domains such as market trading and artificial intelligence (Hendershott et al. 2021), payment settlement, cross-border payment services, lending and deposit services, peer-to-peer (P2P) lending, and robo-advisory (Gomber et al. 2018).

Though no doubt an interesting perspective on innovation, it is not groundbreaking to speculate on the potential innovative disruptions that cryptocurrencies might have on the financial sector. Other less obvious innovations may occur at the environmental or societal levels. The potential for a currency unbound to governments could massively disrupt the social order. Money is the foundation for power and a decentralized money source could shatter that illusion. On the environmental side, there is a debate about the impact of cryptocurrencies on the environment.

The energy consumption in a specific cryptocurrency network is dependent on its transaction validation method. The most common validation methods currently utilized are proof-of-work and proof-of-stake of which the latter one is more efficient regarding energy consumption (Cousins et al. 2019). Despite, the concerns of the energy consumption among the researchers and users (Cousin et al. 2019), bitcoin has lower environmental costs compared to paper money, and banking systems according to the multiple studies cited in Cousins et al. (2019). In contrast, Corbet et al. (2021) estimates that the energy footprint per bitcoin transaction is equivalent to 350,000 visa transactions. Innovation is needed to address this troubling issue in that cryptocurrencies may negatively affect the environment. Given the conflicting research, further studies are needed.

The second area of innovation is on the power structures entrenched by financial systems. Cryptocurrencies can facilitate the decentralization of power over the Internet and of governance in general (Lacity 2022). The potential for research in the area of structures of power is enormous as no technology has enabled the potential for change in the way that cryptocurrencies and blockchain have. Further innovation in societal change can be seen in the potential for FinTech to act as an agent of positive change for the least fortunate. Lagna and Ravishankar (2022) found that business strategies for FinTech-led financial inclusion, digital artifacts of fintech-led financial inclusion, the business environment of FinTech-led financial inclusion, and microfoundations of FinTech for financial inclusion can all have a profound impact on alleviating poverty.

7 Discussion

Cryptocurrencies based on the promising blockchain technology are an intriguing way of payment enabling fast and cost-efficient transactions. In the perspective of information systems, cryptocurrencies require both social acceptance, and the proper technical implementation to function as a convenient payment network for its users. If one or the other is lacking the practical implications of such systems will be too restricted and require further development to meet the criteria of the society. Payment networks should be convenient, trustworthy, and vastly accepted to achieve a user base high enough to act as a currency. The more developed and sophisticated cryptocurrencies and related technologies become, the closer the vast adoption of such digital currencies are.

The future direction of the technology is uncertain while studies identify the prediction of the future of cryptocurrency as one intriguing research topic (Tschorsch and Scheuermann 2016; Siddhart et al. 2020). Further, the difficulty to predict the future of cryptocurrencies is identified. Studies approach the future statements is sensitive and thought-provoking, rather than directive validating the current ambiguous atmosphere in the cryptocurrency industry, which is lacking comprehensive academic sources (Ciaian 2016; Luther 2016; Tschorsch and Scheuermann 2016; Hazlett and Luther 2020; Rehman 2020; Siddhart et al. 2020).

Luther (2016) recognizes the growing electronic transactions made to affect positively the adaptation of cryptocurrencies if the blockchain-based transactions significantly reduce the costs of processing transactions. Moreover, Luther (2016) states that cryptocurrencies '…are unlikely to function as more than a niche money except in the unlikely event of hyperinflation or government support or both'. Trust is an important factor identified affecting the attitudes and perceptions of the future (Albayati et al. 2020). The government support aspect identified by the Luther (2019) might solve the trust issues related to cryptocurrencies at least partly. According to the Rehman et al. (2020) who has researched specifically about the trust of cryptocurrencies concludes that 'achieving a highly trustworthy cryptocurrency ecosystem is not reachable within short time'.

The future of cryptocurrencies is depending not just on the development of the technology, and therefore the usability of it but also on external factors of which the main two identified in this literature review are the trust towards cryptocurrencies and the distrust towards fiat currencies. The latter one might happen due to hyperinflation, while the first one will be achieved through time, and proper research published in the future. Hyperinflation could lower the threshold of using cryptocurrencies, and therefore it could also rapidly speed up the technological development of such digital currencies as interest in the cryptocurrency would increase. The more people use cryptocurrencies the sooner it becomes a convenient currency to use through technological advancements.

The academic literature review available currently indicates that further research is in urgent need relating to cryptocurrencies. Other researchers have echoed the call for more research in the area of cryptocurrencies and blockchain technology. Themes identified in prior research include blockchain governance, human and material agency, blockchain affordances and constraints, as well as the consequences of its use (Rossi et al. 2019). Overlaps in the findings from this inductive research can be seen including governance, end-users. However differences were found whereby affordances and constraints, and consequences are called for. The research since Rossi et al.'s (2019) work has not fulfilled all of the themes called for. Cryptocurrencies and the related blockchain technology have a tremendous opportunity for research in both the areas called for Rossi et al. (2019) as well as the areas identified in this work, including power structures, environmental concerns, and further governance work.

References

Albayati, H., Kim, S.K., Rho, J.J.: Accepting financial transactions using blockchain technology and cryptocurrency: a customer perspective approach. Technol. Soc. **62**, 101320 (2020)

Asheer, J.R.: Taxation of the Bitcoin: initial insights through a correspondence analysis. Meditari Account. Res. (2018)

Beck, R., Müller-Bloch, C., King, J.L.: Governance in the blockchain economy: a framework and research agenda. J. Assoc. Inf. Syst. **19**(10), 1 (2018)

Bezhovski, Z., Davcev, L., Mitreva, M.: Current adoption state of cryptocurrencies as an electronic payment method. Manag. Res. Pract. **13**(1), 44–50 (2021)

Brekke, J.K., Alsindi, W.Z.: Cryptoeconomics. Internet Policy Rev. **10**(2) (2021)

Ciaian, P., Rajcaniova, M., Kancs, A.: The digital agenda of virtual currencies: can BitCoin become a global currency. IseB **14**(4), 883–919 (2016)

Chong, A.Y.L., Lim, E.T.K., Hua, X., Zheng, S., Tan, C.-W.: Business on chain: a comparative case study of five blockchain-inspired business models. J. Assoc. Inf. Syst. **20**(9), 1310–1339 (2019)

Conti, M., Kumar, S., Lal, C., Ruj, S.: A survey on security and privacy issues on bitcoin. IEEE Commun. Surv. Tutor. **20**(4), 3416–3452 (2018)

Convey, L.: Blockchain explained. Investopedia (2021)

Corbet, S., Lucey, B., Yarovaya, L.: Bitcoin-energy markets interrelationships – new evidence. Resour. Policy **70**, 101916 (2021)

Cousins, K., Subramanian, H., Esmaeilzadeh, P.: A value-sensitive design perspective of cryptocurrencies: a research agenda. Commun. Assoc. Inf. Syst. **45**, 27 (2019)

Denison, E., Lee, M., Martin, A.: What do cryptocurrencies do. J. Invest. **28**(3), 57–61 (2019)

Du, W.D., Pan, S.L., Leidner, D.E., Ying, W.: Affordances, experimentation and actualization of FinTech: a blockchain implementation study. J. Strateg. Inf. Syst. **28**(1), 50–65 (2019)

Frankenfield, J.: What is cryptocurrency? Investopedia (2021)

Giudici, G., Milne, A., Vinogradov, D.: Cryptocurrencies: market analysis and perspectives. J. Ind. Bus. Econ. **47**(1), 1–18 (2020)

Gomber, P., Kauffman, R.J., Parker, C., Weber, B.W.: On the fintech revolution: interpreting the forces of innovation, disruption, and transformation in financial services. J. Manag. Inf. Syst. **35**(1), 220–265 (2018)

Hazlett, P.K., Luther, W.J.: Is bitcoin money? And what that means. Q. Rev. Econ. Financ. **70**, 144–149 (2020)

Hendershott, T., Zhang, X., Zhao, J.L., Zheng, Z.: FinTech as a game changer: overview of research frontiers. Inf. Syst. Res. **32**(1), 1–17 (2021)

Ilk, N., Shang, G., Fan, S., Leon Zhao, J.: Stability of transaction fees in bitcoin: a supply and demand perspective. MIS q. **45**(2), 563–692 (2021)

Kohli, R., Liang, T.P.: Strategic integration of blockchain technology into organizations. J. Manag. Inf. Syst. **38**(2), 282–287 (2021)

La Paz, A., et al.: Twenty-five years of the Information Systems Journal: a bibliometric and ontological overview. Inf. Syst. J. **30**(3), 431–457 (2020)

Lacity, M.C.: Blockchain: from bitcoin to the internet of value and beyond. J. Inf. Technol. (2022)

Lagna, A., Ravishankar, M.N.: Making the world a better place with fintech research. Inf. Syst. J. **32**(1), 61–102 (2022)

Luther, W.J.: Bitcoin and the future of digital payments. Indep. Rev. **20**(3), 397–404 (2016)

Mattke, J., Maier, C., Reis, L., Weitzel, T.: Bitcoin investment: a mixed methods study of investment motivations. Eur. J. Inf. Syst. **30**(3), 261–285 (2021)

Parveen, R., Alajmi, A.: An overview of bitcoin's legal and technical challenges. Legal Ethical Regul. Issues **22**(1), 1–8 (2019)

Pernice, I.G.A., Scott, B.: Cryptocurrency. Internet Policy Rev. **10**(2) (2021)

Raddatz, N., Coyne, J., Menard, P., Crossler, R.: Becoming a blockchain user: understanding consumers' benefits realisation to use blockchain-based applications. Eur. J. Inf. Syst. (2021)

Rehman, M.H., Salah, K., Damiani, E., Svetinovic, D.: Trust in blockchain cryptocurrency ecosystem. IEEE Trans. Eng. Manag. **67**(4), 1196–1212 (2020)

Rossi, M., Mueller-Bloch, C., Thatcher, J.B., Beck, R.: Blockchain research in information systems: current trends and an inclusive future research agenda. J. Assoc. Inf. Syst. **20**(9), 14 (2019)

Saiedi, E., Broström, A., Ruiz, F.: Global drivers of cryptocurrency infrastructure adoption. Small Bus. Econ. **57**(1), 353–406 (2021)

Sarker, S., Henningsson, S., Jensen, T., Hedman, J.: The use of blockchain as a resource for combating corruption in global shipping: an interpretive case study. J. Manag. Inf. Syst. **38**(2), 338–373 (2021)

Serapiglia, A., Serapiglia, C., McIntyre, J.: Cryptocurrencies: core information technology and information systems fundamentals enabling currency without borders. Inf. Syst. Educ. J. **13**, 43–52 (2015)

Siddhart, M., Vishal, K., Poonacha, K.B., Arjun, M., Parameshwar, H.S.: CryptoCurrency: a black and white analysis. Inf. Syst. Soc. Chang. **11**(2), 24–40 (2020)

Sun Yin, H.H., Langenheldt, K., Harlev, M., Mukkamala, R.R., Vatrapu, R.: Regulating cryptocurrencies: a supervised machine learning approach to de-anonymizing the bitcoin blockchain. J. Manag. Inf. Syst. **36**(1), 37–73 (2019)

Tschorsch, F., Scheuermann, B.: Bitcoin and beyond: a technical survey on decentralized digital currencies. IEEE Commun. Surv. Tutor. **18**, 2084–2123 (2016)

Tu, K., Meredith, M.: Rethinking virtual currency regulation in the bitcoin age. Wash. Law Rev. **90**(1), 271–347 (2015)

Author Index